THE *Contemporary French* NOVEL

The Contemporary

French Novel

HENRI PEYRE

STERLING PROFESSOR OF FRENCH,

YALE UNIVERSITY

New York · OXFORD UNIVERSITY PRESS

© Oxford University Press, Inc., 1955
Library of Congress Catalogue Card Number: 55-7540
Fourth Printing, 1963

Printed in the United States of America

THE MARY FLEXNER LECTURESHIP

The Mary Flexner Lectureship was established February 17, 1928, at Bryn Mawr College, by Bernard Flexner, in honor of his sister, Mary Flexner, a graduate of the College. An adequate endowment was provided by the gift, the income to be used annually or at longer intervals, at the discretion of the Directors of the College, as an honorarium to be given to an American or foreign scholar highly distinguished in the field of the 'Humanities,' using the term 'Humanities' in its broadest connotation. The lecturers have taken up residence at Bryn Mawr for a six weeks' period and, besides delivering the series of public lectures, have taught graduate and undergraduate students. The object of the Mary Flexner Lectureship is to bring to the College scholars of distinction, who will be a stimulus to the faculty and students, and who will contribute to the maintenance of those ideals and standards of scholarship that will bring increasing honor to the College. The gift provides that the Mary Flexner Lectures shall be published.
The present volume is the tenth in the series to be published.

THE MARY FLEXNER LECTURES

Since 1931 the Lectures have been published as the
BRYN MAWR SERIES *by Oxford University Press*

To the Memory of Howard L. Gray

To Lucy and Samuel C. Chew

To Eunice M. Schenck

THIS BOOK IS GRATEFULLY DEDICATED

IN HAPPY RECOLLECTION OF YEARS SPENT ON THE CAMPUS

OF ONE OF THE NOBLEST SEATS OF LEARNING IN AMERICA

———————————————————

LARGIOR HIC CAMPOS AETHER ET LUMINE VESTIT

PURPUREO

PREFACE

It was the privilege of the author to be invited, in the spring of 1944, to deliver the MARY FLEXNER LECTURES *in Bryn Mawr College. The volume now presented to the public has suffered a long and hardly excusable delay. It was the author's conviction that a few lectures, naturally subjected to the limitations of the 'winged word' and of the fleeting hour, could hardly do justice to the immense subject of the contemporary French novel. It also seemed to him that an evaluation of the literary movement in the ten years following World War II should be part of a volume in which he tried to assess the achievement and the trends of French fiction and to portray some of the deeper concerns of the country as mirrored in its literature.*

H. P.

New Haven, Connecticut
12 January 1955

CONTENTS

tion. The despair and tragic pessimism of most American writers. American literature — crude and brutal at times, antianalytical, gloomy, and morbid, but rich and virile — as an aid in revitalizing the French novel. Bibliographical Notes.

Need for evaluation of contemporary literature, without waiting for the fallible judgment of posterity. The present age of fiction not unworthy of any comparable period in the past. A few of its characteristics: great number, audacity, and high quality of recent women novelists; originality of the North African group of writers; impact of World War II on fiction (defeat, resistance, imprisonment, collaboration). Scant interest in problems of technique and structure. Keener attention brought to the question of language and to weaving the *Surreal* into daily life. Distrust of eloquence and of the social novel. Man's solitude a dominant theme, indicating the recurrence of a romantic mood. Possible explanations. An age of complacent anxiety. Lingering effect on French sensibility of the humiliations of defeat and collaboration, the disillusioned hopes of the resistance, and the insecurity brought about by inflation. The pessimism of French writers often courageous and constructive. Three key words in today's literature: clear-sightedness, sincerity, fraternity.

ACKNOWLEDGMENTS

Acknowledgment is hereby made for permission to quote from the following:

The Atlantic Monthly and Jean-Paul Sartre, for a quotation from the article 'American Novelists in French Eyes,' in the issue of August 1946.

Commentary and Albert Camus, for a quotation from Camus's article 'The Artist as Witness of Freedom,' in the issue of December 1949.

Gallimard, Paris, and the authors, for quotations from Simone de Beauvoir, Albert Camus, André Gide, Jean Giono, André Malraux, Marcel Proust, Antoine de Saint-Exupéry, Jean-Paul Sartre, and Paul Valéry.

Bernard Grasset, Paris, and François Mauriac, for quotation from Mauriac's works.

Harcourt, Brace and Company, for quotations from the novels of Saint-Exupéry, and Mr. Lewis Galantière for quotations from his translations of Saint-Exupéry.

Harper & Brothers, and Aldous Huxley, for a quotation from Huxley's *Eyeless in Gaza*.

The Hogarth Press, London, and Raymond Mortimer, for a quotation from Mortimer's *Channel Packet*.

Horizon and Cyril Connolly, for a quotation from an interview with André Malraux, in 1945.

Alfred A. Knopf, for quotations made from Simone de Beauvoir, André Gide, Roger Martin du Gard, and Jean-Paul Sartre.

The New York Times for quotations from Simone de Beauvoir's article 'An Existentialist Looks at America,' *The New York Times Magazine,* May 25, 1947.

xv

The Philosophical Library, for quotations from Henri Bergson's *The Creative Mind* and from Jean Cocteau's *Letter to Jacques Maritain.*

Random House and Robinson Jeffers, for a quotation from Jeffers's poem 'Joy.'

Theatre Arts, for a quotation from J.-P. Sartre's article of June 1946, 'Forgers of Myths.'

The Viking Press, for a quotation from D. H. Lawrence's *Phoenix.*

The Virginia Quarterly Review, for permission to reprint the substance of an article on 'American Literature through French Eyes,' published there by the author in the summer of 1947.

The extensive reading necessitated by such a work was greatly helped by the resources of the Sterling Library of Yale University, and by the competence, the flair, and the industry of many on its staff, and particularly Mr. Donald Wing, Associate Librarian and Head of the Accessions Department. Our sincerest gratitude goes to him and to all other members of the staff.

Mrs. Raymond Giraud assisted us devotedly and expertly in checking many details and in revising several chapters. Let her find here the expression of our warm thanks. Our debt to Miss Blanche Price cannot be discharged; she assisted us considerably and untiringly with learning, wisdom, and taste. This book would have been much more imperfect without her.

THE *Contemporary French* NOVEL

INTRODUCTION

For a century and a half, the novel has been king of Western literature. Poetry rivals its dominion over a small band of refined spirits, and nonfiction has staged vigorous offensives in the last two or three decades. Still the novel remains supreme, and our picture of the surrounding world and even more of strange worlds is largely the creation of novelists who, in the nineteenth century and to a lesser extent in our own, have depicted the Russia of Tolstoy and Dostoevski, the France of Flaubert and Zola, the Great Britain of Dickens, Trollope, and Galsworthy.

Our vision of foreign lands, however, lags behind the portrait that recent foreign novelists have drawn of England, France, Italy, and Russia since World War I and World War II. Courses on contemporary European literature have been added to the curriculum of many a university, with or without competent teachers to give them. Many foreign novels have been translated in recent years. Lecturers have swarmed to our shores to enlighten audiences on the mysteries of existentialism or on the abstruse myths underlying the fiction of D. H. Lawrence, Thomas Mann, or Franz Kafka. Still it remains difficult for all but the dauntless reader or the professional of literature to thread their way through the literary complexities of our age.

Readers are not altogether to blame for their inadequacy. A

volume of fiction is no longer an entertaining pastime. It requires
the same arduous mental effort and assiduous unraveling of complexities as our ancestors brought to their treatises on theology
and moral philosophy. Gone is the day when any French novel
carried a spicy flavor of sin between its yellow paper covers. Such
novels were universally suspect — and devoured; they were taken
to be the foe of feminine virtue and the temptation that would
set the dreams of Anglo-Saxon ephebi whirling around Parisian
dens of debauchery. In the blissfully naïve days of the end of the
nineteenth century, grave Timothy Dwight, president of Yale,
could censure novels with these serious words that 'between the
Bible and novels, there is a gulf fixed which few novel readers are
willing to pass.' To offer a course on the French novel in an American college then cast an invidious suspicion on the instructor rash
enough to lure undergraduates to Honoré de Balzac's *Physiologie
du mariage,* Gustave Flaubert's *Madame Bovary,* or Emile Zola's
Nana. Today, courses on the novel are designed to frighten all
but the few dauntless souls who are willing to follow the patient
quests for symbolic structure in André Malraux, for the secrets of
temporality in Marcel Proust, or for absurdity, despair, and the
way out of despair in the narratives of Jean-Paul Sartre. Gallic
spice has not altogether deserted recent imports from Paris. But
its taste is acrid.

Fiction reading thus makes considerable demands on persons of
good will. We may lack not only leisure to tackle fiction by André
Malraux, Jean Giono, and Jean-Paul Sartre, but guidance as well.
Criticism of the novel is scarce, and almost nonexistent in English,
for all but a few of the more famous foreign novelists. Legitimate
questions are frequently put to those who should know: Who are
the significant novelists in France today? What important works
of fiction should one read, what works recommend to students
who wish to remain informed? What revelation of the moods of
the French people and of the social and intellectual life of their
country can be obtained from recent French literature? What
trends in technique and psychology are discernible among the
present heirs of Gustave Flaubert and Anatole France?

To these and other questions, the present volume hopes to propose an answer. Not a definitive answer, to be sure, and hardly an
objective one, for it is doubtful whether objective criticism is desirable or possible, especially where contemporary literature is
concerned. But the answer may be honest and helpful. This book
is written by a Frenchman specifically for the enlightened Ameri-

can public, in and outside the universities. It does not pretend to revolutionary novelty or judgment, but it claims some independence of mind and a reasonable familiarity with the material concerned. It wishes to avoid provincialism and the assumption, long placidly accepted by Frenchmen, that their literature is not only central in Western culture (a point that many readers would concede) but is the only one that counts. Frequent reference will be made to other literatures and to foreign influences. Lastly, this book deliberately attempts to keep free of some of the present critical fashions, which have tended to center around a highly technical analysis of structure, time, and style in modern fiction.

Recent technical criticism is, of course, not to be treated lightly. Some of its best products concerning the art of fiction are listed in the bibliography, and use will be made of the results it has attained. No one should quarrel with the critic's right to lend generously a wealth of mysterious intentions and symbols to authors, who may feel flattered by such profuse and unrequited loans. *On ne prête qu'aux riches,* as the French saying goes. The critic's task is indeed to decipher the writer's hidden or subconscious intents. But we contend that criticism of the novel, while it has had to become technical to achieve progress in a field too long given up to pitiful generalities, has, in so doing, cultivated abstruseness and pedantic jargon to excess. It has turned into a private game, in which even the most cultivated layman can hardly participate.

While recent criticism of fiction has favored the patient tracking down of structural secrets concealed by artful authors, it has also proposed another and perhaps more fruitful approach: the study of samples of the writer's style. The close reading of a well-selected passage that epitomizes a volume can indeed be revealing. It reaches deep into the mechanism of the novelist's vision. Martin Turnell has practiced such a method, though not very rigorously and with unequal penetration, in his *Novel in France.*[1] Erich Auerbach, in his important work on the rendering of reality in art, *Mimesis,* has poured into his exegesis of passages from several Western literatures the wealth of an immense culture, deep reflection, and discriminating taste, while remaining clear and urbane and eschewing all dogmatism. Such a method, however, tends to overstress style, which is not all-important in fiction. It fails to seize the novel in its dynamic fluidity. It is best practiced in a seminar, where foreign works can be discussed in the suggestive

1. Martin Turnell, *The Novel in France* (New Directions, New York, 1951).

nuances of the original language, not in the borrowed garb of translation.

The truth is that, if the criticism of fiction has been so disappointing as a whole and has lagged behind commentaries on poetry and on the drama, it has many an excuse. As the keenest of the analysts of the craft of fiction, Percy Lubbock, pointed out, no other reading offers the same dilemmas as the reading of the novel, however little the casual reader may realize it. Teachers of novel courses are familiar with the chief of these dilemmas. Any discussion of a novel demands that we keep in the focus of our attention the whole of its complexity of plots and incidents, its digressions, and its gradual unfolding of characters. Individual episodes and *morceaux de bravoure* cannot be isolated, as they could in the enjoyment of the epic. The beauty of separate passages must not lure us to pondering over them or treasuring them in our memory, as we might do with lyric poetry. The reader must be tempted to rush on to the denouement breathlessly, or the spell is not potent. Yet that comprehensive reading must remain alert for revealing details and be analytical of key passages; it must be seized by the witchcraft of Scheherazade without abdicating critical lucidity. There is a limit to the length and complexities permitted to a drama. There are no such limits today to a *roman-fleuve*, except that 'the weariest river winds somewhere safe to sea.'

Moreover, critics of the novel, who are often also professors, do not enjoy the advantage of being able to desert the work of fiction at will, and to introduce familiar pronouncements uttered by Aristotle, Longinus, Dryden, Lessing, Goethe, Croce, or Richards into their discussion as they can when they criticize poetry, tragedy, or history. Most of these august writers ignore the novel. In antiquity, fiction was hardly worthy of the attention of serious men; the *Satyricon* and *The Golden Ass* were entertainment that did not justify the expense of time that numberless rhetors lavished on oratory. Until the nineteenth century, the novel, since it had not been highly regarded by the ancients, was a mere upstart with which one could experiment at will but which critics would not admit to the literary nobility. It was, as the term indicated, a 'novel' genre, even a popular one, like a *roman* written in the Romance or vulgar tongue for frivolous audiences, at a time when Latin was the proper vehicle for ideas or for the recording of past events.

The novel has had its revenge. In fact, it was a boon for the upstart to escape the pedantry of ancient and Renaissance commentators. It was never codified and tyrannized by rules. No acts and scenes, no unity or unities, no progression of interest, no special style were required for the novel. Some critics of the novel have rejoiced at the youth and freshness of a genre which, they say, is still in its robust adolescence, and they can envision infinite possibilities in its long future. Others periodically insist that their favorite novelist (Balzac, Flaubert, Proust, Tolstoy, Joyce, or Mann) has extracted from the art of fiction all that it can possibly give, and that the novel of the future must meekly follow the 'great tradition' thus established. Every year articles appear on 'the novel of the future.' They are subsequently belied by events. But the role of a minor prophet is a safe one; no one takes the trouble to reread his prophecies and, if he knows his part at all, he makes them ambiguous and contradictory enough so as never to be without honor.

The present writer's conviction is that there is no single approach that is infallible or systematically to be preferred, whether in literature, philosophy, politics — or life. Any dogmatism, while it provides the lover of system with a cheaply acquired consistency and unity of point of view, soon proves detrimental to the most varied of all human pursuits — the pursuit of beauty, truth, and 'greatness' in works of art. Fiction, even more than poetry, music, or painting, sets everything in motion in us: our senses (it would be hypocrisy to ignore the sensuous and erotic motivation of readers of fiction or lovers of pictures), our sensibility, our intellect, our religious, philosophical, and social views, our aesthetic joys, our desire to know ourselves better and to penetrate into other lives and to approve of ourselves in our favorite heroes. Any approach to the novel, therefore, that is honest and intelligently sustained is valid if it draws us nearer to the work of art or to its creator.

The aesthetic approach, including the consideration of the novelist's technique, should reasonably come first, since it is the most mature and the most detached. But the biographical one, looking for the novelist in his works, cannot be excluded; Stendhal, Proust, and Dostoevski fascinate us even more than their fictional characters. Thomas Wolfe expressed more than the pathetic inflation of his ego when he remarked, in his preface to *Look Homeward Angel*, that 'all serious work in fiction is autobiographical . . . a more autobiographical work than *Gulliver's Travels* cannot easily be imagined.' The philosophical study of fiction is equally valid; most great works of fiction become endowed with metaphysical and moral significance as the story mirrors the author's view of the world. In France in particular, long before Stendhal and Benjamin Constant, psychology constituted the warp and woof of many a fictional loom. Finally, in spite of the fear of many aesthetes averse to seeing literature debased to the role of social document, the social approach to fiction has its aims, even if it has been practiced with notorious clumsiness up to now. It is naïve to envisage Proust primarily as the delineator of the decadence of French aristocracy, Zola as the gravedigger of the bourgeoisie of the Second Empire. It is even more naïve to ransack French fiction for information on French family life, French thrift, or French sex manners. But from Balzac to the naturalists, and more recently with André Malraux, Jules Romains, and Louis Aragon, the French novel has been conscious of social values and of social classes. An intelligent social interpretation of the French novel assumes that the novel enables one to gain an insight into French life.

Any work of criticism, like any philosophical treatise, rests upon some assumptions, which are in part arbitrary. The author should, in all fairness, state them briefly, at the risk of seeming to extend his prolegomena with some complacence. Definitions are one half of criticism, and often its better half.

Our first one is a platitude but, like all obvious statements, often disregarded. The modern novel, and specifically the modern French novel, as an entity, hardly exists. There are only contemporary novelists, some of whom are modern. There exist far wider gaps between two novels written in our age than there ever existed between two plays, two poems, even two essays, two symphonies, two churches.

Once this has been said, we shall not, however, shyly refrain from all generalizations about the novel in France. The process of abstracting and of generalizing is inseparable from that of thinking. A suggestive synthesis is more useful to scholarship than one more of those thorough, myopic, and infinitesimal analyses of an ever-diminishing topic. But we prefer concentrating our remarks around individuals who proposed and solved problems *in vivo* to breaking up the art of fiction into components such as narrative, description, dialogue, plot, conflict of characters, and so forth. E. M. Forster has ridiculed some of the textbooks on materials of fiction. He has opened the way to better ones. But the craft of fiction, or the understanding of fiction, or its enjoyment cannot be reduced to recipes.

Fiction, and any movement, trend, or period, is made by individuals. Thus a second pitfall lies before the critics. How will he make a choice among the recent and living authors who seem to have a claim upon his attention? The critic may wish to be polite to novelists who, of course, are also critics themselves and whom he will have to meet next month at some literary dinner party. Moreover, he is not absolutely sure of his own taste and will provide a guarantee against the gibes of posterity if he lists all those who may survive. Many works on contemporary literature, therefore, afraid of appearing schoolmasterish in ranking writers, take refuge in tedious enumerations, granting an honorable mention to every respectable talent. This may save embarrassment, but the criticism will read like a dictionary of names and titles.

Anyone who ventures to treat living literature must be ready to take risks and must abide by his own taste, while broadening it as best he can. Courage is as indispensable as intelligence in such matters. In the realm of fiction, more than in any other, a critic must be selective, for many more novels than any other kind of literature are included in monthly publishers' lists. Out of the fictional avalanche on a reviewer's desk, four or five novels in every decade, that is to say, one per cent or so, may some day emerge. The others are not all mediocre, and we owe to them a few hours of entertainment as well as some understanding of our age and of public taste. The chances are that the best seller will be among these pleasing, soon-to-be-forgotten books. However, these books do not belong to the restricted and magical circle of 'works of literature.'

It is the critic's and often the professor's privilege to decide what literature is and what it is not. But the power of the professor is not arbitrary. He follows not his whim but a test, the most scrutinizing to which a contemporary novel or play can be subjected: Does the new writer stand up under the slow reading, the elaborate dissecting of three or four hours of lecture and of discussion of his work? The teacher and the students who struggle with his volume just off the press are also reading Sophocles, Racine, Tolstoy, Ibsen. To them they will compare Mr. Tennessee Williams, Mr. Christopher Fry, or M. Jean-Paul Sartre. Sad to confess, the rewarding writer who remains on the syllabus is the writer about whom the lecturer does not run dry after fifty minutes and whose solidity resists the irony and the severity of young apprentices.

But the professor is overwhelmed by his responsibility. He is prone to excessive prudence and often seeks refuge in well-established values in order to avoid the brutality of the present. He favors novels which are 'arty,' probably pretentious, and overwritten by an author too conscious of his calculated effects. A clique of an unhappy few may thus cry up Djuna Barnes's *Nightwood*, or Charles Morgan's novels of labored mysticism and impure chastity, or even Graham Greene's weird atmosphere, or, in France, Marcel Jouhandeau, Julien Gracq, and even Jean Giraudoux. They will not succeed in imposing their taste. For, less than any other means of literary expression, can the novel be severed from life for very long. Stylization may rule supreme in some other arts; it does not in fiction. The peril of excluding too much of life, as Henry James did, is greater than that of accepting it too liberally and of running the risk of presenting violence, vulgarity, and sadism as the whole of life.

The very general characteristics by which a novel may be broadly classified may take the place of a definition — necessarily a very loose one. The novel is a story, perhaps borrowed from reality, but reality transposed and reimagined, endowed with form, made fictitious. It is in prose, or it has been since the end of the Middle Ages. It has a certain length; there is no upper limit, apparently, to the number of pages or volumes that a novel may reach, but it should not be so short that it becomes a long short story. All other requirements that have been put forward by critics, those unacknowledged legislators, may be discarded, for they raise too many difficulties to win general approval. A narrative element used to be required in a novel, but it is no longer generally considered necessary. Many moderns are Platonists, who will not allow appearances to count for much, unless they suggest or reveal some deeper significance. Our age yearns for a world of essences transcending our phenomenal and temporal prison. Smooth, vivid, and entrancing storytelling, such as the Italians and Russians once practiced with special mastery, has lost vogue with us. Creation of character is also less essential than it was in the days of Fielding, Dickens, and Balzac. Around 1860–70, literature and art were rocked to their foundations by the writers' and artists' determination to change the world or to re-create a new universe with words, colors, and sounds, instead of placidly depicting reality or letting their picaresque heroes make the best of it and acquire experience, wisdom, and a few good memories thereby. Ever since, the novel has been seized by social and metaphysical ambitions. Some say that its great age then passed away.

Let us not be nostalgic. The greatness of literature, in countries like France, lies in its claim, often made good, of taking the place once filled by religion and dogmatic ethics. Charles Baudelaire, Arthur Rimbaud, and their successors among poets, stark and occasionally cruel novelists, from Flaubert to Sartre, historical writers, from Taine to modern historians, freed from consoling delusions, have poured the virile draught on which the youth of the country has been intoxicated. They did not respect traditions, and they did not encourage man to hope for another world or even for much improvement in this one. But they have steeled many a soul to bear evils with fortitude and, in a world where absurdities and iniquities are triumphant, to take arms against a sea of troubles and to endow a frail life with significance.

The French novel is thus, more than ever before, a novel of moralists more than of storytellers, of seekers of wisdom more than of creators of characters. It aims at increasing the reader's understanding of life, at sharpening his lucidity and his sincerity; indeed, with all its pessimism, it has enhanced the Frenchman's zest for living a life which authors have depicted as sombre, bristling with hostile temptations, unprotected by any Providence, but the more exhilarating for all that.

The present volume deals with the French novelists who appear to be the most significant in the literature of the last twenty-five years. In this sense they are modern, though not particularly modernistic, for, except in poetry and perhaps in music, the years 1925–50 have not been marked, in France, by much technical experimentation, and, since Marcel Proust and James Joyce, the novel has been the least experimental of literary genres. An attempt has indeed been made to innovate in the content of fiction, especially by plumbing depths of eroticism, abnormality, and cruelty as they were revealed by Sigmund Freud, the Marquis de Sade, and other prophets of our era. But these subjects have quickly gone stale; Lesbianism and pederasty have afforded some psychological enrichment, by now fully treasured, or squandered. The most original movement at present is the revolt against language. 'On a touché au vers,' declared Stéphane Mallarmé in 1895 before Oxford and Cambridge audiences awaiting the latest news from Paris. Fifty years later, prose, in its turn, was attacked in its very essence: communication and suggestion.

But experiment is not necessarily the road to the future. It often leads away from the real trend of literary evolution into paths that perhaps have been tried earlier and have proved to be blind alleys. It is possible that one of these paths, diverging from the main road, may one day become a spacious avenue, if a genius forces it wide open. Meanwhile, many experimenters are the martyrs of a lost cause, or of a cause that has not yet found itself. On the other hand, the forces of the past may only temporarily seem to have spent themselves; some genius may instill revolutionary dynamism into them tomorrow. This has often been the case in France.

The French are keenly conscious of their traditions, and no French writer, however iconoclastic he may be, has ever been wholly exempt from some reading of Racine, Pascal, Balzac, and Hugo. Happily for the French, they have not one but several traditions, which more often than not conflict with one another. Periodically, they sort out their legacy of a complex past and advocate a single current as beneficent; the rest become the object of eloquent vituperation.

The position adopted by a literary generation in respect to its past is therefore revealing. No writer worthy of the name and deserving a niche in the temple (or in the stables) of posterity is merely an imitator. Borrowings that may at one time have been permissible in other literary genres would not be tolerated in the art of fiction: the creative imitation of Theocritus by Virgil, of certain Spaniards by Corneille, of Plautus by Molière, of Bion and Moschus by Shelley. Even the patent adoption and utilization of foreign models, such as Lesage practiced with the Spanish picaresque tradition, and many Frenchmen with Samuel Richardson and Walter Scott, would today offend our literary conventions. The American novel has been caricatured in the last decades, somewhat unconsciously, by the Frenchmen who plundered it. But the number of fictional situations, even if a little larger than the restricted number of dramatic situations, is, after all, limited. It is not easy to create a miser or an old man devoured by his fatherly love for his daughters without having Balzac thrown at one's face; a sentimental, cynical young upstart without inviting comparison with Stendhal; a middle-aged, dissatisfied, and tempted lady without conjuring up Emma Bovary. More than in subject matter, the influence of certain past novelists looked upon as masters appears in the tone assumed by some of the moderns. An original history of literature could be written by classifying families of minds in separate chapels, with the name of some patron saint of earlier eras inscribed on the pediment.

The novelists of the past whose prestige and influence in France (and not necessarily elsewhere) have sunk lowest are Anatole France and Guy de Maupassant. The naturalists have not yet regained favor, and many of them hardly deserve it. Joris-Karl Huysmans, who is too often grouped with them, deserves to return to popularity, more so, in our eyes, than do Léon Bloy or Barbey d'Aurevilly, two Catholic but uncharitable souls and novelists of some power. Zola suffered, at least among the self-styled elite, from the trend away from naturalism. He remains, however, with Victor Hugo, the only novelist of the French nineteenth century to have reached the masses and to be actually bought and read widely by the 'common reader.' [2]

Zola is now winning also the admiration of scholars, and one may safely predict a wave of dissertations (*tout finit en Sorbonne,* as a Frenchman remarked) on the structure of *Germinal* or of *La Débâcle* and on the stylistic effects of *La Faute de l'Abbé Mouret.* Few subjects would be richer. It is revealing that one of the warmest admirers of Zola was Mallarmé, the purest and least realistic of poets. Henry James could not help envying Zola's power of dealing with crowds, numbers, confused gregarious movements. In *Notes on Novelists,* he compared him, with more sympathy than irony, to 'some mighty animal, a beast of a corrugated hide and a portentous snout, soaking with joy in the warm ooze of an African riverside.' Arthur Symons, the priest of the symbolist movement, was also partial to Zola; Edmund Gosse, the respectable critic par excellence, who was severe on Charles Dickens's vulgarity and ironical on George Eliot, proclaimed Zola in 1893, in *Questions at Issue,* 'one of the leading men of genius in the second half of the nineteenth century, one of the strongest novelists of the world.'

Flaubert has had to withstand attacks on several scores. His style, on which he had expended much labor and on which he had pinned all his faith, convinced that all else was vanity in a loveless and godless world, meets with few champions among us. Marcel Proust was one of the first to deride its painstaking failure. Paul Valéry mocked Flaubert's ponderousness and his rather weak intellectual grasp (so rules the creator of M. Teste, self-defined by his motto 'stupidity is not my strong point'), which made him an easy prey to the snares of erudition and to the naïve claims of realism. His characters, especially those whom he tried to resuscitate from

2. We are, of course, omitting novelists whom we, and others, do not consider to have a rank in literature: Eugène Sue, Emile Gaboriau, Alexandre Dumas, Georges Ohnet. But they are still read and published serially in newspapers, and preferably in communist ones. *Habent sua fata libelli.*

an archaeological past, are passive and papery. André Gide would not rank Flaubert's novels among the few he would select to bear yearly rereading on the imaginary desert island. André Malraux, in his preface to *Le Temps du mépris* (*Days of Wrath*), and Jean-Paul Sartre, in his manifesto for the opening of *Les Temps modernes*, have been even more blatantly unjust to Flaubert. Some greater measure of justice will eventually be meted out to him, as it has always been among the English and American novelists, whose allegiance he has not lost. But it is doubtful whether he will ever be restored to a supreme place.

Balzac's greatness is overpowering. The number and the quality of the books written about him between 1935 and 1950 exceed any other body of admirative criticism about any French writer. He has traversed most of the avenues which may tempt the modern novelist. Visionary novelists hail Balzac as their ancestor and master; so do several illuminists, occultists, and fervents of mystical correspondences. But Balzac is also the master of those who undertake to embrace in several volumes the social, economic, and sentimental life of a whole generation. Authors who attempt to create monstrous monomaniacs, or to explore the world of financiers, inventors, and even of homosexuals are easily called Balzacian. François Mauriac has confessed his admiration for Balzac; Proust was fascinated by him, and probably reoriented the course of his fictional epic out of admiration for the *Comédie humaine*. Still, because he is too enormous, baffling, and exasperating, and also because his technique, which is subtle despite appearances to the contrary, is closely linked to an imagination that few can emulate, Balzac has not found many imitators in the modern novel. His secrets cannot be appropriated from the outside; and his unsure taste, his liberal digressions, his omniscient generalizations, and his violent or angelic women would impede any disciple.

Stendhal clearly is today, and has been ever since 1920 or so, the novelist of the past who is most, and perhaps too much, with us. Outside France, especially in English-speaking countries, the very small band of the devotees of Stendhal has only lately succeeded in making converts among the youth. But French cultists of Stendhal, like the worshippers of Racine, love their hero all the more devotedly as their passion is not shared by foreign initiates. The psychology of love embodied in Stendhal's novels (which is often remote from the theory of love and its crystallization proposed in the same author's treatise on the subject) together with Proust's portrayal of love obsess younger novelists.

Stendhal's attitude toward his heroes, his nonchalantly adroit manner of intervening in his narrative and of taking us into his confidence as accomplices, his hardly concealed romanticism reveling in passion, violence, and generosity, have left their imprint upon French fiction since Gide. The analytical restraint of his style, classical in appearance but vibrating with tingling emotion, has seduced many moderns in revolt against the barrier of words and especially the lush and vague adjectives that, in the more eloquent writers, interpose a screen between the reader and the object presented to him by the author.

Yet Stendhal can be a perilous master. His models of analytical lucidity and of stylistic sobriety may have proved beneficial to a few authors like Albert Camus who, born to the passionate enjoyment of shapes and colors, needed the lesson of restraint and bareness that Stendhal can teach. 'If I am not clear, my whole universe crumbles into nothingness,' declared Stendhal in one of those lapidary sentences admired by Gide and Camus. However, Stendhal fortunately did not banish shade, mystery, and the whisperings of the subconscious from his novels. His most unforgettable scenes in *Lucien Leuwen,* those showing Fabrice in his prison tower, or Julien and Mathilde fighting with each other's pride in the library of the *Hôtel de la Môle,* are instinct with passion all the more fervid for being analyzed. Stendhal's imitators have seldom pierced through to the romantic ebullience in him, which had to be tamed. They have copied the exterior features of his novels and even some of his mannerisms. However, there is, in most recent novels inspired by Stendhal, a dryness and an excessive fear of being the dupe of feelings and of senses, which betray the secret flaw of many a French novelist: lack of faith in his creation and lack of a true novelist's vocation. As Somerset Maugham once remarked, literature, and especially fiction, is in France a *moyen de parvenir,* quicker than politics, surer than business. Hence there is a proliferation of writers who, in other lands, would be hunting foxes, playing cricket, or selling bonds and television sets. Like all Frenchmen, they are adroit and adept at self-analysis.

Stendhal's influence has been paralleled by the acclaim granted to three earlier novelists, who have lately ceased to be labeled as minor. Indeed, they have displaced many of the once famous classics of fiction in the admiration of our mid-century: Mme de la Fayette, Choderlos de Laclos, and the Marquis de Sade. Sade seems to be grossly overrated as a novelist. Yet an absurd prejudice terrifies many who, for good aesthetic reasons as well as on grounds of common sense and — why not? — taste, see little in Sade, in Henry Miller, in Raymond Guérin, or even in Jean Genet. They are, however, so afraid of appearing to be old-fashioned that they will pay insincere lip service to the cult of these nether-world deities. Laclos is a much greater artist and a keener psychologist than Sade. André Suarés, André Malraux, Jean Giraudoux, and Albert Camus have paid him glowing tribute. His limitations are serious, since they range from some sterility of imagination and lack of narrative skill to a certain poverty of expression and a total lack of that poetical conception of characters in which Stendhal is triumphant. Within these limits, the *Liaisons dangereuses* is a minor masterpiece and perhaps the best novel of the eighteenth century in France.

As to the *Princesse de Clèves,* it deserves unstinted historical admiration as the first good European novel written after *Don Quixote.* It is the pioneer of a long line of French psychological novels treating of the fear of love in a feminine heart and of a Cornelian struggle within a character who is close to some of Racine's heroines. It is a novel by a woman selecting as her heroine an intelligent woman who ironically and vainly seeks moral guidance in her husband, in a lukewarm or nonexistent religious faith, and in a lover who does little to conquer and therefore to silence her scruples, a lover whom she cannot love truly because she does not esteem him fully. Written in 1678, this novel remains the best written in French by a woman. Its imitators, however, have been exclusively men, from Stendhal's *Armance* to Raymond Radiguet's second novel. Stories of love and self-respect at odds with each other, or tales of fear of love cramping the desire for it are favorite subjects with French dramatists and novelists. After Mme de la Fayette, French women writers, beginning with Mlle de Lespinasse, then from George Sand to Mme de Noailles, Rachilde, Colette, and Dominique Rolin, have seldom balked at impudicity, and men, who prefer to retain the monopoly of sensuality in literature or prefer sobbing feminine ones to feminine hearts laid bare, have not easily forgiven women novelists for their boldness.

Are there a few features of the French novel that have persisted to our day and that may help us evaluate it in its recent metamorphoses? The senseless but convenient French saying that exceptions are always to be found to confirm a rule may embolden one to venture a few generalizations.

First, there is order, structure, or, as we prefer to call it, an architectural sense, equally present in French music, painting, drama, landscape gardening, poetry and, naturally, in the foremost French art, that of cooking and of relishing well-composed meals and sipping the attending wines according to a rigid and yet ever-surprising pattern. 'Order the beauty even of beauty is,' said, not a Frenchman, but a Welsh clergyman and rather formless poet, Thomas Traherne, whom Mrs. Wharton liked to quote. John Galsworthy remarked in a vivacious little volume, *Castles in Spain and Other Scripts* (1927), that 'the English novel, though on the whole perhaps more varied and rich than that of any other country, has — from *Clarissa Harlowe* to *Ulysses* — been inclined to self-indulgence: it often goes to bed drunk.' As an antidote, the feeling of enclosure, of planned and self-conscious limitation, which is experienced in Flaubert, has afforded many British novelists a rare and subtle pleasure. 'Never, perhaps, can we hope to bring forth a novelist of such imaginative perfection, so polished, and at the same time so full of fire, as Flaubert,' confessed Osbert Sitwell in *Trio* in 1938 — a confession which can but remain unconvincing to a modern Frenchman. The French, who have been taught rhetorical composition and analytical clarity from their infancy on, are apt to have less admiration for a fairly common virtue that is easily turned into a fault.

The French have rebelled in our time against the worship of composition, which may lead to a dead order and block the irruption of life, which frightens overcareful planners. Paul Bourget's novels were, in a sense, most elaborately composed but also lifeless, for they failed to rest the synthetic organization of the characters upon a previous intuition of those characters. They banish chance, mystery, irrationality, and life itself. Jules Romains is guilty of the same delusion that a character can be welded together out of several fragments elaborately pieced together. Mauriac himself, hard as he tried to avoid becoming another Bourget and to stress poetry in his fiction, constructed some of his bad novels (he wrote a few bad ones) according to a pattern which left nothing to surprise, not even the unfathomable ways of God converting a sinner.

It is easy to assail the teaching of Flaubert, Bourget, and their successors and to point to the greatest novels, *Le Rouge et le noir*, *War and Peace*, and *The Brothers Karamazov* as being, almost purposely, ill-composed. Genius has always defeated all generalizations. Many French novelists annoy us with their emphasis on too-obvious structural effects and with their economy which borders on poverty. But there remain many others (Louis-Ferdinand

Céline, Jean Giono, and Georges Bernanos are among the most gifted of the moderns) who have spoiled a powerful talent and a significant theme for lack of attention to elimination, selection, and grouping. The structure of any work of art must be its own and must be in harmony with the content of subject matter or temperament expressed in that work. It must not be amenable to set rules. The only truth about the French novel as distinct from some others is that it is more sensitive than the American, the Russian, or the German novel to what Walter Pater called 'the necessity of mind in style.' [3]

This may well be, as has often been contended, the legacy of the French classical tragedy to the French novel. For the novel appeared as an autonomous and full-fledged art form at the very time when the last French classical tragedy, *Phèdre,* had been produced on the Parisian stage (1677). To tragedy, it owed its favorite theme: the analysis of couples, with the help of one or more adjuncts, torn by their loves and hatreds, their jealousies, their ambition to possess, be possessed, or elude possession, achieved through a peculiar intensity of self-exploration. To tragedy it owed also the primacy given to women characters in the earliest masterpieces of French fiction; *La Princesse de Clèves* (1678), *Manon Lescaut* (1735), *Vie de Marianne* (1741), *La Religieuse,* and *La Nouvelle Heloïse* (in the early 1760's) all have one heroine. (In the following century only, with René, Adolphe and Julien Sorel in *Le Rouge et le noir,* will young men displace women as protagonists.) To the tragedy of Corneille and Racine the French novel also owed its relative artistic purity, its avoidance of humorous or comic episodes, multiplied in the works of Fielding, Smollett, and Dickens, and its linear development.

Giraudoux once sketched an entertaining parallel between the French novel, *une nouvelle manquée,* a short story which, getting out of hand, became a novel, and the English novel, an abortive epic, multiplying digressions and episodes and rambling leisurely along. He called the effect of the French novel that of a shower, while he compared the English to a bath in which one steeps oneself to one's heart's content and slowly absorbs the benign effects

3. Pater defined it as 'structure . . . that architectural conception of work which foresees the end in the beginning and never loses sight of it, and in every part is conscious of all the rest, till the last sentence does but, with undiminished vigor, unfold and justify the first.' ('Style,' in *Appreciations.*) Such an ideal does not seem desirable in a novel and has not saved Pater's own novel or tales from the threat of oblivion. Even in a poem it might seem too rigid and too naïve.

of the tepid water. From Rousseau, a Swiss, to Proust, a Parisian, and Romains, a son of Auvergne, there have appeared many French novelists undaunted by length. Patience seems to have grown in the reading public since Romain Rolland, beating Balzac and Zola at their own game, let his Jean-Christophe wander for ten volumes in search of himself and his loves.

But even these long sagas are often made up of separate volumes that retain unity and some autonomy. It remains probably true that, even when they disregard it, French novelists feel behind and around them the presence of a tradition of brevity, tenseness, and linear development with one plot and a few characters. Periodically, they return to it, as Mauriac, Green, and Camus have done. Camus, who, among the men born after 1910, has stated the case for classical virtues in the novel most forcibly, takes as symbolic of that tradition the answer of a guard to Louis XVI when the King, being led to the guillotine, begged the man to accept a message for the Queen: 'I am not here to do your errands, but to take you straight to the scaffold.' [4] The essential classical virtue is aptly called by him a passionate monotony. Novelists, like dramatists, treat the same subject over and over again.

Next to the need for a framework in which to insert and set off the variegated unruliness of life, and to the passion for brevity and stylization meant to make art more intense than actual life, the stress on analysis is doubtless the third chief characteristic of French fiction. Existentialist writers have lately taken the French novel to task for its probing into motives and past regrets; they have seen in it an impediment to projection into the future, which alone can form the nucleus of a free personality. They have set up the American novel as a model for a more virile type of fiction. Their reaction was a healthy one. It surprised not a few Americans, who felt that their native fiction, from Ernest Hemingway to John O'Hara and John Steinbeck, could well do with a little more mature analysis of life and a few more nuances in laying bare the secret springs of behavior.

But the best French writers have seldom been able to follow their American models closely. They have already reverted to a compromise between American imports and their own tradition: the exploration of inner life, the weaving of absurd events into an

---

4. The essay by Camus is to be found in an important volume of essays on the novel, prepared during World War II and published in 1943, *Problèmes du roman* (Confluences, Lyon et Paris). Jean Prévost, killed in the *maquis* a year later, supervised and edited it.

almost orderly pattern, the intellectual dissociation of ideas, feelings, and subconscious promptings of men and women.

The point needs no laboring. The emphasis on man and, within man, on his ability to see through himself, to yield to desire, greed, crime, charity, or heroism only after clearly realizing why and how he does so has always been the central force in French literature and art, from Chrétien de Troyes, the Proust of the twelfth century as his ardent admirers call him, and from the painter Jean Fouquet in the fourteenth. *Voir clair dans son cœur,* to read clearly in one's heart, is the constant preoccupation of heroines in French comedy, from Marivaux to Anouilh, in Corneille's Pauline and in Racine's Andromaque, as it is that of Adolphe and of the innumerable progeny of that sterile character in modern French fiction. Emphasis on introspection has been fostered by the Catholic confessional, by the reading of ancient authors at school, by the arts of conversation and letter writing (both so often and so delightfully egocentric) and by the quest for multiple affairs of the heart, which however deceptive or painful, are at least taken to further one profitable end — the lover's progress in his own self-exploration.

Its drawbacks are obvious: one of them is that the story is too often made subservient to the complacent self-analysis of the author; the second, the author's diffidence of unreality, of fantastic or imaginary stories, of epic tales, of mystical novels, in which character portrayal tends to disappear and the links with real life and all-too-human men and women are severed. But the positive contribution of the French analytical novel has amply compensated for any deficiencies. The tradition of the French in fiction, and to some extent also that of the Russians and the Germans, has led them to the perilous, yet valid, temptation of composing novels of ideas. The history of that genre is strewn with misfits. It may degenerate into an over conscious allegory or favor characters who are mere puppets pulled to and fro by the author's tyranny over his creations; it is thus drawn to the Voltairian philosophical tale, to the pleasant but shallow dissertations of Anatole France, and the excessive self-awareness of Aldous Huxley.

It is dangerous indeed to portray a character bulging with ideas, because the ideas will probably be identified as the author's own and will intrude into the narrative. While brilliant paradoxes are bandied back and forth, life may remain in the background. But the distrust of the intellect in the art of fiction has proved a worse peril still, one which has seduced too easily many half-cultured storytellers. After all, the great conflicts of our age are conflicts of ideas, or of myths, that is, of ideas made vital and impelling men to action. The novel has become willy-nilly the most powerful vehicle for the expression of ideas or for their popularization. Even more than history, it has been for fifty years intellectual dynamite. Behind much fiction by Gide, Mann, Malraux, and Camus, there echoes the voice of Nietzsche and that peculiar tragic emotion of our age that the French term *le tragique de l'intellect*. These novelists, with Proust, Joyce, Hermann Broch, Hermann Hesse, and Sartre of course, are men of unusual intelligence, teeming with ideas, and their fiction gains by this fact even if it loses in naïveté. Ideas are lived by them, 'felt in the blood, and felt along the heart,' and are not translated into terms of fiction but conceived in those very terms and impersonated before they appear consciously to the author.

Indeed, the difference between Thomas Hardy, Theodore Dreiser, and Sinclair Lewis and the giants of the novel, between Francis Carco, Georges Simenon, and Jean Giraudoux and their greater French contemporaries is a difference of intellectual as well as of imaginative power. Herman Melville and Henry James appear to us today (since James's death in 1916 and Melville's centenary in 1919, which ended his prolonged stay in Purgatory) as towering above other novelists of the American nineteenth century for the same reason. Melville's intellectual energy, while primarily that of a storyteller and a maker of myths, was also expressed in pregnant reflections on his art, such as are casually scattered in *The Confidence Man*. James's prefaces and letters are famous. Well could he declare with some pride: 'No good novel ever proceeded from a superficial mind.'

Absorption in ideas or in intellectual reactions and in their elucidation by a searching mind has harmed many a French novelist and led him to distrust imagination overmuch. Gide's youthful confession, in his diary of 1893, points to the weakness inherent in an excessive clear-sightedness. 'With me, imagination rarely precedes the idea . . . I have the idea of a work several years before I then imagine it.' Stendhal, in a famous confession, had perceived the foible of that national turn of mind that, with all his worship of energy and passion, was his too. 'I always lay my nets too high; nothing low is ever caught in them.'

Such a charge proffered against the French novel may appear as a paradox to those who remember how often it has been accused of immorality. Traditionally, since George Sand and Balzac, French novelists have been feared by the British as corrupters. A certain sanity and mature courage in refusing to eschew love scenes or to throw a veil over some climaxes which can be the object of serious and even poetical delineation characterize French novels. Sex is treated frankly by the French, and such frankness perhaps indicates more respect than does some of the ponderous sentimentalization frequent in German fiction or the timidity of very brutal American novelists of recent years. In fact, no other nation has probably treated the subject of love with such gravity as do the French. It is usually accompanied by tenderness, mutual esteem, and comradeship; and the physical communion is seldom unaccompanied by the play of the intellect, which watches, understands, analyzes, and occasionally ennobles.

The word by which Frenchmen like to characterize their novelists is hardly translatable; its English counterpart, 'moralists,' fails to convey all that it connotes in French. The ultimate justification of literature for most French people is moral, in the sense that it must push ever further man's knowledge of man, and be easily condensed into precepts that may enable readers to act 'morally,' that is to say, more lucidly and more sincerely. Jean Cocteau, André Breton, Mauriac, and Camus have all proclaimed their concern with *la morale,* which, in the feminine gender, becomes for them a muse, a mistress, the one idol that withstands all assaults. No Frenchman can resist scattering in his larger works a few epigrammatic thoughts summing up his experience of life and his vision of human affairs, with cynicism occasionally but more often than not with earnestness. Through these tablets of compressed wisdom, he naïvely expects to cure some of the illusions, if not some of the diseases, of mankind.

A breviary of higher wisdom can thus be extracted, not only from professional moralists like Montaigne and Pascal, but from Balzac, Proust, and Cocteau. These maxims are incisive, polished, pared down to a few explosive words. Like La Fontaine's fables, they denounce vanity, insecurity, fickleness, and imprudence in the civilized garden of life, from which the Frenchman fondly hopes to expel hazards, blind passions, wild beasts, and obtrusive neighbors. Behind his veneer of irony, which is a mild revenge on life from him who preaches and perhaps practices virtue, the optimistic Frenchman expects that his wisdom, gained through hardships, may keep his readers and their children from venturing into paths of danger. His instinct for economy makes him believe that the experience of one generation can be handed down intact to another in a few neat formulas and save the new generation trial and error. The Anglo-Saxon is a truer cynic. Neither Ernest Hemingway nor Norman Mailer, neither James Joyce nor Virginia Woolf foolishly hoped that, by inserting some such condensed reflections into their tales of war, love, and spiritual adventure they would ever deter their readers and their readers' sons from stumbling into folly and despair.

Modern philosophers are fond of disserting on values. It is hardly in the novelist's role to propose general reflections on the subject. Yet his art, while primarily concerned with storytelling and giving life to characters, is also a creation of values. He weaves a pattern out of the baffling contradictions of reality; he endows with some consistency those strange creatures who surround him in life and seem now empty, now bewilderingly erratic, now steeped in the full logic of unpoetical lives. He singles out a few significant events from the disconcerting disorder of chance happenings, establishes some relation of cause and effect where Fate, with its ironical irrelevancies, appeared to intervene arbitrarily. In so doing, he lays bare the true man in us — a truer man than is heard declaiming on the radio, seen moving jitteringly about on a screen, and myopically observed or belittled by journalists, travelers, and letter writers. And because such a man is a knot of relations, an individual linked by subtle ties to his physical and social environment, willingly held in check by shifting but impressive ethical codes to which he bows even when he disobeys them, the novelist is in our age a worthy successor to the priest and to the moralist. D. H. Lawrence, as good a storyteller as appeared in our century in England, often proved a turgid and apocalyptic reasoner; but he was clear-sighted when, like Proust, Mauriac, Giono, Saint-Exupéry, Malraux, Montherlant, Camus, and Sartre, he perceived the advantages that a novelist who remains an imaginative artist can derive from posing moral problems. He wrote, in a fragment collected in *Phœnix:*

> Morality is that delicate, forever trembling and changing balance between me and my circumambient universe, which precedes and accompanies a true relatedness . . . The novel is the highest example of subtle inter-relatedness that man has discovered. Everything is true in its own time, place, circumstance, and untrue outside of its own place, time, circumstance. If you try to nail anything down in the novel, either it kills the novel or the novel gets up and walks away with the tale.

I

THE CRISIS IN FRENCH FICTION,

1910–1930

THE LAST DECADE of the nineteenth century and the first decade of the twentieth appear to us today as a low point in the history of French fiction. Books published in Paris continued to be sold by the thousands all over the world; Anatole France was for many years identified with all that was subtle and mildly perverse in Gallic letters; Romain Rolland seemed to denationalize and deprovincialize French fiction, and his *Jean-Christophe* drew tears from many eyes. Paul Bourget was proposing first moral problems, then social ones, with convincing dialectic and a few scientific terms attuned to the pre-Freudian era. Henry Bordeaux, René Bazin, and a few other pillars of traditionalism perceived the possibilities of the novel for maintaining scions of noble families, future parish priests, and convent-educated, genteel young ladies on the path to virtue and resignation. Pierre Loti, plaintively tossing his disenchanted soul on strange seas and searching for picturesque feminine puppets and passionate sailors amid exotic climes, carried on the genre of romantic fiction. Maurice Barrès, the least popular abroad of these five masters of French romance, probably the best stylist of them all, and today the least antiquated, attempted a curious experiment in collective fiction with *Les*

24

Déracinés (1897), and, in *La Colline inspirée* (1913), offered the original achievement of a Catholic and mystical novel written by an unbeliever. But ideas that are not transmuted into emotions by the alchemy of imagination soon make a novel monotonous and lifeless. The generation that had been powerfully moved by the Dreyfus trial did not succeed in achieving the significant novel on politics that France awaited. A true novelist needs more faith and less irony, perhaps even a little more vulgarity and occasional stupidity, than these refined and fashionable observers of human folly possessed.

Parallel with this emphasis on the mind and on the psychological novel as opposed to the realistic and naturalistic one, the symbolist trend, in the years 1890–1910, set other pitfalls for fiction. It perceived ethereal and profound symbols behind most appearances. It took flight from earth, its mud, its real men and women, toward blessed damozels, sexless angelic creatures, imaginary polar settings, and perpetual yearning for the Idea underlying all faint representations that reached our prisoners' cave. 'No! bodies are not indispensable interpreters!' exclaims a young character in Gide's earliest volume of prose. And Gide delighted in describing the allegorical *Voyage d'Urien* in which, as the pun in the title suggests, neither scenery nor character has any reality. Symbolist fiction may be credited with a few curious attempts at personal analysis of a young man's soul (in *Valbert,* by T. de Wyzewa, in Edouard Dujardin's *Les Lauriers sont coupés,* which since has won fame as the systematic interior monologue that may have helped James Joyce's *Ulysses*) and with some original, but overwritten and overeloquent, novels, by Joris-Karl Huysmans and Elémir Bourges. But an excessive and 'arty' self-consciousness, a prophetic and declamatory tone, and a uniform haze, muffling all the characters and perfidiously dulling the reader's attention, seem to afflict most of the symbolist novels attempted in any language (and America is not immune from the peril, as readers who have remained allergic to Djuna Barnes's *Nightwood* or to William Goyen's *The House of Breath* will recall). In a splendid series of articles published in 1913 in the *Nouvelle Revue Française,* later collected in the posthumous *Nouvelles Études,* Jacques Rivière, then a young critic of twenty-eight, denounced the pernicious influence of symbolism upon fiction. Soon after, when Proust's first volume appeared, it was imbued with symbolist influences, but the author had assimilated and outgrown them and had made them subservient to his purpose as a novelist.

The French novel in particular stood in need of new blood in the years preceding World War I. It was then wading through one of the low-water tides of its history and ran the serious danger of perishing from drought. Naturalism, whatever we may think of it in retrospect (and a return to it may well be staged within another decade or two), had brought about a triumph for French fiction. But the new vogue for the Russian novel was already, in France at least, undermining the success of Zola and his disciples. Eugène Melchior de Vogüé's book *Le Roman russe* (1882) had made a deep impression; no less a personage than Taine declared soon after to Vogüé that 'Zola, Daudet, Goncourt and others are not worthy to untie the shoelaces of that man [Dostoevski].'

In France, the years 1910–30 have as much unity as any literary period can assume. Elsewhere [1] we proposed the view, which has since won fairly general acceptance, that the new physics (Max Planck and Albert Einstein), the new psychology (Sigmund Freud and his followers), the reactions against Henri Bergson in philosophy and the advocacy of neo-Thomism, the scientific study of literary history and of history (Gustave Lanson, Victor Langlois, and Charles Seignobos), the renewal of sociological, anthropological, religious, and ethical studies (by Emile Durkheim's disciples: Lévy-Bruhl, Rauh, and others) were accompanied around 1910, indeed preceded, by a revolution in literature and the arts. Guillaume Apollinaire sensed the significance of that revolution and was instrumental in effecting it in painting and poetry. Arthur Rimbaud and Stéphane Mallarmé suddenly came into their own, and from their example the surrealists and Paul Valéry were to derive theoretical consequences and felicitous inspiration. Paul Cézanne's lesson at last was proving fruitful, and the postimpressionists were recognized and praised. The superficial drama of the boulevards was battered. New periodicals appeared, new critics took stock of the legacy of symbolism (Albert Thibaudet, André Suarès, Jacques Rivière) and encouraged bolder steps forward. Men who had long waited for an audience (André Gide, Paul Claudel, Charles Péguy, Marcel Proust) suddenly sprang to the fore between 1910 and the outbreak of World War I. Almost all of those who were to be acclaimed in the postwar years began to give substantial proof of their talent around 1910–11. Their names are: Bernanos, Chardonne, Cocteau, Duhamel, Alain-Fournier, Giraudoux, Jouhandeau, Jouve, Larbaud, Martin du Gard, Mauriac,

1. In a volume, now out of print, entitled *Hommes et oeuvres du XXe siècle* (Corrêa, Paris, 1939).

Maurois, Morand, Paulhan, Reverdy, Rivière, Romains, St.-John Perse, Vildrac. Fiction, too, in France in the years 1910–30, is marked by a few features that will naturally leave their imprint upon the subsequent span of twenty years that it is our purpose to discuss.

But first, a brief epitaph on a few graves. The historical novel seems to be dead and gone — deader in France than in English-speaking countries, where Margaret Mitchell and, after a fashion, Robert Penn Warren, or Robert Graves have revived the genre with a measure of success. A case could be made for historical fiction, at a time when history proper has often hedged itself around with footnotes and documents and has ceased to be a part of the reading of cultured men and women.

Romanticized biography has stepped in where historical novels used to reign supreme a century and a quarter ago, when Walter Scott provided Balzac with his impetus and launched Leopold von Ranke on the path to accurate history. Not even nostalgic regret for a glorious past, during the tragic ordeal of the two world wars and of a decline in French power, has succeeded in luring French novelists to their Revolution, their Age of Louis XIV, or the romantic Middle Ages, staged by Gore Vidal in this country as a symbolic setting for his *Search for the King*. The only exception is a Russian-born French novelist, Zoe Oldenbourg, whose novels in a medieval setting, *Argile et Cendres* (1947) and *La Pierre angulaire* (1953), showed skill and narrative talent.

The poetical novel, also dear to the romantics, has likewise disappeared. What in Shakespeare and in Racine is taken to be an effective aesthetic device becomes intolerable in a novel and in prose. Proust, Giraudoux, and Giono have at times ventured dangerously close to the poetical novel; they have been saved, the first by the originality of his psychology, the second by his irony, the third by his robustness as a *surmâle,* as the French word puts it. Description has become a lost art. The influence of painting, then of the cinema has been immense, if seldom recognized, on the reading public far more than on the novelists. Landscape in literature has been divested of its estate.

Finally, the plot as such counts far less than it used to. There again, the movies and the detective story have lightened the weight that used to be borne by the novels of Balzac, Dickens, and Dostoevski. Breathless surprises, thrills of suspense before and after a murder, and patient questioning about when and how the chaste heroine would let her virtue be defeated, appear unsophisticated to many a novel reader today. He enjoys these devices in detective stories read as relaxation and as a geometrical combination to satisfy his logical brain, seeking a cause for every effect and trying to identify murderers of victims who were never very much alive in any case, at least psychologically. But intricacies of plot, subtle progression toward a climax, and unraveling of the knotted threads in the conclusion seem naïve to most modern novelists. What happens is secondary to the question: How are the characters changing under the impact of incidents. In Mauriac, Camus, Sartre, and, to a lesser degree, in André Malraux and Julien Green, the unfolding of events can be guessed from the start or is revealed from the start if the author works back from the present to a reminiscence of the events and motives that resulted in a crime, a trial, a great passion, or a great remorse.

Several times since 1910 or since Rivière's articles in 1913, critics have called for a renaissance of the novel of adventure. They hoped that Pierre MacOrlan or Francis Carco might provide it, after the works of Claude Farrère and Pierre Benoît had ceased to be regarded as literature. Their hopes have hardly been fulfilled. The only adventure that has inspired good novels, from Alain-Fournier's *Grand Meaulnes* to Saint-Exupéry, has been psychological. Men's lives have not been devoid of hazards and contingency in our age, and neither historical determinism nor the revelation of blind impulses from our libido and from primeval forces lingering in us has banished the mystery of *res adventura*, of what is yet to come and surprise us. But the novelist's purpose is to endow the contingent with a certain necessity, to integrate chance accidents into the total and fairly consistent pattern of a man's life, as accepted and even as wanted by him. Adventures in *La Chartreuse de Parme,* in which the structure of the plot counts for little compared with the invention lavished by the author on individual scenes, have delighted many a modern reader whom Balzac's laborious schemes left unimpressed. Many good modern novels are Stendhalian in the sense that they neglect the central plot and the structure and scaffoldings that should support them, but lavish their art on individual scenes that alone will remain engraved in the reader's memory.

On the positive side, the revolution that began in French fiction around 1910 (and that is closely paralleled by a renewal in English fiction about the same time) may be summed up in the word 'disintegration,' stripped of all disparaging connotations. It was, first of all, a disintegration of our idea of reality. Science was then effecting a similar disintegration, which was to usher in the atomic age. But literature owed nothing to science; if anything, the literary revolution preceded the change in scientific thought. Poets and novelists like to be called prophetic, and indeed they have been. French fiction had climbed on the band wagon of science in 1860–90, only to discover that scientific truth is the most ephemeral of all truths. As a German, J. von Uexhüll, declared in 1909: 'A scientific truth is but the error of tomorrow.' Proust, Giraudoux, Virginia Woolf, and Kafka remained unaware of the new physics, probably to their dying day. But they brought about the definitive break with realism in the novel that liberated modern fiction.

Proust attacked realism scathingly in the last volume of *Le Temps retrouvé*. 'The kind of literature which is content with describing things, while it calls itself realistic, is the furthest removed from reality.' Giraudoux and Cocteau depicted life as a pointillist and delightfully confusing welter of impressions. Virginia Woolf, in her entertaining essay railing at Arnold Bennett and his contemporaries H. G. Wells and John Galsworthy, all painstakingly bent upon rendering houses, furniture, silverware, and upholstery of London men of property, inhabitants of the five towns, or of the world of William Clissold, asserted: 'On or about December, 1910, human character changed.' [2] The liberation from too coarse a conception of reality was badly needed at the beginning of the twentieth century. It was effected, thanks to the generation of novelists reaching their manhood or womanhood around 1910. They opened up richer possibilities to fiction as an art.

The second disintegration, now linked with the great name of Freud, was that of our classical idea of man. The notions of libido, the id, the ego, and the superego have not, however, become integrated into the culture of the French common reader as they have in America. Many writers remained unaware of Freud's discoveries or impervious to them as late as 1925 and even 1935. Proust probably never knew anything precise about psychoanalysis. But there again novelists have been ahead of science. They broke up the classical concept of the unity of man, which Stendhal and then Dostoevski had already severely damaged. They freely juxtaposed insoluble contradictions in their characters and sought what Baudelaire had already called antithetic, yet simultaneous, directions toward God and toward Satan. They delved into the subconscious and became fascinated by eroticism. They became especially conscious of the sadistic-masochistic impulses dormant in most

2. *Mr. Bennett and Mrs. Brown* (Hogarth Press, London, 1928).

normal people and often co-existing with moral principles and saintly behavior. To be sure, there was much sadism already, not only in Sade, who was read by only a few until the last decades, but in Balzac, and Emily Brontë, and especially in Charles Dickens (*Nicholas Nickleby, Barnaby Rudge, Dombey and Son*), who was fascinated by it while he condemned it. But our vision of man has been immensely enriched by the novelists of our century, who have torn many of the soothing illusions that used to veil our lower selves from our vision.

This disintegration of our classical notion of personality was helped by World War I, in which many novelists participated (Giraudoux, Mauriac, Duhamel, Drieu la Rochelle, Aragon), while others watched it eagerly, repelled and fascinated (Romains, Colette, Cocteau, young Radiguet). The war itself is treated in far fewer French novels than American. It seems to have inspired many Americans to write, especially ambulance drivers. Nor did it evoke among French writers the same horrified disgust of civilized and sportive gentlemen as it did in English literature (Ralph Mottram, Robert Graves, Richard Aldington, and D. H. Lawrence; and Siegfried Sassoon, Wilfred Owen, and Edward Thomas among the poets). André Gide, François Mauriac, Jean Cocteau, Paul Morand, and Valéry Larbaud preferred to ignore the subject. But the wound was deeper in France than elsewhere, too deep for literary expression, and much of the cruelty and the cynicism depicted in fiction since 1920 originated in the display of man's inhumanity to man that haunted the survivors of Verdun and the Somme.

Linked with the atomization of man's personality, which characterized fiction between 1910 and 1930, is the predominance of two themes or types of characters that gives many of the novels of that age their main tonality. Most of the heroes are devoid of will power and delight in the resulting lack of any axis in their personality, and the majority of them are adolescents, usually of the male sex, if not of an ambiguous or ambidextrous one.

Hamlet has been hailed as the inspirer or the model of many French writers until 1930 or so, and their disease is currently called in France 'hamletism.' Ever since the romantics, the French had been obsessed by the Shakespearean hero. But what had been a literary vogue spread to a larger number of Frenchmen when, after 1918, they were confronted by the need to act and live up to their Pyrrhic victory and also by the unpredictable consequences of their action. The world overestimated French power and even spoke of French hegemony in Europe; diplomats concluded a network of treaties to make themselves believe that time could be stopped and life crystallized by legalistic agreements. But the men of letters, as usual, were more clear-sighted and fifteen years ahead of other observers. They realized that their victory was only luring them into postponing reforms or the needed revolution, that their country was weaker than it appeared to the world, and that the slaughter of a million and a half young men had left their comrades frightened in the presence of the gigantic task expected of them.

Hence the invasion of the novel by young men, devoid of will, weighing on a vast Elsinore platform the skulls of their friends fallen in battle, as Valéry was to say in a famous article. They distrusted propaganda, because war had fed them with official lies; they distrusted politics, since politicians had not averted the war; they distrusted women, because they had helped the patriotic propaganda and admired heroes in uniform and been the mainstay of the pressure of public opinion to encourage men to fight; they distrusted themselves most of all, and the generous but ill-starred *élan* of the youth of 1914. They set about rebuilding the ruins; they rushed to dancing halls, musical *cafés,* jazz orchestras, and cosmopolitan and Bohemian sets populated Montparnasse, and paraded a *joie de vivre* that half concealed their surprise at finding themselves alive after the long ordeal. Like their predecessors, the Julien Sorels and the Rastignacs who grew to manhood after the Napoleonic wars, they rushed insolently to the means of power left after the years of battle: money-making and unscrupulous *arrivisme.* But they lacked the vigor of their romantic ancestors, who, while reading Alphonse de Lamartine and George Sand and carrying their hearts in a sling, had achieved the first French industrial revolution. They took greater delight in pitiless self-analysis than in action. They were sought after by the postwar women in the bustle of the marriage mart, where men were outnumbered and could select, and change their minds or their partners. They disarticulated themselves, and in their novels they complacently analyzed their self-pity, their hesitations, and the finer nuances of their ego.[3]

3. Typical illustrations are many understudies of Gide's Lafcadio in the novel of those years; also, the characters in Edouard Estaunié, Jacques Rivière's two analytical novels, in Jacques de Lacretelle; Philippe Soupault, Marcel Arland, the early Henri de Montherlant, Paul Morand, Betz's *L'Incertain,* Robert de Traz's *L'Ecorché,* Pierre Drieu la Rochelle's *L'Homme couvert de femmes.* Joseph Kessel's *Le Tour du malheur* belatedly (in 1949) depicts the same era and its moods.

The primacy of the adolescent in French fiction from Proust's *Du côté de chez Swann,* Alain-Fournier's *Grand Meaulnes,* Giraudoux's *Simon le pathétique,* and Radiguet's and Cocteau's teenagers to Mauriac and Martin du Gard's young heroes is a strange phenomenon, which has been studied in an excellent monograph by Justin O'Brien and, from another angle, by Mauriac in a revealing little book, *Le Jeune Homme* (1926). Adolescents were not scarce in ancient literature. They had haunted the imagination of many a painter, such as Leonardo and Correggio. But they had hardly ever been analyzed in their contradictions and in their violent impulses to despair, to revolt, and to idealism as they have been in recent French fiction. They have displaced not only the *jeune fille,* who never held a great fascination for French novelists, but their former favorite characters, the mature woman troubled by her 'noonday demon,' and the middle-aged Don Juan unweariedly playing his part of Bel-Ami.

Goethe's Wilhelm Meister, Balzac's Rubempré, and Stendhal's heroes in his three main novels were somewhat different from the adolescents of sixteen to nineteen who have invaded modern fiction. Novelists then preferred to start with the early years of manhood, when the young man, having put on his *toga praetexta,* was completing his education through war, politics, and the affairs of the stage, of literature, or of the heart. George Sand, whose story of her life reveals a much keener psychologist than many of her romantic novels, was the first to remark, in the early chapters of her autobiography, that poets and novelists had unduly neglected the rich subject of the adolescent, worshipping his mother and not yet severed from her spiritually, but ready to transfer to another woman and to another plane some of his feelings, often ugly, rebellious, spiteful, but nevertheless shy and athirst for poetry. Dostoevski's novel *The Adolescent* influenced the modern French more than George Sand's prophetic passage, which Justin O'Brien rediscovered. But the French, try hard as they can, seldom can unreservedly subscribe to the hysterical behavior and to the antics, apparently sincere, that Dostoevski's heroes, and still more his heroines, can stage with much ease. Gide was a more direct inspirer of the French portrayers of adolescence who had been struck by his Nathanael, his prodigal son, and his Lafcadio.

Twentieth-century fiction in France, soon imitated by fiction in other countries, thought it had charted one of those unknown and metaphorically fertile fields in the theme of homosexuality. The theme had been central, twenty centuries or more before, in the literature of antiquity. But it had not assumed the tragic character it received when religion, society, and our prevailing mores, outlawing homosexuality, made it a glamorous forbidden fruit for some, the mark of an ineluctable pursuit by fate for others. If one judges it purely on the literary plane, the theme of homosexual love offers undoubted advantages to the novelist. It lends itself to an atmosphere of secrecy, dear to many readers of detective stories. It affords the thrill of breaking social codes, at a time when adultery and so-called illicit sex relations seem to have lost much of the glamour that surrounded them when *Madame Bovary* revolted French taste in 1857. It cuts across ordinary social strata, and, when men on the wrong side of forty, no longer able to rely upon their charm alone, have to seek their victims or their partners among servants, sailors, and young men whom they bribe, it takes on the pitiful form of social *déclassement,* of venality, and of cruel disparity of ages, well known to readers of Proust and Gide. It has, more, perhaps, than any other single factor, contributed to the predominance of a new type in modern French fiction: *l'homme traqué,* the man hunted by fate, by his passions, by his vice, by his tragic solitude, and yearning for the beauty and formal serenity of a work of art to escape from the night in which he is doomed to grope his guilty way.

Sociologists, who are slow at learning from the insight of fictional works, in which a keener and unhappier sensibility than theirs often senses the most acute problem of the age, may some day look for social, perhaps even economic, causes to explain the vogue of pederasty as a literary subject and the apparently larger proportion of homosexuals to be found among creative writers than among other men, and especially among creative writers since the era of Walter Pater, Oscar Wilde, Paul Verlaine, Pierre Loti, and Marcel Proust. Has the custom of early marriage (often in the early twenties) among students and young men of letters and the consequent financial pressure on them driven the gifted heterosexual writers to pursuits other than literature, leaving the field to those who did not seek the responsibilities of a wife and children? Has the growing comradeship between the sexes and often the effort on the part of the young woman to behave, talk, think like a man divested the woman of some of her traditional charm and convinced some disciples of Plato that intellectual beauty, if it must be sought behind the deceptive appearance of the bodily envelope, can be found more abundantly in young males? Such explorations obviously do not go deep enough. The secret is psychological and individual in the first place. But the increase of self-confessed homosexuals among the gifted men of letters is also in part a social phenomenon, in which imitation and closely knit *confréries* of persons so inclined praising and pushing each other's works may well have a share. The subject cannot be ignored, since it has contributed to the tragic loneliness of many modern heroes and to the now common picture of the family as a prison from which one escapes and no longer as a nucleus around which everything converges.[4]

Paradoxically, at the very time when the novel was taking as its assumptions the disintegration of reality as formerly conceived, the disintegration of personality, and the disintegration of the ultimate social cell, the family, it was also returning to a long, devious, meandering type of epic fiction in several volumes, often grouped around one or several families, the *roman-fleuve*. The reasons for such a vogue are complex. Critics often make the mistake of ignoring the fact that literature is, if not conditioned by, at least produced for a public and for specific publishers aware of the public's buying habits, by authors who have to make a living. A French book will be published, and apparently will be bought, more readily if it falls under a series; fanciful titles for these 'collections' enliven the catalogues of French publishers. Similarly, it was thought, and apparently with good reason, since Romain Rolland's and Marcel Proust's fictional avalanches, that the collector or the thrifty bourgeois who has ventured to purchase the first four or five volumes of a saga-novel would not wish to see his investment interrupted. He might even — who knows? — be so thrilled after volume eight or fourteen that the good will of his purse would continue to respond *in saecula saeculorum*.

But literary motives may also be adduced to account for the extraordinary vogue of the *roman-fleuve*. First, especially after 1920 or thereabouts, the French novelists desired to compete on equal terms with their Russian and English confreres. Parisian publishers

4. John Aldridge, in *After the Lost Generation* (McGraw-Hill Book Company, New York, 1951), notes (p. 100) the intrusion of the same theme of homosexuality in several contemporary American novels by Frederick Buechner, Vance Bourjaily, Truman Capote, J. H. Burns, Gore Vidal, and others. British fiction is now coming to the same subject with *Hemlock and After* by Angus Wilson (Viking Press, New York, 1952) and the extraordinary story of a British officer in Burma by Walter Baxter, *Look Down in Mercy* (G. P. Putnam's Sons, New York, 1951). The most superb example of a novel about a man haunted not by homosexuality but by alcoholism is *Under the Volcano* (Reynal and Hitchcock, New York, 1947), by Malcolm Lowry.

had long worked on the assumption that the French, being a light, fickle, and impatient race, should have their novels brief, compressed, and selective; or that, being self-proclaimed masters in the knowledge of the human, and particularly of the feminine heart, they insisted on their fiction being stripped of all that was not 'psychology.' Then they discovered that the public was ready to welcome *War and Peace, The Brothers Karamazov,* and almost any long novel translated from the English, and, later on, from the German and American. They blamed the decadence of taste and the decline of culture, which were discarding the great classical lesson, the art of omission, and destroying the intelligent group of readers who scorned violent effects and superabundance of details. Incidentally, they forgot all about Balzac and Hugo and a number of Frenchmen whose long serial novels and lavishness of words and overstressed effects had not repelled an earlier public.

Many Frenchmen thus became convinced that a true novel must be long and that their traditional fiction was much too stripped of essential nonessentials, too linear in its hasty ascent to a climax and subsequent descent, too dramatic in its elimination of all that, in the characters, did not bear directly on the central crisis in which they would be the feverish actors.

While the French *roman-fleuve* was often eager to rival Dostoevski in its profusion of seemingly irrelevant details and in its juxtaposition of unreconciled contradictions in men's motives and actions, it also pursued another end; it attempted, in the years that followed the Dreyfus case and seemed to herald the triumph of both sociology and of socialism, to abandon the narrow analysis of one individual, usually telling the story of some episode in his life in the first person singular. The more thoughtful among the French novelists have reflected much, at the time of Proust and since, on the perils of the so-called autobiographical novel, in truth a contradiction in terms. The advantages in credibility and consistency to be gained by memoirs are obvious; the unity of the point of view is easily achieved; the author may yield to poetical evocations, to self-pity, and even more to self-vindication; he leads events and characters safely to a preordained conclusion, which is his present mood of serenity and complacency. But the loss is immense; the multiplicity of possibilities and the thrilling sense for the reader that the novelist is unsure of the future and of the forthcoming development of his characters disappear. Events are relived by memory, but they are not recreated into an animated whole. And the sincerity of the storyteller can be much greater

than that of the reminiscing autobiographical author, hemmed
in on all sides by factual truth and unable to reach toward the
deeper, symbolic truth that fictional creatures of Stendhal or
Proust achieve.[5] Hence the ambition to flee from the self-analytical
ego and from the intimate diary, the perpetual pitfall for French
fiction, and to embrace the vast picture of a changing scene through
a score of years.

The best known of the *romans-fleuves,* reminiscent of Zola's
Rougon-Macquart series more than of Balzac's recurring characters
in his portrayal of the whole of France, are Romains's *Les Hommes
de bonne volonté (Men of Good Will),* Martin du Gard's *Les
Thibault (The World of the Thibaults),* Duhamel's *Chronique des
Pasquiers.* René Béhaine has his admirers, but he has failed to win
an audience, outside of a very small French circle, for his *Histoire
d'une société.* Lacretelle embarked on a *roman-fleuve* with his
Hauts-Ponts (1932–5) and stopped after the fourth volume, out
of breath and deserted by most of his readers. The French Academy, however, soon rewarded him for his portrayal of a woman's
obstinate attachment to her family estate. Later still, a lingering
desire to depict French society between the two wars inspired
Joseph Kessel in *Le Tour du malheur,* Maurice Druon in *Les
Grandes Familles,* Paul Vialar in *La Mort est un commencement,*
and even J.-P. Sartre. It may be confessed, however, that the sociological ambitions of the French novel have been frustrated, and
that its portrayal of French society holds hardly more interest
for younger readers today than do *The Forsyte Saga* and its sequels or H. G. Wells's novels for the new generations of the English. The novel is probably a better document when it is one
without the author's being aware of the fact or when, like Balzac's *Comédie humaine,* it distorts what it renders so powerfully
that it becomes the truth of tomorrow.

After 1930, the social ambition of the novel gave way, in France
and soon in other countries, to its metaphysical ambition. Joyce
confessed that he wished to free himself from the nightmare of
the story; ironically, our successors may someday admire him
primarily as the portrayer of Dublin. Kafka became the model
most oppressive for younger novelists; Mann of *Buddenbrooks,*
probably his best artistic achievement and his most durable one,

5. See especially Duhamel, *Remarques sur les mémoires imaginaires* (Mercure
de France, 1934); Gide's obsession with the problem in his *Journal,* in *Si le
grain ne meurt* (If It Die), and elsewhere; Martin-Chauffier's acute essay on
'Proust and the Double I' (*Partisan Review,* October 1949).

was almost forgotten for the philosophical speculations of *The Magic Mountain* and of *Doctor Faustus*. In France, from Malraux to Sartre and from Cocteau to Genet, no self-respecting writer would sketch a novel without scaling the heights of the difficulty of being, of assuming freedom and responsibility, and of organizing a frail existence constantly threatened by disintegration and nothingness.

MARTIN DU GARD, DUHAMEL,

ROMAINS, RADIGUET

I F A CHOICE had to be made of the most significant novels published in France during the years 1910–30, eliminating temporarily survivors of the older generation (France, Loti, Barrès,
Bourget, Rolland, even Boylesve and Estaunié), and omitting
Mauriac and Green, two novelists of the subsequent twenty years,
our list would include the novels of Proust and Gide; then *Jean
Barois* by Martin du Gard, in preference to *Les Thibault;* Duhamel's *Salavin;* Alain-Fournier's *Le Grand Meaulnes,* for its historical importance; and Radiguet's *Le Diable au corps.* As to the
place of Giraudoux, Bernanos, Larbaud, and Colette, it is permissible to hesitate and to rank the first as primarily a dramatist,
the second as dangerously rhetorical, the other two as authors of
short stories or novelistic sketches. Morand, Maurois, Chardonne,
Carco, and Schlumberger will not, in our opinion, survive as
novelists. Indeed, their stars have already set.

Roger Martin du Gard, who is ten and twelve years younger
than Proust and Gide, respectively (he was born near Paris in
1881), is a less 'modern' novelist than either of the latter. Neither
his technique nor his preoccupations and implicit philosophy rank

38

him as a contemporary of the existentialists and of other new-comers in the field of the novel, whose vision of man is more tragic and whose tone is that of bitter individual revolt. But for anyone who disregards the flux of fashions, the author of *Les Thibault* stands as the most faithful imaginative portrayer of the conflicts that tore France between the Dreyfus affair and World War I, the two great events in the history of French conscience in this century. No history of the Third Republic has yet succeeded in bringing to life the significance of these French crises as have the novels of Martin du Gard. Such an achievement is of a different order from that of technical innovation or the renewal of language, but it is no less valuable, since, for French literature to continue to exist, there must be the country France, and the very existence of the country was at stake in the convulsions of 1900, 1914, and 1940, which novels like these illuminate.

Martin du Gard has been the most modest of all French men of letters in this century. Not one private letter by him has been published; he has not written or revealed any chapter of his memoirs; he has not confided to any interviewer. What is even rarer, he has acted as if he had no opinions whatever on the present and the future state of the novel, on his fellow novelists, or on his own aims, method, and technique. Anyone familiar with French literary mores must entertain an unusual respect for the will to resist and the capacity for silence of a Nobel Prize winner who has refrained from writing a single preface or a single article on his art and its previous or present practitioners. Critics who often balk at dissecting a work of fiction in itself and prefer to fly off on the tangent of the author's opinions and avowals of his loves and hates have been baffled by Roger Martin du Gard's discretion. They have punished him by not writing a single volume, dissertation, or substantial essay on him. But this forgotten man of the French novel, if out of tune with the present mood of cruelty and of complacent denunciation of the absurdity of man's fate, has retained the respect of craftsmen and the attention of readers. His work has worn less thin than that of Romains and Duhamel.

His early training, like that of Mauriac and Malraux, was in history and more especially in archaeology. He wrote a thesis for the *Ecole des Chartes* on the Norman abbey of Jumièges. The future novelist learned how to consult and interpret documents, and his reconstruction of the Dreyfus debate and of the War of 1914 was supported by an impeccable, often obtrusive and lifeless, utilization of the most faithful contemporary accounts. He learned the more valuable art of submitting to his characters as he had created them and to his narrative as it logically and smoothly unfolded. Hence his equanimity appears almost inhuman to some readers who today prefer the vituperations of Georges Bernanos or Louis-Ferdinand Céline and wax impatient at the serene impartiality of a novelist who refuses to intervene and tell us what he thinks of his heroes. The style itself has a uniform transparency, which reveals events and moods without any willful distortion on the author's part.

Some of the volumes in *Les Thibault* have been linked with the French naturalists, especially when Martin du Gard depicts, with clinical precision, a doctor's workday or the onslaught of disease and death upon old Oscar Thibault, then upon Antoine, the warwounded doctor. The author's latent view of man cherishing the pursuit of truth, spurning many of the solaces of traditional religion, and stressing clear-headedness and the senseless inhumanity of war and of fanaticism has reminded some of the positivism of the earlier French naturalists. The analogy is superficial. Unlike the naturalists, Martin du Gard derives no joy from exploring the lower side of man or from exposing the selfish meanness of the bourgeois class. His novel or volume of sketches on peasant life, *La Vieille France,* is doubtless somewhat reminiscent of Zola in its satirical onslaught on the agrarian myth. Sentimental idyls are not to the taste of that clear-sighted observer. But if such a great name is not too overpowering, Tolstoy is the writer with whom Martin du Gard has most in common — except for Tolstoy's faith and crusade. *The Death of Ivan Ilyich,* that extraordinary record of a man feeling himself dying of cancer, is the model, unconsciously perhaps, for the death scenes in *Les Thibault* and in many subsequent French novels. A tone of pity and of generosity, only half audible but excluding cynical contempt for man, a creature more stupid than criminal, and sinned against by fate more than sinning, is the tone of Martin du Gard. Camus, in the following generation more fond of displaying its philosophical reading and more vocal in its revolt, will not be remote from the author of *Les Thibault.*

Lucidity, humanity, and sorrowful, but perforce resigned, evocation of the agony of all his men characters and of prewar Europe are the chief virtues of the fine saga-novel, which it is not our purpose here to analyze or to discuss at length. In spite of some overstressed symmetry, especially in the earlier volumes, between the two families delineated, the novel eschews the characterization of social classes as such. It scathes the tyrannical family pride and hypocrisy of the bourgeoisie, but even the self-righteous old Thibault is treated with sympathy. (Indeed, what services the much-maligned bourgeois have rendered modern fiction, not only by purchasing it but by providing it with three-fourths of its best characters and unweariedly absorbing its fiercest blows!) It moves according to a plan that the author nowhere has made too obvious or too rigid, and the reader remains in suspense and shares in the spontaneity the novelist has maintained in his characters. Though less ambitiously comprehensive than his successor Jules Romains, Martin du Gard has avoided the peril of venturing to describe environments and scenes that he did not know through imagination and feeling. He realized how inadequate is knowledge of the intellect alone, even supported by documents. The limitations of the author are real: he is not enough of a poet in the deeper sense of the word, and his most effective scenes lack the visionary *élan*, the mysterious thrill that alone could engrave them unforgettably upon our memories; and his lighting is probably too uniform, his effects of chiaroscuro or of lurid abysses of night illuminated by sparse rays from the author's projector are too few or too weak. The series of volumes is thus prevented, in spite of the not-undeserved Nobel Prize, from ranking among the great masterpieces of fiction. His own discretion and overready submission to a traditional form of narrative may well have been a disservice to the author.

These limitations, which will be even more conspicuous in other *romans-fleuves*, are perhaps inseparable from the genre itself. No one, except a feverishly inspired genius like Balzac, can turn out one or two novels a year steadily. The author of a long saga-novel inevitably suffers from lapses of inspiration and phases of sterility. He then lets a few years go by without resuming his convict's forced labor, and the sweep of the work, the inspired unity, are compromised. Such was the case with the earlier volumes of *Les Thibault*, interrupted after 1928 and resumed only in 1936 with the series about the summer of 1914. The tone then was altered; the gloom weighing over a universe in which little hope was left for man crushed by physical forces had become all-pervading; the freshness of the scenes of adolescence and love had wilted. In spite of the deep pity of the author for his characters, who are all brooding victims of a monstrous game in which the dice are loaded against man's kindness and courage, we fret at his impassive portrayal of their defeats. Other novelists have proved far less intellectually honest in their description of modern man, less coolly objective;

but we find them less disconsolate, for they at least imply that sin exists and therefore perhaps redemption also, that some grace may call their characters from the most horrible abysses of vice. Evil to them, even to Mauriac and Genet, Céline and Gide, assumes the appearance of a positive, diabolical force, and it is depicted with such truculence that we may, upon closing the book, imagine that *we* are immune from such a violent condemnation. The author of *Les Thibault* leaves us with no such illusion. Science, progress, knowledge, and good will alone could have turned this into a better world; and man has misused them irretrievably. There is no hell; but we are all sick, and no faith illuminates our dismal hospital abode.

Some critics have consequently dismissed Martin du Gard as a man of the nineteenth century who had accepted the benefit neither of neo-Thomism nor of existentialism. Such labels are absurd, for the faith in the possibilities once offered by science was no less valid than the assertion that man's freedom is all-powerful; the disappointment of those who were forced to disbelieve in progress and in ethical behavior severed from religion is no more old-fashioned than the trust of a later generation in a religious, Freudian, or Marxist *mystique*. Physical suffering, stressed by Martin du Gard, is just as revolting and humiliating (perhaps more tragic even if monotonously ancient) as the philosophical anguish of more recent fictional heroes in pondering over the problems of language or of total sincerity. The comparison between our war-ridden twentieth century, with its fanatical clashes of ideas (as we pompously call our propagandized assumptions and our complacently lauded ways of life), and the one that preceded it may well put ours to shame.

Artistically, Martin du Gard had doubtless achieved a greater success with his less ambitious *Jean Barois* (1913). Through its rich content and its symbolical significance, the book may well be one of the most important novels of the years 1900–1918, along with Gide's *La Porte étroite* and Proust's *Swann*. The author experimented with the form of a novel transposed into a dramatic dialogue, which enabled him to avoid some of the smoothness of his later narratives as an omniscient novelist. The conversations between the characters faithfully express the style, the emotions, and the behavior of the interlocutors, without the novelist's having to intrude with comments of his own. High lights can thus be focused sharply, while didactic parts (on the background and details of the Dreyfus case) and especially descriptions, the dead weight in so many novels of Balzac and Dostoevski, are cut short. A few stage directions conjure up the setting of the main scenes.

Such a technique, however, cannot avoid some artificial devices or some monotony. Martin du Gard, who has written farces for the stage with marked dramatic flair and is not without a bitter comic sense, does not succeed in animating some of his crucial scenes. His women characters in particular are too reserved, closer, even in their scenes of anger and protest, to women as men want them to be in life — composed, outwardly resigned, inwardly sure of their own ultimate victory — than to women as men like to find them depicted in novels of other nations — hysterical, as in Dostoevski, shrieking with orgiastic laughter, clinging to the man who has scorned her most and following him to Siberia after his inevitable crime. The passions that impel Jean Barois, Luce, and the other characters are mainly intellectual. The love element is restricted. The noble impartiality of the novelist disconcerts readers who like to have the author's position stated unambiguously.

This dramatized novel is likely to remain as the most vivid portrayal of the two crises lived by the author and by France between 1880 and 1910: the struggle waged between Catholicism and science, and the loss of the traditional faith in many minds that had received a historical and exegetic training; and the Dreyfus case, which drove some of the same minds to anticlericalism. These crises go a long way toward elucidating the attitude of France even in 1950 and help explain how, to this day, Frenchmen may, in the face of grave exterior perils, refuse to compromise on such questions as the state support of clerical schools.

The drama of Jean Barois lies in his anxiety to fill the gap left by the breakdown of the Catholic faith of his youth, shattered by the study of natural history and exegesis. The rigidity of the Church dogmas and his own uncompromising temperament drive him to an active crusade for new values, which he cherishes and which he opposes to traditional Christianity. He soon clashes with his pious wife, Cécile, whose religion has become narrow and superstitious. They separate. The Dreyfus affair breaks out. Jean Barois plunges into it on the side of the defenders of Dreyfus and, even more, on the side of liberalism and abstract justice. After seven years of trial and retrial, of organized lying by the anti-Semites and by the defenders of the army, prone, as Goethe once confessed he was, to prefer an injustice to disorder, Dreyfus is vindicated. Socialism, tinged with anticlericalism and antimilitarism, triumphs. The noble *mystique* of liberal champions of justice and truth has to give way to a spoils system in which the army is weakened, the Church is persecuted, and the mediocrity of profiteers of politics replaces the lofty dream of elevating the people and of teaching them socialism as an untarnished Messianic faith.

Jean Barois does not moralize on the event. The novel gives us insight into the minds of some of the fighters in that great duel of consciences. Jean himself has had his nerves shattered by the long fight. He sees death close to him in a carriage accident, and his lips voluntarily whisper a prayer memorized in his pious childhood. He admits that he fears death. His own daughter, whom his wife alone has brought up, chooses to be a nun. Her father realizes that any onslaught on dogmas and rites, any historical and philosophical refutation leave the will to believe, the hope of triumphing over death, and the solitude of human beings yearning for charity and love untouched in many a heart. On his death bed he prays and is comforted. Roger Martin du Gard, who had the 'irony' of an artist and has never forsaken his intellectual honesty, avoided the naïveté of letting his own unbelief win in the denouement. The overtones of sadness in the final pages, however, half reveal his own sorrow at man's inability to act rationally.

To people who read about the Dreyfus case only in history books, *Jean Barois,* better than any other novel written on that tragic civil war, which tore irretrievably the conscience of France and moved that of the world, offers an accurate, yet a significant and stylized, account of the events then lived and of the problems involved. It constitutes indeed fiction truer than truth.

The aftereffects of World War I on French psychology, ethics, and will to live have been enormous, and thus far underestimated by many, especially in other countries, who still expect from the French patriotic and idealistic reactions and a faith in their future, which could never again be the same after 1914–18. The history of the war itself has been told in the minutest detail. Still the significance of World War I in French, and therefore in world, history has not been brought out strikingly in fiction, and no painstaking historical account can replace that. Will a Tolstoy or a Balzac appear, forty years after the event, to comprehend the magnitude of the subject?

Many novels were written about the war itself, half a dozen excellent ones among them. Proust and, regrettably enough, Gide, Mauriac, Bernanos, and Green left the subject out of their fiction.

Cocteau wrote an ironical but very subtle and even moving novel, in its brevity, of war in the rear and of an adolescent, unscathed by his own imposture and the sordid plots around him, dying a modest hero's death, *Thomas l'Imposteur*. Céline rendered the horrors of war with Goyaesque visionary power in his *Voyage au bout de la nuit* (*Journey to the End of the Night*), and Giono with even more grim horror in realistic and pacifist volumes. Henri Barbusse hardly ranks with authors assured of survival. Three writers seem to us to stand out as the chief portrayers of the war in several of its aspects, one of them, Radiguet, utilizing the war only as a background for a story of adolescent love. The other two, Duhamel and Romains, are far more than war novelists; their forty- or fifty-volume work is, at the present date, still in progress, if such a word may be used to denote a decline following maturity. But their pictures of World War I, drawn from life by Duhamel, reconstituted from research and from imagination by Romains, represent the climax of their success as novelists.

Duhamel and Romains, and a number of other novelists, J. R. Bloch, Chardonne, Alain-Fournier, Carco, Jouhandeau, and Bernanos were born around the middle eighties and were profoundly impressed by the years that followed the Dreyfus affair. They witnessed a good deal of soul-searching in France. World War I came as a shattering blow to those young men of thirty who had been dreaming either of a strong traditionalist France worthy of Saint Louis and of Louis XIV or of a rapprochement between literature and the people and an enrichment of the intellectuals from the comradeship with the masses initiated during the Dreyfus struggle. This generation of novelists was endowed with remarkable gifts and opened itself to some fecundating influences, chiefly that of Russian fiction. It poured a new content into effete art forms and, for all its sentimental and occasional socialistic fervor, it remained sensitive to artistic values. Yet very few great novels by these men are likely to emerge as achievements to be ranked on a par with those of Proust, Gide, and Colette, their elders by some fifteen years. Overproduction may be one of the causes of that relative failure, but a very partial cause indeed. For Flaubert, alone of all the novelists of England and France in the nineteenth century, and Joyce in the twentieth, cannot be called overproductive. The temptation to crusade for a political or social cause and to become a journalist dealing out wisdom in daily articles is probably the most baneful temptation to which a novelist may yield; and many have succumbed to it.

Georges Duhamel enjoyed the advantage of clear prose and an apparently effortless and smooth narrative, which designated him as the successor to Anatole France. His work, however, wore thin after he had drawn on his war experience and on his postwar vision of men bound by friendship and a kindly desire to rebuild a better world. His long and facile saga-novel, *Chronique des Pasquier,* in spite of occasional charm and freshness, fails to hold the attention of readers; Duhamel's one determined attempt to renovate his inspiration, after World War II, with *Le Voyage de Patrice Périot* (1951) resulted in an unconvincing picture of a doctor's family torn by ideological feuds and of naïve scientists becoming the playthings of political exploiters. These novels start auspiciously and are delineated in pleasing and precise outlines, displaying a gift for draftsmanship, which has become a rarity nowadays. They breathe a human warmth that is also rare in the pessimistic literature of our age. But they fail to expand and to be sustained to the end by sufficient creative fire. It is sad to have to confess once again that anger and hatred seem to nourish an author's energy more persistently than pity and love.

Duhamel's father was a doctor who started practicing medicine late, never became very successful for lack of order and efficiency in his life, and bequeathed little else to his family but the memory of an entertaining visionary buffeted by life but always obstinately smiling. He appears several times in the novels of his son. Duhamel was also a doctor, one of many in Europe who turned to literature; Céline and Luc Durtain were also medical men who won fame as novelists, as other doctors — Elie Faure, Henri Mondor, even Alexis Carrel — became outstanding essayists. 'Anatomists, physiologists, I find you everywhere!' exclaimed Sainte-Beuve, himself a former medical student, when reviewing Madame Bovary. It has been contended that doctors' sons (Flaubert, Proust, Mauriac) lean heavily to intense analytical study of life and to melancholy brooding over man's inability to escape from his physical and physiological limitations. If this is so, Duhamel is an exception among doctors and doctors' sons. But he owed much to the practice of medicine, the most fertile training ground for one who would be a novelist. He probed the secrets of men and women and diagnosed the psychological causes of some of their diseases. He observed the concrete instead of theorizing from books and systems. He visited people when they were off their guard, in a disorderly bedroom, with their hair, faces, and clothes unprepared for the social comedy that one plays in healthy life. He heard confessions from wives hating their husbands, from heartless husbands, and from human beings suddenly become abject in their fear of disease and of death. But that experience did not make Duhamel bitter or cynical. It did not even make him gruff and imperious, like many doctors who think they will be obeyed and respected more by their patients if they utter laconic oracles and scold with sharp finality. Pity is the controlling sentiment that Duhamel tried to reintroduce into literature, after the naturalists and certain intellectual cynics had disaccustomed readers to such an outmoded feeling.

Duhamel as a child had been poor, a not-uncommon feature among men of letters, who are mostly drawn from the lower middle class. He neither resented his poverty nor revolted against it. Even less did he affect the worldly manners of young men who want to forget their origins and the sacrifices made by their families so that they may tempt fortune in Paris. Duhamel never made a speciality of the study of misery, as did the proletarian novelists and later a short-lived group of 'populist' novelists (Henri Poulaille, André Thérive, Eugène Dabit). He liked to choose his characters from among shabby office clerks and petty government employees, and he tried to steer halfway between the sentimental idealization of their mediocre lives and the propagandist tone of Upton Sinclair or of John Steinbeck that weaves misery and injustice into much too colorful an epic.

Duhamel succeeded where others failed, without having the inverted pride in his social origins that drove D. H. Lawrence, for example, to grant the monopoly of sexual attraction and potency to miners, soldiers, gamekeepers, and American Indians. The stumbling block of such a literature is sentimentality, and sentimentality, which occupies a large place in life, is granted only a small place in literature. Duhamel tempers his picture of man with humor. His sentimentality is closer to the tragic kind that is found in Russian fiction. His characters lay their hearts bare with humility and a passion for abject confession of their weaknesses and sins; but they do not revel in it with the pride of sinners who wish to unbosom their secrets so as to make room for more sins in their unburdened souls.

The lifelong concern of Duhamel, apparent in all his essays, reminiscences, and novels, is one that he shared with Charles Péguy, Romain Rolland, Jules Romains, and other writers of his period: an idealistic impulse to save men. Duhamel, like young Péguy, then an unbeliever, turned all his meditations around the

categorical imperative inspired by Joan of Arc: 'One must save.'
But save whom? For men are stubbornly reluctant to be saved.
As the Utopian socialists had done, as Péguy did, Duhamel and
some of his friends dreamed of harmonious life; in their youthful
fervor they attempted life in common in the phalanstery of an old
abbey. But the French, who are likely to cherish mankind in the
abstract and to undertake distant crusades in the interest of humanity, are notoriously bad neighbors when it comes to silencing
their individualism, their envy, and their irony. Duhamel smiles
at the men and women whom he wants to continue loving in spite
of themselves. He is not blind to the disappointments that an optimist must endure, and all his novels display the gradual collapse
of a rosy dream. He will not seek a solution in an easy catchword,
tendered by Christianity, which he respected but never professed,[1]
or in science, which he always admired, though he was aware of its
limitations. Friendship is the feeling of which he spoke most nobly
(in *Deux Hommes* especially); like Romains, Vildrac, and later
Malraux and Saint-Exupéry, he would have liked to build a virile
and warm regeneration of mankind upon friendship, that is, upon
the most beautiful of all words and ideals proposed by humanism
and by Christianity — fraternity.

After completing his medical studies, Duhamel had written
plays, of slight dramatic value, and critical essays, when World
War I revealed to him a new and richer vein of his own talent.
In 1917, he brought out, under a pseudonym then required by
his position in the army, *La Vie des martyrs;* he followed it up
with a sequel, *Civilisation,* in 1918; and, thirty years later, he returned to the same subject in one of the best volumes of his old
age, *Récits des temps d'affliction.*

Duhamel's point of view toward the gigantic catastrophe into
which Europe was plunged in 1914 is original. Others, most numerous, chose to depict war as monstrous and ghastly, caused by
the greed of statesmen and of industrialists. A few, found among
the fighters as well as among the profiteers and those who love to
command from a safe desk job, actually enjoyed the war and explained why in memorable books: Ernst Jünger in Germany,
Montherlant (*Le Songe*), Drieu La Rochelle (*La Comédie de Char-
leroi*), Vercel (*Le Capitaine Conan*). Some, to avoid being crushed
by the inexorable and devouring machine, undertook to laugh the

1. He published during World War II (in 1941) a series of very personal literary
studies, stating his own religious and philosophical position, notably apropos
of Pascal: *Les Confessions sans pénitence* (Plon, 1941).

strain off by stressing the humorous or entertaining moments in the soldiers' lives; thus did André Maurois who, like Duhamel, hit upon his best vein in his two war books of conversations with Colonel Bramble and Dr. O'Grady. Giraudoux pretended that he enjoyed the war because it was a liberation from prosaic life, an opportunity to dream freely about women, transfigured by the soldiers' love-starved imagination, an ordeal pleasantly interrupted by furloughs and hospitals. The poet Apollinaire, before he died from his wounds, likewise sang the romance of modern war, of galloping artillery horses and 'phallic' antiaircraft guns pointing to the sky.

Duhamel was a doctor in the front lines. He had no ax to grind, having no political cause to uphold. He was not naïve enough to believe wars to be the contrivance of munitions makers. He did not attempt a panoramic picture of the war, with the strategic plans of generals and the intricate transmission of orders and an elaborate analysis of the emotions of men before and after an attack. Like Stendhal in his famous account of Waterloo, he was determined to describe only what he saw. As a doctor, operating in an ambulance close to the line of battle, in a war in which the medical corps was conspicuous for its poor organization, he saw wounded and dying men. To weld those fragments of experience into a continuous novel would have been untrue to the author's purpose. He did not compose a novel, which would have been more vivid perhaps than reality but which would have betrayed the bare testimony of a witness and destroyed the gloomy unity of the author's experience, obsessed by so much suffering. The war books of Duhamel are composed of vignettes and short stories, with a minimum of touching up. They are told dramatically, because Duhamel's artistic sense prompted him to restore to reality, through literary skill, some of the tragedy it contains. But the author expressed himself in the first person, an eyewitness who, as an army doctor, participated in the scenes enacted and endured.

Those war books are an impassioned, though restrained, indictment of war. They use satire effectively to scathe the ridiculousness of hierarchy and discipline and the vanity of otherwise intelligent men, who fondly believe that they belonged to 'the most intelligent people' on earth and suddenly, having donned a uniform, abdicate all critical spirit. Doctors, who were accustomed to following exacting professional standards, become fascinated by gold braid on a cap and the voice of a higher officer who may hold their promotion in the palm of his hand. Men whose survival cannot be reasonably hoped for deceive themselves stubbornly unto the last and expect a miracle. Gravely disabled soldiers, for whom life can be only a slow death, cling to the hideous wreck that is their maimed body. They even laugh at their own martyrdom and joke about their misery. The resilience of men is the most eloquent challenge to pessimism about the human race.

While sparing no realistic details, Duhamel is moved by devotion and sympathy for the new martyrs whose flesh was tortured in the bloodiest war in history. Moralists and preachers have given physical suffering too much credit for its reforming effects. It may sober up and mature a few sufferers who might otherwise remain plain hedonists (a beautiful word, which we have allowed to degenerate into one of opprobrium), unconcerned with an afterlife. But how degrading sickness and pain are to our bodies and to our minds! These ills are unjust, stupid, humiliating, and, especially if inflicted through war, a mockery of all the hopes and aspirations of mankind. Duhamel's first war book was merely descriptive. The second becomes more bitter as it develops and, discreetly, suggests the author's message. In an operating room, the most handsome men of France, cavalry soldiers transferred to the infantry, have been pouring in since morning, wounded in the lungs, in the stomach, in the head; the surgical tools shine resplendent on all sides, devised by the ingenious techniques of modern 'civilization.' Negro stretcher-bearers from those black regiments that France had recruited all over Africa to come and take part in the slaughter of 'civilized' whites by other whites come and go, silently and gently carrying the groaning men. The author looks at that nightmarish scene, ashamed of what may be going through the dim consciousness of those African soldiers, ashamed of his own race. The lofty words of our religion, to which we have been paying lip service for almost two thousand years, sound ironically in his ears: 'Love ye one another'; 'Thou shalt not kill.' His whole being shudders in protest. Civilization does not lie in the tools of the surgeon or in the perfected anesthetics of the operating room. 'If it lie not in the heart of man, it is nowhere.'

Duhamel's qualities appear most conspicuously in the best novel (in our opinion), which he wrote after his war books: the central book in the Salavin series entitled *Journal de Salavin*. The subject is one of the most commonly treated in fiction: the failure of an ideal and eventually of a life. Duhamel handles it deftly, with kindly, though frank, humor and without the obstinate insistence on crushing men's aspirations that marked the French naturalists,

American pessimists like John Dos Passos, and even the author of *Of Human Bondage.*

Salavin is a well-meaning, honest, thoughtful man of about forty, essentially undistinguished but determined to rise above his own mediocrity. He decides to keep a diary and realizes in so doing that his life thus far has been empty and useless. He will rise, not through money, for which he cares little; not through action, for he is not ambitious and is hardly the stuff of which heroes are made; not through art, for he is not gifted. Failing those, he will try to become a saint. His inability to have any religious faith fails to deter him. Saints, the dictionary informs him, have done good and lived in humility and devoted themselves to others. He will do as they do and record his saint's progress in his diary. He promises to himself the utmost sincerity.

His mother is puzzled when he declares to her that he wants to be good. His wife, noticing that he no longer protests at the dishes he used to dislike and that he rises earlier in the morning, thinks he is sick or queer. He is forced to lie to the two good ladies. Saints have borne suffering; he inures himself to pain by inserting his finger between the door and the doorframe every morning and closing the door on it a little more each day until it hurts. But his wife, unsuspecting, one day slams the door and his finger is crushed. He goes about the streets of Paris looking for old ladies carrying parcels whom he may assist, since helping young ones might be misinterpreted, and lepers whom one may kiss in brotherhood have become rare in our cities. He goes into movie houses, hoping for the day when a fire may break out and he will extinguish it, help the audience to escape, and save them from the stampede. When a fire once actually occurs, he must confess in his diary that his reactions were not those he had rehearsed; he had scurried toward the door, forgetting about women and children to be rescued. A fellow employee at his company had been stealing for some time. Salavin deprives himself and his wife to give him money, so that he may restore what he had subtracted from the cashier's desk. He thus becomes party to an offense, and the culprit never reforms. Telling the truth to others, he soon discovers, brings only embarrassment and ill will to them and to him.

Salavin must confess that he is a failure. It is hard to be a lay saint. Religious faith would help him if only he could acquire it. He visits a Protestant pastor famous for his influence, who hurriedly psychoanalyzes him and sees a crank in him. He goes from the Protestant pastor to a Catholic priest, expecting much from the atmosphere of the Church and from the confession. The priest pities him, offers to take upon himself the burden of Salavin's mistakes, and suggests prayer as a cure. The solution is too easy for the unquiet soul of the would-be saint. Will not God bestow a sign upon him and help him in his spiritual ascent? More confused than ever, he wanders in the snow, distraught, and awakes in a hospital bed, feverish, disillusioned, and ready for further crises of remorse and aspirations, which will fill the last volumes of the Salavin series. The very abnegation of that pathetic character was tainted with pride. His sincerity only wrought havoc around him and failed to satisfy him. He acted upon a system instead of truly loving with a spontaneous overflow of his heart. He wanted to be humble, but humility also can be false and affected or exaggerated. In that entertaining and skillfully drawn portrait Duhamel has delineated one of the typical characters of the postwar era, eager to reform a world bent upon its own perdition, pitifully incapable of achieving too overwhelming a task and admitting his failure.

Jules Romains appeared for some time likely to rank as the most important French novelist of his age group. He possessed the breadth of culture and knowledge, having early mastered philosophy, literature, and even natural history, traveled in several lands, observed varied environments, and even evolved a philosophical system of his own, which attracted and deserved notice. He had attempted poetry with determination, if not with an inspired gift, and seemed capable of putting poetry in a broad sense into the novel. Several of his plays had met with success; they held the promise of a novelist who would perceive the comic potentialities of situations and was endowed with one of the primary gifts of a creator of fiction, the gift of mimicry. Lastly, Romains (whose real name was Louis Farigoule and who, some scoffers have hinted, had chosen the first name of Julius Caesar and an impressive pseudonym suggestive of Roman grandeur) met at least one of the requisites of genius, an infinite capacity for taking pains. His *Les Hommes de bonne volonté* (*Men of Good Will*) sprawled over twenty-seven volumes in the French original and might well have been extended still further if the good will of the readers had responded to the dauntless obstinacy of the author.

Novels hailed as timeless masterpieces age quickly in our century. Many flaws have appeared in the ambitious fabric of that long saga. The author has provided his readers with weapons against himself in the artificiality of his composition and the papery thinness of many of his hundreds of characters stretched across seven thousand five hundred pages. Such an immense undertaking required far more imaginative sweep than Jules Romains possessed; its ups and downs are too painfully obvious, and the ups do not carry one along loftily enough to help one forget all the swampy stretches that must be waded through. But some ultimate failures are not only more courageous but also more informative than successes easily achieved through fear of risks. Romains has fulfilled at least one of the ambitions of many *romans-fleuves* — he is to be reckoned with, through sheer weight and comprehensiveness. And his very shortcomings have taught his successors some lessons.

The son of a schoolteacher from the center of France, on the border of the Auvergne, Romains spent his childhood and adolescence in the busiest and most populous districts of Paris, on the right bank near Montmartre. He showed great promise as a schoolboy and student, being equally proficient in the humanities, in philosophy, and in science. He entered the celebrated Ecole Normale Supérieure, took his advanced degree in philosophy, did experiments in biology and experimental psychology, and wrote a scientific treatise on the paroptic, or extraretinal, vision, which failed to convince many biologists but attracted others among them. He had also, although he has been reluctant to acknowledge it and was perhaps unaware of it, been influenced by the startling development in sociology associated with Gabriel Tarde, who saw in imitation the most powerful factor explaining the behavior of human beings (a doctrine that denied sociology properly speaking, since it started from individual phenomena, which spread through contagion) and with Emile Durkheim, who tried to give the new science its laws and its rules. When Romains was studying in Paris (he was twenty in 1905), sociology was renovating the study of history, anthropology, and several branches of law. It was natural for literature to react against the cult of the individual and to analyze groups and the forces that endow groups with a semimystical power incommensurate with that of the individuals whose gathering around some creeds constitutes a group.

Romains always maintained, and there is no reason to doubt his word, that his literary work had not originated in any preconceived theory or been subjected to philosophical influences, but that it had stemmed from observation of the concrete and from an almost mystical intuition. Like many moderns who do not subscribe to Christian faith but try to find substitutes for religious experience in poetical experience, like Rimbaud and Proust, among others, Romains has secularized mysticism. Repeatedly, in his early works, even in some of his farces, then in several volumes of *Les Hommes de bonne volonté,* he has depicted the action of a few individuals giving a soul to a group or controlling their own bodies, even the mechanism of their breathing or the beating of their hearts. And he has described their hallucinations. He is a mystic, not only without God (not an uncommon occurrence after all) but with more rationality than sensibility and with an unflagging practical sense. He has related how, at the age of eighteen, walking along the rue d'Amsterdam, near the Saint-Lazare station, at the end of the afternoon, while *midinettes* rushed to their buses or to their rendezvous, commuters to their trains, loafers to their favorite *cafés,* he had experienced a trance. Suddenly, he had become conscious of the crowd in its bustle and confused unity; he had merged his own identity into that of the group. His calling was then decided; he would become the literary interpreter of the group and unleash the explosive forces latent in gatherings of men.

He had the good fortune to coin a word for his intuition, which soon became a reasoned and consistent view of men — 'unanimism.' The original significance of the Latin words enclosed in that '-ism' must not be lost sight of: single-minded, or one-souled. Social environments and huge collective events are not, for the founder of unanimism, a mere series of diverse settings in which his stories may be laid. He also discards the invention of character and incident conceived as an illustration of the play of those social forces, for, thus conceived, individuals dwindle and tend to become types. Romains aimed at being the magician unleashing and controlling spiritual forces latent in groups. He always contended that he was not an analyst of social phenomena but a captor of magnetic currents passing through and electrifying crowds and transfiguring them into conscious, dynamic organisms with a collective soul.

His most conspicuous success was in rendering the life of a street or of a quarter of Paris. There his greatness is assured. He blended knowledge of all the haunts of the big city with tender sympathy for its little people and an intense perception of the erotic thrill of men and women seeking each other in desire and passion, as Lucretius evoked them in the woods under the sway of Aphrodite.

The fourth volume of *Les Hommes de bonne volonté,* entitled *Eros de Paris,* is in that respect among the freshest and most tender in the whole work. But in all his writings, plays, short stories, poems (if Romains's prosaic and desperately wingless verse can thus be called), the founder of unanimism has pursued the implications of the truth that had been revealed to him one afternoon in a Paris street. If he is, as he likes to be considered, an inspired mystic first, Jules Romains is also an adept at dissociating ideas and at reasoning. He has repeatedly and very deftly laid bare the mechanism through which a random gathering of persons in a school, in the army, in an audience, in a bus, or in a railway carriage is suddenly transformed, turned into a unanimist group, with a soul, or a 'divine' presence, different in nature from each of the individuals merged into the group, yet present in each member of the group and endowing him with a new personality. The two persons who make up a couple are three and not two, for a third living being, the couple, hovers between them and molds them. The five members of a family are all permeated by the spirit of the family, a sixth being more potent than each of them separately. A new and higher symbolic, yet living, presence pervades the mediocre, isolated, soulless human beings who were gathered in a bus or in a street (as in John Steinbeck's *The Wayward Bus* and in Waldo Frank's *City Block,* which indirectly owe much to unanimism). They become endowed with a collective soul, enhancing their individual personalities.

Romains gave the most successful illustrations of his unanimist view of man in his early and brief stories, like *Le Bourg régéneré* (1906), *L'Armée dans la ville* (1911), and *Sur les quais de la Villette* (1914). He has never recaptured their contagious humor and their robust concreteness. As is to be expected, unanimism was more effective in rendering humor than sorrow, and the process of giving a soul to a group is more easily practiced in a comic spirit than in the lyrical or tragic mood; *Les Copains* is one of the very few excellent works of comedy of an age that has not displayed much mastery in rivaling Molière. *Mort de quelqu'un,* which was translated into English by Desmond MacCarthy as *The Death of a Nobody,* was more ambitious. It delineated the concentric zones of spiritual influence, forging unanimist groups around a banal incident: the solitary death, in Paris, of a retired employee, who had remained without friends and without any unanimist radiation while he was alive. His old father in his native village takes a train to Paris; he is afflicted by the death of his son, yet proud of the important news, which he must share with his fellow travelers in the railway carriage. Gradually, until the burial takes place with mourners, neighbors, and sympathetic onlookers, a new group consciousness is momentarily aroused around a man who had been a mere somebody or nobody when he lived alone and left everyone unconcerned.

Later on, especially in his trilogy, *Psyché,* Romains tried to raise unanimism to the plane of mysticism. After a first volume, which was modest and rich in restrained poetry, *Lucienne,* the author attempted, with *Le Dieu des corps,* a description of the physical mutual adoration of a man and his wife, which is as infelicitous as all the erotic scenes in *Les Hommes de bonne volonté.* (There are many, regularly scattered here and there, as if to help the sales of each volume.) The third volume, *Quand le Navire,* is a totally unconvincing, though painstaking, description of a hallucination, by which the husband, traveling on the seas, conjures up his absent and ardently loved wife. Repeatedly, Romains ventures into the zones that lie beyond consciousness and rationality, and into the realms of communication with the unknown. It is difficult, however, to be a mystic without faith and without some naïveté. Those excursions into the mysteries of the beyond, into which the prophet of the unanimist religion was lured repeatedly, have been ill-starred. A later work along those lines, which takes place in New York, *Violation de frontières,* is among his poorest pieces of writing (1950). It is a melancholy sight to observe almost every writer bent upon verifying at his own expense the saying of Ruskin that 'no great man ever stops working till he has reached his point of failure.'

Romains's wish was to stand or fall, as a writer, by his huge cyclic novel, *Les Hommes de bonne volonté,* one of the most determined and intellectually powerful fictional attempts of the century in France. In it, Romains undertook to be the Balzac or the Zola of his age. The similarity between his ambitions and theirs led many a critic to compare him, much too hastily, to those giants of the last century and probably induced Romains to take the comparison too seriously. Unlike Balzac, however, Romains wished to write a collective novel that would not be just a collection of separate parts on the army, the church, provincial life, the peasantry, and so forth. It would have a unity of its own, at the risk (which it ran, alas, too liberally and hardly victoriously) of depriving itself of the fresh *élan* of a new work, loosely, if at all, tied to its predecessors.

Unlike Zola, he wanted to avoid the easy trick of a family, with its several members serving as pretexts for exploring a different segment of life in the country at a certain time.

Romains has boldly attempted to avoid the single hero going through an incredible variety of experiences and environments, and the family or the selected group of friends to which earlier novelists limited their field of vision. He chose to create an extremely large number of characters, with no one of them being for long 'above the rest proudly eminent.' He took them from a purposely bewildering variety of social environments: students, scientists, writers, actresses, aristocrats, journalists, murderers, workmen, priests, politicians. An index appended to every other volume enabled the reader to thread his way among the successive plots and the thousand small and big characters. The action would vary, at times resembling or aping a detective story, at times disappearing altogether to make room for the Battle of Verdun or the idyllic life of the survivors of the war rediscovering the 'douceur de la vie.' Romains tried to steer midway between purely objective recording of the behavior of the characters and supposedly deep probing into their inner secrets, which several contemporaries have sought through the interior monologue. The first method could hardly satisfy a writer who insists upon understanding mysteries and upon reconciling some of the contradictory manners in which men behave with some concealed or semiconscious unity. Romains found it easy and a little cheap to multiply strange actions and unpredictable behavior in his characters, as some Russians, many Americans, and even Joseph Conrad do in their fiction, and then to gape at the profundity of their contradictory, hence unfathomable, creations. On the other hand, he found fault with the systematic use of the interior monologue made by Valéry Larbaud in France, by James Joyce in England, and by their followers. For that monologue seizes only what flits through the consciousness as words, but hardly or not at all what cannot be formulated in words and often lies much deeper. What is worse, it puts everything indiscriminately on the same plane, the silly unuttered jabbering with ourselves in which we indulge when walking on a street and monologuing about a dog, a fly, a speck of dust, a letter we have forgotten to write, the shape of a body we may desire, as well as the deeper emotions, the original thoughts in us, which may also be part of our stream of consciousness.[2] The possibilities offered by the interior

2. Romains slipped many of his views on the novel into his *Les Hommes de bonne volonté* sometimes under the guise of satire of his fellow writers. He

monologue, which seemed revolutionary when Joyce first came into fashion, have indeed narrowed down to an occasional and often artificial device to which a novelist may resort. It cannot, any more than the novel written as an intimate journal (also the object of Romains's sarcasm), replace the narrative of events and the analysis of character by the novelist himself.

It would be idle and carping criticism that would find fault with Romains's saga-novel because the novelist's method is not revolutionary, certainly much less revolutionary than he himself assumed. The results have to be assessed independently from the method and from the doctrine of unanimism, which may for all practical purposes be ignored by the reader of those novels. In the best volumes, like *Verdun,* neither theories nor technique are primary. We have an acute and extremely intelligent study, in imaginative form, of the reasons why men fight and continue to fight in a war, of the impact of war upon soldiers and generals, upon civilians, including profiteers, upon women, and upon the forces (gigantic even more than collective, tragic, and baneful, and no longer comic and partly or pseudo divine) that buffet human creatures at odds with hostile fate. The book came out at an opportune moment: in France just at the time of Munich (in the fall of 1938), in America in the fall of 1939 when the reality of another war faced the West. The praise lavished on the book was almost boundless. In December 1939 *The New Yorker* critic, typical of many others, called it 'the most adult' of books written about World War I, 'a war novel in the grand style,' able to 'see war steadily and see it whole.'

Much of the praise still seems deserved, after the lapse of a dozen years or more and the completion of another world war. The behavior of the traders supplying the army, of the workmen turned into fattened bourgeois by their war profits, of the ladies selling patriotism in the salons, of the generals, some cowardly and grotesque, some well meaning but crushed by the enormous task to be accomplished, has been observed by a sarcastic and lucid eye. The discussions on strategy are said to have satisfied many a staff officer; the precise details of the French units fighting at Verdun, on the geography of the battlefield, on the thousand local fights that went into the bloodiest battle of the bloodiest of wars; the letters and conversations of the two intellectuals discussing the wherefore and

---

has expressed himself in lectures on his own work, not yet collected into a volume, notably, as concerns the interior monologue, in *Les Annales-Conferencia* (November 1950).

the how of war — all have met with the approval of those who actually fought at Verdun. Romains himself was not there and does not speak as an eyewitness, though he nowhere mentions straightforwardly the fact that he depicts war at second hand.

The undoubted merits of the author are his intellectual equipment and his broad sympathy, as well as his gift for lucid narrative. The book is impeccably documented. He studied newspapers of the time, memoirs of soldiers, diaries of officers, logbooks and histories of regiments and divisions. He reconstitutes events logically and integrates them into a pattern, distributing light evenly, shifting impartially from the French front of battle to the German lines, from Verdun to the rear, from officers to privates. He explains, with commendable didactic talent, the motives for the actions of some individuals and, with even greater skill, the motives that cause soldiers to fight: patriotism, to be sure, and an ideological attachment to a way of life, to a cultural past, to the soil and the landscape and the eating habits of their country; a sense for risk, which cannot be underrated and to which many conquerors and dictators have appealed; and an exaltation toward greatness to which even cynics occasionally respond. But Romains does not overlook the liberation that army life brings to young men; they are suddenly uprooted from their families, from their wives and home life, from their small towns and the conventional watch of society, of women, of group meetings, of professional behavior. Wars are caused by far different forces, but they are made possible by the pitifully inadequate appeal that modern life makes to imagination. All the boyish instincts for destruction, the adolescent instincts for male comradeship, coarseness of language, violent sport, and the male instinct for polygamy seem to be unleashed by war.

Verdun is a valuable historical document. It is remarkably lucid, exact, and exhaustive as psychological analysis. It is impartial even when it is ironical, and it leaves the reader with respect for the author's intellect and for the range of his knowledge and the acuteness of his dialectic. But is it a very great book? Our own answer must be negative, and that is not disparaging a fine work, for very great books are scarce. It is exact as history, painstakingly documented, but it lacks the kind of poetry that would be truer than history, the lie inherent in all art that makes art not just a copy but a new truth parallel to reality and more meaningful. The profound truth of the Verdun battle, which even the humblest participants in that fight experienced, was one that eludes Romains through his patient explanations: soldiers and civilians alike felt then that the decisive moment of the war had come, that they had to resist at all costs, with a unanimist and grim determination that made their silent heroism worthy of an epic. That epic, that concentration of energies around a *mystique,* called for an imaginative rendering, enhancing reality in order to express its latent *élan.* The founder of unanimism, when weighed against the immense subject he had assigned himself, is found wanting.

His very gifts of a clear intellect and the detachment of a cool professor expounding his view of history in an orderly fashion fail to serve the novelist in him. He knows too much about his characters, about the whys and the hows of war, and the fundamental irrationality of history and of men is consequently left out. If Romains's fiction has aged fast in ten years, it is because he will not accept or depict the absurdity of man, which has become very dear to another generation. Even mystery is absent from his picture, as is shade. Everything receives an equal lighting and is pitilessly analyzed, as if by a professional psychologist. But less intellectual novelists have managed to reveal far deeper secrets with fewer words and less dissection; the secrets of human beings flash to us through a smile, a gesture, the way a person walks or sits down, his drawn features, a gleam in his eye. Romains fails to render the physical or spiritual presence of his characters. His women in particular are all pitifully unconvincing. His art, in a word, is one of combination. He resembles a pharmacist or a grocer, taking a few ingredients from a shelf or from one glass jar, then another, and eventually concocting his panacea. A more cruel reviewer (a woman) has even compared him to a manufacturer of synthetic rubber, drawing his elongated or overextended plastic material through volume after volume. But the intuition of life, the sudden creation that does not juxtapose fragments of observation but makes them spring alive, the global synthesis that is not made up of a conglomeration of neatly cleaned and sized-up particles — those gifts are not primarily those of the author of *Les Hommes de bonne volonté.*

Even if it has not yet created masterpieces of fictional literature, unanimism has been a significant force in the first half of the twentieth century and one of the most determined attempts to broaden a limited field, which writer after writer has been content with tilling. The nineteenth century had not ignored the play of great social forces: Zola had animated crowds, in *La Débâcle* and in *Lourdes,* as few novelists have been able to do; Balzac deserved the praise of Karl Marx, who saw a revolutionary delineation of the corruption of the bourgeoisie in the novels of that monarchist and conservative.[3] But it remains true that the collective factors were hardly sought by most authors and by most heroes in the literature that extends from Chateaubriand and Byron to Ibsen and the symbolists. The favorite characters, from Byron's Childe Harold, Vigny's Moses, Stendhal's and Balzac's young men rushing to the conquest of Paris, to Baudelaire's cursed poet and Ibsen's enemy of the people, were those who branded the masses and almost any group as contemptible and deified the man who chose solitude. The hero was 'immovably centered,' as Baudelaire defined him after Emerson, reluctant or unable to establish communication with others even in love. When a reaction against the romantics set in, men began feeling nostalgic for earlier ages, which as they fondly imagined, had witnessed a closer communion between the creative individual and the group inspiring him, supporting him, interpreted by him: ancient Greece and the age of the cathedrals. Their social conscience, after the Dreyfus case and the 'democratic' wars of the new century, tormented them. Was it right, and was it beneficial to literature, to continue enjoying the advantages of a culture and of a civilization without contributing anything to its spiritual enrichment? Were not the essential forces, which are collective in our gregarious age, to be captured by writers powerful enough to renounce the easy self-analysis of a lonely individual, to attempt the tragic subject of what has been called 'a lonely crowd'? The fear of solitude and the fear of insecurity have become such anguishing motives in the lives of moderns in the second half of our century that hymns to solitude and odes to the spirit of adventure have become as unthinkable in modern poetry as odes to enthusiasm and vituperations against an unfaithful mistress. Poems in praise of wine have likewise regrettably disappeared, while drinking has become general but unpoetical. Novels are boldly attempting to depict men, in search of fraternity, huddled together in labor unions, army squadrons, suburban communities — and hating each other more bitterly than ever before. Never was hatred of man for man — ideological, political, sexual, racial — so bitter as it has become in our era, which preaches the virtues of getting along with people and of mutual assistance and international understanding.

3. Both Marx and Engels praised Balzac to the skies. See Karl Marx and Friedrich Engels, *Literature and Art* (International Publishers, New York, 1947), pp. 42-3, 135-9.

If Martin du Gard, Duhamel, and Romains counted, perhaps mistakenly, on the massive impact of their sagas upon posterity, Raymond Radiguet owes his survival to two slim, youthful, yet extraordinarily precocious, novels. Death carried him off at the age of twenty. Whether he would have matured into a full-blown novelist, creating a world of his own and perhaps rivaling Stendhal, or would have lapsed into overconscious analysis and the tricks of a moralist writing novels in the classical tradition must remain matter for speculation. It is dangerous for a gifted writer not to have passed through a romantic phase, with some unsure or bad taste, an unpruned growth of sentiments and unruly emotions, and an undisciplined abundance. But it would be ungracious to be squeamish about the achievement of Radiguet. Many Frenchmen consider his *Bal du Comte d'Orgel* a masterpiece to be ranked with *La Princesse de Clèves,* which was obviously Radiguet's model. We do not, and we confess that our disbelief when reading that novel is constantly aroused by the author's intrusions into his narrative and by the sententious tone of these reflections of a very young man who thinks he has nothing more to learn about life and love. But *Le Diable au corps* is a minor masterpiece of French fiction in this century, and it inspired one of the best French films of the last twenty years. Radiguet, born in 1903 in the suburbs of Paris, along the river Marne, which serves to endow his novel with reality and with poetry, composed some delicate and strange poems when he was fifteen; they were collected in *Les Joues en feu* (1920). They do not warrant comparison with Rimbaud's far more powerful genius, but they reveal a combination of sensitiveness, restraint, and familiar irony, the original vein of the year 1920 and those following, as the postwar poetry of Max Jacob and Jean Cocteau, Radiguet's two sponsors, was to demonstrate. *Le Diable au corps* appeared in 1923 and was translated into English in 1932. On December 12, 1923, Raymond Radiguet died of typhoid fever. Three days earlier he had whispered to his friend Jean Cocteau: 'Listen to something dreadful. In three days, I shall be shot by the soldiers of God.' Cocteau, Lacretelle, and Mauriac mourned him as one of the 'inheritors of unfulfilled renown.' Aldous Huxley, prefacing Kay Boyle's translation of *Le Diable au corps,* recalled young Mozart and remarked that the author 'set out in possession of those literary virtues with which most writers end.'

Precocious as he was, Radiguet could not but write an autobiographical novel under a disguise. But most of the usual faults of adolescent writing have been avoided by the youthful author, except a tendency to summarize the lessons of his experience in those neat, imperious maxims of which French novelists have always been fond. The book has been called a *'Daphnis and Chloé* in modern dress,' and the author himself mentions the falsely naïve Greek pastoral that his mistress and he are living over again. But the idyl becomes a tragic one, and the adolescent blends cynicism and cruelty with tenderness. It assumes universal value by the remarkable talent for selection of significant details displayed by an author in his teens who had read Mme de la Fayette, Stendhal, and perhaps Mérimée. It is the definitive portrayal of the adolescent in wartime, rushed into manhood and unequal to the emotional demands and responsibilities thrust upon him.

War is mentioned in the opening sentence of the book; to the boys then entering their teens, it was a four-year holiday, with freedom prematurely won from their parents, who spoiled their sons, threatened by the draft; the young women, temporarily deprived of their husbands, were prompt to initiate these youngsters to love.

The narrator is still a child who has to creep out of his home stealthily at night for his first rendezvous and to forge lies to conceal that he has missed school. He tries hard to appear cynical, but he faints when he watches, with the crowd of his little town, a mad woman leap from the roof of a house. He meets Marthe, who is a few years older, engaged to an officer, and very much of a 'petite bourgeoise.' A common interest in literature arouses their curiosity about each other. He skips school to accompany her when she buys furniture for her future home. He imposes his own taste upon her, and he naïvely wonders at her feminine pleasure in yielding to his self-assured male reasoning. He meets her again after she has married, having been invited to look at the bedroom decoration he selected for her. He has now lost his pose and his cynicism in playing at inspiring love. He is the shy and clumsy adolescent, fearful of the mystery in the woman, intimidated by his own body and the gestures of profanation that love seems to require. She leads him tenderly to physical union, after the subtle gradation from 'vous' to 'tu,' from respect to carnal union, and from passion to the tenderness that outlives and justifies the physical passion. Some details of the idyl, such as the basket filled with eatables that the boy had to accept from his mother; his fear of ridicule; his arrival, soaked from the rain, when Marthe has to make him undress and don her husband's dressing gown; the fire of olivewood beside which they lie down in silence — all are exquisitely selected and treated with skill.

But the adolescent is still a child intent upon breaking up his toy and killing his happiness. There is no sense of sin or remorse in him, but an unexplained cruelty, as of a boy bent on hurting his devoted mother and jealously picking quarrels on the flimsiest pretexts. A demon of analysis, instilled by literature, makes him question whether he really loves her. He becomes impatient over her angelic look when she wakes up beside him or after she has become pregnant. Their love, meanwhile, has become a scandal in the little suburban town. She must go and stay with her family. Once Marthe and he attempt a trip to Paris for a night; in an unforgettable scene of boyish cruelty, he makes her walk for hours (she is then pregnant) in search of a hotel, while he is too shy to ask for a double room. She catches a lung affliction and dies soon after. Her young lover faints when his younger brothers break the news to him. 'My jealousy,' he confesses when tragedy has at last overwhelmed him, 'pursued her even in the grave, and I hoped that there would be nothing after death.' He understands that he was probably never really happy but that he loved Marthe profoundly, even if their love was doomed in advance by all the conventions of their class and the ineluctable necessities of life.

Le Diable au corps, which is strikingly but unfaithfully rendered by *Devil in the Flesh* (for neither the suggestion of flesh nor that of the Devil as evil is connoted by the French phrase, whose meaning is closer to being full of devilment and restlessly sowing one's wild oats), cannot be ranked with the more mature and relentless analytical novels of French literature, of which *Adolphe* is the prototype. Its study of analysis of love and of a self-tormenting adolescent hurting the woman who has unreservedly given herself to him shows flashes of deep insight, but it is not woven into a finished artistic whole, as are Gide's shorter novels or Proust's poetical developments. It is remarkable for its restraint and its structural organization, with episodes, concrete details, and symbolic incidents marking the phases of an implacable tragedy of love and death. Except for the few unpleasant didactic remarks strewn here and there, the novel stands out for its perfect naturalness; the adolescent and the woman accept themselves as they are, submit to their love and its consequences, quietly ignore and challenge society, and reach a bareness in stating their feelings, as they discover them, which was to remain unequaled in the novels of the decade 1920–30.

There is more tenderness and more sincerity, more art, in its naïve excess of sophistication, and more mystery in this little book than in most of the more ambitious volumes of Romains, Duhamel, and even Martin du Gard. Once again, a novel may survive owing to the restrained poetry that breaks through in patches in spite of the author's endeavor to be a detached and lucid moralist. Radiguet's promises were great indeed. Like Rimbaud, to whom he is often and unfairly compared, like Cocteau himself, who became, for a brief while, a convert following Radiguet's death, the author of *Le Diable au corps* was athirst for purity when he analyzed himself and others most mercilessly, a fallen angel or, as Cocteau put it, a glove of heaven:

> You know what I call 'gloves of heaven': To touch us without soiling itself heaven sometimes puts on gloves. Radiguet was a glove of heaven. His form fitted heaven like a glove. When heaven takes out its hand, it is death.[4]

BIBLIOGRAPHICAL NOTES

General works on the fiction of the years 1910–30 are listed in our general Bibliography on the novel, at the end of the present volume.

Both *Jean Barois* and *Les Thibault* have been published in English translation by The Viking Press (New York). One or two able reviews of *Les Thibault* were written by Jean Prévost and Benjamin Crémieux, both victims of World War II. The essay by André Rousseaux in *Littérature du vingtième siècle* (Albin Michel, 1938–53, 5 vols.) is neither distinguished nor very informative. René Lalou has a slim pamphlet on Martin du Gard (Gallimard, 1938) and Howard C. Rice wrote one in English (The Viking Press, 1941). The only illuminating discussions of Martin du Gard are those by Claude-Edmonde Magny in her *Histoire du roman français* (Editions du Seuil, 1950) and by Jean Prévost in *Problèmes du roman* (Confluences, Lyon et Paris, 1943, pp. 95–100).

Marcel Saurin published, in 1951, at the Mercure de France, a very useful bibliography of Duhamel's writings, interestingly prefaced by Duhamel himself. Articles on Duhamel are very numerous; a special number of *Le Capitole* was devoted to him in 1927. Little books on Duhamel have been written by Luc Durtain in 1920, André Thérive in 1925, and Achille Ouy in 1927. A collective work on *Duhamel et nous*

---

4. Jean Cocteau, *Lettre à Jacques Maritain,* translated by John Coleman as *Art and Faith* (Philosophical Library, New York, 1948), p. 21.

(by Claudel, Madaule, Archambault, and others) constituted one of the 'Cahiers de la Nouvelle Journée' (Bloud et Gay, 1938). Other essays may be consulted, by Henri Massis (*Revue Universelle,* March 15, 1922, pp. 738–61), Christian Sénéchal (*La Vie des peuples,* July and August 1924, pp. 456–83 and 681–716), by André Rousseaux (in *Ames et visages du vingtième siècle,* Grasset, 1932), and by Louis Chaigne (*Etudes,* December 20, 1935, pp. 721–35). The most recent books in French are *Georges Duhamel ou le bourgeois sauvé* by Pierre Henri Simon (Le Temps présent, 1947), and, by William Falls, *Le Message humain de Duhamel* (Boivin, 1948). Other admirers and interpreters of Duhamel in America have been Hélène Harvitt and Clark Keating. Duhamel himself wrote a suggestive, though slight, essay on the novel, *Essai sur le roman* (Marcelle Lesage, 1925) and some interesting considerations on the 'I' in fiction and memoirs in *Remarques sur les mémoires imaginaires* (Mercure de France, 1934).

Jules Romains has not lacked enthusiastic critics. The first volumes of *Les Hommes de bonne volonté* were warmly and intelligently appraised by Benjamin Crémieux, Jean Prévost, and Marcel Thiébaut. Reference is made in our text to the remarks of the woman critic Claude-Edmonde Magny (*Esprit,* February 1941) and to a review of *Verdun* by Clifton Fadiman (*The New Yorker,* December 30, 1939, pp. 53–5).

André Cuisenier has two solid books on Romains: *Jules Romains et l'unanimisme* (Flammarion, 1935) and *L'Art de Jules Romains* (Flammarion, 1952). Other monographs are by Marie-Louise Richli-Bidal, *Après le symbolisme: retour à l'humain* (Presses modernes, 1938), W. Ehrenfels, *Das unanimistische Bewusstsein im Werke J. Romains* (Greifswald, 1940), Henri Blaser, *De l'influence alternée et simultanée des éléments sensible et intellectuel dans les oeuvres de Jules Romains* (Zurich, 1941), Madeleine Berry, *Jules Romains, sa vie, son oeuvre* (Le Conquistador, 1953), and Madeleine Israel, *Jules Romains* (Kra, 1931). André Figueras presented a selection of Romains's poetry at Seghers's in 1953.

Radiguet's two novels have been translated: *Devil in the Flesh* has appeared as a Signet Book (New York); *The Count's Ball* has been published by New Directions (Norfolk, Connecticut). There is no substantial criticism of Radiguet to date. An Australian, Keith Goesch, presented a Sorbonne thesis on Radiguet in 1952 (as yet not printed) containing many curious texts and documents.

III

THE LEGACY OF PROUST AND GIDE

MARCEL PROUST died in November 1922. There can be little question, thirty years or more after his death, that his place is secure among the French novelists, indeed, that he must rank with the four or five greatest among them. Gide, born two years before Proust, survived him by almost twenty-nine years. Gide's influence on French novelists and probably on French life was wider. His literary activity was diverse, and his polymorphous personality stood at many a crossroad of religion, psychology, politics, aesthetics, and ethics. He was a great prose writer and a *touche-à-tout* of genius, such as Voltaire had been and such as Sartre is today. But Gide's ultimate position as a novelist and as a writer is likely to be a far more modest one than Proust's. He will soon appear more remote from us than Proust. No novelist in the present century, not even Thomas Mann, James Joyce, Joseph Conrad, or William Faulkner, has left a gallery of characters — tragic and ludicrous, vain or pitiful, profoundly analyzed or fleetingly episodic — as rich and as teeming with life as the hundred or so characters of *A la recherche du temps perdu* (*Remembrance of Things Past*). Balzac, Dostoevski, and perhaps, though it is doubtful, Tolstoy and Dickens alone tower above Proust in that respect.

Proust's untimely death in his fiftieth year, only fifteen years or so after he had decisively embarked upon his career as a novelist, left the second half of his monumental work imperfect; and his text suffered from the haste and the carelessness of the posthumous editing. But his early death proved a boon for Proust's ultimate reputation. He was not afforded the time to attempt paler copies of his own great work or to caricature its subtlety, occasional morbidity, or its stylistic mannerisms, as has been the sad lot of aging writers. After his death, his novel was submitted to many attacks. Since adversaries are proverbially more clear-sighted than admirers, they helped rid the Proustian monument of much superfluous accretion and shift the emphasis away from secondary features to the more vital ones, where Proust victoriously resisted both criticism and the corroding of time. Several alternate, if not necessarily conflicting, interpretations of the greatness of Proust have been proposed since 1922. The first test of literary immortality has been met: the ability of a work to assume different faces for succeeding generations and to lend itself, with the sovereign indifference of beauty, to a variety of transfigurations.

English critics and admirers were, characteristically, the first to pay Proust a discerning and enthusiastic homage; a volume entitled *An English Tribute,* published as early as 1923, contains valuable contributions by Clive Bell, Joseph Conrad, Compton Mackenzie, Middleton Murry, Logan Pearsall Smith, Arthur Symons, Alec Waugh, and others. Several of the best recent appraisals of Proust have come from Great Britain and America. Between 1930 and the year 1941, when war-ridden England welcomed the two-volume new edition of *Remembrance of Things Past* (Random House, New York, 1941), ironical or severe attacks against the adulation of Proust poured in from English pens. A certain moral revulsion from the Proustian obsession with abnormal love was to be expected, even from post-Puritan England, and the lack in Proust of a social conscience or of any political enthusiasm for a better world was to be resented by the young Englishmen who 'thought continually of those who were truly great' and were inflamed by the Russian five-year plans and the Spanish republican cause. W. H. Auden and Louis MacNeice, venturing to appraise the literary stock market in their *Letters from Iceland,* prophesied — wrongly — 'some further weakening in Proust.' Philip Guedalla had, much earlier, coined one of his bons mots in announcing that the vogue for Proust would hardly outlast a 'Marcel wave.' 'Water jelly,' exclaimed D. H. Lawrence to characterize that strange cold-blooded animal who scientifically and patiently dissociated ideas, emotions, and sensations. 'Ploughing a field with knitting needles' was George Moore's description of Proust. Aldous Huxley, one of the very few living writers who had the honor of a flattering mention in Proust's novel, placed some ungrateful lines in the mouth of one of his characters in *Eyeless in Gaza*.

> How I hate old Proust! . . . that asthmatic seeker of lost time squatting, horribly white and flabby, with breasts almost female but fledged with long black hairs, for ever squatting in the tepid bath of his remembered past . . . There he sat, a pale repellent invalid, taking up spongefuls of his own thick soup and squeezing it over his face . . .

The disappointment and the impatience that many expressed between 1930 and 1940, when the newness of Proust's psychology and poetry had worn off, can easily be explained by several converging causes. First came the mechanical working of one of the few effective laws of literature: the law of reaction of one generation against the previous one. Proust had appeared impossibly difficult in 1913 — to the point where Gide himself had refused his manuscript for the Gallimard firm and where critic after critic confessed he could make neither head nor tail of *Du côté de chez Swann* (*Swann's Way*). But obscurity is short-lived in modern letters and was in this case. Ten years after Proust's death, most young readers declared Proust's writing occasionally involved and needlessly exacting, but hardly obscure — in fact, not enough so. Too many passages are too well written to suit the present fashion for bare simplicity, and for some the author falls too readily in line with the French tradition, which stems from Chateaubriand or even from Montaigne. Kafka and Joyce seem to many young readers to retain their 'virtue' of obscurity longer than Proust, now read as a classic the world over and revered as a model prose writer in many anthologies.

The personality of Proust as it came to be half revealed after his death (many letters probably still remain to be unearthed and many ugly secrets still to be brought to light) was a second source of disappointment for the early admirers of the novelist. It dawned on many that the author had lent much of himself not only to the narrator as a child crying for his mother's kiss and spoiled by his grandmother while vacationing in Balbec, but perhaps also to Mlle Vinteuil indulging in sadistic profanation of her father's image, to the morbid inquisitor into Albertine's past debauchery after the girl's death, and even to Morel, Jupien, and some of the most dubious or frankly discreditable characters in fiction. There were glaring contrasts in Proust's personality, polite to a fault and treating his friends to sumptuous aristocratic dinners, then repairing to some shady establishment where he would evince more concrete admiration for the handsome or vicious servants of the dukes and barons with whom he had associated. That ambivalence of the man in Proust obviously served the artist in him. He had good reason for forcing his own fictional characters into sudden contradictions or abrupt changes of personality that no gradual evolution could account for. Staid critics have been repelled or unconvinced by those dramatic metamorphoses that plunged Saint Loup or Gilberte into vice and exalted a former prostitute like Rachel to the pedestal of an actress loved and idealized by one of the most intelligent members of the aristocracy. In *La Prisonnière* (*The Captive*) Proust expressed his admiration for the buffoons and the women in Dostoevski, similar to people painted by Rembrandt, alternately exuberant in their humility and haughtily insolent, charitable to a point that hurts our Western idea of self-respect, then suddenly lecherous or drunken.[1] He compared Dostoevski's fantastic creatures to Rembrandt's 'Night Watch,' and implied, with his own characters in mind, that only the lighting and the costumes exalted to the status of visionary phantoms people who were perhaps average men and women.

Revelations, as first half-whispered and lately more frank, from friends and acquaintances of Proust threw some light on facets of Proust's personality that could not but disappoint the least squeamish among his readers. His high-flown compliments to women concealed a profound lack of interest in all but the superficial aspects of their nature. His interest in servants, chauffeurs, butlers, and elevator boys hardly sprang from social charity. Even his proverbially lavish tips were an unpleasant manifestation of his desire to be liked and to pay for his loves or for friendship. The publication of Proust's letters proved especially harmful to the cult that might have developed for the author of the most intimate novel of the century. He reserved his genius for his book, fearful as he was of dying before he would complete it, and veiled his life under a screen of flattering politeness that was little more than a defense

1. Claudel likewise acknowledged Dostoevski's enormous influence over him; he admired in him the rapid and sudden changes in the characters, through which they discover elements in themselves that simply were not there before — the way stressed by the biologist De Vries in which nature proceeds in its sudden mutations.

reaction. There was a rare gift for mimicry in Proust's ability to observe and reproduce other people's idiosyncrasies, and not a little hypocrisy in the adolescent who had cultivated his disease in order to retain his mother's lenient love and who had to conceal from his beloved mother and from all those who were dear to him the less orthodox sides of his nature.

Other grievances harbored by many readers of Proust concerned his excessive preoccupation with sexual abnormality and his snobbery. Our moral notions are, it is well known, elastic, and the literature of the last two decades has accustomed many of us to a more than frank treatment of sodomy and Lesbianism. Jean Genet makes Marcel Proust appear rather tame. But even the broadest-minded among Proust's readers may protest, on aesthetic grounds, against a vision of the world that sets up abnormality as the norm. When practically every character in Proust turns homosexual in the latter part of the novel, we remain unconvinced and wonder how 'universal' such a vision can be. Proust, perhaps fascinated by Balzac, and in terms Flaubert or Zola might have used, defined himself in his last volume as an 'anatomist' and quietly wrote to one of his friends: 'I obey a general truth which prevents me from being concerned with friend and foe alike. The praise of sadists will distress the man in me when my book comes out. It cannot alter the conditions under which I experiment with truth and which I do not choose arbitrarily.'

Only naïve sociologists will demand from an artist that he depict the world as it is and be true to statistical proportions established by scientists. Obviously, the world of Balzac, that of Dostoevski, or that of Faulkner are no more normal, in other respects, than that of Proust. Even the France of Louis Philippe was less preoccupied with money than the characters in the *Comédie humaine* appear to be; and Temple Drake must have few prototypes among Southern American college girls. But Proust's saga-novel rests upon the assumption, occasionally made explicit by the author, that sexual anomaly and sadism are linked with moral goodness and superior intelligence. M. de Guermantes, unhappy enough to be afflicted with normal love habits, is a fool when compared with his extraordinary brother, M. de Charlus. Jupien, Proust assures us, was in truth highly gifted, whatever the average reader may think of the use to which he put his talents. The scene in *Swann* that shocked Edith Wharton and many French friends of Proust, where Mlle Vinteuil displays and spits upon her dead father's picture when indulging in Lesbian caresses, is strangely followed by an apology for sadism, in which Proust betrayed his hidden purpose. A sadist like her, he explains to his reader, is an artist in evil. She is a purely sentimental creature, naturally inclined to virtue, and, when yielding to evil momentarily, she merely 'escapes from her scrupulous and tender soul into the inhuman world of pleasure.' Elsewhere, in *A l'ombre des jeunes filles en fleurs* (*Within a Budding Grove*), he asserts that 'only in truly vicious lives can the moral problem be posed with its full anxious force.' There is much didacticism in Proust, and too much of it, less blatantly but more perfidiously than in Gide's *Corydon,* is devoted to proposing a justification of unorthodox sexual behavior and of effeminacy in some men, which remain exceptional in the eyes of many of us.

It seems hardly to be denied that Proust, in his youth at least, was a snob. He strove hard and long, he, a half-Jew, to be received into the most aristocratic Parisian circles. To this end he spared no effort of his naturally kind personality. He was almost obsequiously anxious to please; he was generous, but convinced that any affection is venal and could be purchased with enough presents and favors. But hundreds of writers in the past have been snobs and many are today, or inverted snobs in their brutality toward wealthy and well-mannered people and in their courting the popularity of the uncultured. Proust denied, in letters to Paul Souday and to his English friend Sidney Schiff (alias Stephen Hudson), that he was a snob. And he certainly outgrew most of his early admiration for the fashions, etiquette, and conventionality of the Faubourg Saint-Germain. He became ruthless in displaying their selfishness and their vanity. But he lost also 'whatever poetry there may be in snobbery,' as he had called it in writing to Lucien Daudet. In any case, snobbery exists; it is a powerful social force, occasionally a force for good. Proust deserves no blame for having turned his telescope, as he liked to call it, on that phenomenon.

He has, however, been severely taken to task for concentrating almost exclusively on the feudal nobility, the bourgeoisie, and the servant class. The charge is naïve and rests upon a misunderstanding. Neither Racine nor Kafka has depicted workmen on strike or humble housewives struggling with the Monday-morning laundry, and the depth and the truth of their work have not suffered thereby. Kitchenmaids and milliners have been known to admire such 'class products' as the Duchess of Guermantes and Gilberte; a New York commissioner of police, in 1950, was depicted by a weekly magazine as reading Proust at night in his kitchen while drinking (was it an antidote?) a glass of milk before retiring to bed. British prisoners of war, in 1940–44, displayed a passion for reading Proust, and it is reported that Proust had to be branded officially as dangerous to communism and as too subtly corrupt, even as an example of the decadent bourgeoisie, when his success in Russian translation frightened Moscow's cultural masters; proletarians had to be protected against his insidious poison.

Several brave critics, however, between 1930 and 1940, announced that Proust's fame was on the wane because he had sadly lacked a social conscience. Others ventured the thesis, in 1940, that he would remain as an illustration of French decadence and as providing the key to France's failure of nerves and to Vichy. Sociological maniacs, who flourish in some academic circles, maintained that Proust's survival would be attributable to his description of the ascending bourgeoisie absorbing the descending aristocracy. They overlooked similar assertions, which had characterized in closely parallel terms the memoirs of Saint-Simon, the satirical portraits of La Bruyère, Balzac's fiction, and many other famous works. In truth, the vision of the narrator, and of the author, having become gradually blurred by pessimism and by the stress on abnormality, is responsible for the changes in the characters and groups delineated by Proust. The fusion of the middle and upper classes had occurred a long time before Proust and would not have been a very original subject for a novelist. Just as convincing a case could be made for Proust as the champion of the servant class! He is tender to Jupien and Morel, lyrical in his irony over Françoise's culinary talents, and when a certain young man who had served him as a chauffeur died in 1914 in an airplane accident, Proust praised him in a letter to Gide as a 'young man with a delightful intelligence' who, with no culture and of a lowly estate, had written him 'letters which are those of a great writer.'

Proust's fame has survived these charges and others; it has emerged unscathed from World War II, from the new stress on *littérature engagée* and on man's freedom in his denial of a God on whom to lean, and finally from the admiration for unanalytical American novels. If the convergent attention granted to a writer by scholars of all ages and by critics is a sign of his continued reputation, Proust has certainly received that tribute. At least twenty full books on him have been published in French and English since 1940. Proust's niece, by distilling very sparingly the notebooks left by Proust and hinting at further revelations,[2] has in-

2. Other letters of moderate interest have come out in 1952–3. The most important posthumous work is *Jean Santeuil*, published in 1952, a long manu-

creased the curiosity of many for the details of Proust's life and the mysterious and critical years between twenty-five and forty when he elaborated his future work through fruitful waste of time. But the emphasis is no longer on the man, obsequious, tormented, hypocritical, self-centered, vicious as he may have been, and equally kindhearted, sensitive, secretly courageous, and extraordinarily intelligent. It stresses the long novel created by Proust, which proved to be greater than its creator.

An interesting French novel, in 1949, *Une Lecture* by Roland Cailleux, turned the Proustian novel itself into a fictional character. The protagonist of that book actually had his whole life changed by reading Proust. The author, Cailleux, and many who agreed with him, confessed that their own and many other lives had been determined at some critical moment by the intrusion of Proust's characters into their own careers. Only Balzacian creatures seem ever to have fascinated French readers to such a perilous extent. Contrary to what suspicious critics might expect, it is not the homosexual obsession suddenly irrupting into 'normal' lives that acted most potently upon devotees of Proust. For it soon dawns on the reader that, while Proust derives much that is universally valid and profound from his delineation of abnormal love, he has established those truths upon a fundamental lie; his most impressive scenes, such as those in which Albertine is kept prisoner, are too obviously incredible in their data. The hero of Cailleux's novel and many readers of Proust in actual life are much more struck by the critical about-face of the narrator in *A la recherche du temps perdu*. After many years seemingly wasted in social vanities and the melancholy conviction that he was unfit to devote himself to

script apparently composed between 1892 and 1903 or perhaps 1908 (and not just 1896–9 as claimed by the publisher). It was unfortunately badly edited, put together very arbitrarily and preceded, thus far, by a very inadequate introduction. It can be called a novel only in parts, for many of its chapters rather resemble portraits, sketches, comments on literature and politics. But several parts already give evidence of Proust's stylistic gifts and of his early awareness of some of the essential themes of his future work: the mother's kiss, the conventionality of the father, the son's revolt against his parents, the ambivalence between sadism and kindness in the imaginary novelist portrayed, the children's loves in the Champs Elysées, the death of love, jealousy. But neither Saint Loup, Charlus, Swann, nor Vinteuil is yet present. And Proust has not yet developed the type of fictional technique that felicitously blends the directness and intimacy of memoirs in the first person singular and the novelist's art through which he assigns full significance to the remembered past and recreates it imaginatively. *Jean Santeuil*, valuable as some of its chapters are, fails to come to life as a whole and to be lightened of the weight afflicting memoirs that adhere to reality too closely.

any serious achievement, the Proustian narrator suddenly shifted
from the past to the future. He vanquished death, perceived the
serpentine but sure direction of all his past life, and embarked
upon artistic creation. Future Ph.D.'s will most certainly write
theses on the beneficent moral influence of Proust's work.

The admirer of Proust need have little worry about the survival
of Proust among the most eminent novelists. The difficulty lies
rather in determining the most lasting reasons for that survival.
We have enumerated the main grounds on which Proust could
well antagonize or disgust the generations that followed him. Other
flimsy assertions have been neglected, such as the prophecy, advanced by Léon Pierre-Quint in a disappointed or defeatist article
in *Europe,* in 1935, that new generations being brought up in sports
would find Proust distasteful. By the same reasoning, Joyce, Kafka,
Eliot, and Sartre would hardly appeal to those who have practiced
boxing, football, golf, and cricket! Proust has enjoyed an advantage
that has not often been granted to great works and that the four
authors just mentioned have been denied: he has had practically
no imitators. Jean Stafford's *Boston Adventure* in America and
Stephen Hudson's *A True Story* in England have been described
as Proustian novels. In French, it would be hard to quote one book
written unambiguously under Proust's influence. Proust has thus
been spared the harmful tribute of disciples who caricature a great
work and popularize it, a tribute from which Debussy, Cézanne,
Matisse, and Gide have not been saved.

The legacy that Proust bequeathed French literature is as rich
and diverse as the whole of his extant work and as the series of conflicting interpretations and misconstructions of which that work is
susceptible. Among the manifold aspects from which one may
look admiringly and with renewed wonder at Proust, a few, however, seem to us to deserve being singled out, thirty years after
Proust's death. Others, which immediate successors of Proust had
stressed, were soon dwindling into relative insignificance; or rather,
they may well be the 'wrong reasons' that have always at first
attracted the earliest admirers of great innovators to their least
significant merits, as was the case, for instance, with Diderot,
Baudelaire, Mallarmé, Henry James, and Yeats. Thus the so-called
philosophy of Proust, which has been repeatedly referred to Plato,
Schopenhauer, Schelling, and Bergson, seems to us today a secondary factor in Proust's originality. Hailing Proust as a 'forerunner'
of Freud, whom chronologically he followed, or as a rediscoverer

of Freudianism, of which he had probably never heard, is similarly irrelevant and injurious to Proust since Freudian psychoanalysis, epoch-making as it is likely to remain, is being superseded by other doctrines and newer forms of soul therapeutics. It was equally naïve to multiply articles on the impeccable composition of Proust's novel, variously termed 'Wagnerian,' *'en rosace,'* 'circular,' even a model of 'a perfect circle,' and 'Gothic,' like a cathedral of Ile de France. It is true that Proust stressed the ingeniousness of some of the props on which he was raising his structure, rich in gargoyles and buttresses and dark, suspicious aisles, and built many of his volumes with a view to the final aesthetic revelation of *Le Temps retrouvé.* But it is none the less true that few great novels, even Russian and American ones, are so liberally encumbered with digressions and extraneous accretions.

Whether organic structure, in spite of the immense prestige in which the word 'organic' seems to be held by many readers today, who approach literature with the minds of engineers, is an essential, or even an authentic, virtue in a novel seems to us a debatable point. Proust's tricks of *petites phrases* and leitmotivs and foreshadowings of the future evolution of his characters are in fact tricks and clumsy devices used by a writer who was far too mindful of the traditional French stress on composition and who could not help respecting Flaubert, Anatole France, and even Bourget (Bergotte has all the letters of Bourget's name but one) far too much. Lastly, to define Proust's position in literature as the crowning achievement of symbolism, as Edmund Wilson did, is to overemphasize one of the aspects of the early Proust and his theoretical aesthetics. Only rarely was Proustian symbolism artificial and intellectual, as the search for subtlety in correspondences had often proved to be with the minor symbolist poets. Proust himself liked to stress the naturalness and inevitability of metaphors not only in style but in our very perception and sensibility. 'Is it not logical,' he asks somewhere in his novel, 'through no device of symbolism but through a sincere return to the very root of the impression, to represent an object by another which, in the flash of an original illusion, we had mistaken for it.' But Proust, whatever he may have said in praise of dreams, of the imagination, of the magic lantern of his childhood reminiscences, of ethereal women's dresses, and of languid flowers, also stands the furthest removed from Henri de Régnier, Albert Samain, Maurice Maeterlinck, and other symbolists. A virile intellect, a relentless mental courage, comic realism, a grasp upon prosaic life, and the awareness that women are not blessed damozels nor marmoreal Herodiades, that men and even children are not angels of purity and innocent Pelleases — these were Proust's gifts also.

Proust possessed the primary privilege of the great novelist: he could, and did, create a variegated and haunting gallery of characters, the richest in French literature next to Balzac's. In spite of the philosophy that is generously lent to him, in spite of the psychological and moral didacticism, of which he was often guilty, and of the aesthetic theorizing in his last volume, Proust never created his characters in order to illustrate pre-existing views or as mouthpieces of his own ideas. Even Bergotte and Elstir are primarily real people. Elstir is the most complex and profound painter ever portrayed in fiction. Proustian characters are not all as convincing. The women who are loved (in what strange ways!) seem to have been endowed with the most elusive characterization. Odette and Albertine are almost negative in this respect. But Andrée, Oriane de Guermantes, Françoise (in spite of Proust's wearisome obsession with the language of his characters), the old aunts at Combray, Mme de Villeparisis, the narrator's grandmother — all are splendidly alive.

So are the 'flat' characters, as E. M. Forster calls them, of which any novel must count a good many, because they are actually flat in real life and are likely to become easily adopted as types. We dare laugh at them as we cannot do when we have discovered the true complexity of M. de Charlus or the tragedy of Swann frittering his life away not only, as he confesses somewhere, on a woman who was not worth it, but on empty social values from which he could not free himself. Proust is probably the greatest master of comedy since Dickens. M. de Norpois will for many decades remain the fatuous diplomat, Cottard the pompous doctor. Legrandin's nose, M. and Mme Verdurin's gestures, cruelty, and silliness are unforgettable. Proustian readers have actually been known to shed tears at St. Loup's disappointing evolution and death, and others to choke with sobs when reading the grave pages in *La Prisonnière* on Vinteuil's greatness or the Dantesque passage where Swann recognizes his own tearful eyes in a mirror while listening to the *petite phrase* and living over again his disappointed love for Odette in his torturing memory.

While Charlus is the incomparable hero of Proustian fiction, perhaps of twentieth-century fiction altogether, Swann, though less dominant in the saga, lays bare more clearly Proust's process of character presentation and delineation. Like all the others, he is a blend of several persons observed by the author in reality. He first appears to the narrator when the latter, a sensitive child, surrounds him with mystery and accumulates baffling contradictions on the wealthy neighbor of Combray. Proust depicts his physique in rapid touches, renders his language, gradually suggests him among his family, his sets of friends. Like most Proustian characters, Swann leads a double life and is himself ambivalent. He is one of the very few exceptions who, perhaps because he dies before the middle of the work, is never carried away in the infernal homosexual round. But he cherishes dolorous and languid women, Botticelli-like, in art, yet, in real life, concretely embraces Rubens-like cooks, servants, and unrefined country girls. He is addicted to dreaming and sharpens his acute nervous sensitiveness to the point of welcoming pain, but he is not capable of the effort needed to mature in solitude and to create a work of art. He thus fills an essential function in the novel. He opens up the world of art to Marcel but fails to show him how to penetrate deeply into it, as Elstir will teach him. He points to the peril of living a purely mundane life and of being engulfed by it to the point of losing the ability to concentrate and to create. And he prefigures for Marcel all the tortures of sickly love, anguish, lack of will, and jealousy that will punctuate with their monotonous burden every subsequent passionate pilgrimage within the long novel. In the revelation of his characters, which is never continuously dramatic, Proust is gradual, second to no novelist, except perhaps Dostoevski. The character is imagined and magnified by the narrator long before he appears; then he reveals his several facets, always keeping some mysteries in reserve, and to the last he retains his capacity to astonish us and baffle us. Well may a discerning English critic, Raymond Mortimer, have declared:

> No novelist has made his characters more real to us than Proust, and we know much more about them than about any other figure in fiction. For this reason alone, I believe him to be incomparably the greatest writer who has flourished in my lifetime.

Much will doubtless continue to be written on Proust's psychological revelation and on his aesthetics, the two aspects of his work best calculated to tempt commentators. Both the psychology and the aesthetics of Proust contain much that is already being assimilated by other novelists and by a large portion of the public,

even if that public has not actually read Proust. Our way of looking at nature and our manner of falling in and out of love and
complacently undergoing the tortures of jealousy have today become definitely Proustian, so much so that the originality of the
finest Proustian analyses are already blurred for the generations
that have grown up in a Proustian climate. The secrets Marcel
read in the sudden thrusts of involuntary memory have likewise
lost some of their magic for us. Too many of us have thought ourselves favored with a Proustian revelation because dipping our
cake into a cup of tea, smelling a woman's perfume, hearing the
distant hum of a train in the night, or stumbling on a flagstone
have, thanks to Proust, become meaningful events laden with
what we seriously take to be half-mystical ecstasies. In truth, these
multiplied episodes in which an involuntary reminiscence re-
leases the Proustian narrator from his anguish and interrupts the
otherwise inexorable flow of time do not constitute the most lasting part of Proust's revelation. They may indeed appear to some
as a very frail and artificial foundation for the immense cathedral
they have to support. Only the unusual depth of Proust's analysis
and his poetical gift of transfiguration have saved such episodes,
in the last volume, from appearing somewhat childish and arousing
our disbelief.

Placed, however, in the course of the novel in general, these
flashes of involuntary memory take on a different significance. The
Dantesque voyage of the narrator through his childhood and his
loves, through the turmoil and vanity of social life, even through
the revelations of the spires of Martinville, of the hawthorn and
of the medieval stones will end in futility. Society people are empty
and cruel; the bevy of girls cycling about the beach is just as heartless; loved ones are mere pegs on which our illusions are hung for
a brief respite; death is preying on us from all sides. But one involuntary memory suddenly reveals to the narrator the pattern
for which his life had in vain striven. The past is recaptured, the
essences shine from behind the painted veil of appearances, the
hero's vocation is at last discovered. He composes his work and
triumphs over death.

We have also disfigured Proust by our unjustified harping on
the theme of his unconscious or latent Bergsonism. Since the task
of men teaching young men is apparently to explain more than
can be explained and to present annoyingly unpredictable masterpieces as linked to a society or to a philosophy, scholars and critics
like to stress the unity of a culture or of an age. Their keenest joy

is to discover a philosopher (Descartes, Hegel, Comte, Freud, or Dewey) who will be considered, preferably once he has been safely tucked in his grave, as having formulated the creed from which artistic creations of that age radiated. Bergson has been that scapegoat for the symbolist movement and for the aftermath of symbolism, with Claudel and Proust, even Valéry, presented as his astonished disciples. Proust's repeated denials availed but little, for a touchy author is always suspected of denying most vehemently what secretly pinches him most. The question of Proust's Bergsonism is highly complex and concerns us little here. Clearly, however, Proust does not stem from Bergson and cannot be explained by him. He differs from the philosopher of *Matière et mémoire* (*Matter and Memory*) radically in his conception of memory, in his neglect of the Bergsonian theses on freedom and on the heterogeneousness of cerebral and psychical elements in us, in his stress upon the past, and in his total disinterest in will power, in contrast with Bergson's orientation toward the future and toward action. Proustian aesthetics may remind us of the all-too-scarce passages in which Bergson (notably in *Le Rire* and in *La Pensée et le mouvant,* translated as *The Creative Mind*) had some lineaments of a Bergsonian aesthetics. But there again the parallel should not be strained.

Proust may more convincingly be presented as the Christ heralded by Bergson the Baptist. He was the novelist whom Bergson might have wished to appear and might have announced, even if the prophet did not hail the Messiah with enthusiasm when he finally arrived. For, however perfidiously Bergson may have been lauded by other philosophers for his literary style — a double or multiedged compliment on their lips — he himself never confused the two separate provinces of philosophy and literature. In a passage of *La Pensée et le mouvant,* he declared: 'It is the province of literature to undertake . . . the study of the soul in the concrete, upon individual examples; the duty of philosophy, it seemed to me, was to lay down the general conditions of the direct, immediate observation of oneself by oneself.' In the same volume, in an essay on 'La Perception du changement,' Bergson had granted the artist a privileged function and added: 'What is the object of art if not to make us discover . . . outside and within ourselves, a vast number of things which did not clearly strike our senses?' And in his first work, *Les Données immédiates,* translated as *Time and Free Will,* he had praised the anonymous, bold novelist who might tear the deftly woven cloth of our conventional self and put us back in the presence of ourselves.

Proust's original vision may well remain priceless where it indeed rent the delusive veil that conceals true life from us. He escaped from the dull narcotic of habit, removed the superficial layers we have allowed to accumulate over our perception, espoused essences, and arrested time. He belonged, through some features of his genius, to the same family of minds that included Bergson, Rousseau, and Montaigne. He uttered diffident warnings against intelligence, also ingloriously treated by Bergson in *L'Evolution créatrice*. It is a saving grace for France, as Etienne Gilson has remarked, to count periodically some prophets who bid their countrymen to distrust the intellect and flout reason. But for them, it would be harder for Frenchmen to remain intelligent with the due corrective of humility.

More aptly than the much-abused adjective 'Bergsonian,' the broader word 'romantic' would designate the best in the Proustian vision. The romantics restored 'the pleasures of imagination' to the forefront. Romantic heroes, and, even more, romantic heroines, enjoyed the expectation of all joys, and particularly the sinful ones, far more than the fulfillment of such expectations; for reality regularly disappointed them. Like Emma Bovary after she had decided to seek the realization of her bookish dreams with pitifully selfish lovers, they confessed to 'experiencing nothing extraordinary' even in forbidden pleasures. But, and on another plane, imagination was the goddess worshipped by Coleridge, Poe, Baudelaire, and Proust. It alone constituted the whole of love according to Proust; it lay at its source in any case, and it provoked all other pleasures, transfiguring to secondary characters fleetingly colored by the narrator's magic lantern persons from M. de Charlus, Mme de Guermantes, la Berma, and Bergotte to Mlle de Stermaria or the dairy girl of whom he caught a glimpse from the train taking him to Balbec. Proust's claim to greatness lies in part in that irradiation of imagination, enriched by a retentive and transfiguring memory, which turns a weight of matter into gold, and transmutes vices, jealousies, and suspicions into beauty. The lyrical novel, in every language, has usually ended in failure. The Germans, the French (from Chateaubriand to Barrès), the English, including Walter Pater, George Moore, perhaps James Joyce himself, have regularly failed in their attempt to incorporate lyricism and a highly wrought prose into fiction. In his poetization of objects, persons, the cries of street vendors in Paris, and the butlers and lackeys standing in the antechamber of Mme de Saint-Euverte, Proust has succeeded in remaining a convincing and fascinating novelist and in filling the novel with all the poetry it can hold.

But Proust, like all writers who tower above mere talents and who retain their freshness through and despite generations of commentators, cannot be reduced to one formula. He unites in himself contradictory qualities. He 'pushed analysis to the point where it becomes creative,' said one of his earliest English admirers. On the one hand, he belongs with the romantics and the symbolists and goes beyond all of them in centering the whole of life and the whole of his long novel on art. The world, his own remorseful loss of past time, and his plunging into disease and vice receive their only possible justification in being suddenly raised, by the artist's magic wand, to the plane of an aesthetic phenomenon. On the other hand, Proust is a pitiless analyst of all that he uncovers in man, and of himself. He had been compared by the man who understood him most deeply among his contemporaries, Jacques Rivière, with Kepler, Galileo, or Newton. His sharp and cruel vision pierces through all our illusions. He dissociates, even more lucidly and relentlessly than the founders of psychoanalysis, the emotions of love, before which most philosophers, except perhaps Plato and Schopenhauer, had recoiled.

The miracle is that such analytical dissociation is not affected by separating the object from the subject but by a more intimate penetration into the object itself and a spiritualization of matter, which breaks up its material substance into atomic particles and infuses new life into them. The greatest virtue that Proust possesses can probably be best represented by one word — depth. Where others would have passed by, content with rendering the world of appearances, Proust dislocates, assimilates the shattered fragments, and reconstructs them. Like his hero Elstir, he spares no effort to 'dissolve that aggregate of reasonings that we call vision.' His own vision has the newness and the same quality of wonder as that of a child. But it is supplemented by memory, by knowledge of other artists who have already penetrated into the secrets of reality, by an intense concentration of the attention, and by knowledge. Proust probably appreciated the impressionists most among the painters of his age, but Cézanne, and before him Chardin, are those to whom he stands closest. His treatment of concrete objects (the brioches eaten at Combray after the Sunday Mass, the asparagus on Françoise's table, the telephone set at Doncières when he hears his grandmother's voice transfigured by the instrument) has all the solidity and the multidimensional quality of a post-impressionist painting. And it retains motion or the potentiality of motion, grace, and elusiveness as well.

In a curious preface to *Tendres Stocks,* by Paul Morand, Proust wrote lines that may well apply to his own unique gift.

> In all the arts, it seems as if talent consisted in a greater close-ness between the artist and the object to be expressed. As long as the closeness of the one to the other is not complete, the task is unfinished . . . In other centuries, we feel that there always had remained a certain remoteness dividing the object from the highest minds which hold discourse about it.

These words may well be the most fitting to designate the unique features of Proust's eminence as a novelist. He has most of the other qualities for which we praise the greatest of novelists.[3] In range, he cannot rank with Dickens, Balzac, and Dostoevski. In nat-uralness, Tolstoy outshines him. But his deep penetration both into reality and into man's emotions and thoughts is hardly equaled anywhere. As a foreign commentator, and one who is not partial to fiction or to French literature, the Spaniard José Ortega y Gasset declared:

> He [Proust] stands as the inventor of a new distance between things and ourselves . . . The whole of the novel that pre-ceded him suddenly appears like a bird's eye literature, crudely panoramic, when compared to that delightfully near-sighted genius.

'My function is to disturb,' Gide was fond of saying. His in-fluence has been profound and always a fecundating one, partly because Gide's own achievement seldom reached such greatness as would discourage emulation in others but also because he will-ingly sacrificed some of his potentialities to teaching others how to become more truly themselves. His own artistic failures or his limitations have in that sense proved more valuable than several of his better-known volumes. Indeed, the triumphant Gide, the one whose *La Symphonie pastorale* was adapted to the screen with

3. In fact, a German critic, Ernst Robert Curtius, did not hesitate to write in the *Nouvelle Revue Française* issue devoted to Proust in 1924: 'He [Proust] excels Flaubert in intelligence, as he excels Balzac for his literary qualities and Stendhal for his understanding of life and beauty.'

great skill and whose *Caves du Vatican,* staged at the *Comédie Française,* reached new and wider layers of the public, struck his truest admirers as a dissonance. There were not a few lapses of taste in the elder Gide. The most glaring one was *Robert ou l'intérêt général,* a ludicrously mediocre and uninspired play, which his critical self should have strangled before it reached the printer. His compilation of a banal and conventional *Anthology of French Verse* was another mistake, which revealed how one of the acutest of critics could err in dealing with his own literature, as he had erred repeatedly when carried away with enthusiasm for Rabindranath Tagore and the lesser poems of Robert Browning, by Arnold Bennett and Dashiel Hammett. His flippant *Thésée* was hardly better inspired; and even the claim to sincerity failed to excuse the publication of long, dull stretches of Gide's later diaries. Early in his career Gide sensed that the peril for him would lie in replacing the vibrating fervor of desire, transfiguring the whole of life, with the didactic utterances of a moralist. He has not always kept clear of it. But Gide seems to have been bent, through some Protestant passion for self-mortification, upon providing his critics or his enemies with a plentiful arsenal of weapons against himself. Some even suspect him of coquettishness (he was occasionally guilty of that charming minor vice) in disarming eventual critics by handing over to them the weapons with which to assail him. His future biographers may look back nostalgically upon the earlier part of Gide's career, when he struggled in vain for public recognition and veiled his avowals and his conflicts under artistic restraint. He might well have heeded Proust's advice to him that a writer may say anything provided he does not use the first person singular. Our own conviction is that Gide's *Journals,* which have been hailed in Europe, then in America in Justin O'Brien's excellent translation, as his main achievement, have been dangerously overrated. Only a slim anthology containing the most significant excerpts from that collection of notes, maxims, and confessions jotted down over sixty years of an overlong career and, added to them, the dozen or so critical and aesthetic articles in which Gide has proved a singularly perspicacious critic might be likely to reach posterity. Not a few chapters of Gide's autobiography, *Si le grain ne meurt,* already rank as classics of French prose. *Gidisme,* like *Beylisme* or *Renanisme,* is likely to remain as a typically French illustration of the influence of literature upon life. Like Voltaire, or rather like Goethe, to whom he prefers to be compared, Gide never summed up his very diverse gifts into

one or several masterpieces that might survive independently of
the author and of his life. The potentialities that one detects in
him remain superior to his actual achievement. Perhaps his preoccupation with his own problems and with the ethical and aesthetic solution he pursued for them, while it communicated a peculiar *Schaudern* to Gide's writings, prevented him from cutting
the navel cord, as the French like to put it, and hampered the
expansion of his inventive gifts.

The case of Gide is by no means an isolated one in French literature, although an infrequent one in other literary traditions in
which fewer writers attempt to compose novels while not especially
endowed with the conventional gifts of the novelist. The gradual
loss of the essay — literary, fanciful, whimsical, polished, even
political and philosophical — for which our periodicals apparently
no longer find the space or the patience, is responsible for many
twentieth-century men of letters embodying their abortive or repressed essays into a work of fiction. The parallel disrepute into
which the short story has fallen forces these writers to compose
novels when they should have been content with a more constrict-
ing and deepening framework. *Philoctète* and *Le Retour de
l'enfant prodigue,* perhaps also *Saul,* may remain as the finest
works of Gide to reach posterity. *Les Nourritures terrestres (The
Fruits of the Earth)* would have gained by being cut to half its
length.

But it would be a senseless mutilation to insist that a literature
be reduced to the very few great works of fiction for which their
authors seemed to be predestined. 'What is great in a great book?'
is a question no theorist of literature has ever yet answered adequately. Many of us, mildly impressed by the ballyhoo surrounding the hundred best books in the world, would gladly remain
blissfully ignorant of two-thirds of those recognized or loudly pub-
licized 'classics' and grant our partiality to works just below the
greatest. Gide's novels have moved generations of readers to their
depths, in part because they were not the easy outpouring of a
born novelist but a painful conquest over obstacles and over himself.

Gide *had* to compose novels in order to escape from the pitfall
of solipsism, to which not only his own physical temperament and
his education but the example of many self-centered symbolists in
Paris *cénacles* exposed him. Only through half-imaginary creatures
could he, at first, prolong and liberate some of the obsessions that
tormented him. Only thus could he solve in some measure the

dilemma posed by his search for sincerity. But Gide's sincerity never went quite so far as to condemn him or caricature him remorselessly. His novels remain, under several insidious disguises and in spite of some prefaces (not too genuine, like that of *L'Immoraliste*) and of Gide's insistence on the critical or ironical character of his books, self-defenses. That rebel against Protestantism could never rid himself, any more than could Rousseau, of the lurking conviction that he was right and that his most abject avowals ultimately would vindicate him.

If that elusive 'synthetic and magical power,' imagination, is the primary gift of the born novelist, Gide was not one of its recipients; neither were many of the most respected novelists of several Western literatures. But few acknowledged it as nakedly as did Gide, for imagination, even more than taste, is the last quality of which a writer or an artist may confess to being deprived. As early as 1893, Gide jotted down in his *Journals* that imagination, with him, rarely preceded the idea. He would conceive the idea of a work and even its organization before his imagination took fire. He paid himself elsewhere the dubious compliment: 'And then, I do not know how to invent anything,' and, at the very end of that strained and stilted satirical tale, *Paludes,* for which the author has expressed such surprising tenderness, he half-ironically noted: 'My aesthetic principles are opposed to conceiving a novel.'

Not a few important works of fiction, to begin with *Don Quixote* and *Joseph Andrews,* were born from a satirical intent. Their very irony became creative. After he outpoured the fervor of his *Les Nourritures terrestres,* Gide wrote nothing, as he himself confessed, but 'critical' and ironical works. But the irony in *L'Immoraliste* and in *La Porte étroite (Strait Is the Gate)* is not of the Voltairian kind. It is so artfully conveyed that many a reader has shed tears at reading these strangely ironical works, in which the half-stifled sobs of the author's ardent sympathy break through his suggested criticism of his characters. Gide's chief virtue as a novelist is probably his ever-renewed capacity for sympathy. His friends have often portrayed him in society or at gatherings of intellectuals, listening intently to all that others glibly uttered, sharing their eagerness, lending himself generously to them, hardly able to resist the first impulse of admiration and even of self-humiliation. He would soon after, when alone with his thoughts or with his diary, withdraw with equal eagerness — like a kiss, said Rivière of his ability to give himself and take himself back again — and revenge himself for having rushed to admiration too soon.

In his diary, he has recorded more than once how he would open a volume with raptures of joy or even of tears, then would lay it down and take it up again with disenchanted boredom. Indeed, his gift of sympathy, which enabled him to become all his characters as he wrote his novels instead of modeling his characters after their creator, was matched only by what Cocteau has pointed out as his gravest flaw as a novelist, his inability to bear boredom.

A writer of fiction probably should possess a more plentiful supply of patient tolerance toward his characters than Gide displays toward his imaginary counterfeiters or even toward the parson in the *Symphonie pastorale*. But many other novelists have knelt down ecstatically before the children of their brain and marveled at their own inexhaustible fertility. It is refreshing to come across a novelist who, at the risk of being less authentic, also remains humorous and intelligent and stubbornly rejects paludal stagnation. Gide is not a powerful thinker, and his fiction may suffer thereby. But one of his most precious messages has been that of continuous development, through contradictions, sharp about-faces, and impious denials. He adopted as one of his mottoes the beautiful sentence of John Keats: 'Better be imprudent moveables than prudent fixtures!' He spurned all systems as prisons for willing captives. He ridiculed the pompous attitudes in which literary potentates often consent to posture. He stood on the lookout for new small facts, historical, biological, psychological, through which the pretentious edifice of a system collapses. Passionately, he hoped to lead into uncharted lands. His early *Les Nourritures terrestres* (*Fruits of the Earth*) was a canticle to joy; but he soon repudiated any joy, any happiness that would fail to be progressive. And he soon discovered that through restraint and voluntary impoverishment alone can our joys take on an ever-new intensity.

Gide the novelist should be judged by three volumes: *L'Immoraliste* (*The Immoralist*) (1902), *La Porte étroite* (*Strait Is the Gate*) (1909), and *Les Faux-Monnayeurs* (*The Counterfeiters*) (1925). *La Symphonie pastorale* (*The Pastoral Symphony*) (1919), while exemplary within its limits, suffers from an excessive haste in the development of the plot and from some improbability in the denouement. The lyrical vein has been silenced by the author; sobriety and simplicity are carried almost to the point of asceticism. The symmetry between the spiritual blindness of the pastor and the gradual discovery of light, of love, of evil by the blind girl is too deftly contrived. The irony toward the ecclesiastical unctuousness of the clergyman undergoing a second youth and rationalizing his impulses is a trifle facile. Yet, once again, Gide only half-disguised the deep personal tragedy of his own life from which he was trying to find deliverance in a work of art: his own passionate affection for a young person, called Michel (in truth, Marc) in Gide's diary, with whom he traveled in 1917–18, and whom he attempted to mold amorously, and the consequent sorrow of his wife to whom the pastor's wife, Amélie, is not unrelated.[4] *Thésée* may be dismissed as a skillful neoclassical pastiche, lacking in force and naturalness. *L'Ecole des femmes* (*The School for Women*) and its two brief sequels are, in our eyes, an uninspired attempt to write within the tradition of the analytical novel, of which Constant's *Adolphe* is the model but also the *ne plus ultra* beyond which lies the peril of dryness, a tradition that has misled more than one French novelist. *Les Caves du Vatican* is entertaining buffoonery.

L'Immoraliste was slowly and probably too laboriously composed by Gide. Several incidents, easily identifiable, are borrowed directly from life, obviously a legitimate procedure; but the author may have respected their literal data overmuch, instead of transfiguring them through some impetuous rush of an imaginary re-creation. Gide repeatedly reported that he discovered the work of Nietzsche while he was writing that novel and rejoiced that Nietzsche had said before him much of what he, Gide, was thinking; the novel could thus be lightened of an unwelcome burden of didacticism. Indeed, the weight is not all gone, and the preaching by Ménalque to his friend in search of his own liberation constitutes a superfluous and unconvincing hors-d'oeuvre. The preface, written in a somewhat stilted manner, offers the author's plea that he be dissociated from his hero and that his book be judged as an objective work of art, in which, as Flaubert had taught the young admirer of his correspondence, the artistry alone matters and no conclusion need be sought. The conclusion of the novel also betrays traces of imperfection. But Gide is fond of intriguing denouements that, untying little (the plot was frail in any case), seem to prolong the story into the reader's perturbed

---

4. It is not indiscreet to hint at the living sources of *La Symphonie pastorale* after Gide's death and *Et nunc manet in te.* A very acute literary historian, A. Adam, has analyzed the critical years of Gide's life (1915–23) in an excellent article in *Revue des Sciences Humaines* (Lille) (No. 67, July–September, 1952, pp. 247–72). See also Léon Pierre-Quint's excellent volume on Gide (1951) and its valuable appendix.

mind. But elsewhere, in the descriptions of Normandy, in the slow recovery of the hero in North Africa, and in his naïve egotism asserting itself at the expense of his wife's very existence, the book reaches one of the few summits of Gide's career. It is indeed, as Charles du Bos aptly called it, 'the masterpiece of luminous cruelty.'

The themes woven into the novel are complex, although they hardly enter into struggle with one another. Gide keeps sedulously shy of conflicts in his strangely anti-novelistic novels. On the surface, *L'Immoraliste* is the portrayal of the individualist who breaks free from his past, from his education, and from his environment and asserts his determination to live authentically. Such a subject was hardly original and has today become a current one in international fiction, from Franz Kafka to Georges Simenon. The liberated individualist in this case is a scholar who, like Gide in his earlier crisis, rapturously celebrated in *Les Nourritures terrestres*, bidding farewell to his youth, realizes that true life has passed him by. Michel decides to scratch beneath the varnish of culture and to embrace a more primitive mode of life, to flee both the aridity of scholarship and the effete existence of the salons. His journeys to more sunny climates are flights away from his earlier and tamed self, responses of a Faust hardly of epic stature to some Mephistophelic calls, and yearnings for some Walpurgis night.

Gide, not unmindful of his own private life, smoothed the path of his hero's liberation beyond the bounds of psychological verisimilitude. Michel has married, impelled by no particular passion or affection. He has loved no other women and thought it natural not to experience any particular warmth toward his fiancée. He then gradually discovers, with some astonishment, that his bride has a personality of her own. He falls gravely sick while traveling in North Africa. She nurses him with admirable devotion and restores him to health. Meanwhile, he has belatedly become conscious of his own body. He absorbs with voracious joy the sunlight, the gentle African winter air, and the fragrance of the night. And he becomes aware of the special charm that young adolescents and especially 'the sunlight that lingers on tawny skins' hold for him. An Arab boy whom he had seen stealing his wife's scissors especially fascinates him.

The second part of the novel, too symmetrically contrived in relation to the first, relates Michel's new passion for all that is primitive, robust, spontaneously vicious, including wrestling with handsome young farmers and poaching on his own estate. Ménalque, a predicating and not too witty Oscar Wilde, teaches Michel in ponderous formulas to believe in his own pleasure and to cultivate his own uniqueness. He incites the former archaeologist to forget all yesterdays and to welcome every hour that strikes as virginally novel. Meanwhile his wife falls gravely ill. He takes her to Switzerland; but, impatient with the dull honesty and the unimaginativeness of the Swiss, he sets off with her southward. While she pines alone on her sick bed, distressed by the doctrine now preached by her husband, which advocates the suppression of the weak, he worships 'an unknown god.' He gives free rein to his homosexual bent and rises at last beyond conventional good and evil. 'In every being, the worst instinct appeared to me as the most sincere.' His wife dies in desperate solitude. Thus each man kills the thing he loves. Gide's message had not essentially varied since *Les Nourritures terrestres* and would vary but little in years to come: liberation is arduous and perhaps genuine only if it is bought with the suffering of others. One must not indulge possession after possession has ceased being an enrichment and has become a stale prison; for then one is in truth possessed by what one loved. Gide was ready for the message that he was, some ten years later, to hail in Blake: 'Sooner murder an infant in its cradle than nurse unacted desires.'

To a correspondent who praised *L'Immoraliste* with exaggeration, at the expense of his next novel, Gide replied, as he reports in 1909 in his *Journals:* 'If I were but the author of *L'Immoraliste* which you admire so much, then truly would I feel myself shrinking.' Although Gide, in his Goethean ambition, always refused to let himself be summed up by one single work and coyly dissented from admirers who singled out one of his volumes for their eulogy, he may well remain for future ages the novelist of *La Porte étroite*. Once again, the book may be biblically said to be 'a bone out of his bones and flesh out of his own flesh.' There is little invention in it, as there was little in many eclogues and epics and tales of the classical ages; but the incidents and the dreams of his own youth are harmoniously fused by the author into one of the most restrainedly tragic novels of the century.

The elements Gide borrowed from his own peculiar inclinations are here transmuted into universal motives. The fear of love is also the fear of all the accumulation of mediocre habits, banal gestures, half-sincere formulas, and legalized boredom that bourgeois married life may bring. The dream of the two young people is that of many couples in the present age, obsessed by Rimbaud's disturbing cry: Love is to be reinvented. Too often love is a comedy in which the pursuer attempts to conceal the bestial avidity of his face and of his desire under soothing romantic assurances, and the pursued one practices elegant feints and coquettish wiles, combining what Laclos has called 'the glory of defense and the pleasure of defeat, woman's two favorite passions.' Yet some women insist upon being esteemed in their own uniqueness and respected as minds and souls, while sought for their physical charm; they include not only the *précieuses* of all ages but many of the noblest idealists of their sex. But an ominous severance of pleasure from sentiment, of the senses from the respectful and spiritual love may take place in the pursuer. It did in Gide. And, rather than become exposed to such a dereliction and to the wreckage of their youthful dreams, some young women, like the heroine of this novel, may prefer to enter the narrow gates of saintliness and of spiritual widowhood.

Gide's limitations as a writer of fiction are here turned to actual advantages. The type of novel attempted in *La Porte étroite* required a minimum of incidents, few or no exterior intrusions, an extreme purity of structure, and the effective use of silent pauses. The souls of the protagonists had to be engaged in an inward exploration of their own depths in order to offer to each other the noblest of tributes: a clearer insight into themselves and a fervent striving after perfection, laid at each other's feet. It was thus natural for Alissa, Jérome, and Juliette to avoid the brutal explanation or conflagration of scenes, to shun the harsh words, the swoonings, or the hysterical flow of tears dear to earlier fictional heroines or to Dostoevskian ones. Gide's rather easy device, the laying bare of the private diary invariably kept by the leading character, thus becomes fully natural here, as does the exchange of letters indulged in by the idealistic lovers. 'More than kisses, letters mingle souls,' said Donne. The Jamesian question of the point of view is happily solved by the device of the narrative in the first person singular, which appears fully natural and even inevitable in *La Porte étroite*. Jérome, the witness and recorder of the tragic story of failure, had to have, as seemed natural in his case, a discreet, modest, even a weak, personality. He had to be intelligent and analytical, but neither avidly possessive nor scathingly ironical. He only half understood the drama in which he was a semipassive actor, and Gide was thus able to launch his reader on several divergent tracks without ever imposing one set of symbols or of explanations upon him. The extreme brevity of the volume enhanced its beauty further; for, unlike Balzac and the novelists who insist upon leaving nothing unsaid, Gide wants to remain as far as possible from the perilous effect of saturation produced by Richardson, Zola, or Dostoevski. The past is subtly guessed. A few sentences suffice to conjure up Lucile Bucolin, the only sinner in the family, to whom perversely curious readers would have liked a whole chapter devoted. Juliette's life of resigned domestic bliss is left for us to imagine. The natural scenery and the passing of the seasons are conjured up in a few haunting poetical touches.

La Porte étroite stands in some respects closer to some of the late nineteenth-century novels than to more recent ones, in which obstacles laid before the fulfillment of passion spring from physiological or psychoanalytical motives, seldom from spiritual aspirations. In very few of the great French novels (neither in La Princesse de Clèves, in Manon Lescaut, nor in Rousseau, neither in Stendhal, in Balzac, nor even Mauriac) did love enter into conflict with religion. It wrestled with honor, ambition, pride (Mlle de la Môle), maternal affection, social conventions, the fear of hell occasionally, or even the sense of duty to one's spouse, but seldom with the aspiration toward saintliness. Alissa spurns, like her creator, any happiness that would be easy to reach. 'What one undertakes above one's strength is what goes by the name of virtue' was the Protestant saying uttered by a Greek character in Gide's Philoctète. She will not marry and then play to herself the comedy of conjugal happiness, even less carry over a complacent self-satisfaction to her children and forsake her earnest, girlish ideals. Her idea of happiness is a steep and perilous one. It must, like true love, feed on the sacrifices that it entails. She cherishes difficulty, wants a human happiness that leads not away from Christ but closer to mystical love. The dream proves an impossible one, and she mutilates herself in pursuit of inhuman purity.

But Alissa is more complex than that. The fire that burns within her soul stirs also within her body. Her father, early in the novel, remarked how closely she resembled her sinful mother, who eloped long before, but is not wholly forgotten by those who now keep their lips sealed about her. Alissa is ashamed and afraid of her heredity. She had, very early, to substitute for her absent mother and to assume the responsibility of the household. Her acquired seriousness has not, however, killed her zest for life. There are dormant possibilities in her that love might awaken.

She has not yielded to them up to the present. Her implacable Protestant habit of soul-searching has taught her to be lucid and has given her the pride of dignified self-sacrifice in favor of her more earthly and less exacting sister Juliette. She tries to persuade Jérome to marry Juliette and be content with banal domestic happiness. But Jérome loves Alissa, and Juliette marries a worthy, uninspiring man of affairs. She fears she may be too old for Jérome, for she is indeed not only a few years older but wiser, more cerebral, more clear-sighted. Does he love her with the whole of his nature or only with a noble chivalrous exaltation mixed with some pity, for he was aware of the grief caused in her by her mother's irregularities? Will he not someday dissociate desire from respect, physical passion from tender affection, and cruelly wreck her ideals? Will he not turn — like Michel — and, belatedly, discover that another kind of love is more meaningful to him? Nothing in the novel entitles one to surmise, as critics have done, that Jérome may be afflicted with impotence, like the hero of Stendhal's *Armance,* or with latent homosexuality. But nothing precludes such a conjecture, however crude it may seem where such a masterpiece of delicate understatement is concerned.

Jérome is an essential agent in the development of the volume, even if a passive one. It would have taken the tricks of a coquette or the harmless poutings and whims of an average girl to stimulate him into less cerebral a passion and to hasten the marriage he steadfastly but shyly contemplated. He quotes reams of poetry to Alissa, dreams of kisses of the soul and spiritual bonds. He studies ancient poets at the university, and perhaps Virgil's third *Eclogue,* in which Galatea throws an apple at the young shepherd and flees toward the willows, wishing first to be seen. But he will not read between the lines of Alissa's letters. She bids him not to come, and he naïvely refrains from coming. 'Suddenly,' she writes him, 'I wished you right here, I felt you here, close to me, with such violence that you will perhaps have shared it.' Later, she distressedly remarks to him that each of them in his letters writes to himself alone and seeks a mirror, and she expresses her diagnosis that his love 'was mostly in his brain, a fine intellectual obstinacy in tenderness and fidelity.' He does not reply, does not even rush to the train to come and deny the indictment. Only later will he read in dead Alissa's diary: 'Poor Jérome! And yet if he knew that at times he would have only a gesture to make, and a gesture which at times I pray for . . .' Gide has never written more heart-rending pages than those that follow the tragic misunderstanding between two exalted natures, perhaps not born for happiness, and too averse to anything low or vulgar ever to reach it at the expense of

their spiritual or religious ideal. Alissa's slow death was a prefigura-
tion of the premature aging and forlornness of Gide's own wife,
as his posthumous revelation of Mme Gide has showed. Never did
Gide explore the abysses of sorrow more tragically than when he
turned her irretrievably away from him. But he knew the Goethean
art of converting sorrow into art. 'We make out of the quarrel
with others, rhetoric, but of the quarrel with ourselves, poetry.' [5]

During the fifteen years that elapsed between *La Porte étroite*
and *Les Faux-Monnayeurs,* Gide went through several crises. The
first was intellectual, the impact of Dostoevski, which revolution-
ized many of his views on the novel and drove him to seek for
more complexity in the multiplicity of plots, to prefer surprise to
continuity of effect, and to forsake the western dogma of the essential unity of man. 'Oh do not believe in the unity of man!' is among
the Russian master's pronouncements. The years of World War I
also coincided with a profound sensual and religious as well as
sentimental upheaval in Gide, from which he emerged, after a
bitter struggle, more self-assured, determined to reject religious
conversion and to flout the conventional censorship of pederasty
through the publication of *Corydon* and of his memoirs. The
youthful uncertainty and the frailty of the young novelist, as yet
unsure of himself, communicating his own vibration to his tales
and instilling poetry into them gave way, in *Les Faux-Monnayeurs,*
to a prolonged intellectual attempt and to a work that springs
from will power as much as from inspiration. The mastery of the
craftsman is evident. The elaborate organization and the utmost
care spent over details concealed under an apparent nonchalance
have caused the novel to be compared with the three greatest works
of the years 1920–26: *Ulysses, A la recherche du temps perdu,*
and *The Magic Mountain.* The comparison, however, can only
bring out Gide's lesser power. The value of *Les Faux-Monnayeurs,*
more than thirty years after its appearance, probably lies in the
ingeniousness of its psychology and its technical lessons for novelists
and students of the novel.

The unity of a single plot and the intimacy of a narrative in
the first person, which marked Gide's earlier novels — or *récits* as
he was to call them according to a *distinguo* that we need not adopt
— are gone. There are as many as five or six separate stories in
Les Faux-Monnayeurs, and the links established among them remain tenuous. Gide sought new starts with every chapter and at-

5. W. B. Yeats in *Per Amica Silentia Lunae,* Macmillan, New York, 1918.

tempted very hard not to take advantage of any earlier and cumulative *élan*. The tone itself is no longer as clear and bright as that which irradiated Gide's early prose. There is something abrupt and disconcerting in the succession of the chapters and in the very last sentence, which does not close the book but with which Gide delights in appearing as the demoralizer. The structure of *Les Faux-Monnayeurs,* also, even judged by its own laws, is not above reproach. Far too much has to be presented through Edouard's diary and is colored through his tinted glasses. But there is much also that could not be thus encompassed, and the fusion of heterogeneous data is not felicitous. The omniscient author himself asserts his presence and pulls the strings of his puppets with some irony. One is too deeply conscious that he had earlier selected the material his characters have observed. The characters are very artificially linked to one another by the busybody Edouard, who reads Vincent's last book and Laura's letter, and receives Bernard's and Olivier's secrets. Old La Pérouse, borrowed from life, is movingly true but hardly essential to the plot. Passavant, perhaps a caricature of Cocteau, and Lady Griffith are hardly convincing. Gide's purpose, however, was not so much to create characters able to compete with the *Etat civil,* like those of Balzac, but to depict the characters' own progressive self-discovery. The author purposely wanted them to remain unfinished, endowed with diverse and unexhausted possibilities and, if not like Pirandello's in search of their author, at least in search of the reader of good will who would prolong their frail existence.

The chief interest of the novel, next to its delineation of the complex psychology of adolescents, has been found to lie in its being a novelists' novel; its theme is 'the rivalry between the real world and the representation we make of it,' as Gide formulated it. A sophisticated modern novel must comprehend within itself the critique of the novel and its own genesis: how reality can become stylized into art. Such is the contention of self-conscious or technique-intoxicated readers, who rejoice in a novel about a novelist writing a novel about a novelist trying to write a novel. We confess to a mild interest in such disquisitions when carried outside the critical seminar where they rightly belong.

Stronger features of *Les Faux-Monnayeurs* are the central symbol of counterfeit coin and the dramatized position of the question that permeated all the meditations of Gide in his last thirty years and that will probably remain the most valued part of his legacy to the world, the question of sincerity. Most of the characters in the book are themselves counterfeit: Robert de Passavant and Lady Griffith most of all, for they do not even know what it is to be sincere; but so are Vincent, who lacks the strength to become himself, Olivier who, after brushing past suicide, is driven back to Edouard, La Pérouse, whose married life has been futile and who was a dupe always, and others, such as the Pastor and Azaïs, whose professions should have implied the practice of truth and virtue. Bernard himself rebelled vigorously against hypocrisy but exhausted his vigor in the process and failed to live his love for Laura. However, many people go through life without having ever been sincere in the sense of being authentically themselves. The true hypocrite, as Gide remarked in one of his many reflections on the subject, 'is he who is no longer even aware of a lie, who lies with sincerity.' His name in our midst is legion. All our moralists, Berdiaev, Pirandello, Aldous Huxley, Kafka, but none more consistently than Gide, have denounced the prevalence of insincerity toward oneself as the gravest of all our intellectual and moral lapses.

Gide is the novelist of sincerity. Therein lies his chief claim to the gratitude of moderns who are determined not to live forged lives and who wish to throw away the forged coins of social conventionality, of religious conformity, of sexual Pharisaism, of literary and rhetorical embellishment. Montaigne, La Rochefoucauld, and Rousseau had paved the way for him. For, in spite of the Socratic message and of the Roman elegiacs, even of St. Augustine and of the Christian analysts of the tormented human conscience, it was hardly before Montaigne that the ideal of sincerity became the *unum necessarium* of modern letters, as it is today in France. Most of Gide's novels and all his intimate journals and confessional writings have revolved around that question, which colored all others. Among these other questions was, first, style. Can style cease being an adornment, a sumptuous drapery folded over the object, become bare and apparently artless, and yet not betray thereby the intensity of the feeling to be expressed, the force of the idea? And is spontaneous, speedy, almost automatic writing the more faithful, or writing that, through art, succeeds in curbing and concealing art? Gide oscillated between the two poles.

He also pondered the next obvious question. Does sincerity demand that we reject all that was acquired through education, reading, social adaptation, moral censorship, and that we restore in ourselves the primitive, presumably the violent and the irrational? Is there more truth in the heart than in the brain, or in the solar plexus as D. H. Lawrence contended, or in what in ourselves used to be considered base? The Olympian Goethe confessed, in a remark that was to haunt Gide, that there was 'no crime, however monstrous, of which he did not feel himself to be capable.' Gide attempted to find the core of one's sincerity in gratuitous acts, unexplained crimes, waves of folly surging beyond the dull routine of habit, beyond repression and logic.

'Who will deliver my spirit from the heavy chains of logic?' Gide cried, in a Rimbaldian *élan,* in his sequel to *Les Nourritures terrestres* in 1935. To him, as to most of his logic-conditioned compatriots, sincerity lay beyond clarity, beyond consistency and neatly aligned ideas. He chided Corneille, Descartes, Balzac, and the influence of society life, which tends to laugh our naturalness away, and the traditional teaching, which assigns to us a model personality according to which we try to build ourselves. Gide cherished contradictions, sudden upheavals originating in our senses or in imperious desires, disintegrations of our personality preluding a rebirth and doing away with what he called 'clear-cut ideas, the most perilous of all, for they are in ourselves a premature death.'

The search for sincerity is perilous, for the Devil may lurk behind it, as he does in *Les Faux-Monnayeurs.* He may suggest to us that indulging our vices, gratifying our desires, and rebelling against laws observed by more conventional members of our society are forms of sincerity. He may lead us to mistake 'sincerity' in crude avowals and shameless confessions for a moral virtue and hold that all that is boastfully confessed is thereby purified. Sincerity may also lead us to mistake a momentary exaltation for our truest mood, as Gide did when he thought he was undergoing religious ardor (in *Numquid et Tu*), or communist fervor, or some short-lived literary admiration. It tends (this is even more dangerous for our art) to reduce literature to the direct expression of the ego; but memoirs, confessions, and private diaries are often the most mendacious of writings. They boast or they disparage, they reinterpret the past in the light of the present, they stress the silliest deeds or gestures of Pepys, Boswell, Rousseau, or Gide. But they leave out the dreams that reality may have aroused, the imaginary lives that have often meant more than our mediocre existences, the imaginative liberation that the writing of a novel or a poem will afford us. Writing inevitably implies a public, hence a pose, and Claudel, whose theological virtues have been other than charity, may not have been far wrong when he stigmatized his great contemporary and rival as a man fascinated by mirrors and trying out attitudes before others and himself. Narcissus is one of the undying myths of literature.

BIBLIOGRAPHICAL NOTES

Essential titles on Marcel Proust as a novelist are listed below. None prior to 1939 is included. Consult A. L. Bisson's excellent review of recent Proust criticism in *French Studies* (Oxford), I, 3, July 1947, pp. 191–217.

Brée, Germaine, *Du temps perdu au temps retrouvé*, Belles-Lettres, 1951.

Bret, Jacques, *Marcel Proust, étude critique*, Geneva, 1946.

Chernowitz, Maurice, *Proust and Painting*, Columbia University Press, New York, 1944.

Coleman, Elliott, *The Golden Angel*. Coley Taylor, New York, 1954.

Etiemble, René, *Proust et la crise de l'intelligence*, Editions du Scarabée, Alexandria, 1945.

Fardwell, Frances V., *Landscape in the Works of Proust*, Catholic University of America Press, Washington, 1948.

Fernandez, Ramon, *Proust*, Nouvelle Revue Critique, 1943.

Golstine, Enid, 'La Renommée et l'influence de Proust en Angleterre,' Paris, 1949. (Thesis, not yet published.)

Green, F. C., *The Mind of Proust*, Cambridge University Press, Cambridge, 1949.

Haldane, Charlotte, *Marcel Proust*, Arthur Barker, London, 1951.

Hindus, Milton, *The Proustian Vision*, Columbia University Press, New York, 1954.

Leon, Derrick, *Introduction to Proust: His Life, His Circle and His Work*, Kegan Paul, London, 1940.

March, Harold, *The Two Worlds of Marcel Proust*, University of Pennsylvania Press, Philadelphia, 1948.

Maurois, André, *Marcel Proust: Portrait of a Genius*, Harper and Brothers, New York, 1950. (In French: *A la recherche de Marcel Proust*, Hachette, 1949. English translation: *The Quest for Proust*, Jonathan Cape, London, 1950.)

Mouton, Jean, *Le Style de Proust*, Corrêa, 1948.

O'Brien, Justin, 'La Mémoire involontaire avant Proust,' *Revue de Littérature Comparée*, XIX, 1, January 1939, pp. 19–36.

——, *The Maxims of Marcel Proust*, Columbia University Press, New York, 1948.

Rivane, Georges, *Influence de l'asthme sur l'oeuvre de Marcel Proust*, La Nouvelle Edition, Paris, 1945.

Taumann, Léon, *Marcel Proust: une vie et une synthèse*, A. Colin, 1949.

Vigneron, Robert, Several important articles, not yet collected into a volume, in *Revue d'Histoire de la Philosophie* (Lille), 1937;

Modern Philology, May 1945, November 1946, February 1948; *The French Review,* May 1946.

Allusion is made in our text to Léon Pierre-Quint's articles, 'Une Nouvelle Lecture: Marcel Proust et la jeunesse d'aujourd'hui' (*Europe,* XXXIX, 1935, 185–98 and 382–99); to Roland Cailleux's *Une Lecture* (Gallimard, Paris, 1949); to Raymond Mortimer's *Channel Packet* (Hogarth Press, London, 1943); and to a superficial article by Edwin B. Burgum, 'Into the Night: Proust's Account of the Collapse of French Civilization' (*Accent,* summer 1941, pp. 202–12).

The important works by Gide (except for the beautiful *Le Retour de l'enfant prodigue*) are all available in translation. A very abundant biographical and critical literature has accumulated in the last few years on a writer who concealed little about his own life and earnestly wished to interest and to disturb after his death. Much of it is ephemeral: the books by Pierre Herbart, Maurice Lime, Maurice Sachs, for example, and even the imposing but disappointing special number of the *Nouvelle Revue Française* devoted to Gide in 1951. The *Conversations* with Gide by Claude Mauriac (Albin Michel, Paris, 1952) and especially the brief *Notes sur André Gide* (Gallimard, 1951) by Roger Martin du Gard are the most valuable posthumous testimonials.

Among the special numbers of periodicals in which a varied and solid crop of articles on Gide may be found, two deserve to be set apart: *Le Capitole, Hommage à Gide* (1928) and *Yale French Studies* (No. 7, 1951).

The most useful bibliographical items will be found to be the following, Hytier's and Pierre-Quint's being the most valuable of all:

Adam, A., 'Quelques années de la vie de Gide,' *Revue des Sciences Humaines,* No. 67, July–September 1952, pp. 247–72.

Alibert, François-Paul, *En Marge d'André Gide,* Oeuvres Représentatives, 1930.

Arland, Marcel, *Essais critiques,* Gallimard, 1931.

Bendz, Ernst, *Gide et l'art d'écrire,* 1939.

Davet, Yvonne, *Histoire des nourritures terrestres,* Gallimard, 1948.

Du Bos, Charles, *Dialogue avec André Gide,* Au Sans Pareil, 1929.

Estève, Claude, *Etudes philosophiques sur l'expression littéraire,* Vrin, 1938.

Fayer, Mischa H., *Gide, Freedom, and Dostoevski,* Middlebury, Vermont, 1946.

Gandon, Yves, *Le Démon du Style,* Plon, 1938.

Guérard, Albert J., *André Gide,* Harvard University Press, Cambridge, Massachusetts, 1951.

Hytier, Jean, *André Gide,* rev. ed., Charlot, Alger, 1945.

Lafille, Pierre, *André Gide romancier,* Hachette, 1954.

Lalou, René, *André Gide,* Heissler, Strasbourg, 1928.

Lang, Renée, *André Gide et la pensée allemande,* Egloff, 1949.

Lièvre, Pierre, *Esquisses critiques,* Le Divan, 1929.

Mann, Klaus, *André Gide and the Crisis of Modern Thought*, The Creative Age Press, New York, 1943.

March, Harold, *Andre Gide and the Hound of Heaven*, University of Pennsylvania Press, Philadelphia, 1952.

Michaud, Guy, 'Genèse des Faux Monnayeurs. L'Art de la fugue. Morphologie-Syntaxe,' *Dialogues*, II, 2, January 1951, pp. 37–86.

O'Brien, Justin, *A Portrait of André Gide*, Alfred A. Knopf, New York, 1953.

Pierre-Quint, Léon, *André Gide*, Stock, Paris, 1951.

Rivière, Jacques, *Etudes*, Nouvelle Revue Française, 1911, and articles in *Chronique des Lettres Françaises*, January–June 1926.

Schwob, René, *Le Vrai Drame d'André Gide*, Grasset, 1932.

Scott, J. D., 'André Gide,' *Horizon*, No. 64, April 1945, 267–79.

Thomas, D. L., *André Gide*, Secker and Warburg, London, 1951.

Wilson, Edmund, *The Wound and the Bow: Seven Studies in Literature*, Houghton Mifflin Company, Boston, 1941; new printing with corrections, Oxford University Press, New York, 1947.

FRANÇOIS MAURIAC

I
F THE FRENCH CRITICS of 1930–45 had been asked which novelist, in their estimation, was the most likely to outlive the wreckage of time and to rank next to Proust in greatness, more votes would probably have been cast for Mauriac than for any other living French writer, his rivals being Malraux, Giono, and Bernanos, probably in that order. Mauriac's eminence was comparatively unrecognized in English-speaking countries, long after his election to the French Academy in 1933 and even after the Nobel Prize had been bestowed upon him. Translations of his works have been coming out timidly. The utmost tribute, that of a Pocket Books edition with a seductive or a sickening cover (as tastes may go), came to the *Desert of Love* only in 1953. The brevity of Mauriac's *récits* may have appeared unorthodox to publishers who like a novel to conform to the supposed demands of solid readers who insist that they get their money's worth in weight. The poetic finish of his style may have frightened off translators. But the pessimism of Mauriac's novels and their Roman Catholic view of sin and of love must have proved the chief deterrent to Anglo-Saxon readers. Pessimism, to be sure, abounds in their own fiction, but it dons youthful violence, and evil is somehow depicted in glaring and alluring colors.

There were signs of a change in the tastes of many educated

readers, at the very time (since 1945 or thereabout) when the compatriots of Mauriac tended to dismiss him as a classical writer who,
afraid of spoiling his earlier successes through imitating himself,
was driven to dramas and to journalism. Many students in American colleges were fascinated by Mauriac as a craftsman and also
by the use he has made of the religious theme. Religion once again
has become fashionable in fiction. It has been found by reassured
critics to permeate James Joyce's work, to explain William Faulkner's portrayal of an evil that was original and hence ennobling,
and to give a Catholic hue to Eugene O'Neill's plays and James T.
Farrell's saga. The adjective 'Catholic' paired with the word
'novelist,' has, in the eyes of some readers, enhanced the stature
of Graham Greene and Evelyn Waugh. Somerset Maugham made
skillful use of the theme in *The Razor's Edge,* and Aldous Huxley
wrote fondly of Machiavellian mystics like Father Joseph. But
Mauriac's place in contemporary letters owes little to sectarianism
or to tides of changing taste. Out of the score of novels he has
published, four or five seem clearly destined for survival. Few are
the novelists in any language of whom such a prophecy could be
ventured.

If the factors at work at any one time in life and in art may be
grouped into the conflicting forces of tradition and of experiment,
Mauriac seems to rank with those novelists who have shunned the
loudly advertised paths of experimentation. At a time when the
roman-fleuve appeared as the order of the day and when jug-
gling with the old-fashioned structural unity and with the continuous flow of time had become the first gesture of a writer asserting his modernity, Mauriac chose to compose isolated novels,
strictly organized, with few of those contradictions and violent
plunges into the unconscious that other Frenchmen took as evidence that they lived in a post-Dostoevskian era. Once or twice, the
same characters recur in two different books. But their creator had
enough humility not to presume that his readers might, after several years, remember the earlier doings of certain women of ill
repute or of angelic adolescents. He rightly feared the lack of
freshness and the artificiality of novelists who have chained themselves, volume after volume, to the drawn-out career of a Forsyte or
of a Jean-Christophe. Every one of Mauriac's novels is a fresh
attempt and an adventure into the unknown, though every one
of them ends monotonously with the gift of grace that the novelist
insists upon imparting to his sinners.

Mauriac's fiction has been charged with monotony. It moves in a world that indeed is, geographically and socially, narrowly limited. It revolves around the same perennial obsessions with money, property, the enticements of the flesh, and the wages of sin. Within these confines, however, it explores in depth. What is more, it conjures up that diseased and haunted world, and gains in vivid intensity what is sacrificed in diversity. In contrast with several experimenters among contemporary novelists, Mauriac stands as the upholder of the traditional virtues of the French novel. He is fully aware of the new complexity that Stendhal, Dostoevski, and Proust have led us to expect from fiction. But his purpose is not to experiment with new fictional forms or to explore recesses of the unconscious with awe, or with the naïveté of one who has lately discovered the jargon of clinical psychology. He writes because he must rid himself of the obsession of his characters and endow with shapes and sounds the desolate world that he carries within his imagination. The traditional form of the French novel, condensed, linear ✓ in its development, and strongly tempted to return to the unities of the classical tragedy, suited his talent as it did the themes he treated. Like Racine's plays, his novels are dramatic presentations of a psychological crisis. The plot permits very few incidents, and only those that help bring out new aspects of the characters. His novels move swiftly to a relentless denouement. Indeed, their tension is so feverish that they could hardly last longer without becoming painful to the reader. They are no more relieved by humor, by the restful oasis of pure description or of lyrical escape than is Racinian tragedy. Within the traditional mold of the French novel, classical in its economy, swift in its pace, written with elaborate care for stylistic values, Mauriac subtly cast the molten lead of dark motives and destructive passions, such as we have come to expect from modern fiction since Balzac, Melville, and the great Russians.

Mauriac's date of birth, 1885, makes him one of the group of gifted French novelists who were to reach full manhood on the eve of World War I and to stage, in the years 1910–13, a literary renaissance in Paris. Martin du Gard, Giraudoux, Duhamel, Romains, Maurois, Alain-Fournier, Jouhandeau, and Bernanos belong to the same age group. Their ascendancy over French letters reached it height in 1925–35, when, with the exception of Alain-Fournier, who was killed in the war, they were to meet with an audience attuned to their music, and to produce their most accomplished work. Most of them belonged to the middle or lower strata of the bourgeoisie, whose creative vitality has remained astounding in France, despite savage attacks repeatedly launched against it by its own scions, from Flaubert to Mauriac himself. Most of them were provincials; and Mauriac's fiction, even after he had taken up residence in Paris, fed on the observations and memories accumulated in his provincial childhood.

The section of France to which he belongs with all his being had already given birth to many men of letters, most of them of a cheerful and humorous disposition, inclined to skeptical enjoyment of the varieties and inconsistencies of mankind. But Mauriac has little in common with Montaigne or Montesquieu, even with elusive Fénelon or with Rivière, also born in Bordeaux, in 1886, who searched for faith with the secret fear of being imprisoned in it if he once found it. The power of literature is such that the Bordeaux region and its inhabitants will henceforth appear to many in the gloomy hues lent to them by Mauriac's fiction, as Georgia and Mississippi have been stamped as lands of oppressive tragedy by contemporary American novelists. The traditional Gascon, with his bravado or with the playful irony that Renan thought he owed to his Gascon mother, the smiling beauty of his vineyards, and his Epicurean delight in choice food, never appear in Mauriac's stories of frustration and of remorse.

Yet Mauriac loves his native city of Bordeaux, its wine merchants and its lawyers, its *cafés* and its public gardens, where his characters repair, pleasure bound, when they leave their country estates to celebrate a rich crop or an advantageous sale of timber. Rather, he hates Bordeaux because he loves it too much, as he confessed at the end of his fragment of an autobiography, *Commencements d'une vie*. 'We hate our city as we do the being whom we love, for all that is usurped by that being, for the limits which it imposes upon us; it sets irreparable bounds upon our existence, and defrauds us of a higher fate.' His debt to his provincial childhood has been loudly and repeatedly proclaimed.

In fact, he confessed his inability to place any of his novels in a setting other than the one in which he grew; he compared the fascination thus wrought over him by his province to the blinding of a mule doomed to grind corn in its circular prison. When his characters rush to Paris, eager to escape for a brief respite from the passions that hold them captive in their drab familiar surroundings, they appear suddenly less real. The dance halls or the *cafés*, where they attempt to drown their regret for their childhood and for their native village, are depicted as some devil's den in a modern Babylon. The characters who had hoped to escape from themselves remain provincials in exile. 'The provinces are Pharisaic,' said Mauriac in a small book of notes and maxims on that subject, *La Province*. 'Only in the provinces do people know how to hate well . . . The provinces condemn most women to chastity.[1] How many of them lacked the vocation for it . . . Every writer leaving his province for Paris is a fugitive Emma Bovary.' But life is more intense because it is less subject to idle diversion than in Paris. The human heart can be more easily laid bare to one who, as a youth in his teens, had silently observed his elders, dreamed about women whom he would never approach, tamed his wild desires, and stifled his rebellious sobs.

The child, in Mauriac, is father of the man. He was molded by his early memories. Malagar, the country house in which he takes refuge every summer, has been repeatedly transfigured by him into a setting for his stories. Langon, which has become a gloomy abode of the dying wife and of the domineering mother-in-law in *Genitrix*, situated near the railway line between Bordeaux and Sète, was his grandfather's property. That grandfather, stubborn and anticlerical, who was converted on his dying day, has provided his grandson with a few features of the pathetic old man in *Le Noeud de vipères* (*Viper's Tangle*). Thérèse's house, named Argelouse in the novel, was that of Mauriac's maternal grandmother. The rumbling, packed streetcar in which, every evening, young Courrèges first met Maria Cross, was familiar to Mauriac when he was completing his secondary school in Bordeaux. Mauriac's own father died when he was but eighteen months old. The child, along with three brothers and one sister, was brought up entirely by the young widow. The father had been an unbeliever, the mother was sternly religious, with a deep tinge of Jansenism to her Roman Catholic faith. The evening prayer, uttered by the mother with her five children gathered around her under the crucifix, was a solemn rite. Then the children would go to sleep, their arms crossed on their breasts, as demanded by God. They scrupulously observed the strictest rules, to the point of not eating the crust of their bread on Friday if it appeared slightly yellow, hence tainted with the yolk of eggs, thus infringing upon the observance of fasting. The fear

1. The French word is nobler or more pretentious — *la vertu*. Nietzsche scathingly remarked somewhere how the term that used to denote the virile courage of man had been degraded to signify a 'merely negative' attribute of some women.

of sin, first conceived as disobedience, haunted them; God was the formidable chastiser of the Old Testament rather than the merciful forgiver of the Gospels. Death was often present to them, as the dire event that might at any moment force them to appear before their Creator in a state of unreadiness.

Yet Mauriac's childhood was a happy one. He liked solitude and found it, even at school, where he seldom took part in games and sports. His faith was a source of deep inner joy to him. His meditative habits developed in him a precocious sensitiveness to nature. He feared the beauty of the fields and the hills, yet drank it avidly. Unlike the Psalmist, he could not read the glory of God's bounty in the starry nights and the fragrant orchards in springtime. 'Cybele has more worshippers in France than has Christ,' he wrote, denouncing the religion of the earth as the most potent religion among French peasants. He, too, was swayed by that pagan cult; the struggle between earthly and earthy attachments and a thirst for divine grace is an ever-recurring one in his characters. His early studies in a religious school near home developed religious sensibility in him and the other schoolboys but did little toward fostering religious intelligence, as he later remarked. Pascal was the favorite writer of the youth; although he later took him to task for his Jansenism, Mauriac remained his spiritual descendant. His fiction has aptly and skillfully been defined, by those who defended its orthodoxy against timid souls who smelled heresy in it, as the concrete expansion of a title suggested by Pascal for a whole section of his *Pensées:* 'Misery of the world without God.'

Mauriac completed his secondary studies at the *lycée* of Bordeaux. He passed his baccalaureate and went to Paris to pursue his scholarly education. Paleography and medieval archaeology then attracted him, and, after passing the required tests, he entered the *Ecole des Chartes,* where curators of French archives and medievalists are trained. However, he soon resigned from the *Ecole des Chartes.* His was not the scholar's patient and modest gift. He carried an ardent world within him, made up of memories of his province, of human desires and temptations, and, even more, of an impossible conflict between human and divine love. His ambition was to translate that inner universe into words.

Along with Pascal and Racine, who were, among the French classics, the chief builders of his soul, the writers he admired were the more sincere and the more tormented of the romantics. He admired Alfred de Vigny, whose thoughtful poetry attracted him in spite of, or perhaps because of, its passionate revolt against God, which Mauriac tended to prefer to conservative religious complacency. He felt close to Maurice de Guérin (1810–39), who worshipped nature with a burning fervor that set him apart from other French romantics. Guérin was a pagan and a pantheist tempted by Christ, struggling to be a true Christian but engulfed by the worship of the elements celebrated in his famous prose poem, *Le Centaure*. A centaur himself, he aspired toward the serenity of the heavens but was held back by animal life and earthly beauty. Jean Lacordaire and Félicité de Lamennais were also his spiritual and literary intercessors, the first for his eloquent charity and because 'he dares call human love by its name; the flesh and the blood are not silenced by him,' the second because he rejected the placid comfort of orthodoxy and a religion unmoved by the sufferings of the poor. Baudelaire's fame was spreading among the French youth in 1905–10, when Mauriac was himself courting the muse. One of his early essays vindicated *Les Fleurs du mal* against the Catholic critics who tried to reject such poetry on account of the poet's life or his occasional blasphemies. Mauriac, already, advanced the assertion that a sinner who half repenteth or who, like Baudelaire, with remorse and anguish damns himself is more truly Christian than many a virtuous man who has, like the philosopher Taine, led an impeccable life.

Among the writers then living, Mauriac, on the threshold of his literary career, was attracted by Barrès. At the age of sixteen, he drew comfort from a formula in *Un Homme libre,* one of Barrès's early novels, which described what the provincial adolescent was then practicing: 'to feel as much as possible while analyzing oneself as much as possible.' Mauriac rejoiced in his youthful sorrows, which made him a younger brother of those men of letters whose biographies he was devouring at that time. During his solitary years in Bordeaux and later among the temptations of the metropolis, the young Mauriac was followed by his familiar daemon, the daemon of self-knowledge (the title of his most searching short story was 'Le Démon de la connaissance'). Soon, however, he discovered, like all born novelists, that it is easier to know oneself by lending one's own feelings to imaginary creatures and developing them to the full than by remaining confined to complacent introspection. He cultivated in himself 'the fondness for taking a voluptuous interest in souls' that he attributed to one of the characters in his earliest novel.

Mauriac's literary debut, with two volumes of verse, was hailed by Barrès in 1909 and 1911. Soon after, the young poet, having married, gave up formal poetry, in which he felt his style was always cramped, and adopted the form of the novel. He returned to poetry only after his fiftieth year, in *Atys*. His early attempts at fiction, *L'Enfant chargé de chaines* (1913) and *La Robe prétexte* (1914), are immature and overinclined to lyrical exuberance, which detracts from the convincingness that the plot and characters might have had. The author, already the father of a child, served in the army during World War I. The war, as a theme, left little trace in his work; but, in its gloomiest year, while a member of the expeditionary force on the Macedonian front in 1917, he meditated on the French moralists of whom he knew himself to be the heir. He strengthened his resolve to follow in their footsteps. But his ambition was to be a Christian moralist because he considered the Christian as the truest of all humanists since, 'to reach God, he must cross the whole of himself, and see the light dawn only through and beyond his own heart.' [2]

On his return to civilian life, Mauriac brought out two brief, ardent, but still unconvincing and youthful novels: *La Chair et le sang* (1920) and *Préséances* (1921). They, as well as a stronger work, *Le Fleuve de feu* (1923), are permeated with the obsession of the flesh. The delight of the senses is depicted as mysteriously entrancing, driving the characters to wild forsaking of all self-control and even to suicide. Yet those carnal pleasures are not merely the snares of the Devil. The power of love is great because we are aware of its frailty, we desperately try to embrace a beautiful body and to discover a soul behind it because we dread soon to be deprived of such ephemeral loveliness. Fear of the passing of time and of our own hasty march toward old age and death, search for self-oblivion in the abysses of passion, dim realization that the sufferings of love and the disgust of our sins draw us nearer to religion — such are the feelings lurking in the frantic adolescents depicted in Mauriac's early novels.

With *Le Baiser au lépreux* (1922), Mauriac composed his first masterpiece. Weaker novels were still to alternate with others of rare finish and power. *Destins* (1928), *Ce qui était perdu* (1930), *Le Mystère Frontenac* (1933), *Le Mal* (1935), *Les Anges noirs* (1936), *Les Chemins de la mer* (1939) are considered definitely feeble products of the novelist's pen. Even *La Fin de la nuit* (1935), 'Insomnie,' and 'Thérèse chez le docteur,' two striking, long short stories included in *Plongées* (1938), and *La Pharisienne* (1941), while far

2. Preface to *Petits Essais de psychologie religieuse* (Société littéraire de France, 1920), written during Mauriac's service on the Eastern front.

from negligible, suffer from blemishes that impair their effectiveness as a whole. The best of Mauriac lies, for us, in the five works to
which closer attention will be given in these pages.

Jean Péloueyre, the lamentable hero of *Le Baiser au lépreux*, is
depicted with relentless lucidity by Mauriac. He is hideously ugly,
tortured by shyness and the consciousness of his ridiculousness,
afraid of girls; he resorts to religion and especially to confession
as a refuge from his inferiority. He discovers one day a page of
Nietzsche branding the inferior breed of 'slaves' as ready prey for
Christian ethics and exalting the will to power in man.[3] He resolves to shake his gnawing timidity and to ask a young woman,
from a poorer peasant family, to marry him. She cannot say no,
for the Péloueyres are a well-to-do family, envied and respected in
the district, and, as the priest explains to her, 'one does not refuse
a Péloueyre.' Noémi, the husky peasant girl, like most of Mauriac's
heroines, hardly looks for any physical pleasure in marriage; she
will obey the law of religion and of her husband, and retain,
through several pregnancies, a candid and almost virginal innocence. But the ugliness of Noémi's husband, the leper, whose soul,
haunted by desire, becomes even more repulsive than his face, is
too much even for her naïve good will. She embraces him, solely
out of pity, and he, aware of the horror that he inspires, convinced
that he never will be loved, flees to Paris for an impossible respite.
He languishes away from her and from his familiar country surroundings, returns thin and pale, while she has involuntarily
thrived in his absence. He dies, mourned by his wife, to whom he
has bequeathed his fortune on the condition that she shall not
marry again. Repressing her buried youth and silencing the call
of her flesh, she resigns herself to the eternal mourning clothes of
the provincial widows and enters the only path open to her, that
of self-denial.

In that brief, inhumanly hard novel, all the greatness of
Mauriac's art is already fully developed. The vision of nature is
vividly suggested, contrasting in its magnificence with the cring-
ing and self-ashamed hideousness of the hero. The characters are
powerfully sketched in their physical personality with a few harsh

3. Mauriac, broad-minded and often unorthodox Catholic that he is, has confessed to a curious fondness for Nietzsche. He wrote in *Le Bâillon dénoué*
   (Grasset, 1946) that 'no philosopher had remained dearer to him than
   Nietzsche, the poor antichrist' and that, although Voltaire always repelled
   him, he counted more than one friend in the posterity of Voltaire: Stendhal,
   for example, and Giraudoux on whom the Voltairian smile, no longer 'hideous,' sat like a radiant light.

touches. The stifling rites of bourgeois existence imprison in a strait jacket the latent paganism of those who dare not rebel against them. The tone of the novelist is one of satire blended with pity and enhanced by poetry.

Genitrix (1923) is laid in the same setting of a gloomy country house near Bordeaux. Fernand Cazenave is the son of a domineering mother, who eyed his marriage with suspicion and treated his bride with hostility. Her animosity grew when the young woman became pregnant; she feared that her son would then escape her for good. The baby, fortunately, was stillborn, and Cazenave's wife is now dying in a solitary room in the bleak, cold house. Her whole past appears in the mind's eye of the abandoned woman: her melancholy childhood spent in poverty, her marriage to a man older by a good many years who trembles like a little child before his authoritarian mother. He had consented to be lured into wedlock through a futile effort to free himself from the maternal tyranny. But he had never given his wife the slightest joy. 'This body of hers was soon to be consumed by death, and it had not known love. No annihilation in the ecstasy of caresses had prepared her for the eternal dissolution.' She dies. Her memory will henceforth live with her weakling husband; it is so much easier to love the dead, as Mauriac says somewhere, for they do not annoy us any more. Remorse, bitterness against the engrossing love of his mother who can think only of watching his appetite, his sleep, his clothes, his comfort, and of coddling him as if he were still a little child, and contempt for his own selfishness and avarice now turn him against the triumphant Genitrix. She, who thought she had recaptured her son with the death of her daughter-in-law, now finds herself rejected. She dies in her turn and leaves her son to his solitude. He, like many a man, should have gone through life without even trying to know what love is.

Genitrix is, in its condensed beauty, almost unbearably harsh; the theme of maternal love driven to tyrannical excesses, worthy of Greek tragedy, has seldom been approached by a novelist with such stark courage. The three characters are depicted with cruel truth, unrelieved by any touch of irony or tenderness. The beauty of the flesh and the fond transfiguration of the loved one by the lover have little place in such a novel. Children and domestic animals hardly ever seem to inhabit Mauriac's world. Only the changing seasons or the tragic grandeur of the night, with the whistle of express trains in the distance and the sounds of the owls or the nightingales in the garden, bring a momentary vision of external beauty, contrasting with the feverish emotions of the characters, bent on mutual torture.

Le Désert de l'amour has more ample scope. Not only is the novel longer, with changes in place and time, but it offers a subtle orchestration of diverse themes and varies the novelist's focus by presenting three protagonists of almost equal importance. Dr. Courrèges has led a life of incessant labor; his wife, absorbed by the material worries of daily living, has gradually lost all spiritual companionship with her husband. Professional success has come to him, but he is profoundly lonely. He, who has pierced through the secrets of many patients and listened to their confessions, cannot break through the wall of shyness and misunderstanding that separates him from his own son. The latter, an uncouth and gawky adolescent, frets in the atmosphere of cold suspicion that prevails in the home; he neglects his studies, affects a brutal cynicism, and awaits the experience of love, which might transform him.

When the novel opens, fourteen years after the events, Raymond Courrèges is sitting in a bar in Paris. A woman enters with an older man. He recognizes her as an old acquaintance from Bordeaux, Maria Cross. The train of memories takes him back to his life as a schoolboy of eighteen, when he used to take the evening streetcar back to the suburbs of Bordeaux. On it he met Maria Cross, a woman of doubtful reputation, kept by some rich merchant. Maria Cross was no lady of vice, not even a coquettish or sensuous woman. She had fallen into her existence out of weariness; she harbored sentimental yearnings and became fondly and maternally attached to the clumsy lad who, every evening, sat opposite her in the dingy streetcar. At the same time, his father, the doctor, was falling in love with her, respectfully and naïvely, like a man of science having suddenly, in middle age, discovered romantic tenderness. The woman worshipped the doctor as a saint and fondly accepted the affection of the adolescent until, one afternoon, he brutally tried to rape her. He was repulsed and mocked. Vexed in his male pride and hurt in having been judged both silly and repellent, he left her, eager to take revenge upon other women for the wound inflicted upon his vanity. He embarked on a dissolute life but never would forget or forgive the woman who had treated him like the clumsy child that he was.

The last pages of the volume take us back to the bar in Paris. Maria Cross, after years of a semirespectable liaison, is now married. She has recognized Raymond, vaguely recalled the ridiculous adventure that, for her, never counted. Her husband is suddenly seized by a stroke. And it is the old Dr. Courrèges, who had telegraphed his son that same morning to announce his visit to Paris, who is called by him to attend to the sick man. Father and son briefly meet near the woman whom they both had fondly dreamed of, still vainly trying to understand each other, solitary pilgrims in the desert of love.

A similar technique of relating the events in retrospect, as they flash upon the memory of the chief actor reliving every gesture, every sensation or thought that once was his, is used to superb advantage in *Thérèse Desqueyroux.* The point of view of the protagonist is thus adopted without any artificiality, and the reader shares the sense of solitude that afflicted the heroine, to the point of excusing her criminal attempt. Of all his women characters, Mauriac has drawn Thérèse with the deepest sympathy and with the finest nuances of convincing verisimilitude. Twice he felt impelled to return to the same heroine and perhaps to bring her to God. He shrank, however, before the conversion that might have saved Thérèse in the religious sense but would have imperiled her complex humanity.

Thérèse was a provincial *jeune fille,* the daughter of wealthy proprietors of acres of pines and vineyards, who accepted marriage, with no more love than is customary in such unions, to Bernard Desqueyroux, a landowner who seemed cultured and handsome. But Thérèse finds no happiness in married life, not even in maternity. She reads, thinks, smokes cigarettes, and judges her mediocre husband with lucidity, soon with severity and hostility. He is brutal and animal in his physical seizure of his bride; her senses are repelled by his complacent male coarseness. Every one of his thoughts revolves around the land and the family. Thérèse feels forever imprisoned in a dreary cage. Hatred for her husband creeps into her heart, and fear that her own daughter may have inherited too much of the paternal coarseness and conventionality haunts her. One day, while a fire was raging outside, in the pine forests, Bernard unwittingly pours himself a double dose of the arsenic that had been prescribed for him. She fails to warn him. She then is tempted to pour poison herself for her husband, and she falsifies the doctor's prescription to obtain it. Her husband survives, and her crime is discovered. She is saved from a prison sentence by Bernard's wish that the family be spared such a scandal. She is taken back to her husband's house and sequestered there until, one day, stifling in her prison, she decides to break away and live by herself in Paris. Appearances have been preserved. The family can exult, and Bernard can go back to his truest concerns, those of a landowner, sportsman, and voracious eater.

Thérèse, the sinner, the unbeliever, is the heroine of Mauriac. For she has suffered and revolted; and she is lamentably misunderstood by her middle-class family, who are aghast that one of them should insist upon thinking and acting in her own way. Mauriac delineated her with tender care, while apologizing for not creating characters 'streaming with virtue and pure in heart.' He presented her with the most precious gift a novelist can make to his heroes: he endowed her with mystery. She herself never knew what had impelled her to poison her husband. Shade plays with light, and half-shades with more glaring color in Thérèse, the most subtle and the most pitiful of Mauriac's oppressed women.

Mauriac's most successful novels eschew the confusing turbulence of the fiction in which life seems constantly to erupt with fresh incident and new characters. The novelist's most powerful stories are also the barest. Artistic unity is achieved through our perceiving every detail through the lens of one central character. But our vision remains impartial, for the protagonist who tells the tale is pitiless to his own failings. The form of reminiscences or of a diary occasionally interposes remoteness between the events remembered and the reader, keeping the reader at a distance and in a state of tranquility. In Mauriac's use of the form, on the contrary, the reader is carried away by the torrent overflowing from the tormented heart of the protagonist. The feverish, broken-up style of the interior monologue wins the reader's participation in sordid calculations and venomous hatreds.

Le Nœud de vipères is an artistic masterpiece, somber as a Shakespearean tragedy without comic relief and momentary escape into the ecstasy of the lyric. The hero is a King Lear with no Cordelia at his side, a Balzacian miser without the fierce passion for gold that transfigures Père Grandet. Everything in the middle-class family described by Mauriac is sordid. Jealousy, hatred, spying on one another, lying, and the sadistic infliction of wounds through words poison the family circle, which Mauriac, himself the happiest of family heads, refuses to see in rosy hues. But the true viper's tangle is the heart of the old man, Louis, who has kept a diary for years so that his wife might one day peruse it and marvel at how much he scorned and distrusted her.

Her 'crime' was that she had married him for money, after having broken an earlier engagement into which, presumably, she had poured more sincere feeling than she was ever to experience for her husband Louis. She belonged to an old family, which had lost its fortune, and she thought she honored Louis by accepting his hand, for he was but a son of peasants who had risen through their stubborn thrift. He had received a good education, had worked with zeal to be able to eclipse in intellectual achievement the young men whose greater social ease and worldly success he envied. Succeeded he had, and when he discovered that his bride had married him solely for his position and his money, while scorning his humbler origin and clumsy manners, he was wounded for life. Money-making became for him the only joy; or rather, a wild drive for possession of material good replaced in him the affections of the heart. His wife raised their children against him, as her potential allies; she nurtured them in a conformist and Pharisaic religious attitude, which professed horror at the father's unbelief. He lived on in his alienated home, surrounded by children and grandchildren who feared him and who speculated avidly on the amount that the old man was likely to leave them on the day of his death. He, in the bitterness of his heart, fed on revenge and plotted to hand most of his securities to an illegitimate child he had once had and thus deprive his family of the coveted legacy. The scheme is foiled through the cowardice of the bastard son.

His wife, for whom the venomous diary was intended, died before him. To the old man, long starved for affection, who had been waylaid by possessiveness and retaliation for the blows he had suffered early in life, another path now opened. Like most people, he had deceived himself only to be able to live. Hatred and vengeance had been vain pursuits for him. 'I have always been mistaken as to the object of my desires. We do not know what we desire, we do not love what we think we love.' Beneath the vipers entangled in his hardened heart was a nugget of charity. He inscribed in his mournful diary the name of the one true Love; he was drawn to Christ by his sufferings and sins, before he died.

But for its final pages, where the move toward divine charity appears too sudden and unexplained — a common feature of literary works in which supernatural grace invades a soul through an illumination, which can neither be prepared nor accounted for rationally — Le Nœud de vipères ranks among the most masterly novels of the century. Within a brief compass and through a voluntarily restricted technical medium, Mauriac has explored depths of evil and potentialities for good in a human creature. He has given concrete form to a vision of life and of man that is dark but is lighted up by charity. Without any elaborate description or ideological digression, he has afforded his reader an insight into social problems proposed by a middle class gnawed by avarice, Pharisaism, conventionality, and relentless selfishness.

Only one other of Mauriac's novels, in our opinion, ranks among his best, and even in that one the flaws are more conspicuous than in the earlier masterpieces, and the emphasis on the Catholic psychology of the characters is overstressed for the non-Catholic reader. The novel is *La Pharisienne* (*A Woman of the Pharisees*). The leading character, Brigitte Pian, is a deeply religious woman who might be called an unconscious or a sincere hypocrite. She forces others to practice virtue and thus drives them to revolt or hatred. She ruins a priest whose faith she finds too weak, dooms a frail young woman who insists upon knowing love of the flesh,[4] and turns her own religion into a caricature of Christian mercy. With his usual subtlety, Mauriac allows us to infer only that impure elements may enter into the making of such an imperious propagandist of enforced virtue, who may combine greed for power over souls, sexual unbalance perhaps, and sincere striving after saintliness. But he refrains from intrusive analysis and from the comments of a moralist. Several paths are opened before the reader down which he may venture to seek an interpretation of the novel. The technique differs from the retrospection or from the diary device of most earlier stories. A narrator is introduced, who participates in the action yet abstracts herself from it at times to interpret it to the readers. Some of the stark unity of Mauriac's more vivid masterpieces is thus lost.

Much in Mauriac must be explained by his determination not to become another Bourget, who preached the validity of Christianity for political and social reasons and praised Catholicism as an adjunct of order and an instrument for discipline. The author of *The Pharisienne* is Catholic but not clerical. Faith is, to him, not a haven of security and serene joy. Good does not reign on earth, and the hearts of the faithful are far remote from the purity of little children. Indeed, St. Francis celebrating the naïve beauty of birds and flowers, and Christ pointing to the lilies of the field

---

4. Mauriac lends to the narrator of the story in *La Pharisienne* the following words, which reveal one of his obsessions and explain the ardent and constant attraction and repulsion that the theme of love holds for him: 'I believe that all the miseries of our human conditions spring from our inability to remain chaste and that human beings vowed to chastity would not be afflicted with most of the evils that oppress them.'

are infrequent visitations in modern Catholic literature. Evil lurks behind every shape and perfume that is beautiful; the ultimate descent of grace into disturbed hearts takes place most surely once sin has paved the way to regeneration. Mauriac's Catholic novel insists upon remaining bold and powerful; it is Catholic and Christian because it respects the ugly truth of life and conforms to reality. Its characters are not docile believers bent at will by their creator; they resist him, rebel against being led to Paradise. In a little book written in memory of a friend of his youth who died during World War I, Mauriac clearly defined his purpose: 'A certain literature of edification falsifies life. The transcendence of Christianity appears most manifest in its conformity with reality. Do not then fake reality. To depict man in all his misery is to unmask the abyss opened, in the modern world, by God's absence.' [5]

It is strange that it should be in our time, when faith is less widespread than in the past centuries, that Catholic literature, long relegated to an unenviable place, has regained ascendancy with Péguy, Claudel, Bernanos, Mauriac, and certain Catholic writers of note in England and America. Catholicism, by once more placing disquietude at the core of religious literature, has tapped the sources for a new tragic feeling for life.

The advantages derived by Mauriac from his Catholic conception of the world are to perceive life as unceasingly torn between contrary forces and to picture man as restlessly preyed upon by the powers of Evil. Christianity, says Mauriac, enters into souls in order to divide them. The world is an arena for the struggle in which the Devil fights against God, vice against virtue, the animal part of ourselves against the call of the spirit. To the honest observer, virtue is not triumphant, as it may be in edifying novels; nor can vice win in the end, for that would be a denial of Providence. Thus a conflict is perpetually being waged. Man finds in his own ability to doom himself the very proof of his freedom. He revolts against God; but the life he makes for himself is, but for a few unreal moments of bodily and sensuous exultation, afflicted with an oppressive sense of dereliction.

Life assumes a significance to the Catholic novelist, in contrast with the naturalist author in whose fiction one felt only the slow, meaningless gnawing of an average existence, abandoned to forces of heredity, environment, and instinct. The Catholic novel portrays a struggle, with an end at least dimly perceived, sometimes

5. *La Vie et la mort d'un poète* (André Lafont), Bloud et Gay, Paris, 1924, p. 32.

attained with the help of divine grace. Sin also takes on a significance.

The Catholic novel rests on a sharp distinction between Good
and Evil. Man surrenders to the call of his desires or to the violence
of his passions voluntarily and, what is more, fully conscious that
he is breaking a moral law. 'La conscience dans le mal' [6] gives added
zest to his pleasures, but works for his remorse, and in some cases
for his salvation. Mauriac goes much further. Sinning appears in
his fiction as the prerequisite for entering through the strait gate
and winning 'more room in Heaven' after the sinner will have
atoned for the sin by repentance. This concept reassures his disturbed characters that they were not born to the conventional
existence of a timid Pharisee; they are not, therefore, incapable
of the *élan* that plunges them into hell only to raise them all the
more securely into the abode of the elect.

> Those who seem vowed to evil were perhaps elect before all
> others, and the depths of their fall measure the extent to which
> they have betrayed the task to which they were destined. There
> would be no blessed in Heaven if they had not received the
> power to damn themselves; it may be that they alone rush into
> perdition who might have become saints.[7]

The doctrine is not without its dangers, which moralists could
denounce.[8] But it offers unambiguous advantages to the Catholic
novelist, who uncovers snares laid by demons in the beauty of an
April morning, in the loveliness of a youthful face, in the encounter of a young man and a young woman in a restaurant or on
a bathing beach. While Anatole France and many another novelist
traditionally called Gallic accepted the pleasures of the flesh as
the most valuable adornment of our brief life, Mauriac pictures
them as unreal and followed by unspeakable misery. 'Christianity
makes no allowance for the flesh; it suppresses it,' asserts our
theologian-novelist. And, as he elsewhere adds, we cannot love both
Cybele and Christ. Conflict waged against one half of ourselves and
vigilance against all in outward nature that could seduce us into

6. The line concludes one of the darkest poems in *Les Fleurs du mal*, 'L'Ir-
rémédiable.' Mauriac's affinities with Baudelaire can hardly be exaggerated.
7. Mauriac, *The Mask of Innocence* (Farrar, Strauss and Young, New York,
1953, p. 138).
8. Indeed, a moralist had denounced the doctrine in the second century A.D.,
for the view that sin gives the sinner a moral superiority and a prior claim
to the Kingdom of Heaven is as ancient as Christianity — the pagan apologist
Celsus, as reported by Origen in *Contra Celsum*.

paganism give Mauriac's novels a tragic meaningfulness that Epicureans and skeptics seldom achieve in fiction.

Not all Catholic readers feel secure in the presence of such stories of temptation and subsequent remorse. Some openly regret that this Frenchman from the south should be relentlessly oppressed by the vision of sin. They would prefer the harmonious balance between the flesh and the spirit achieved by Hellenic culture and attempted by humanism after its discovery of antiquity. They contrast the hideousness of caresses exchanged between lepers in Mauriac's world with the splendor of the kiss bestowed by Cleopatra on Antony in Shakespeare's play, when the Queen of Egypt, who had mastered the art of sinning with grace, proclaimed herself and her lover peerless before the world.[9] Others, less nonchalant in their tolerance of the charming evils that flesh is heir to, have wondered which of the two phases often described alternately in Mauriac's novels was the more powerfully delineated and the more likely to remain engraved in the memory of young readers: the descent into the abysses of vice, or the ultimate dipping into holy water and the visitation of faith when sinners were no longer able to bear their strenuous life of sin?

Mauriac, in the sincerity of his faith, has pondered over some of these criticisms, of which his coreligionists have not been sparing. But he has remained convinced that his duty is to depict man as he sees him and to describe the world with the truth from which great Christian artists have seldom flinched. 'To dare say everything, but to dare say everything chastely. Not to divorce ardor from purity.' The most unchristian view of life would conceal the power of temptation to carry away the frail and even the most resolute of creatures. Like many Catholics and like many Frenchmen, Mauriac is primarily anti-Rousseau; man, to him, was not born good and can only with much effort become so, seldom through his own light. Not desire and lechery alone, but pride, avarice, bourgeois complacence, hatred of one's neighbors and family, the vanity of petty pleasures, and, most of all, the incurable stupidity of many human beings testify to the pervading influence of original sin. 'Men are all fools,' said another Catholic, an Englishman, G. K. Chesterton. 'This doctrine is sometimes called the doctrine of original sin. It may also be described as the natural equality of man.'

9. The criticism was offered with others, in an ironic, yet sympathetic, speech delivered by André Chaumeix when he received Mauriac into the French Academy (November 17, 1933).

Mauriac's originality as a novelist lies in his Catholic vision of the world, in his analysis of love and especially of middle-aged women and adolescents led by a love affair to explore the bitter depths of love. It lies, too, in his craftsmanship, which, conscious and subtle as it is, contrives to leave in the novel the element by which it is most likely to challenge time — poetry.

Love hallowed by the sacrament of marriage and embellished by the devotion of the Christian couple to the service of God is hardly a theme for Catholic novelists. Happiness does not interest a creator. The radiating joy of lovers who might find an absolute in physical love is the foe Mauriac pursues relentlessly, either in the second act of *Tristan und Isolde,* where, to Mauriac's relief, the lovers' raptures can end only in death, or in *Lady Chatterley's Lover,* against which he has shot the arrows of his bitterest irony, in 'Eros,' *Journal* I and 'Une Gorgée de poison,' *Journal* II. To him, desire is always hideous. 'It transforms the person who draws near us into a monster that is no longer like him. Nothing then stands any longer between us and our accomplice.' His married women have, of course, ceased to expect any pleasure or joy. No mutual esteem, no admiration ever precedes or prolongs physical love. Love is nothing but a delusion that makes us feel our loneliness more acutely, or a fleeting sadistic impulse to humiliate our partner. More often still, with Mauriac, love is the inordinate power to torment us with which we have suddenly invested another creature. 'There's beggary in the love that can be reckoned,' whispered Shakespeare's Antony. The French novelist, listening to Wagner's opera, mourns: 'How can love ever be reckoned, except by the tears that we draw from our partner?'

Mauriac indicts the flesh because he fears its power. Like the ascetics, he brands its pleasures as lamentably brief and preposterously vain, since they rest on illusions about our partner and delusions about ourselves. Love cannot live on if the lovers renounce the martyrdom of separation. Let lovers understand their true role, which is that of being the executioner of one another, he exclaims in a very pregnant preface to *Trois Récits* (1929). Human love will fill its only true purpose if it serves as a tool to inflict suffering upon us, a hook to catch us unawares and lift us to the only love that disappoints not — divine love.

His partial view of passion, his denial of the mere possibility of happiness illustrates the limitations of Mauriac. He never aimed at universality and he did not claim objectivity. 'The novel does not reproduce reality; it transposes it' is one of the many lucid remarks made by the novelist on his art. The novel falsifies life for many a technical reason: for example, it cannot render silences, and must resort to dialogues far more than we do in life; and no fictional device is perhaps more artificial than the much-vaunted interior monologue, in which the novelist conceals his intervention and blends confusedly the perception of a series of events and the consciousness of such a perception. Mauriac cannot hold the mirror up to nature because he starts from an a priori vision of the world. The word metaphysician recurs in critical essays devoted to Mauriac, who is nevertheless hardly a philosophical mind, and he has used it himself in the most fitting characterization that he has made of himself in *Journal* II: 'I am a metaphysician working on the concrete. Owing to a certain gift of atmosphere, I try to make the Catholic universe of evil perceptible, tangible, odorous. The theologians give us an abstract idea of the sinner; I give him flesh and blood.'

Not only must he resort to exaggeration and distortion but he must (or so Mauriac thinks) focus his lens on the inner man and on the isolated individual. Even the portrayal of a family is, with Mauriac, the portrayal of divergent members of one group, impatiently fretting at the prison where they must gather for meals or for the evening rest. They hardly ever communicate. Mauriac repeatedly contended that factory workers do not differ from duchesses in the quality or the manner of their feeling and that love and hatred are fundamentally the same in a farmer's daughter and in Racine's Hermione. He does not attempt to delineate groups or a whole society. He says of himself and of novelists in general, we 'can only depict with some adequacy beings oppressed by a law . . . The art of the novelist is a bankruptcy.'

Brevity is another self-imposed limitation with him. It keeps him from gaining for his stories the slow collaboration of time. The effect of the corrosion of the years on his characters does not interest Mauriac any more than it did the French tragic writers of the classical age. His manner, to use the Jamesian terminology, is not panoramic (except when characters survey their remembered past) and it is seldom dramatic in the literal sense, for there is very little drama enacted in the presence of the reader. Several of the best novels begin after the climax of the action has been reached, after Raymond Courrèges has lived his life of futility, after Thérèse has been judged for her attempt at poisoning, and after Louis has undone some of the viper's coils oppressing his heart. The passing of time matters less for Mauriac than the exploration in depth of the inner man. Variety in his gallery of characters matters less for him than grappling repeatedly with a few stubborn souls and unearthing more of their secrets.

Sartre, in a scathing article,[10] has pitilessly pointed out the truest weakness of Mauriac: the absence of freedom in his characters. Everything in them is predetermined by heredity, by the curse of original sin, and by their creator or by God. Mauriac once defined the novelist as 'the ape of God.' Sartre concludes his article with the oft-quoted words: 'God is no artist. Neither is Mauriac.' He charges Mauriac with first identifying himself with his characters, then suddenly forsaking them in order to act as a stern judge. Like God, he decrees that his wretched creatures be such and such, but he does not show them in the process of becoming what they are to be. The reader is not uncertain enough about the fate that will ultimately be meted out to them. The element of indetermination, which Sartre, the philosopher and the novelist of freedom, boasts of having restored to fictional characters, is indeed woefully lacking in Mauriac.

But he has other gifts, which compensate those he may lack: that of the tragic writer, hasty, feverish, eager to integrate the discoveries made by Dostoevski and Freud into the French mold of strict construction and swift, unrelenting ardor; that of the moralist, whose concern is to bring to light the still-unexplored or dark recesses of the human heart and to explore the perilous force of passions; above all others, that of the poet. In an interview with Frédéric Lefèvre, Mauriac indirectly hinted at his finest achievement when he declared:

> There is little danger in the novel's invading the rest of literature. I believe that only poetry counts, and that only through the poetical elements enclosed in a work of art of any genre whatever does that work deserve to last. A great novelist is first of all a great poet. Both Proust and Tolstoy were because their power of suggestion was boundless.

BIBLIOGRAPHICAL NOTES

The most valuable material on Mauriac is that which he has untiringly provided himself, in many biographical essays: *Commencements d'une vie* (1932); 'Cinquante Ans' (*Nouvelle Revue Française*, No. 313, October 1939, pp. 535–51); in the four volumes of his *Journal;* in his wartime

10. The article is listed in the Bibliographical Notes. Mauriac has never forgiven it and has seized every opportunity to attack Sartre in *Le Figaro.*

essays *Le Bâillon dénoué* (1945); in excellent analytical essays on *Le Jeune Homme* (1926) and *La Province* (1926). Mauriac has published three important little books on the art of the novel as he envisages it: *Le Roman* (1928), *Dieu et Mammon* (1929, reprinted in 1935), and *Le Romancier et ses personnages* (1933).

No volume on him is thus far wholly satisfactory, not even Nelly Cormeau's, which Mauriac praised as the best on him. Useful information may be found in the following titles:

Bendz, Ernst, *François Mauriac, ébauche d'une figure*, Elanders, Göteborg, 1945.

Boerebach, 'La Place de la métaphysique dans le roman de Mauriac,' *Neophilologus*, October 1946, pp. 151–64.

Catalogne, Gérard de, 'Mauriac ou le sens du péché,' in his book *Une Génération*, le Rouge et le Noir, 1930.

Cormeau, Nelly, *L'Art de François Mauriac*, Grasset, 1951.

Fernandez, Ramon, Essay introductory to the second edition of Mauriac's *Dieu et Mammon*, Catalogne, 1935.

Fillon, Amélie, *Mauriac*, Malfère, 1936.

Greene, Graham, 'Mauriac vu par un Anglais,' *La France libre*, April 16, 1945.

Hopkins, Gerard, 'Mauriac et les Anglais,' *Mercure de France*, April 1, 1948, pp. 590–95.

Hourdin, Georges, *Mauriac romancier chrétien*, Le Temps présent, 1945.

Jaloux, Edmond, Essays introductory to Mauriac's *Le Romancier et ses personnages*, Corrêa, 1933.

Magny, Claude-Edmonde, 'Un Romancier de la passivité, Mauriac,' *Esprit*, September 1949, pp. 444–54.

Majault, Joseph, *Mauriac et l'art du roman*, Laffont, 1946.

O'Donnell, Donat, *Maria Cross: Imaginative Patterns in a Group of Modern Catholic Writers*, Chatto and Windus, London, 1954.

Palante, Alain, *Mauriac, le roman et la vie*, Le Portulan, 1946.

Prévost, Jean, 'De Mauriac à son œuvre,' *Nouvelle Revue Française*, I, 1930, pp. 349–66.

Sartre, Jean-Paul, 'Mauriac et la liberté,' *Nouvelle Revue Française*, I, 1939, pp. 212–32, reprinted in *Situations*, Gallimard, Paris, 1947, I, pp. 36–57.

——, *Hommage à François Mauriac*, La Revue du Siècle, July–August 1933.

V

<hr />

JEAN GIONO

HISTORIANS and philosophers, with their faculty for proposing impressive generalizations, will some day speculate on the 'necessary' correlation between society and literature in France during the period between the two world wars. In the view of these thinkers, artists and writers stand in close dependence upon the environment in which they have grown up and reflect the prevailing mood of their age. Those who have remained aloof are ruled out as solitary exceptions confirming the common rule, as the absurd saying puts it; or they are branded as dwellers in an ivory tower, who refused their duty to society.

The truth is that the spirit of an age as it is reflected in history is often contradicted by the image of the same era mirrored in its art and letters. In western Europe the period from 1919 to 1930 was a time of economic reconstruction, of relative political stability, of social optimism, and of the pursuit of prosperity. Yet the literature of the period was characterized by an all-pervading sadness, even when it advocated hedonism. This generation cared little about stability and unambiguously dismissed any concern with eternal values. While official prophets celebrated the creed of social service and the steady improvement of man and his world, the rebels of letters bewailed the solitude of the modern civilized individual, and his failure to reach harmony with others and find peace within himself. The writers stressed introspective self-analysis as never before. When many declared that woman had at last come of age and would henceforth share man's role in the world, heroines practically disappeared from literature or were depicted with ferocious severity. While the world, one was told, was entering upon a century of indefinite progress, literature expressed discouragement, describing the disintegration of man and his world and the disintegration of the novel and other art forms.

France was struck last by the economic crisis of 1929–33, and for a time she seemed only mildly affected. Yet a worm undermining her political structure was gnawing more and more deeply. A cleavage was widening daily between antagonistic social elements. The country, with her nostalgic attachment to the past and her innate turbulence, avid for innovations, seemed reluctant to accept the modern world, with its methods of mass production, its faith in machines, and its worship of efficiency. While other nations were artificially fostering their much-advertised 'dynamism,' they revived the old accusation that France was backward and 'decadent.' Yet intelligence, subtlety, humor, and originality were as abundant as ever in Paris. Unfortunately, action seemed to be divorced from intelligence, and subtle minds seemed unable to envision the forces of the future and to harness them in the interest of their country and of mankind.

At the very moment when her political and economic leaders seemed powerless to avert an impending catastrophe, France produced a number of writers whose robust audacity and faith were scarcely equaled elsewhere in Europe. Jean Giono is probably the most original among these men; his appearance in the French literary firmament was truly meteoric. At the very time when Marcel Proust seemed to have established his supremacy in French fiction and to have oriented it toward the minute analysis of man's remembrance of things past, when Jules Romains, Jacques de Lacretelle, and André Maurois were delighting in the delineation of hypercerebral and sensual characters, when François Mauriac was populating his fervid *récits* with miserly bourgeois men and love-starved wives frantically seeking God to put an end to their isolation, a new voice rang from the remote Alpine countryside. It sang of nature, of the starry skies, of the wind, of ardent and simple creatures, and of intoxicating sensations, with the accents of a primitive bard. The novels of that newcomer to literature were not skillfully built; they ignored academic subtleties and the fashions of the day. Their heroes were not poisoned by complexes, nor did they blend desire and hatred in 'that mutual torture,' which was, for Proust, synonymous with love. In them the tone of a psychological dissector had given way to that of a poetical master of suggestive language and an epic storyteller.

Giono was also a prophet, and his message was soon acclaimed by eager disciples. He rejected much of our urban and analytical civilization; but he held out hope for despairing moderns. He aimed at rebuilding a new unity in man and endeavored to instil in him the sweet, or bitter, 'lore that nature brings.' The shades of other prophets of revolt were recalled by critics: Rabelais, Rousseau, Rimbaud. Once again, indeed, from the land most famous for analytical introspection and destructive irony, there sounded an appeal to listen to nature alone and to delve into the mysteries of precivilized life. This new hymn to nature and to joy at once found echoes in other lands. Giono's prose, unusually difficult because of its wealth of vigorous words, was enthusiastically deciphered by students in foreign universities. The screen consecrated first *Harvest* (*Regain*), then the *Baker's Wife* (inspired by an episode in *Jean le bleu*), a typically Gallic picture, which caused American journalists and commentators to throw moderation to the winds in their praise.

Giono is a Frenchman of the south, but there are many varied domains within the vast and vague realm called 'southern France.' His *petite patrie* is not the playful Southwest of Montaigne, Montesquieu, and Gobineau, nor the mysterious land of the Basques. It is not the Provence of the cavalcades and of the *Félibres*, of colorful costumes and a sonorous language revived, not without some artifice, by Mistral and his circle. Alphonse Daudet's graceful tales, fragrant with rosemary and thyme, are pale sketches when placed beside Giono's flamboyant description of mountains and storms and floods. The ferocious logic of Charles Maurras and of other southern Royalists clinging to a bygone order, or the subtle Greek intellectuality of Paul Valéry, are no less alien to this new romantic. Although Giono's native city is not many miles distant from the Mont Sainte-Victoire, now familiar to museumgoers of two continents, his luxuriousness seems to set his landscape in a different world from that of Cézanne's essential sobriety. With Zola, Cézanne's compatriot, Giono seems at first to have more in common. But he embellishes reality and exalts man, while Zola, a romantic at heart, found bitter rejoicing in the somber poetry of vice and too often cultivated ugliness.

Giono is not merely a provincial novelist or what the French

call *un écrivain du terroir*. His appeal is to all modern men, as is
Thomas Hardy's or William Faulkner's, even though the setting
and the characters of their books are narrowly localized. But
Giono's reader cannot divorce the message implicit in his books or
in the beings to whom he gives life from the landscape, which is
always part and parcel of the story. His Provence is not the conventional Riviera with its cosmopolitan tourists, its equable climate gentle to invalids, retired officials, and undersexed esthetes. It
is not the Provence of imposing Roman ruins or of pine-clad prom-
ontories still haunted by Greek memories. It stretches between
the Durance Valley and the Italian frontier, north of Aix and
Draguignan. Its soil is poor; indeed the Basses-Alpes, being one of
the least favored of all the French departments, has remained unspoiled by industry and by the tourist trade.

Manosque, Giono's birthplace, is a town of some five thousand
inhabitants, whose history, as a few picturesque relics still testify,
goes back to the Middle Ages. Its narrow lands, contained within
the perimeter of old fortified walls, afford vistas of the countryside
studded with dark tapering cypresses, long rows of century-old
ashen-gray olive trees, and, in the early spring, the delicate beauty
of almond trees in bloom. Beyond stands the mountain of Lure,
a familiar presence in Giono's novels. On its slopes there are scattered farmhouses with their ancient wells shaded by a broad fig
tree, and a threshing ground for the wheat that grows sturdily in
the dry, red earth. Farther up, there stretch green pasture lands to
which shepherds repair in the summer with their flocks, after driving their sheep and a few male goats along the dusty roads of the
plain all the way from Camargue. Stags and birds, depicted with an
uncanny insight into their physical being and their wild, delicate
nature in some of Giono's books, haunt the many glades, which
resound at night with their calls. The fauna of Giono's landscapes
is bewilderingly rich: swarms of insects buzzing in the trembling
noonday heat, partridges and larks and nightingales, rabbits, mar-
tins, and weasels appear in his stories, not as a pretext for elaborate
descriptions, but briefly characterized in the felicitous images of
a sensuous pantheist. Snakes are especially dear to him, as they
were to Shelley, for their strange gracefulness and peaceful communion with the earth in which they wind and burrow. The river
Durance is ever present; now almost dried up by the summer
drought, with innumerable islets overgrown with osier and tall,
marshy grasses in which the baker's wife and her lover take refuge;

now impetuously overflowing the plains, swollen with the thaw of Alpine snows and swinging against its banks in wrath.

The chief actors in Giono's stories are the great elemental forces: the wind, the torrents of spring unleashed over field and marsh, the parched earth in summer, the Dionysian dance of reeling odors, which intoxicate his men and his women, and above all, the stars that guide their works and their humble meditations. The novelist's purpose is to create living beings not unworthy of such a simple and yet grandiose setting, and the best of Giono's books are those in which he has conjured up the people who enchanted his childhood and taught him the meaning of life and the acceptance of fate. They are his father, a few women with their wise intuition and their revelations of the mysteries of physical delight and of spiritual otherness, an occasional artisan or peasant, now and then a village healer or an itinerant acrobat who attempted to cure the evil in souls. These characters are robust children of nature, hardly literate, little addicted to pondering mental problems or to repressing their healthy enjoyment of all senses by inhibitions of religion or culture. Yet they are never coarse, like the degraded peasants of Zola or of Erskine Caldwell. Their passions are ardent when aroused, but they never become abnormal nor indelicate. Clumsily but with earnest good will, they grope toward an end; and that end is almost always charity, the gift of themselves to others, the fraternal desire to help their fellow creatures reach joy. Idealized though they may be, and sweet-tongued or figurative in their language, they seldom appear false to those who are familiar with their native province. The humble shoemaker in *Jean le bleu,* the simple and devoted journeyman from Baumugnes, the farm laborers in *Que ma joie demeure,* even the more primitive men and women struggling against fate and against each other in *Le Chant du monde* are as true to life as any other peasants in French literature.

Giono was born at Manosque on March 30, 1895, the first of a brilliant group of writers who came into the world before the dawn of the new century. His father, who died in 1920, was a shoemaker in his small town. Giono learned much from watching his father at work with his leather, awl, and cobbler's wax, and from listening to his slow, thoughtful conversation with friends and customers. Unlike other writers born in humble condition, who hasten to become members of the middle class or to knock at the doors of salons and academies, Giono always took pride in his humble origins. His semifictional autobiography, *Jean le bleu,* movingly portrays his father guiding his son through the awakening of adolescence to the shrewd wisdom of inner contentment and fraternity. He has often alluded to three other French writers of some repute (Jean Guéhenno, Louis Guilloux, and Lucien Jacques), also sons of shoemakers, as constituting with him the brotherhood of cobblers in present-day literature.

Giono's father, like Zola's father and Valéry's mother, was of Italian descent. His grandfather, who had conspired with other Italian *carbonari,* had fled from Italy across the French Alps, then served with the French in Algeria in 1835. Giono's father, born near Marseille, had eventually settled at Manosque; there he married, in 1892, Pauline Pourcin, whose father came from Provence and whose mother came from Picardy. She was a laundress by trade, and *Jean le bleu* as a child roamed from the tools of the shoemaker's workshop to the lower floor of the laundry where the smell of clean linen, of hot irons and, as he proclaims, of perspiring women delighted his precocious adolescence.

His father was his most influential teacher. To him Giono owes a spirit of indomitable independence in his political and social views, a seriousness of purpose, which may have been strengthened by certain leanings in his father toward Protestantism, and a durable attachment to the concrete and the palpable in life, which recalls a craftsman plying his wood, leather, and thread. Giono's sense of touch is second only to his extraordinary sense of smell. The boy went to school in Manosque from the age of six to that of sixteen, then entered a local bank as a petty clerk and remained there until the war broke out. His amazing mastery over one of the richest stores of words ever handled by any French writer was apparently acquired not in lecture rooms and university libraries but at the truest fountains of language: a few great books, read and reread, and the talk of peasants, shepherds, and artisans.

Little is known about Giono's sources, and even the most inquisitive scholar need not know much more; except for a few reminiscences of Gide's *Nourritures terrestres,* Giono owes little to the works of his contemporaries. The two great events in his youth were his discovery of the classics and his initiation into music, related with emotion and humor in the early chapters of *Jean le bleu.* To his love of music, especially that of Bach and Mozart, different as Giono is from them, some of his ideological essays will later bear witness. His novels, with their alternating phrases of sonorous exuberance and of slender flutelike melody, occasionally recall musical symphonies. They certainly aim at seizing the whole of the reader's sensibility and they unleash the same elemental forms that Beethoven and Wagner translated into sounds. They hardly reflect the preference for design, often accompanied by too sharp a relief given to lines and too conscious a control of one's material, that has marked the French novel since Stendhal.

The reading of ancient poets in translation was for the young Jean the supreme revelation. Others, born comfortably into the middle class with the advantages of a liberal education, have derived nothing but boredom from their enforced construing of the lines of Homer and Sophocles. Giono had not learned Greek, but he grew up in a land where peasants to this day winnow their grain, pluck their olives, and milk their goats much as their Mediterranean forefathers did in the time of Ulysses or Theocritus. He felt the classics spontaneously and lived them in his body. They gave him, according to his favorite phrase, 'a kick in the stomach.' They aroused in him at fifteen an impulse to write, which he was to obey only many years later. In one of the few passages in which he has enlightened us on his training and technique, Giono declared:

> Born in a poor family, the son of a shoemaker, then a small clerk in a bank, I bought one day the ancient classics in the cheap Garnier collection. The Greeks were revealed to my dazzled mind . . . I have revived, or rather I have made actual, the heroes of Homer and of Sophocles whom I found unchanged in my native province . . . From that day on, I had found my path: to renew the great Greek tragedies.[1]

In his autobiographical novel, *Jean le bleu* (blue because he loves to close his eyes and to feel his dizzy head all filled with blue), he recalls the intoxication of his fourteenth year. Once, at harvest time, a mysterious farm laborer lent him a copy of the *Iliad* in translation. He read it among the yellow ears of wheat, while scythes were creaking and long forks were pitching the sheaves.

1. The passage is from an interview given to *Les Nouvelles Littéraires* on March 13, 1937. Most of the other details about Giono's family, his manner of living, his reading, and about the successive drafts of his novels, as well as several very valuable quotations from unpublished manuscripts, are to be found in the only essential book on Giono, *Jean Giono et les religions de la terre,* by Christian Michelfelder (Gallimard, 1938).

The text penetrated into his very senses and marrow. 'Into me was Antilochus throwing the spear. Into me was Achilles ramming the soil of his tent, trampling in the wrath of his heavy feet. In me was Patroclus shedding his blood.'

Homer, Aeschylus, Sophocles, and Aristophanes are still the authors most often taken from their shelves; then Shakespeare and Spinoza. Hardly any of the French classics and only, among the moderns, Melville (for whom he wrote an eloquent preface, *Pour saluer Melville*, in 1940), and Walt Whitman, whom he has frequently read aloud to the peasants of Provence. With the Old Testament he is obviously familiar, and some of its myths have lately haunted his imagination. Unlike many of his contemporaries, he refrains from belittling Hellenic themes with irony and facile anachronism when he goes to them for his inspiration; he also refrains from technical tricks and from such manipulations with time, syntax, and words as have tempted many moderns, naïve in their sophisticated desire to disconcert their readers. His only principle is to grasp the subject fully, squarely, banishing all subterfuge; the rest follows slowly but surely.

When the war suddenly broke out in 1914, the bank clerk, then nineteen, was soon called to the colors. For almost four years he served as a private in an infantry regiment, exposed to the sordidness of mud and carrion, watching men intoxicate themselves with the smell of blood or resort to the lowest pleasures in order to forget. Miraculously, he escaped wounds and death. But he saw his dearest comrades fall in combat by his side; he returned home on brief furloughs, to watch desolate parents and widows pining in grief and to count the friends of his youth whom war was ravishing one after the other. Giono hated war. His anger against Christianity springs in part from the lamentable record of modern history, with war condoned or incited by religion. Leaving Nietzschean hymns to the virtues of the dangerous life and the heroism of hardhearted warriors to the lucky or timid ones who had stayed behind at their desks, he spoke as a plain soldier who had seen too much actual shedding of blood ever to celebrate the mystical value of that rite. 'I have stayed at Fort de Vaux [near Verdun] for forty-two days, and it is difficult for me to get excited over a corpse . . . The stupidity of war is what disgusts me most in it. I love life.' Indeed, his war stories, ferocious in their bitter emphasis on the grim aspects of the fighting, contain some of the most haunting evocations of the butchery of Verdun and Kemmel. But the bruised flesh and the eyes of dead soldiers eaten up by rats and vultures revolted Giono less than the immense waste that characterizes war. Peasant that he is, he cannot be reconciled to the senseless mowing down of young bodies and ripe crops and cattle, and the laying waste of old trees and carefully tended meadows.

In 1919, Giono finally came back to Manosque, sad in mind although unharmed in body. Other young men who had shared the same experience were driven by the lust of escape to exotic lands; or they were eager to make up for their lost years and rushed to Paris, the eternal goal of all provincial Frenchmen with literary, political, or financial ambitions. Giono did not share in the post-war race for pleasure, speed, and 'intense living.' He quietly took up his former position at the local bank, worked underground in the vaults at the *Service des Coupons,* endlessly clipping off bits of strangely colored and engraved paper and crediting them in big ledgers. But a banker he was never meant to be. He resigned from the bank when, in 1929, his company offered to send him to Antibes to direct a new branch there. Money inspired him with neither respect nor greed. He will later contrast 'the true riches' with those squares of green-backed or yellowish thin paper that most men worship. In 1920, he had married and soon had had two daughters.

After he had resigned from the bank, he devoted most of his day to writing. He began by composing poetical tales of nature and delicate eclogues set in the Manosque region, then a more ambitious volume inspired by the *Odyssey,* or rather reinterpreting the old epic imaginatively, *La Naissance de l'Odyssée* (1930). His friend Lucien Jacques took one of his manuscripts to Marseille and had it published there. He was thus encouraged and in 1929, *Colline,* printed in a Parisian review, revealed him as a writer of original talent. The doors of the literary world suddenly swung wide open.

Giono did not rush to conquer the salons and the *cénacles* of the French capital. He chose to remain a provincial. The streets of the busy metropolis appeared inhuman to him, for they were filled only with vacant eyes and the hurried steps of people who had lost contact with trees and rocks, horses and foxes, even with the sun and the sky. He traveled there seldom, to visit his publisher or to watch the performance of his plays, two of which were given on the Parisian stage with scant success, for Giono's talent is not truly dramatic. He avoided literary circles, but fame came to him as it had come to few modern French writers since Proust and Valéry. Still Giono lived on in his old house in Manosque, writing in his 'lighthouse' as he calls his clear sunny room overlooking the valley. His friends remained the humble folk of the country: the postman, the grocer, the shepherd, and their wives, whom he persuaded to bake their own bread, as the first step to the recovery of pristine wisdom.

Giono, however, is no modest hermit singing in unadorned language of simple life and the joys of the earth. He soon became conscious of his rare power over words; at times he became intoxicated with it. He was not content with portraying what he saw or writing of the feelings and the sensations that he imagined. His later tales had a message, and the message was in danger of devouring the tale. In the years immediately preceding World War II, Giono turned into a Tolstoyan prophet. Many men and women of France, and still larger numbers from central Europe, flocked to Manosque to seek the counsel of the Master. Tourists on their way to the Riviera included Manosque in their journey and came in the luxurious comfort of their automobiles to revere the advocate of simple living. Enthusiasts, reported a German friend of Giono who became a French writer of no mean talent, Ernst E. Noth, even claimed that pilgrims to the Giono abode should not walk or ride but crawl on their knees from the railway station to his house!

Giono's career was, from 1929 to 1937, an uninterrupted flowering, which brought forth over a dozen volumes and probably another dozen that have remained in manuscript to this day. These works can, without too much artifice, be divided into several groups.

In his first attempts, the sage from Manosque was trying his hand at stories of limited length, sketching only a few characters but already investing his tales with symbolic significance and discovering his gift for the earthy, striking metaphor. Along with *Naissance de l'Odyssée,* a fanciful tale of Ulysses' home coming (written five years before its publication in 1930), Giono first revealed himself with a collection of short stories, *Solitude de la pitié.* Several of them are intensely moving because of the simplicity of the theme and the directness of the style. The two words linked in the title point toward the leitmotivs of the book. Giono has none of the impassive objectivity of Guy de Maupassant. He is less intent on building his stories up to a dramatic climax; he seems to whisper his tale into the reader's ear with a heart-rending, though unsentimental, force of emotion, rare in the short-story writers of our century. Giono already draws upon some of the mainsprings of his inspiration: his hatred of urban civilization and of Paris, against which he launches a burning anathema (in 'Destruction de Paris'); the visitation of Pan, herald of rapturous joy, to a village ('Prélude de Pan'); and his ambition to write a book in which man will be merged into the surrounding world, attuned to its supreme harmony ('Le Chant du monde'), a brief tale with the same title as the novel.

Soon after, three short novels appeared, which Giono grouped as the *Trilogie de Pan: Colline* (1929), *Un de Baumugnes* (1929), and *Regain* (1930). The second of these volumes was translated into English as *Lovers Are Never Losers,* and the third is known as *Harvest;* both were made famous by screen adaptations. This trilogy revealed Giono to be a master of adroit stylistic effects; his sentences are short and concise and seem to grasp the object in its very shape and mass and odor. They render, more faithfully than Giono's later exuberance succeeded in doing, the dry heat of Upper Provence and the parched earth strewn with pine needles. Great God Pan, reborn after centuries of Christianity, or, rather, never dead in spite of Plutarch's sailor hearing the voice announcing his end, reigns supreme in that pagan land. *Colline* is a tale of peasant witchcraft as well as a hymn to the true life that flows in communion with nature. *Regain* is the new grass growing on reclaimed meadows and again mown, and the new crop of wheat in fields that had long remained untilled: a victory of man over the earth he had misunderstood and over his own selfish and bitter solitude. The story ends in fairy-tale fashion, with too obvious a moral lesson, which detracts from the artistic quality but was made more palatable in the moving picture.

The middle book of the trilogy, *Un de Baumugnes,* on the contrary, is a masterpiece of its kind. The novel has a moral purpose, but it is not obtrusive, and the tale in itself is breath-taking. The scenery is suggested with subtle restraint, so that the description remains secondary to the plot and creation of character. The story is told in the first person by a farm laborer who, at harvest time, met in the village *café* a tall young man with a heavy weight on his heart. He is Albin, from the village of Baumugnes (Vaugnières is the real name of the village on the map, but it has also been identified as St. Julien en Beauchêne, where Giono occasionally spent the summer months), a silent, clumsy, kindhearted giant, who inherited from his Huguenot ancestors an uncanny gift for playing the harmonica. Persecuted by the people of the plain because they clung to their different religion, these Huguenots had had the tip of their tongues cut off by their Catholic enemies during the religious wars, so that they would no longer be able to sing their hymns. They fled to the mountains, and, unable to speak, they called each other through the music of their harmonicas.

Albin was strolling in the village one evening after work when he was struck by the apparition of a tall, slim girl from one of the farms. But another lad had seen her too, a rascal from Marseilles, who was eager to earn his living more speedily, if less honestly, than by threshing corn. More wily and eloquent than Albin, he lost no time in arranging a meeting with the girl, Angèle, lured her with mendacious promises away from her home, and, after a child was born to her and she was ashamed to go back to her parents, forced her to sell herself to other men. When she broke away and returned with her fatherless baby to the farm where she was born, her parents, nearly crazy with shame, imprisoned her in a silo so that she would never again be seen. But Albin could not forget the vision of Angèle. His friend, the narrator of the story, undertook to discover her; he had himself hired at the desolate farm and, risking the wrath and the gun of the old father, discovered at last the subterranean prison and called for Albin. Albin's harmonica, played at night with skill and with feeling, revealed to Angèle the faithful young man who had once gazed at her. The novel ends when, after eluding the attacks of the old maniac, Angèle eloped with Albin, taking her baby, which became his. They went to the mountain village to live happily ever after. The story is simple but told with consummate art, with none of the complex layers of motives and desires dear to the novels of the nineteen-thirties. It is credible throughout, flowing with life. Unashamedly, it portrayed in postwar literature a man who was sincerely and naïvely in love and a woman worthy of being loved.

These early novels of Giono reflected the radiant search for joy of a young man exulting in his rediscovered bonds with the mythical forces of nature and eager to rebuild a new communion through love. Soon, however, the author became obsessed with the memories of war. Giono is the author of two war books, *Le Grand Troupeau* (1931) and *Refus d'obéissance* (1937). A third one, *Jean le bleu* (1933), receives its full significance from the last chapters on the tragic massacre that buried the rosy dreams of his adolescence. 'Beyond this book, there is the huge gaping wound by which all men of my age are gangrened,' he writes as a mournful conclusion to that enchanted autobiography.

Refus d'obéissance is vitiated by too crude an emphasis on the bloodcurdling aspects of the carnage in the trenches; its propagandist intention almost defeats its own purpose. It recalls the era when well-meaning pacifists thought they would undermine fascist appeals to the heroism of battle by dwelling on the horrors of gore and blown-out brains. The war scenes in *Le Grand Troupeau* are horrifying too, but so was the reality they describe; they do not try to provoke or convert the reader, and they strike one as graphically true to life. But the splendid part of this book is the delineation of civilians; for example, the opening scene with its epic descent of the flock of sheep through the dusty Alpine villages, the solitude of women dreaming of their absent husbands after the day of hard physical labor on the farm, haunted, in Giono's usual manner, by odors: 'When he was undressing, it would swell your nose; an odor of leather and of perspiring hair on his body. It smelt as when one prepares the dressing for the big Summer salads and crushes vinegar and garlic and powdered mustard in the salad bowl.' The volume, which is less a novel than a series of disconnected vignettes of the front and the villages in the remote rear, with the omnipresence of death contrasted with the resilience of life, ends when an old shepherd visits a newborn baby on the farm and wishes for him the true blessings of life.

> If God may listen to me, it will be thy lot to love slowly, slowly in all thy loves, like one who holds the arms of the plow and digs a little more deeply every day.
> Thou wilt never weep the watery tear through thy eyes, but, like the vine, through the cleft opened at random.
> Thou wilt often carry the burden of others, and be by the roadside like a fountain.
> And thou wilt love the stars!

The last word of the grim war book is an appeal to lead the great flock of men, and not let oneself be led, a message of hope, which Giono will henceforth regularly propose to his contemporaries.

Jean le bleu similarly lacks the well-balanced unity of a carefully composed novel. It meanders among the profuse reminiscences of the author's childhood and adolescence, treasures the sounds and the smells through which young Jean awoke to the exterior world, and conjures up, in an order as capriciously alien to time sequence as that of Proust's saga, visions of nature, farmers, animals, all reeling in a dizzy feast of the senses, amid the pagan setting of upper Provence. The book overflows with vitality; its very images are heavy, like pendant clusters of grapes. Yet there is wisdom in that debauchery of sensations, and purity in the pagan naturalness with which these peasants face the basic realities of life. The personality of Giono's father, the reflective shoemaker, dominates the book. Toward the end, the old man, his heart weakened, feels death approaching. In magnificent language, he explains to his son the meaning of the words 'God,' 'Death,' 'Life,' and tells him how much more difficult it is to suffer all alone than to live all alone, and how soothing it would be to invent God to console one's suffering if one has failed actually to find Him.

The news had just reached the quiet Southern village of the American who had succeeded in keeping in the air for one hundred and fifty feet. Some day it would be one hundred and fifty miles and many more, but the village sages nod their heads dubiously.

All that will not change anything, for the happiness of man is enclosed in small valleys.

Close to us, against the wall, there were swallows' nests, and mother-birds came to feed the little ones . . .

The tragic thing about our lives is that we are nothing but halves. As long as inventions are made in mechanics and not in love, men will not reach happiness. We are still only halves. The curse of heaven on us had been to make our hearts single. One for each. Once halved in two, you must find your exact counterpart, or else you will remain alone all your life . . . You are not any the happier for these magical inventions, for you have invented nothing new in the call you send around you for the other half of your heart.

And while the milk of the earth streams through all the blades of grass, while tree and beast are in all their glory of early summer, the young men leave for war, singing. Half of them never again will gaze at the beauty of this world.

Giono had proved himself a master of the robust idyl in *Un de Baumugnes* and had given in *Jean le bleu* a happy blending of fancy and of warm and sensuous realism. His next masterpieces, *Le Chant du monde* (*The Song of the World*) and *Que ma joie demeure* (*Joy of Man's Desiring*), can best be defined as epic novels. Giono was predestined among the French novelists of the century to attempt an epic novel. His humble origins and his obstinate determination to remain a provincial and a man of the people preserved him from the cleverness that gives a veneer of charm, but nothing more, to many brief French novels. He did not aim at speed and did not shrink from the plodding gait of the farmer pacing his furrow. His gift was one of the imagination rather than of analysis, and his instinct kept shy of the studies of desire, passion, and jealousy in which his compatriots think they excel. He had no cynicism and hardly any irony, not even much of a sense of humor, which is a saving grace in some writers but which occasionally paralyzes creation.

Le Serpent d'étoiles, published in 1933, is a strange tale of Provençal and Piedmontese shepherds gathering their flocks on the high pastures of the Alps during the summer. At the end of their long trip across the parched plains, they improvise a splendid epic drama in which the dialogues and the choruses leap with the untrammeled freedom of primitive inspiration. If, as he avers, Giono has preserved the original integrity of these folk songs and folk dramas, the book contains some of the most unique documents ever recorded in popular and spontaneous literature. The setting is described with a splendor of imagery that recalls the greatest of primitive epics, the Vedas and The Iliad. The reader feels the wind graze the palm of his hand, drinks the sky in long gulps, sniffs the smell of the hay in rapture, marvels at the multitudinous stars 'sown into the night as from a sack of rice' and as brightly pure as if they had never before twinkled in the luminous darkness. In this book, Giono first decided to apply to his writings the Whitmanian question: 'Can your work face the open countryside and the ocean shores?'

Le Chant du monde (1934) takes us back to the world of man with its passions and hatreds. It is, of all Giono's works, the one nearest to our idea of a novel, with characters presented in motion, struggling against each other, and integrated into a closely woven plot. Antonio, a fisherman, starts on an expedition along the river banks to a high mountain, with an older man, Matelot. The latter, having lost one of his twin sons in some wild fray, has resolved to explore the country for the other twin, a red-haired young man who has lately mysteriously disappeared. The pasture lands above the valley and the fantastic city halfway up the mountain are ruled over by a much-feared tyrant by the name of Maudru. Cowherds for leagues around obey Maudru's bidding. Antonio and Matelot reach the town and repair to the house of a hunchback, who is versed in old books, herbs, and plasters. The hunchback, who had been frustrated in some early love, had retired into that spacious house, the old palace of the bishops, and had devoted his life to healing the sick and the lunatics, who flock to him in long caravans from the countryside. There he had given refuge to the red-haired twin, who had dared fall in love with Gina, a girl of the Maudru family, and had eloped with her, after killing her fiancé, Maudru's own nephew, in a fight. He had promised her escape into the plains far away, freedom, and joy. But freedom is slow in coming; and the girl's hot blood boils while she is kept in concealment by her husband. But the couple cannot face the wrath of Maudru and his vassals in midwinter. They must wait until the snow melts and uncovers a raft, which the husband has built and concealed in a lonely creek.

Meanwhile, Matelot is killed in an ambush by Maudru's men, who have sniffed an enemy in him. His son, outraged and furious, with Antonio's help, sets fire to Maudru's stables and frees the bulls, which, maddened by the smell of fire, race wildly across the fields and overpower the cowherds. Then, while the great disorder of spring sends off steaming clouds from the forests of firs, quickens their trunks with sparkling sap, and thaws the face of the earth into rivulets and swamps, the two men launch their raft and float down the swollen river. Gina at last sees her dream of freedom fulfilled and admires in her husband the fearless killer, as tender in his love as he was furious in battle. With Antonio is a blind woman, Clara, whom he had met one day in the woods, while she was giving birth to a baby. He had tended her clumsily but devotedly and had accepted her insight and her faithful gratitude, while she worshipped his smell of a robust male. The two young couples sail down the river on their Noah's ark, as if determined to remold their own lives and the world. Slowly the blind woman deciphers the names of the trees, of the mud, of the stars, through the eyes of her lover; and he listens to her strange metaphors, which translate nature through other senses than sight; through her, he learns that seeing is deceptive. The secrets of life have to be questioned patiently, in humble submission.

Throughout the novel, the forces of nature — mountain and river and snow and the tender spring buds — are united with the wild passions of men, clan hatreds, vengeance, and desire. The story takes on a frantic violence at times, then subsides in the end, where the dominant feelings are those of protective love bestowed on the frail by the strong and of tender pity for the meek. The actors, except Toussaint, the healer, the meditative character who always appears among Giono's primitive souls, are above the common stature of men. They are epic heroes not because they accumulate feats in violent battle but because they are the very forces of nature embodied in simple, strong creatures; they echo the song of the world.

Each pair of lovers, at the end of *Le Chant du monde,* reaches happiness in mutual love and in bowing humbly to nature in her moods of fury or of gentleness. But man cannot long ignore other men; even the senses and the passionate desire that fully rewarded love had momentarily appeased will soon aspire beyond the walls of their selfish retreat.

Que ma joie demeure, published one year later, in 1935, is a more ambitious attempt. It portrays a group of diversified human beings who want to reach happiness and to preserve it when once won. The title is taken from the opening of Bach's choral, from which the first word, Jesus, considered by Giono as a limitation, has been erased. The volume, an ample and at times meandering novel of five hundred pages, is one long, surging aspiration toward joy. The plot is too loose to be summarized. A peasant has risen in the middle of the night to plough his field, vaguely disturbed by a brooding sense of the incompleteness of his own life and of that of the farmers around him. Suddenly a stranger appears on the ploughed furrow, under the dance of the stars, asks him to look up at Orion so like a carrot flower, questions him on his secret sorrow, and promises joy to him: let him leave some strips of land unsown, and grow lavish daffodils, and daisies, and merry hawthorn. The thrifty farmer listens, and obeys. And his neighbors, amused at first, also fall under the sway of Bobi the stranger, a mountebank and a prophet. They understand that to live is not to economize and to hoard in selfish possession. To live is to seek joy and to find it in what is useless. 'Youth is a passion for what is useless.'

The new faith spreads. The farmers banish the mutual diffidence that had caused them to live like lepers. They learn to co-operate and to trust each other and to listen to nature. Their consecration of a new community bond is sealed at an epic dinner, in which meat and game and fragrant herbs and wines pour out with Rabelaisian lavishness. Their senses and their hearts vibrate with the new fraternity. They let their colts and mares roam free about the pastures; they uproot the fences that jealously enclosed their fields; they harvest their wheat and mow their hay in communal glee. Bobi had brought with him a stag. The men start on an expedition to a nearby forest, described by Giono with exuberance and splendor; they surround and catch hinds as companions for the stag. It is like the dawn of a new world.

Tragedy soon breaks the idyllic dream. Aurore, a girl in her teens, an Ophelia-like creature, who has secretly fallen in love with Bobi, the wise man working his natural magic, commits suicide in her grief at seeing her love unrequited. Hearts are stung with jealousy. Greed proves hard to eradicate. Joy, easily attained in an *élan* of youthful faith, is hard to retain. Bobi knows that he has gone too fast and aimed too high. The world cannot be transformed overnight. His message must, once sown, slowly germinate. He decides to go away. He is ascending a mountain path, alone, when a storm gathers around him. Rain streams on his body, gusts of wind buffet his back; he walks on; and a lightning stroke, like a dagger, pierces him between the shoulders.

Although the meaning of the novel is cloudy at times and contradictory, the book is made alive through Giono's splendid art. The ardent love of nature, the insight into the life of animals obeying sovereign forces, mating in the woods with a grave delight worthy of Lucretius' evocations, the portraying of the changing seasons and of the works and days of peasant life reminiscent of Hesiod — these are the finest merits of the book. Its magic descriptions unite the splendor of the epic with a familiar simplicity of dialogue that few realistic novels have struck so felicitously. The volume is probably too long and its plot too thin or too unconventional, the behavior of the characters too insufficiently motivated and their pronouncements on life, joy, and fraternal love too cryptic to rank *Que ma joie demeure* among the most satisfying novels of this century. But nowhere has Giono risen higher than in certain chapters of this book.

Batailles dans la montagne, which followed in 1937, is an even more ambitious attempt at the epic and is even more disconcerting to the common reader of fiction, who expects the smooth flow of narrative and true-to-life characters. The story leaps almost beyond human bounds; the actors are hardly made real. Saint-Jean, the chief character, a carpenter who saves the village from a threatening flood, is more a symbol than a living man: Jacob wrestling with the angel or Prometheus defying the gods to serve men. After his superhuman feat, he aspires only to the calm serenity of death. His epic stature alone fills the novel; but the dramatic and even the plain human equality of Giono's earlier works seems gone. Words are rich in sap and juicy as sunny grapes, but their impetuous torrent appears no longer controlled by the author. Giono's epic qualities have swollen dangerously.

The novelist then appeared to be attracted by another medium. The next phase of his career was similar to that which came at the end of Tolstoy's and D. H. Lawrence's literary careers. (In all likelihood, Giono's evolution was accompanied by a loss of artistic creation similar to that of Tolstoy and Lawrence.) More and more, as he became sensitive to the evils of the world, the prophet in him triumphed over the teller of tales.

His gift of style has not left him. His message, earnestly felt, is often expressed with great force. An anthology of Giono's thoughts, detached from a certain verbose repetitiousness, which weakens them in their context, would include some of the most convincing denunciations of the social and moral wrongs of modern life, couched in sumptuous language. But Giono's books have become loose in structure, occasionally declamatory, and wearying in their revolt against the inevitable. The distinction the Stoics make between evils that we may hope to cure and evils that are not under our control is not observed by this son of old pagan wisdom. *Les Vraies Richesses* (1936) recalls Gide's paean to the sensuous joy of living in *Les Nourritures terrestres* and, even more, the Nietzschean assertions of Zarathustra. It is an impassioned protest against the dehumanization of men in our industrial age and the ensuing reign of greed and fear. *Le Poids du ciel,* published in 1938 with sumptuous photographs of stars and interplanetary spaces, also contains pages of beautiful prose. Giono, Antaeus-like, seems to draw unto him the strength of the earth and Atlas-like, carries with ease the weight of the skies on his shoulders. He interprets the lessons of nature with convincing eloquence.

His reasoning is less cogent when he attacks our civilization indiscriminately, and it is difficult to think that he could have seriously believed that his message of nonresistance to war was timely preaching in 1938, before the Munich capitulation and when one half of Europe was bent upon annihilating the other half. 'All conquered people have become the masters of their conquerors. Violence and force may satisfy those who think only of what is temporary; it might be time to think of what is eternal.' These words of Giono were to bring little solace to Frenchmen in their years of oppression. His message was one of resignation to the inevitable enjoyment of the simple pleasures of life, of poetical familiarity with the great forces of nature; it was also one of peace at any price. At a time when tanks and airplanes were rumbling out of German factories, Giono became an ardent pacifist. When

Austria and Czechoslovakia were suffering their supreme national humiliation, he was preaching passive resistance against the call to arms.

Only the greatest, that is, the humblest of masters can resist the wine of flattery, which worshipful disciples dispense to them. A group of rebels against modern civilization gathered around the sage of Manosque. With his friend Lucien Jacques, Giono founded *Les Cahiers du Contadour,* from the name of the plateau on which the new gospel was preached; communal living in harmony with nature was practiced there by these pagan cenobites. Much vain declamation was poured forth. Giono issued two small pamphlets to his friends the peasants: *Lettre aux paysans sur la pauvreté et la paix* and *Précisions* (1938 and 1939). These advocated resistance to war through nonobedience, resistance to the state, which serves nothing but its own tyranny, contempt for money and machines. 'No political regime ever gave men in a thousand years the thousandth part of the happiness which they find in one night's sleep.' In 1942, in a volume of long and rather diffuse reflections on the same themes, Giono, apparently unperturbed by the plight of his compatriots who had lacked machines and had been crushed, continued his preaching. The logic of his position led him to espouse some of the doctrines of collaboration with the Nazis, for instance, to contribute to an abject periodical, *La Gerbe,* inspired by a traditionalist Breton nobleman who was also a gifted novelist and a blinded admirer of the 'New Order,' Alphonse de Chateaubriant.

Giono practiced passive resistance himself when France mobilized her men in 1939. He was thrown into prison for a brief while, then released. While the Germans oppressed his country, he failed to realize that if war is evil, it is a far worse evil when waged by a Frenchman at the behest of German conquerors than by a Frenchman and his logical allies against his oppressors. His volumes published during the war years, while not actually praising the enemies of his country or supporting the absurd doctrines of Vichy, did not bring added glory to his name. He was imprisoned for a little while after the liberation of France, but apparently left unharmed or ignored by the reprisals that ensued. His part as a leader of French youth or even as an inspired writer of epic fiction seems to have been brought to a close when World War II broke out. In 1947, he emerged from the war years a completely different writer, content once more to be a storyteller. Could he, at fifty, find himself attuned to a changed world?

Giono is significant in French letters because he is, primarily, a great artist. This son of a Provençal shoemaker enriched the French novel of his age with an infusion of virility and of poetry. He broke with the tradition of the psychological novel of Stendhal, Proust, and Gide, as well as with the tradition of huge realistic sagas that Roger Martin du Gard and Jules Romains had tried after Zola.

His first astonishing gift is sensation. Giono plunges into the world with a freshness of perception denied to most adults. But that freshness is not the delicate sensitiveness of children, which blends the concrete and the magical. His sensations are as robust and earthy as they are intense. They do not diffuse objects in a halo of evanescent glimmering light; they accept them whole and capture their essence, concrete and spiritual. The novelist's world is a world of smells, tastes, palpable masses and shapes, caressed by the body; visual sensations account for little, and the intellectual content of perceptions is sacrificed to their sensuous revelation.

What he has perceived is almost instantaneously rendered through images. Giono is one of the most prolific creators of images in modern literature. He has occasionally abused his gift, but he has seldom indulged in the tricky metaphorical phrases for which Jules Renard, then Paul Morand and Jean Giraudoux became famous. Giono's images do not aim at surprising the reader, even less at debasing the person or the object, as was the fashion when a 'gentleman' would compare his lady's pale complexion to 'that yellow paper in which butchers wrap up meat.' Giono's rarest gift is his inexhaustible ability to create precise, yet expanding and soaring, images. He fixes the essense of reality through them and ennobles it at the same time; he simplifies, and yet transfigures.[2] Later, when he became conscious of his gift of coining metaphors and became more ambitiously epic, Giono developed his metaphors into ample comparisons. 'Intelligence is a miserable and stately Antigone: it appears, leading man by the hand . . .' And, in a passage of *Que ma joie demeure* not unworthy of Homer, the simple farmer gazing at the distant village at night, perceives fiery

2. Here are a few examples: 'Through the slit of the vale, one sees a country russet-red like a fox.' 'The air, full of flies, creaks like a greenfruit that is being sliced.' 'Aubignane clings to the edge of the plateau like a small nest of wasps.' 'That beautiful round breast is a hill.' 'The lizards sleep in the sun; then they jump, snap up and slowly chew bees which taste of honey. And they shed golden tears which sizzle on the burning-hot stone.' 'The transparent shade of the olive-trees holds in its spider's web the siesta of a little girl.'

signs flickering; they are, of course, the rays of light filtered irregularly through the shutters. But before he realizes their origin, the old man slowly spells them like letters of the alphabet: 'L', f, o, m, l', f, o, m, . . . like one of those great shapeless words which must have designated the sun, the moon and the stars in the mouths of early men.'

Giono is no master of the art of fiction in the traditional sense of the word; and his wealth of digressions and lavish use of description deprive his books of the purity of outline associated with many French novels. The structure and the pattern of his volumes (with two or three exceptions, such as *Un de Baumugnes* and *Le Chant du monde*) would not stand the strict critical scanning of a disciple of Henry James or Gustave Flaubert. They are often loosely built. Even in character creation, where Giono is far stronger, he can lay no claim to having molded individuals overflowing with life, as are the heroes of Balzac or Proust. His women in particular remain indistinct. We know much of what takes place in their sensations and, as it were, along and under their skin, but much less about their feelings and less still about the intellectual side of their nature, their moral or social reactions.

They are nevertheless real human beings and as true peasants as exist in fiction. It is not easy to give life to simple, robust, uncouth people, naïvely groping for joy, clumsy in the expression of their emotions, but unafflicted with the contagious disease of Gide's, Huxley's, and Mann's heroes, who discourse endlessly on their view of the world or conveniently reveal in a diary all the reader should know about them, and more. Giono's characters are not made of elaborate synthetical combinations of disconnected elements patiently pasted together; they surge into life at one stroke, as if impelled by a powerful creator to appear and haunt us. We may know little about them and their reflections and their inhibitions; but, as might be said of D. H. Lawrence's heroes, we become aware of their mysteriousness and live with them through three hundred pages.

Giono is also an artist with words. His vocabulary is extraordinarily varied — one of the richest in French since Balzac and Hugo. He seems to have the right word always ready at his disposal to express any part of a flower, of a tree, of an animal, or of a house, for the precise sensation received from the wind or the rain. His language is as robust as it is rich. The reader actually smells Giono's verbs, breathes the fragrance of his adjectives, feels the caress of his adverbs on his skin. A voluptuous artist was born in the son of the Manosque cobbler. 'Before I write a word,' he confessed to his biographer, 'I taste it as a cook tastes the ingredient that he is going to add to his sauce; I examine it against the light as a decorator gazes at the Chinese bowl that he will place in its proper setting.' Elsewhere one of his characters speaks of the magic of images that transfigure reality, of the legerdemain practiced, as by a dyer, by the artist in words, who changes the colors of objects. 'Poetry is the dynamite that blows up and tears away the rock.'

Where he has avoided the traditional pitfall of southerners, verbosity and lavish eloquence, Giono has indeed proved one of the finest masters of contemporary French prose. One is at times uncertain whether this primitive artist is not a false primitive, pretending to write clumsy dialogue or endeavoring not to compose his descriptions with the obvious artistry of a more conventional writer. But in his best moments, when rendering the cataclysms of nature or the sensations of men, Giono has succeeded in creating a style that appears devoid of artifice, more naïvely natural than the poetic prose of Chateaubriand or Barrès, more animated than Flaubert's dead cadences, less 'clever' and self-conscious than that of most moderns.

If art is the chief quality to be demanded from an artist, the artistic gift of creation and of expression that distinguishes a novelist like Giono is nevertheless nourished by a personality that feels and thinks. Giono's 'thought,' when reconstructed with some consistency by the critic, is neither profound nor original. Tolstoy's was no more so when he undertook to elucidate art or to comment on Shakespeare, nor Lawrence's when he pontificated on the fantasia of the unconscious and the 'dark mysteries' of sex. Even Shakespeare's pronouncements on life's brief candle and dusty death and self-slaughter, if translated into dull prose, would appear shallow or commonplace. The value of an artist's 'ideas' lies in the intensity with which they have been felt and clothed, and in the dramatic fitness with which they are expressed by the imaginary characters of the drama or the novel at a chosen moment. Giono feels his ideas with a burning ardor and makes his creatures live them.

But the critic's task is to restate in his own colorless language, and probably with clearer logic than his subject would like, a 'philosophy' that was merely implicit in the novelist or the poet. He cannot shirk this task if he studies writers like D. H. Lawrence and Giono, Claudel and Dostoevski; for their ideas, profound or shallow, trite or original, counted vitally for these men, and for their followers. Giono's message shook many a European in the early 'thirties; and its influence, assimilated and transformed, has probably not yet ceased acting as a ferment in the emotional aspiration of our age.

Giono, like Lawrence whom he often recalls (although the southern Frenchman, accepting sex with the sanity and restraint of the peasants of his country, is remote indeed from the mysticism of the flesh preached by the inverted Puritan of the Midlands), rejects the civilization that surrounds him. The modern world is utterly bad if it dooms man to be a cog in a crushing wheel. Greed, gregarious pleasures, meaningless ambitions, and aimless and soulless efficiency for efficiency's sake drive most modern men to a death-in-life worse than death. 'You must have been told,' Giono declares to his imaginary disciple in *Les Vraies Richesses,* 'that you should succeed in life; and I tell you that you should live: that is the one true success in the world.' And again: 'We have forgotten that our only purpose is to *live,* and this is a thing we must do every day, and at each hour of the day we fulfill our true Destiny if we live.' Let us therefore go back, and abandon the path of death and war which has misled us so lamentably. We can and we must recover deeper sources of life today, and thus make it possible for our sons to become harmonious beings once more.

Not only have we forgotten how to live, but we foolishly revel in our inner emptiness. We even lack the courage to look for the remedy, which lies within our reach. 'Modern times have not merely solved the problem of the disintegration of the atom; they have accomplished the disintegration of our beings, needlessly freeing and wasting spiritual forces that were necessary to us if we were to lead a human life.' We build and drive machines, we go to the bank and sign checks and clip off coupons, we read books and dissect them, we dictate from an office chair to a meek and neatly manicured secretary who obeys us punctually, and we give the name of life to that routine activity. But no true contact with the realities of life enters into that stultified existence. We devise mechanical contraptions that we force our customers to buy from us, through wars if need be; but we do not know how to make our own bread any more. We talk of mastering economic forces, but we have allowed the wind and the rain and the snow and the forests to be taken from us.

The secret of happiness is to recover our lost unity; the road lies through the restoration of a threefold communion. First, with nature. Such a communion, more necessary today than in Rousseau's times, as our urban lives have become more mechanized, is not to be effected through spending a few weeks at a seashore resort, not even through diligently mowing our lawns on week ends or sawing trees in a summer camp. Only through humility can we penetrate into the secrets of nature. 'Now I understand why we are the salt of the earth,' exclaims the prophet of *Les Vraies Richesses*. 'The wide still fields cannot of themselves express their deep intentions; silently, they blow a foam of vegetals. The extraordinary thing about our human destiny is not the intelligence that we have carefully molded for ourselves and that we direct at will like a revolving beam . . . it is our power to fuse ourselves with things; it is that divine part of ourselves, always in rebellion, which makes us the mouthpiece of the world.' Earlier, in a preface to a deluxe edition of *Colline*, Giono had already proclaimed in striking language: 'All the errors of man spring from his imagining that he is treading a dead earth, while his footsteps are imprinted in a flesh full of good will.'

The lessons of nature must bring us back to a sense of unity with the world around us. But the storms that tear our own world are no less tumultuous than the fierce rending in the clouds and the salubrious gusts of mountain wind that sweep across Giono's novels. It is easier to find contentment in submission to nature than to reconcile our own inner conflicts. Ignoring the call of our senses or repressing it is a false way of reaching an illusory peace with ourselves. Giono, to be sure, never advocates gratification of the senses; his novels do not contain precise love scenes, and bodily embrace and sexual indulgence are remarkably absent from his stories. But he knows that true wisdom is not of the intellect alone. Asceticism is to him a criminal mutilation. The obsession of the senses is never worse than when the unhealthy lover has to gird himself daily for the fight against his desires and his poisoned thoughts. Full acceptance of one's body is more chaste and wiser, Giono declares, echoing perhaps unconsciously Zarathustra's aphorism: [3] 'To satisfy our intelligence is not difficult; to satisfy our mind is not difficult either. But to satisfy our body seems to humiliate us. Yet the body alone partakes of a dazzling knowledge.'

Thus the novelist who has rendered sensations with unrivaled vividness and reveled in their richness happens to be one of the

3. 'There is more reason in thy body than in the best of all wisdoms.'

least morbid and least libertine in contemporary French literature. Giono does not leave women out of his stories, as Malraux does, except for Malraux's few scenes of eroticism. He is completely alien to the subtle perverseness that fills many French stories of amorous friendships of adolescents. Proust's sadism is equally remote from him, as well as the recent fashion that, under the guise of friendship and equality of the sexes, reduced many heroines to the role of willing partners to man's drinking bouts and amorous games. Giono's women do not resort to the hysterical screams dear to movie actresses, nor to the hardhearted calculations of would-be and accomplished spouses destined to arouse and maintain man's desire before and after marriage. His peasant women always win the esteem and affection of men, as well as their love. Seldom do their senses overpower their will; or rather the two hardly ever enter into conflict. There is little brutality and much mutual respect in the free giving and receiving of their love.

Yet it may be relatively easy to reach communion with another being in the passionate ecstasy of love or through the painted veil woven between lovers by the magic of desire. The truly rare communion is that which may spring from love between a man and a woman and outlive it, or link several men and women together in unreserved trust and the common pursuit of a higher goal. Giono, like Duhamel, Malraux, and Saint-Exupéry, is obsessed by the necessity of nurturing among us the plant of true friendship, rarer, as La Rochefoucauld once said, than true love. For friendship is more than comradeship of youth, of students or soldiers who have not yet been thrown into divergent paths by ambitions, selfish pursuits, or routine habits. It requires an unstinted sacrifice of our self-centeredness, a victory over secret jealousy and spite, a determination to spread joy around us and to accept it from others. It is perhaps the highest fulfillment that men can accomplish, for it demands the greatest immolation of our pride. It should combine the spontaneous gift of oneself that youth is prone to offer with the patient tolerance and the wise humility that mature years alone can bring.

It is such a purification of the soul that Giono advocates in his disciples. This prophet of a new paganism [4] here concurs with

4. Giono professes paganism, not atheism. 'The atheist says no; he is content with refusing. But the pagan wishes, wants, hence destroys and rebuilds . . . atheism retains something of the sour atmosphere of spiritualistic religions; paganism truly liberates.' Thus spoke Giono in a conversation reported by Christian Michelfelder.

the sages of Christianity and of oriental religions. He spurns the denial of the body, which is a mutilation of our being, but he decries no less vehemently the lavish attention paid by many to their feminine or effeminate bodies. Modern times provide us with luxurious pink, pistachio, and sky-blue bathtubs, with a whole pharmacopoeia of almond creams and odorous and deodorant perfumes and nail polishes. But who attends to the pustulant rash of our souls? Where are the hygienic experts to wash away their crust of filth?

This is the function of the artist. He creates beauty; but he must also extend his prophetic gaze beyond the narrow horizon of other men, discover and radiate joy, teach hope. 'The true artist always stands at the vanguard,' says Giono. 'He leans over from the top mast; he is the discoverer of new lands, of all the joys, the delights, and nourishment which await men — not for men to capture such riches greedily and shut them up in a safe, but for him to live with this treasure in a harmonious integration.' And again: 'The poet is a professor of hope . . . the horizon of men having fallen lower, his gaze flies far beyond, and the fragrance of stars is wafted to him.' Joy is the keynote of Giono's pagan message as it is of Claudel's Catholic teaching.

But can joy be long possessed? In the resplendence of his early creative years, Giono had seemed content with the delineation of humble characters reaching joy and living content in its fulfillment. That, however, gave an appearance of unreal idyls, almost of moral Sunday-school teaching, to his first novels. For joy is not all.

> If joy is better than sorrow joy is not great;
> Peace is great, strength is great.
> Not for joy the stars burn, not for joy the vulture
> Spreads her gray sails on the air
> Over the mountain; not for joy the worn mountain
> Stands, while years like water
> Trench his long sides . . .

Thus, at the remotest end of the world from Giono's Provence, wrote Robinson Jeffers, the tragic pessimist of California in one of his finest short lyrics. In his more mature works, Giono became aware of suffering and of the inevitable brevity of joy. 'I believe that one cannot make joy last, and even that one should not desire it . . . Suffering is an inventor of remedies; an inventor of hope. When man suffers the most hopelessly, then also has he the most hope. Suffering is then an immense apple-orchard in Autumn, under the rain, with beautiful washed apples at the end of the branches.'

It is on that word 'hope' that Giono's message concludes. He realizes that no regression is possible for men; machines will not be scrapped and probably should not be; but 'the true riches' should be shared by many of those who are at present absorbed in machines. If we cannot deny or undo mechanical civilization, we can go beyond it. To the suffering man of today, oppressed by a load of monstrous drudgery and living in terror of fierce cataclysms, Giono extends words of solace and hope. 'I can no longer accept the works of art unless they serve man, and the sign of the highest is that they express at the same time the strange misfortune of man's fate and man's reasons for hope.'

A passionate protest against man's fate — this is the significance of Giono's work. Some will smile at these outbursts against modern civilization and affix the familiar labels: romanticism, primitivism, anti-intellectualism. There will doubtless be a measure of truth in their scoffing. But Giono's art laughs in turn at such philosophers who treat man as a purely logical and reasoning animal, or rather as hardly an animal or plant at all, while he differs only in degree from trees and horses. His creed is not likely to be long discussed by professional thinkers or to be weighed carefully by experts on economic science. But it is the living faith of a poet, the passionate and anguished cry of a sensitive man protesting against 'what man has made of man.'

Giono, like Rousseau, Tolstoy, Thoreau, Rimbaud, and Gauguin,[5] has written about one of the most significant moods in the psychological history of mankind in the last two centuries: dissatisfaction with modern civilization. We have changed the face of the earth, filled the air with our engines and our sound waves, mastered explosive energy, but we have hardly scratched the surface of man's spirit. Can we not change man also and bridge the chasm that has too often separated our hearts and our heads, our religion and our philosophy? A Chinese sage of our time, Kou Houng Ming, has aptly expressed our tragic dilemma: 'Europe has a religion which satisfies its heart but does not satisfy its head,

5. As a prophet, Giono belongs with these men; as an artist, however, and as a powerful delineator of peasant life and of men living in harmony with nature, his spiritual family counts more central Europeans and Scandinavians than Frenchmen or even than English writers who, like Mary Webb, lack a certain robustness and elemental vigor. The Pole Ladislas Reymont, the Scandinavians, and the Swiss Charles Ramuz are perhaps nearest to Giono in modern literature.

and a philosophy which satisfies its head but fails to satisfy its heart.'

A Note on Giono's Novels Since World War II

Giono has not recovered his earlier prestige with the youth of France and of other countries; his writings since the conclusion of World War II have commanded respect from the more conservative part of the French public, which Giono's paganism and pacifism used to frighten, while the young have acclaimed philosophical literature stressing the absurdity of man's fate and see little meaning in a creed of harmony with nature. The resentment noticeable among the new readers is in no way due to Giono's marked lack of heroism during the war and his sentimental pacifism, which was respected for its sincerity. Admirers of Montherlant and of Jouhandeau, who both have enjoyed a new lease of glory after adopting an attitude to the war and to the resistance even less heroic than Giono's, and many disciples of another son of Provence, the Marquis de Sade, have turned away from Giono's romanticism and from his prophet's message. Like many men of letters who have once known the intoxication of success, Giono writes too much; but, unlike some others who, like Duhamel, Romains, Mauriac, and Maurois, have coveted official honors and multiplied ephemeral writings on the problems of the day, Giono has remained free from the deterioration that allows famous men to dispense advice to newspaper readers and to sell in ever-thinner slices the memories of their lengthening lives. No articles of importance have appeared on Giono since 1938, and no serious study of his work in any language has yet been attempted, while books on Saint-Exupéry, on Bernanos, and on Malraux are multiplying. Pierre Bergé has promised one, which would stress the later phase of Giono's career, supplementing the disconnected and uncritical, but valuable, pages of Michelfelder's earlier hagiographic volume.

On World War II itself, his attitude and his experiences then, Giono prefers to remain silent. He devoted most of his time during those years to writing. The stage tempted him, as it did every writer in those years, and one of his plays enjoyed some temporary success in a very small Paris theater. But the practice of the dramatic form mostly helped Giono to strip his prose and cultivate terse dialogue. His dramatic attempts were published in one volume in 1943, including *Le Bout de la route, Lanceurs de graines, La Femme du boulanger*, to which a *divertissement romantique* in three acts, *Le Voyage en calèche,* was added in 1947. They do not gain for Giono an enviable rank as a dramatist.

Giono also tapped the vein of *Jean le bleu* in a few sketches of his native Manosque; in an introduction to selections from Virgil, which first appeared in August 1947 in the periodical *Hommes et mondes,* he conjured up with great charm his reading of the Latin poet in translation and his rapture over those ancient writers who illuminated his creative understanding of his Provençal countrymen. Through Aeschylus and Virgil he learned to perceive in the women of Manosque selling or buying in the market place 'daughters of Minos and Pasiphae, Electras, Clytemnestras, perhaps even Jocastas.' Dido was alive around him. Through their friendly presence he interpreted his native city anew and could survive the inferno of his years as a bank clerk.

Between 1947 and 1951 Giono published five volumes of a long, loosely connected series of novels with the very general title *Chroniques.* He made no secret of the fact, which must have daunted the most enterprising of publishers, that the remaining fifteen of the twenty volumes of the work were ready in manuscript, as well as eight other novels composing a second parallel saga.[6] The *Chroniques* are said by their author to remind him of Froissart, perhaps because of a certain colorful truculence and naïveté in the narrative, while the other series would be closer to Alexandre Dumas. Giono may, indeed, almost rival the fertility of Dumas. He confessed to interviewers that work is everything and imagination is never wanting or never necessary. He goes to bed every night at seven and writes every morning from four to twelve. Posterity may wish that obstacles had impeded such a smooth flow of inspiration.

The break with the prewar Giono is complete. The style is concise, bare, familiar; the exuberance of metaphors and of comparisons is gone. Gone also are the elaborate descriptions of nature. A few vignettes suffice to picture the colors of the dawn, the marvel of the stars, the smell of hay in the fields, the winter roads slippery with snow and ice. The trees and the rivers, whose impetuous life Giono used to recapture in torrents of imagery, are still the kings of his landscape, but sketchily evoked. The scene of the novels themselves is not specifically laid in the Upper Provence dear to the earlier Giono. *Un Roi sans divertissement,* the first of the Chroniques, is a 'regionalist' story, supposed to have occurred in

6. See *La Gazette des Lettres,* September 6, 1947, and two articles by Maximilien Vox and Pierre Bergé in *Livres de France,* II, 1, January 1951, published by Hachette.

1843, somewhere in Dauphiné. The fifth, *Les Grands Chemins,* shifts from some Alpine region to the Rhone valley and a landscape of dry bushes beaten by the wind. Nature has ceased to be the protagonist in Giono's novels. His manner, humorous and familiar, now cuts short all the poetical *élans* of the cosmic pagan. Eloquence is pursued and banished. The stories are usually told in the first person by some observer and narrator who has been an actor in the events related. His own language is rendered with some realistic accuracy; it is never coarse, as in many recent writers, but earthy, picturesque, close to the 'green' language of slang, and it moves in a swift tempo.

The volumes themselves are brief. They leave much unsaid, so much indeed that the inquisitive reader may think himself inadequately repaid. The novelist makes little effort to enter the minds of his most important characters (such as the dying old lady in *Mort d'un personnage,* the domineering peasant woman in *Les Ames fortes,* or the card player and thief who inspires the storyteller in *Les Grands Chemins* with a strange fraternal and maternal devotion until he is shot by him, almost tenderly). He alludes to some events, briefly sketches a scene, describes bewildering behavior, sometimes bordering on the fantastic (as in the short story, 'Faust au village'), then passes on. It would take extraordinary power in the novelist to win the credibility of his readers, and Giono does not always win it. The novels strike one as a little thin, their psychological depths insufficiently explored, told with ease and verve but not truly compelling belief.

The admirer of Giono is ready to concede that the author had to renovate his earlier manner, which had been in danger of stifling plot and characters with an overgrowth of poetry, allegory, and imagery, and that the cosmic or epic novel should not be attempted too often. He may also, however, resist the latest 'chronicles' of peasant life delineated by Giono and his attempt at sketching real characters. The most successful are those of *Mort d'un personnage,* with the skillful picture of a home for the blind in the late nineteenth century and of a strong and spiritually blind woman withdrawing from the visible world. Giono's mastery is that of a superb craftsman. His sensitiveness is more human, more attuned to our average statures, than it was in his former volumes. But none of the *Chroniques* thus far published would be enough to grant Giono an exalted place in French letters today. His portrayal seems strangely detached and cool. His narrative technique is too smooth.

Le Moulin de Pologne, published in 1953, is in our opinion equally remote from Giono's earlier achievement. Some scenes, that of the ball especially, are related with a rare skill for creating suspense, and the character of Monsieur Joseph, who baffles all the inhabitants of the slumbering provincial town, is delineated with much verve. The tragic story of an implacable series of misfortunes striking three or four generations of the Coste family, owners of the 'Moulin de Pologne,' appears gratuitous. Too little is explained, and the pace is too swift for the reader to become absorbed in the tragicomic tale of Atrides or Amalecites transplanted into Provence.

Le Hussard sur le toit (1952), which, unfortunately, Giono has followed up with a lengthy sequel, *Angelo,* is on the contrary one of the most youthful and freshest novels of the last fifteen years. The hero is a young Piedmontese and a colonel of hussars, a very close relative of Stendhal's Fabrice. He had to flee his country for political reasons in 1838 and, on returning home, he encounters a terrifying epidemic of cholera in upper Provence. He escapes from the hostile inhabitants over the roofs of the city, falls into the room of an aristocratic young lady, and meets her again on the road while escaping both the plague and the fury of the populace dreading contagion. They flee together, respect each other to the end, and their comradeship, their virile restraint and their chivalrous sense of humor prove stronger not only than love but than the plague and the wickedness of men. This long adventure novel does not win the reader's credence throughout; the contrast between the lurid scenes of drought and cholera and the fantastic heroism of the Italian colonel appear lacking in nuances; the Stendhalian tone is too conspicuous, and one wonders whether the author intended a historical novel or a pastiche of *The Charterhouse of Parma.* But alone among the seven or eight volumes published by Giono since 1946, *Le Hussard sur le toit* gives evidence of true original power and promise of a renewal in a novelist who will be a sexagenarian in 1955.

Bibliographical Notes

The Viking Press, New York, published a translation of *Regain (Harvest)* in 1937, *Que ma joie demeure (Joy of Man's Desiring)* in 1940, and *Jean le bleu (Blue Boy)* in 1946. Knopf published *Le Hussard sur le toit (The Hussar on the Roof)* in 1954.

Useful information, much of it given by Giono to the author, will be found in Christian Michelfelder's *Jean Giono et les religions de la terre* (Gallimard, Paris, 1938). A German thesis, *Giono als Dichter der Provence*, was done as early as 1934 by Heinz Ciossek from Posen, and published at Greifswald. A French thesis, far more important, was done by the translator into English of *Blue Boy* and *Joy of Man's Desiring*, Katherine Allan Clarke, *L'œuvre de Jean Giono* (unpublished).

There are only a few good articles on Giono. Keen reviews of novels by a compatriot of Giono, Henri Fluchère, appeared in *Les Cahiers du sud* (March 1932, pp. 144–49; July 1935, pp. 588–91), and by Christian Michelfelder (Ibid., February 1938, pp. 144–47). Pierre Varillon had two essays in *Etudes* (Vol. 230, 5 and 20 February 1937, pp. 337–51 and 469–83). Henri Pourrat, himself a gifted provincial novelist, discussed 'La pensée magique de J. Giono' in the *Nouvelle Revue Française* (October 1938, pp. 646–58). In this country, Hélène Harvitt studied Giono's comparisons and the excessive use he makes of them in *The French Review* (March 1934, pp. 284–99), and Alphonse Roche undertook a solid and precise study, which met with Giono's approval, 'Les provençalismes et la question du régionalisme dans l'oeuvre de Giono' in *Publications of the Modern Language Association*, LXIII, iv, December 1948, pp. 1,332–42.

VI

ANTOINE DE SAINT-EXUPÉRY

OF ALL THE French writers who sprang to fame around 1930 (Giono, Bernanos, Céline, Malraux), Antoine de Saint-Exupéry is the one whose popularity, not only in France but in other countries too, grew most suddenly. There was nothing spurious about the enthusiasm that acclaimed the author of *Terre des hommes* (*Wind, Sand and Stars*), no undue publicity encouraged it. Neither the stories that his books told nor the manner of telling tried to lure the reader with superficial charm. Their author shunned the publicity of newspapers and lecture rooms. It was clear that the chief concern of this aviator with a legendary past was that of a seeker after wisdom and of a classical craftsman.

Popular acclaim is no conclusive proof of greatness, nor, in spite of some cynical scoffers, of mediocrity. We do not believe that Saint-Exupéry will go down the ages as one of the truly great names of modern French letters. But piety and admiration surround his memory, more than ten years after the author disappeared, a new Icarus, flying over the Alps and German antiaircraft artillery. Saint-Exupéry's influence on the youth of France is deep. He is one of the very few of his immediate predecessors of whom Sartre, the philosopher of *What Is Literature?*, wrote with respect. The new province of literature that he opened, the literature of aviation, is proving to be an important one; but none of the French successors of Saint-Exupéry (Jules Roy and Pierre Clostermann are the most gifted), or Anne Morrow Lindbergh, or heroic Richard Hillary have eclipsed the pioneer. The significance of Saint-Exupéry transcends literature. He was the mouthpiece of some of the deepest aspirations of the French people, perhaps even of Western man, between 1930 and 1944. He sensed and concretely expressed some of the most harrowing problems of his age. He was less — and far more — than a novelist. Steeped as he was in Gide and Giraudoux, who had been among the purest men of letters of the decade 1920–30, prone to *préciosité* himself and to the cult of imagery, Saint-Exupéry nevertheless charged his writings with a new density. He eschewed politics, felt more at home in the sands of Africa than in Parisian *cafés,* and died before the phrase *littérature engagée* became the order of the day. But he had been among the first to realize that the era that saw Hitler crushing democracy at home and that saw Abyssinia, Spain, Austria, and Czechoslovakia falling prostrate and betrayed was entitled to more than the introspective complacency of the writer of 1920–30. The gravity of the moralist and the wrath of the prophet could hardly be out of place in the new novel, even if it ceased to be the traditional fiction bent upon telling a story and upon creating characters similar to living men.

Saint-Exupéry's fiction is concerned with the anguish of man facing himself, war, and death rather than with the verisimilitude of a few puppets or the adroit contriving of a coherent plot. He is a moralist and a poet even more than a novelist. Three characteristics may be said to mark his anxious quest and that of many of his French contemporaries: intellectual lucidity, a profound sense of the tragedy of life, and unconquerable hope. Most of the writers of today are agnostics nostalgic for religious faith, or, more curiously still, believers nostalgic for the inquietude and the torment of negators. They are also contemptuous of the easy delusions with which a previous century had imagined it had put an end to bloody wars and revolutions. Saint-Exupéry, Malraux, Sartre, and Montherlant never forsake intellectual lucidity, even when they desert clarity in their sentences and scorn the pedestrian linking of ideas.

Such a lucid gaze at the stark truths of life brings to modern writers a sense of tragedy. The word 'tragedy' is at present being discredited by being dragged into every book of criticism, every sermon, every philosophical article. But Saint-Exupéry, always modest and touchingly *pudique,* shied at such easy words. He lived tragedies and did not discourse about them. Death was close to him many times; he had grappled with its most excruciating forms, perishing from thirst and hunger, in the solitude of mountains. He returned from his overtures to death all the more eager to live and to endow life with a meaning. His hope for man and for his country never faltered. Not a professional thinker himself, although he toyed with the ambition of being one in his unwieldy posthumous volume, he meditated incessantly on some of the dilemmas that confront modern man. Dilemmas they are, rather than problems. For they can never be solved once and for all but only perceived intensely and, at best, embraced in a higher dialectical synthesis. Four such dilemmas seem to haunt the French writers of the years 1930–50, and most of all the moralist Saint-Exupéry.

The first is the necessity of conciliating the legacy of the past and the forces of the present. Western man today, and the Frenchman most of all, is obsessed by history; he is prone to lament all that has happened to his country after a certain date — 1914, or 1870, or 1789. His nostalgic and reactionary attitude provokes other Frenchmen to assert that the true tradition of France is revolutionary. Hence the conflict that incessantly opposes those who are unable to prepare for the future or accept it imaginatively and those who scorn all earlier achievements, the paralytics and the epileptics fighting for the control of history, as Ortega y Gasset has called them.

The second dilemma is to reconcile thought and action, ideal and reality. A woeful divorce of the modern age is the growing rift between intelligence and politics, abstract thinking and the techniques of practical life. Idealists who expect to change man in the near future are often naïvely chimerical; pseudo-realists who accept him at his lowest and flatter Caliban in order to leave him to his low estate are cynics. Too much action, in politics and diplomacy, is futile because it has not been preceded by careful meditation.

Third is the antinomy between concern for the individual, respected as a human being, and subordination to a group, which should enrich him spiritually without forcing him into gregariousness. Historical evolution has, in the last hundred years, tended to enhance the power of the centralized state, and impressive results have been achieved. But the habit of herdlike thinking and of passive conformity has also poisoned many a soul. The Frenchman distrusts intellectual monotony, quantitative accumulation, and even the modern techniques of mass production and of efficient government. But he wonders today how long his individualism can survive. Saint-Exupéry, Malraux, and their contemporaries foresaw that the task of the second half of their century would be to evolve a synthesis between the individual, with his creative gifts and his dignity as a person, and the collectivity, claiming more and more sacrifices from its participants.

A fourth dilemma haunts these writers: the machine versus the soul. Men like Saint-Exupéry, Malraux, and Chamson, who have flown thousands of miles in modern airplanes and witnessed the power, first of German, then of American, machines to enslave or to liberate men, do not scoff at the machine as Duhamel and an earlier generation did with some complacency. It is futile and probably foolish to declaim against modern mass media, as it once was to indict the cinema or photography or modern newspapers, which once drove Baudelaire to an abortive or a simulated suicide attempt. The task confronting us, however, is to utilize mechanical help to the full while remaining aware of its limits. Beauty, mystery, and sentiment have not been expelled from our world by the machine. The thinking man need not be awed into silence and submission by mechanical civilization. 'The airplane is a machine, but what a tool for analysis!' wrote Saint-Exupéry.

Around 1930, Antoine de Saint-Exupéry, whom no early essays had yet revealed to critics, was suddenly hailed as a writer marked for glory. Success came to him overnight; literary prizes crowned a man of action, who had remained innocent of all literary strategy. Then, with a grave volume that had none of the features of the usual best seller, Saint-Exupéry conquered the North American public. Soon, the readers of ten countries praised in that Frenchman a writer with a sumptuous gift of style, who lavished images as in a shower of stars and renovated the traditional novel; a man of action, who had lived his stories and, describing his adventures without bravado or egotism, had annexed to literature the virgin domain of men conquering aerial space; a psychologist and a moralist eager to probe into the secret springs of action; a poet in prose whose restrained fervor sang a hymn to friendship, to the earth, to men.

He was born with the century, on June 29, 1900, in Lyons, the fourth of a family of five children. His name suggests the nobility of his family. It is said that one of the ancestors of the twentieth-century flier had fought in the American War of Independence and had been present at the siege of Yorktown and the surrender of Cornwallis.

Little is known about the private life of 'Saint-Ex,' as he was usually called by his friends, and the discreet reserve of this spiritual son of the French classicists must be respected. His books, however, are all colored by what Baudelaire has called 'the green paradise of childhood loves.' The life of the man was irradiated, at times saddened, by the nostalgic memory of too happy a childhood. Repeatedly, when stranded in the desert or surrounded by the fire of enemy bullets, the airman was to remember the wide park in which he used to play with his sisters, the wild games they would invent, and the Tyrolean governess Paula, who took such good care to protect them against 'adventure.' From that sheltered world, he emerged to enter the most audacious career open to modern man and to face the most extreme hazards of a deadly war.

But the child in him never died, with its tenacious loyalty to comrades in peril and its silent wonder at the big words and vain discussions in which grown-ups feel they must periodically indulge. Saint-Exupéry always preserved jealously the integrity of his dreams against the intrusion of bleak reality. During the darkest days of his vigil of arms in New York in 1941–2, the famous writer would spend hours toying with complicated mechanical gadgets or flying small paper airplanes of his own making over the strollers in Central Park. Of many a poet and artist of our times, the saying of William Wordsworth seems truer than ever: 'The child is father of the man.' The first novel of Saint-Exupéry, *Courrier-Sud* (*Southern Mail*), announced already his nostalgic concern with childhood, which his last published work will triumphantly proclaim. 'You have integrated the course of the star, O generation of laboratories, and you no longer know it . . . Your knowledge does not measure up to that of a small child.'

Two main influences molded Saint-Exupéry's formative years: Catholicism and humanism, the two, of course, meeting at many points. After his very early years at St. Maurice de Remens, near Ambérieu, he was educated at the Jesuit College of Notre Dame de Sainte Croix, at le Mans, then at Fribourg in Switzerland. The dogmas and the ritual of the Catholic Church were not to play an important part in his later life; while his sisters remained deeply pious, their brother seemed detached from all strict orthodoxy. In the most critical moments of his career as recorded in his books, his preoccupations were not with a future life but with man and his world. But the lasting effect of his Roman Catholic upbringing is felt in more elusive ways; he never sloughed off the habit of moral stocktaking and of searching confession acquired in childhood. The study of the classics strengthened his concern with the analysis of inner life and his emphasis on man as the measure of all things. These classics were, in the French use of the term, both the ancients (a pregnant density, reminiscent of Latin, marks his sentences) and the French writers of the age of Louis XIV. To Montaigne, Pascal, La Rochefoucauld, and other 'moralists,' Saint-Exupéry owed in part his refusal to allow the lucidity of his vision to be blurred by the rationalization of perfidious wishes of the heart.

Saint-Exupéry's school years came to an end while World War I was raging. His vocation for literature apparently dawned early and he had, while still a child, dreamed of writing poetry. The first book that he loved passionately was Andersen's *Tales,* then, a little later, *Les Indes noires* by Jules Verne, whose subterranean wanderings may have lingered in his memory when he wrote *Vol de nuit* (*Night Flight*).[1] Balzac's *Père Goriot* then fascinated him. In 1915 he discovered Dostoevski; it was a revelation. 'I felt at once that I had entered into communication with something vast, and I proceeded to read everything he had written, one book after the other, as I had done with Balzac.' This in no way implies that Saint-Exupéry's gifts lay in the direction of the imaginative giants; to admire is not to imitate. More than a creator of plot and characters, the author of *Wind, Sand and Stars* was a sensitive prose poet. He related himself how he was seized in his teens by the adolescent's passion for poetry and learned by heart many lines from Baudelaire, Leconte de Lisle, Heredia, and Mallarmé. Among his immediate contemporaries, Rilke charmed him by his feminine delicacy and plasticity and by the intensity of his inner life. He also cherished Giraudoux, especially in his early works such as *Simon le pathétique,* steeped in gentle and humorous emotion.

The desire of the future flier was to enter the French Naval Academy. Pierre Loti, Claude Farrère, and Alain-Fournier had similarly been attracted by the sea and the long meditative leisure

1. Saint-Exupéry confessed it himself in an article he wrote for *Harper's Bazaar* in April 1941. He has generally been very discreet on the subject of his reading or of influences by other writers. Quotations are conspicuously absent from his works. Yet one influence at least, that of Gide, is clearly felt in his early writings. Reminiscences published by Saint-Exupéry's friends since his death have added little to our knowledge of the man. See Stanley Walker's article in *Tricolor* (October 1944) and André George's essay in *La Nef* (September 1945). In English, E. M. Bowman's introduction to the school edition of *Vol de nuit* (Harper's, 1931) remains one of the best summary accounts on the author. Curious details are added in 'Pique la lune' (*The Cambridge Journal,* VI, 1, October 1952, pp. 40–50), an article entitled after Saint-Exupéry's nickname, by Peter Green.

of ocean voyages, conducive to literary labor. But the irony of fate (or the legend) would have it that young Saint-Exupéry, who excelled in mathematics, failed the entrance examination to the Naval Academy because of incompetence in French composition! He then turned to architecture for a brief time, served his term of military service in Strasbourg after the peace of Versailles, and contemplated vaguely and unenthusiastically a business career.

But aviation was his true mistress. He had already taken a few flying lessons; he received his pilot's license in 1921; in 1926, he was accepted as a regular air-mail pilot on the Toulouse-Casablanca line. Those years were the heroic era of French aviation: the planes were often antiquated; machinery was scarce; radio communication was lacking or in its incipient stage; but flying attracted daring young men all the more.

Saint-Exupéry was no rebel against society, no voluntary exile contemptuously shaking the dust of Europe off his feet. He went back to Paris on his furloughs and enjoyed the delicacies of life, especially the choice meals in which the gastronomes of his native city proverbially indulge. He was fond of the company and the conversation of women and was said to display his charm most when engaged in the playful sport of flirting. But the most refined human comedy soon appears ludicrous to a man whose profession it is to risk death. For a year, Saint-Exupéry was placed in charge of the airport at Cape Juby, where airplanes made brief stops in their flight from Casablanca to Dakar. The country around, poetically called the Rio de Oro, was far from safe. Many of the natives took their theoretical allegiance to Spain more than nonchalantly; to them, a stranded airman was a valuable captive to be held for ransom. Saint-Exupéry learned how to deal with the natives, and undertook many missions, as diplomatic as they were bold, to rescue pilots grounded among dissident tribes. He loved the chivalrous code of those natives, their virile pride, their loyalty to their friends, and their capacity for solitude.

While on that assignment, Saint-Exupéry made the acquaintance of the already legendary figure of Mermoz. The men who worked with Mermoz all revered him as a pure hero of our time; they admired his daring and his skill, his unfailing devotion to his team, his unselfish pursuit of tasks for higher than individual reward. His little book, *Mes Vols*, reads at times like a fragmentary epic. Another French writer and airman, Joseph Kessel, wrote the story of his life. For ten years, Mermoz, who served in the same air line as Saint-Exupéry, the Latecoère company, stood at the vanguard of all aeronautic progress. He opened the air-mail service to Dakar, then across the South Atlantic, then from Brazil to Argentina and, most perilous of all, across the Andes. Paris and Buenos Aires had thus been linked by five-day airplane communication. Then, on December 7, 1936, Mermoz, who had defied death repeatedly, disappeared with his crew while on his twenty-fourth flight across the South Atlantic. Saint-Exupéry was to succeed him in the admiration of French youth until he, too, mysteriously disappeared in another flight of Icarus.

During his years at Cape Juby, Saint-Exupéry enjoyed for the first time the leisure necessary to literary creation. His first book, published in 1929, was entitled *Courrier-Sud*. It met with moderate success. *Vol de Nuit,* two years later, brought him wide fame. Many another flier might then have exchanged his life of hazards for the comfort of a promising literary career. But Saint-Exupéry chose to remain silent for eight long years, thus setting an example rarely followed by modern novelists. That silence enabled him to enrich his experience of life and to mature his talent. The famous writer retained his modest simplicity and his freshness. He flew planes across the Atlantic Ocean and the South American continent, and became a pioneer of mail flights south of Buenos Aires through the dreary solitude of Patagonia. He gained administrative experience as director of the station of Commodoro-Rivadavia, in southern Argentina. A reorganization of the French air lines, which reduced the number of pilots, occurred in 1933. Saint-Exupéry made way for younger men, took to journalism, and visited Russia and most of Europe and the Near East. Late in 1935, he started on a record nonstop flight from Paris to Indo-China, against adverse meteorological conditions. He had to make a forced landing in the Libyan desert, was stranded without food or water, and for several days was given up as dead. Bedouins dramatically rescued him and his mechanic when thirst had conquered their resistance. Once more the flier-writer took up his itinerant career. He was sent to Spain as a correspondent from the daily *Paris-Soir* when Madrid was heroically holding against the troops of Franco.

In 1938, for the second time, Saint-Exupéry had a narrow escape from death. He had reached New York in a monoplane, which he planned to fly all the way along the American continent to Patagonia. But when taking off from Guatemala, his plane crashed to the ground and he suffered serious injury to his shoulder. He was then warned that he should never again attempt parachuting, for the shock might prove too much for his bruised shoulder. He did not, however, give up his passion for flying, and he had a third accident that nearly cost him his life: He was almost drowned in the bay of Saint-Raphael, in southern France, when trying a new hydroplane. Meanwhile, *Terre des hommes* had made him the literary hero of the year 1939, crowned by the French Academy, adopted by all the book clubs. He again courted danger, first in piloting a heavy flying boat from France to New York, then in insisting, in spite of his forty years, upon taking part as an active flier in World War II. Once again, during the disastrous days of June 1940, he miraculously escaped death. He survived to write a grave tribute to his torn country and to his friends of the French air force who had fallen in the fight.

While a semblance of order was succeeding the disorderly turmoil in France of the summer of 1940, Saint-Exupéry, spurning the advances of the Vichy regime, decided to settle in New York until events took a turn for the better. He spent two tormented years there. It was clear that, while impatient to re-enter the fight against the Germans, Saint-Exupéry was not altogether in sympathy with some supporters of the Free French cause in America and retained a prejudice against General de Gaulle. Only much later, when he heard the leader of Fighting France deliver an impassioned speech to the Provisional Assembly in Algiers, in that terse and lofty language that has won for him a place among the soldier-writers of his country, did Saint-Exupéry acknowledge that his prejudice had been unfounded.[2]

In America, Saint-Exupéry worked silently, avoiding many of his countrymen, whose idle talk angered him. He had seen with his own eyes the tragic inequality of forces, which had doomed the French to German bondage in 1940; he resented the *émigrés* who argued that the defeat might have been averted by some last-minute palliative. He knew that only America's entry into the war could ultimately liberate France from the German yoke. But the reluctance of many Americans to admit that the cause of oppressed Europe was also their cause, that freedom and democracy were everywhere endangered, caused him, until Pearl Harbor, to be grieved by the attitude of a country that he deeply admired and loved.

Saint-Exupéry traveled little about the United States. He refused most invitations to lecture. But he was working hard with his pen

2. See the article by André Gide, who then saw much of Saint-Exupéry in Algiers, as reported in *France-Amérique* (New York), (March 25, 1945).

all the while. He labored patiently, as he always did on his manuscripts, over *Pilote de guerre* (*Flight to Arras*); he was also keeping the record of his thoughts in a thick notebook, which has become *Citadelle* (*The Wisdom of the Sands*). He had other books in mind, concerning spiritual and moral problems. He avoided the polemics then rife among Frenchmen in foreign countries; his own record in the battle of 1940 had spoken eloquently for him. In November 1942, when the Americans landed in North Africa, he published an open letter to Frenchmen abroad, in *The New York Times*. 'Let us be infinitely modest,' he told them. 'We do not represent France; all we can do is to serve her . . . Men of France, let us be reconciled in order to serve.' Some saw in these words an excessive leniency to the Vichy regime and a preference for General Giraud against General de Gaulle. The philosopher Jacques Maritain took the philosophically minded aviator to task with some bitterness. But such divisions, however important at the time, have already been blurred by events. Saint-Exupéry was to serve his country in one supreme task. He asked to leave for North Africa; he took up active service in the reconstituted French Air Force and insisted upon flying in spite of his forty-three years, although he was implored to stay with the ground forces. The integrity of his intentions was soon proved by his actions and ennobled by his death.

Saint-Exupéry's literary output is comparatively scant: four volumes, which one may call novels by stretching the word a little; a fairy tale, *Le Petit Prince* (1942), more revealing of its author than many a page written in the first person singular; a slim collection of reflective essays, *Lettre à un otage* (1943), and posthumous reflections. This restraint is only another mark of Saint-Exupéry's stark sincerity. He never indulged in writing merely to retain the attention of the public or because of tempting contracts offered by publishers. He patiently waited until he had matured inwardly what he had to say and had mastered the form that would say it most adequately. Saint-Exupéry's books are usually brief, almost to a fault; there is no redundance in them, few irrelevant digressions, no trace of superfluous fat, as it were. In his rare moments of confiding in his readers, he would compare himself to a diamond cutter or to a sculptor, chiseling away from the first drafts of his writings all extraneous substance; or, better still, to a baker kneading his dough over and over again until it developed enough resistance for him to fight successfully against its plastic matter. Indeed, his manuscripts showed whole pages crossed out after successive and pitiless revisions.

Southern Mail (translated under this title by Stuart Gilbert in 1933) was composed while the author was stationed at Cape Juby. He read it, seated on his camp bed in the sun-baked tent, to the man whose approval he most earnestly desired, Mermoz. The book enjoyed moderate success, and so did the film based on it. It is faulty in many respects and immature in technique. Saint-Exupéry is not skilled in inventing incident interwoven with character or in handling the traditional form of the novel. But the gifts of the author as a stylist, and his concern with discovering a deeper purpose to human life are already discernible. The hero, Bernis, an air-mail pilot stationed in the West African desert, is obviously a projection of the writer. His story is told in part through laconic radiograms of weather reports and of the progress of his flight, in part through his own confession woven into a novel. The interest of this early work is twofold. It sheds light on the life and moods of a pilot, away from civilization, alone with his machine and with the clouds, restraining his regrets and his dreams to bow to a self-imposed discipline and to the biddings of fate. But Bernis is also the one character in Saint-Exupéry's works for whom love might almost challenge 'military servitude.' During a leave spent in France, he has met a former childhood friend, Geneviève. The only woman who plays any part in Saint-Exupéry's books, she is delineated with delicacy and tenderness. To the flier, she embodies the golden years of his boyhood. But she is not happy. Her husband is ambitious, selfish, and without understanding. When their son dies, his brutal behavior drives her to leave him in a rage; she seeks refuge with Bernis. For a brief while they try to recapture the beauty of their adolescent dreams. They leave Paris together and drive to a provincial city. But, realizing the sordidness of a conventional liaison, they decide to master the force that had drawn them together. Their love, perhaps, is too weak; all love, perhaps, is weakness; childhood visions, embellished by rosy memories, cannot be relived. Bernis also understands the meaning of his vocation. A flier is no longer a man like other men. Geneviève belongs to another world in which comfort, security, and serenity are real things. How could he ever draw her into his world? In spite of the sentimental link between them, they are separated 'by a gulf of a thousand years.' Bernis returns to his flying in Africa. A few days later, his plane is lost and his body is found in the desert.

The originality of this early volume lies in its sketchy but subtle portrait of Geneviève, frail, illogical, unhappy, yet tied down to her worldly life. In Bernis's career of aviation and exploration, love sinks into relative insignificance. After his first two books, woman disappears from Saint-Exupéry's work. She remains in the background, as the precious symbol of that other world to which the flier returns after his inhuman challenge of the hurricanes. He will concentrate on what he knows best. The meaning of life as perceived by men of action thrown together on some common adventure will be to him a more fitting subject than any interpretation of feminine psychology.

Vol de nuit is artistically far superior to *Courrier-Sud*, more strongly welded, with a skillful fusion of moral reflections and of dramatic action that the author was never again to accomplish as felicitously. The slim volume, a *récit* more than a novel, enjoyed a surprising success on its appearance, in 1931. It was soon translated into ten languages. Strangely enough, the author who had, through his introspective stories, his very frank confessions of the least orthodox aspects of his life, and his prestige with youth, symbolized the literature of the postwar years, André Gide, was the first to point out the significance of Saint-Exupéry's book. He seemed ready to burn what he had once adored when he declared in his preface to *Vol de nuit:*

> Too well we know man's weaknesses, his inner surrender and his shames, and recent literature has been only too skillful in exposing them: our need is for authors to show us how the force of will can lift man above his own self . . . I am grateful to Saint-Exupéry for having illustrated this paradoxical truth, that man's happiness lies not in freedom, but in his acceptance of a duty.

There are only three characters in the short novel: two men and a woman. The pilot, Fabien, is engaged on night flights between Buenos Aires and Patagonia or the Andes. These flights are perilous but indispensable if the air lines are to compete with ships and trains. In these pioneer days of aviation, many of the pilots flying at night will never return, but, because of the risks they have taken, others may one day safely carry business letters and lovers' messages with greater speed. A pilot has been married only a few weeks. One morning, before dawn, a telephone message orders him on a flying mission. His young bride watches him sleep a few more minutes, answer the call to duty, which rings for him alone in the silent city, glance at the moonlit darkness, and don his helmet and his leather breastplates. Like a medieval knight leaving on a single fight, he then goes. Meanwhile Fabien, carrying the mail from Patagonia, is surrounded by a hurricane. He loses his way in the clouds. The fuel tank shows that his respite is decreasing from one hour to half an hour, to a supreme quarter of an hour. The radio stations on the ground hear him no longer. Soon he has disappeared, forever.

Fabien's wife appears only fleetingly in the drama. She has counted the hours since her husband took off, felt reassured when the moon shone in a clear sky, disturbed whenever the overcast sky brought an omen of storm. He should by now have safely arrived. She calls up the air line, receives elliptic answers mentioning unforeseen delay. She understands and utters only an 'Ah!' from her wounded flesh. Revolt is vain. She represents the absolute of love and individual happiness, opposed to that of duty and action. She bows to the mysterious law that bids men play havoc with humble affections, gentle memories, the soft light of a lamp on a table, and the comfort of family life.

But the chief character in the book is not the flier or his wife, and the true conflict is not that of love and duty. Saint-Exupéry has avoided such conventionality. Rivière is the hero. He is the director of the office of the air lines. His task is to impose discipline, to defend the regulations as if they were sacrosanct, to order pilots on the night flights. He appears harsh, but it is only in order to extract from men their latent energy and to raise them above self-pity. He kneads them as virgin wax and instills a will into them. His curt language superficially recalls that of a Nietzschean superman, ordering an inferior race ruthlessly and singing the paean of Zarathustra — 'Let us be hard.' In truth, he is deeply human. He will not display his sympathy for others in order to win their love. Events have to be controlled by men, and men must be emboldened so that they will conquer events. Repeatedly, Rivière, meditating upon the loss of human lives, ponders: 'Is this worth the life of one man? Is anything worth the life of a young man, carefully nurtured, patiently educated, tenderly loved?' And he replies: 'Human life may be priceless, but we always behave as if there were something higher in value than human life . . . But what is it?' When Fabien's plane is overdue, a pin is removed from the map in the office; a card is withdrawn from a drawer. Death is a victory. Through the unending task accomplished by successive men, aviation will conquer the night. As Renan used to say, man is like the worker at the Gobelins tapestry, weaving from the reverse a design that he does not perceive.

Vol de nuit is, in its condensed form, worthy of a classical tragedy. The theme itself recalls the torch race of the Greeks, in which relay runners pass the torch to each other with the spirit in which men and women devote themselves to a higher purpose dimly understood. The tone is that of a tragic dialogue, chary of words, devoid of declamation. There are three characters, as in the early Aeschylean plays, and they meditate while they act. Their struggle is not among each other; it is rather a threefold combat. Men challenge the elements, while the radio stations on land, sending messages across the air, seem to play the part of the chorus witnessing the doomed human challenge to fate. Man has to face woman and the values that she opposes to duty, profession, and risk. Man fights chiefly against himself, for it is in Fabien's and Rivière's very hearts that tenderness, pity, and love have to be ultimately mastered.

After eight years spent in accumulating varied experience and meditating on it, Saint-Exupéry published *Terre des hommes*. The new volume was acclaimed instantaneously. It brought its author the coveted reward of the Grand Prix du Roman, bestowed yearly by the French Academy. In it, however, Saint-Exupéry made no pretense of retaining the form of the novel. Man in general concerns him more than individuals; and his creative gift is more suitable to the presentation of suggestive details chiseled into striking images than to the invention of an arbitrary plot.

Terre des hommes is indeed primarily the work of an expert in the artistry of style, but it is not overwritten, as elaborate French prose is apt to be. Saint-Exupéry occasionally indulges in a perilous fondness for rhetorical questions and invocations to departed friends, but he soon restrains these expansive emotional outbursts. He is usually remote from the joyful exuberance of Gide's early prose and from the excessive dryness that marks imitators of Stendhal, from the unnerved and pale style of Maurois and from the rigid prolonged tension of Malraux. His sentences are brief; the words are the simplest possible, with hardly any technical expressions. The cadences of poetic prose are sedulously avoided. The flavor of the style comes from the splendor of its imagery contrasting with the sobriety of the general tone. Whirlwinds tearing across the Atlantic skies are transfigured into pillars of an awesome temple or grotto inhabited by giants. The moon often pours its lurid light over the stormy scenes described by the author, now dying in the sky like pallid embers, now playing with the fog and the clouds. The earth and the sky are often merged into one vast indistinct substance hostile to the rash flier. At times also, he rejoices among the stars, shimmering as in green water, glittering like hard diamonds, or shooting across the blue darkness in a mad gambol.

For the volume, composed of separate vignettes linked by a profound unity of meaning, is that of a cosmic poet. The adjective has been abused, but to few men does it belong by birthright as to Saint-Exupéry. Shelley, Hugo, and Rimbaud had dreamed of wild rounds of planets in fantastic skies or had lent a voice to the clouds and the moon. Saint-Exupéry has actually conversed with these divinities, has received from them now guidance, now treacherous delusion, and he humanizes them in the simplicity of his prose. But his true theme is not the firmament; it is the earth. And the first essential word in the title of his book, unfortunately omitted in the English version, is *Terre*.[3] The lakes of twinkling diamonds and the wild tornadoes rending the sky are but a setting for the only abode that really counts, the earth. The originality of this poet-airman is that he has, through his adventures in the air, rediscovered the earth.

The earth seen from above is not the familiar and orderly landscape to which we are accustomed. It is only a small archipelago, hemmed in by oceans; and on that narrow stretch of land, spanned in a few hours of flight, how many expanses of hostile sand, of uninhabitable mountains and glaciers! The airplane alone could reveal to us our globe as it is, by lifting us out of our well-tilled plains, fertile valleys, and winding highways. To the flier swooping down in search of his landing field, the thatched roof of a farmhouse, a shepherd girl grazing her lambs near some Andalusian village, or a little fort guarded by a sergeant and four soldiers in the African wild appear suddenly invested with a frail and moving beauty. If the earth appears frail seen from the skies, men should revere it all the more tenderly; and tenderness is indeed the note that best describes many of Saint-Exupéry's evocations. Among his perilous cosmic wanderings, the warm security of a soft bed and, in the morning, hot *croissants* and *café au lait* appear as goods of unattainable, haunting value, which will again link the knight of

3. Lewis Galantière has revealed, in a very interesting article in *The Atlantic Monthly* (April 1947), that Saint-Exupéry himself had chosen *Du vent, du sable, des étoiles* as the title of his manuscript, then changed his mind in the French edition so as to avoid appearing romantic or too literary.

the air to plain but dear realities: the flour and the wheat field recalled by the *croissants,* the cows that produced the milk and the
butter, the poetry of the earth that is never dead.

Such was Saint-Exupéry's discovery, which renovated the literature of aviation. The miracle of the airplane, he writes, is that 'it
plunges man straight into the heart of the mystery.' It even reveals
mystery where man had heretofore failed to perceive it. For years,
loud innovators had proclaimed the advent of the machine age
in literature; they had baptized 'futurism' a childish rendering of
mechanical objects through broken-up phrases and juggled allitera-
tions. They had encumbered their writings with blast furnaces
and electric wires, worshipped dynamos and airplanes. Or else they
had been intoxicated with the power that men draw from their
illusory mastery over machines and, like an Italian flier bearing
a famous name, they sang the rapturous joy of bombing defense-
less Ethiopian villages. Saint-Exupéry is true to the traditions of his
people in considering the machine as a tool, beautiful because of
the materials of which it is built and because it attains the purity
of a stripped body and a perfect simplicity of outline, as well as an
exquisite fitness to its purpose. But, as he declares at the conclusion
of his book:

> The airplane is a means, not an end. One does not risk one's
> life for an airplane any more than the peasant plows for the
> sake of his plow. But, through the airplane, one leaves cities
> and their accountants and recovers a peasant reality. One ac-
> complishes a man's work and knows man's cares. One enters
> into contact with the wind, the stars, the night, the sand, the
> sea . . . one envisions the airport as a land of promise and
> questions the stars for one's truth.

Terre was the first essential word in the title of the book;
Hommes, also omitted from the traitorous English title, is the
second. And the true leitmotiv of the book is indeed men, in the
plural. Through flying, charting new lands on his frail globe, and
spanning boundless oceans, man makes one gain alone: he is given
the means of knowing himself more deeply. The ghost of Pascal
haunts the reflections of the twentieth-century aviator. For man
is weaker than a reed when tossed about by the winds, lost in the
fog, stranded on a peak in the Andes, reduced to licking a few
drops of dew on the wing of an airplane in the parched Libyan
desert. His courage then rises to radiant summits.

Saint-Exupéry does not prize physical courage very highly; most

men will develop it under the stress of circumstances and will endure what had seemed insufferable. The trite motto 'live dangerously' has more appeal to sickly philosophers muffled in their dressing gowns amid books than to true men of action. Saint-Exupéry
despises the risk that gamblers with their lives incur for the mere
thrill of it. Intense living is to him only a means of penetrating
more deeply into the secrets of the universe and of developing a
keener consciousness of our duties and potentialities as men. And,
in man, reasoning counts little and seldom grasps the essentials.
Logic too often remains a shell of ponderous words with which we
disguise the real truth about ourselves and our living contradictions. Our truth is what fosters in us a grave sense of inward fulfillment, liberates us from the trivialities of life, and endows our
smallest acts with a meaningful virtue. 'Spirit alone, blowing over
the loam, creates man.'

Action enables man to know himself better and to define his
conscious purpose in this life. It also brings men together. *Terre
des hommes* and, indeed, every work of Saint-Exupéry, is in its
essence a hymn to friendship. Flying over oceans, imprisoned in a
solitary airport in Africa, sharing thirst, hunger, and extreme
fatigue when thrown by a forced landing into a ravine that may be
their grave, two or three men, stripped of every earthly good and
almost of every hope, relish the treasure of true comradeship. Then
they know and understand each other without effort. There is
dignity and loyalty in their relation, unreserved mutual devotion,
tolerance and even admiration for their differences, and an exaltation that comes from pursuing a common purpose together. The
machine has helped create such friendship, as have sports and
wars. Love dwindles to a selfish and anarchic or disturbing force
when compared with the cool, restrained friendship enjoyed in
the midst of ordeals; men will often yearn for friendship when
rivalries, ambitions, the selfish exigencies of family life again draw
them apart. The concluding pages of *Terre des hommes* sing the
unique and well-nigh mystical joy of men who, freed in their
perilous career from all the false values of life, suddenly become
alien to hatreds, jealousies, and desires, and reach the true fraternity of co-operating, with body and soul, in a disinterested effort.
'When joined to our brothers by a common purpose which is placed
outside ourselves, then only do we breathe and understand that
to love is not to gaze into each other's eyes, but to look together in
the same direction.' National rivalries and wars appear senseless
at such moments. For if war does provide these grave and loyal

comradeships, other experiences can create them at lesser cost. 'War deceives us. Hatred adds nothing to the exaltation of the race that we run. Why hate each other? We are all in the same solidarity, carried away by the same planet, as crew of the same ship. It is good indeed for civilizations to compete in order to bring about new syntheses, but it is monstrous for them to devour each other.' Thus, a few months before World War II unleashed its orgy of destruction from the air, ran the message of one of the noblest fliers France had yet produced,[4] and the most thoughtful of them all, in a book hailed by a critic in *La Revue Hebdomadaire* as 'The Song of Roland' of our modern age.

Saint-Exupéry, who happened to be in New York in the spring of 1939, sensed that a war was inevitable and hurried back to France in time. He was soon attached to a reconnaissance squadron, one of the few in the French army. To his experiences in the fateful days when the whole of his country seemed to be disintegrating under the impact of the German Panzer divisions, we owe the finest prose work that World War II seems as yet to have produced. It appeared in French in New York in 1942 as *Pilote de guerre* [5] and in English as *Flight to Arras*.

It is not a conventional war book. The circumstances in which Saint-Exupéry wrote it were the most tragic in which his country, and perhaps mankind, had ever lived: in 1940–41, Russia and the United States had not yet been thrown into the conflict and a German victory seemed a dreaded possibility to all but a few daunt-

4. There is only one other book that we would rank high among the works inspired by aviation: the moving autobiography of a British flier who met death in World War II, after having endured ghastly ordeals, *Falling through Space* (Reynal and Hitchcock, New York, 1942), by Richard Hillary. (*The Last Enemy*, Macmillan & Co., London, 1943, was the title in the English edition.) Its artless charm and winning humor stand in contrast with Saint-Exupéry's gravity and studied artistry. In French, Jules Roy wrote a fine volume, *La Vallée heureuse* (Charlot, 1945), on the bombing of the Ruhr in which he took part; another pilot of the R.A.F., Pierre Clostermann, like Jules Roy an ardent admirer of Saint-Exupéry, has written *Le Grand Cirque* (Gallimard, 1948; *The Big Show*, Random House, New York, 1951), a fresh and unpretentious account of his airman's experiences, and *Feux du ciel* (1951), a more technical volume.

5. It was reprinted in French in Paris after the liberation. The Germans, having allowed it to circulate freely in France, banished it on the denunciation of a French collaborationist writing in *Je suis partout,* who pointed out to the master race that the book praised a Jewish aviator, Israel. Captain Israel was in fact one of the members of Saint-Exupéry's outfit in 1940; his name was not invented.

less optimists. The author, miraculously safe after a fierce though unequal fight, resented the lack of understanding with which many then spoke of the collapse of France and of her too-easy acceptance of her humiliation; a note of bitter impatience before much idle talk creeps at times into the volume.

But *Pilote de guerre* is primarily the objective record of a mission and the exposition of the author's philosophy. Few books are more stripped of all superfluous details. The classical principles of economy of means and of understatement have seldom been more strictly observed: no grandiloquence, no stylized imagery, not the faintest trace of pose. On one of the last days of May 1940, six reconnaissance groups out of twenty-three are left in the unit to which Captain de Saint-Exupéry belongs. The first phase of the war is already hopelessly lost for the French. German fighter planes outnumber them ten to one; and any information that French reconnaissance could bring back is clearly of no avail. The enemy himself does not conceal his position, while the French staff is disorganized, its telephone transmission cut off, and its orders delayed and inapplicable. But the cruel game of war has to be acted to the last: as glassfuls of water are poured over a huge forest fire, French crews are being ordered out one by one and, stoically, they fulfill their mission.

Saint-Exupéry's turn has come. He and his friends are stationed in a schoolhouse, among desks, maps, and blackboards. A door is flung open now and then; an order is shouted, which calls for a crew to take to flight. The chances are exactly two to one against their returning alive. At night, at the officer's mess, a laconic remark will be uttered: '*Tiens!* so and so is not back at the base'; an oppressive silence will follow for a minute, and that will be all. The reconnaissance plane of Saint-Exupéry is given the mission to observe the enemy deployments over Arras; to do it, he must fly over the German lines, over roads clogged with refugees fleeing from the dive bombers, and face several barrages from German fighter planes enjoying unchallenged mastery of the air. Repeatedly, the fliers' lives seem to hang by a thread. The pilot's controls freeze when he has to climb to thirty-three thousand feet to escape enemy fighters; he drops to twenty thousand feet to watch Arras in flames. Bullets pierce his fuel tank, hit his wings; he runs the gauntlet of intense flak, goes up again, baffles his pursuers by losing himself in the setting sun, and miraculously returns to his base, where he has already been given up as lost. Within a few hours, packed with intense living and ardent thought, he has gone through the acts of a fierce tragedy, challenged fate and death, and accumulated enough reflections for him to ponder over for years.

The tragedy is not a merely personal one, however. The action of the book (a meditative action, for the author is all along a Hamlet, who welcomes action as a road to clearer self-knowledge) takes place on several levels. He returns alive, but with no exhilaration. For he has witnessed the defeat and misery of his country. From the air, he has seen the roads of France clogged with refugees fleeing toward an unknown fate, blindly obeying orders that bid them evacuate their villages, starve by the roadside, be shelled by German planes. The picture of that population fleeing in panic, mixing with the remnants of a broken army, driving in pitiful old cars, which soon will run short of gasoline and will be abandoned along the road as scrap iron, is sketched in lamentable and vivid colors. Babies are born in ditches, others vainly cry for milk, grandmothers perish exhausted. The whole of France is like a huge anthill kicked open, the ants swarming aimlessly. Yet no complaint is heard; it is war, and although the sacrifice is apparently useless and illogical, it has to be.

It would have been out of place for Saint-Exupéry to weave artistry out of such human misery. Once or twice he catches himself coining a precious image while pursued by the enemy fighters, imagining the wake of gossamers left behind his machine, and eluding his pursuers by skillful turnings, like a pretty lady proudly holding the train of her dress, spotted with stars of ice, and suddenly eluding her suitors. But he is the first to smile at his own far-fetched fancy. The poetry of *Pilote de guerre* is never superadded; it is harmoniously integrated with the book. It calls up idyllic memories of childhood, which contrast with the terrifying present, the joy of hearing a fire crackling in the hearth before jumping out of bed on an icy morning, the fighter planes around him like 'a people of jugglers throwing their missiles,' and the trajectory of the bullets is like a slender needle or a stalk of wheat.

> The German on the ground knows us by the pearly white scarf which every plane, flying at high altitude, trails behind like a bridal veil. The disturbance created by our meteoric flight crystallizes the watery vapor in the atmosphere. We unwind behind us a cirrus of icicles . . . our wake will thicken bit by bit and become an evening cloud over the countryside. The fighters are guided towards us by the ostentatious luxury of our white scarf. Nevertheless, we swim in an almost interplanetary emptiness.

Such is, in Lewis Galantière's very sensitive translation, a sample of the poetry woven by the flier out of peril and death, a moment's relief amid terror and pity. But *Flight to Arras* taken as a whole is not a serene work of art on the misfortunes of war. It is a book written in the throes of defeat by a Frenchman who fully accepted responsibility for his country's mistakes, took pride in her moral greatness asserted in the midst of chaos, and tried to rise above national considerations to the formulation of a faith valid for all men. There is not one word of hatred in these pages, composed while the Germans were plundering the land of France and killing innocent hostages; not one boastful sentence, such as a soldier who had risked his life might utter against those who stayed at home or emigrated abroad and wrote books and articles on what should have been done. Defeated army generals were then in Vichy bestowing medals upon each other and laying the blame for the defeat on politicians; politicians were throwing the burden on their predecessors or on the institutions of the Third Republic. Foreign observers, disappointed by the debacle of the French army, which should have served as their shield against the German menace, coldly sat back to remark that sacrifices had been too scant, that not enough bridges had been blown up, not enough cities offered to destruction.

Saint-Exupéry's answers unite humility with nobleness. While flying to and from Arras amid the tracer bullets, watching villages burn and civilians shelled, he meditates on his country's right and wrong. Much, to be sure, was wrong with France. But she had played her part and was then helpless. She could not possibly have won in 1940 and she knew it; she went to war against logic, and lost. In so doing, she was a victim, and it was hardly fair of the outside world to look upon her as sinning rather than sinned against. By her readiness for sacrifice she should be judged. Because she plunged headlong into disaster, she did not betray the conscience or the confidence of the world. For the final assault to be successful, many a victim must first fall in the vanguard. The defeat of France, fatal as it was, was made worse by incompetence and laxity. But no Frenchman can disown responsibility for it; to his country and to the whole world, he is bound by solidarity. 'Each is responsible for all. Now for the first time I understand one of the mysteries of religion, from which originated the civilization which I claim as mine. "Bear ye one another's burdens." Each of us bears the burdens of all men.'

But in that very defeat lie the seeds of rebirth and of spiritual victory. Frenchmen, suffering together, discovered a new meaning to brotherly communion, to charity, to love. When the evil consequences of starvation and humiliation have been obliterated, Europe may well discover that the cruel lessons of the war have not been learned in vain. There was little good to hope for in the world of 1933–8, and stagnation and fear might still be ruling if, by some series of 'Munichs,' the war had been averted. Russia in 1917 and Germany in 1918 had seemed even more prostrate than France in 1940. They rose again. A defeat, or a victory, is what we make it. 'One victory exalts, another corrupts. One defeat kills, another brings life. Tell me what seed is lodged in your victory or your defeat, and I will tell you its future.'

Through this message of indomitable hope in his country's future, Saint-Exupéry rises to a broader lesson, addressed to all men. He is no professional philosopher, and he is no virtuoso player with abstractions. But his manifesto, diffuse and wordy at times, groping toward an approximation of his own truth, is a generous statement of faith; it rises to a strange greatness without being novel or profound, for it is the creed of a man of action who, while ready to give his life for a higher cause, discovers the meaning of the great struggle. Logic and intelligence are by themselves of little avail. Our key words — democracy, culture, religion — have gradually become emptied of their substance. We must imbue them again with fervor; each must strike new roots in a soil of reality. And the chief reality is that we are all bound together; we participate and commune, and, in Coleridge's words, 'we receive but what we give.'

But, 'in my civilization, he who differs from me, far from impoverishing me, enriches me.' The uniformity of spirits and their consequent leveling down are to be sedulously avoided. Differences bring us a truer gain; minorities, instead of being suppressed or even artificially assimilated, must be harmoniously fused so that they will retain some of their original essence while contributing to a larger whole. Men are equal in the dignity due to all of them, and political and social organization should help correct the natural inequalities that separate them. But equality is not identity. And equality, like liberty, should be conscious of a higher purpose, and enable men to reach, all together, new heights. The goal is not a collective deity that crushes men; it is rather the cult of Man, superior to isolated individuals. Charity and humility, generosity and self-devotion are revered virtues in the humanism propounded by Saint-Exupéry, which unites the best of the Christian teaching, transposed into lay formulas, with the best of ancient pagan wisdom, and endows with renovated meanings the most beautiful word ever coined by man — 'fraternity.'

Such is the conclusion of this war volume in which a pilot in a defeated army, obsessed at first by the magnitude of his defeat, gradually vanquishes it in his soul, draws upon his deepest spiritual sources, and recovers his own center by redefining his reasons for living. He does not offer a doctrine, but forges new links between himself and other men. He has demonstrated nothing. His teaching retains no trace of sophistry; it eschews the much-vaunted French clarity; it proceeds slowly, at times confusedly. But it is worthy of the man who has lived it, fought for it; it fulfills the saying of the Spanish thinker of our day who defined true culture as lying not in the accumulation of knowledge or in the weaving of consistent reasonings, but in 'feeling more and more intensely a small number of mysteries.'

Le Petit Prince, published simultaneously in French and English in 1943, is a fairy tale of infinite charm, in which gentle satire of the dullness of grown-ups, of the pomposity of scientists, and of the aimless feverishness of businessmen is delicately blended with poetical evocations of the African desert and of cosmic wanderings among planets and stars. It illustrates the truth of Baudelaire's celebrated definition of genius as 'childhood recovered at will.' The Little Prince, whose fancy roams in interstellar spaces, also asks a few questions, intensely grave as children's questions can be. It incarnates Saint-Exupéry's passionate regret for the fervent faith of a child and his imaginative freedom, unspoiled by the hypocritical calculations of adults. The tale is written with a purity of outline and a terse simplicity of dialogue that recall the exquisite blending of reasonableness and supernaturalism that marks the seventeenth-century French fairy tales of Perrault. It makes no concessions to absurdity or cheapness of effect, as too many of our writings and films for children, unsuccessful imitations of *Alice in Wonderland* or of Walt Disney, are inclined to do. Its simple dialogue between a flier impatient with the evils of the world and a terse unsmiling child clinging to his dreams receives a tragic significance when read as the author's farewell to this gross earth over which millions of young men were then shedding their blood, their sweat, and their tears.

Saint-Exupéry published another little book in the year 1943: a slender collection of personal reminiscences and reflections, dedicated to a friend who had remained in France, one of the millions of 'hostages' before whom the flier, safe in America, bowed in humility; for they could only suffer in silence and wait for the long-wished-for dawn of their liberation. In his *Lettre à un hotage,* Saint-Exupéry reiterated his philosophical message; its key words were 'weight' and 'substance,' designating the chief virtues that any man's thought must possess if it is not to lose itself in airy nothings; then 'friendship' and 'joy,' the latter to be experienced not in the conventional pleasures of social intercourse, not even in the ecstasies of mutual love, but in the rare moments of life when a man feels, through a smile or a radiant look, that he has forged bonds with another man.

Saint-Exupéry had had little opportunity to meditate on social and political problems. The discipline of the life of airmen waives many issues with which the civilian and the politician have to cope. But gradually his thought faced the complexities created by free men colliding against each other with their ambitions and their jealousies. He denounced the source of all that was most nefarious in fascism as contempt for man. Conversely, he reasserted that the prerequisite for democracy is respect for man.

Modern man must borrow from religions their keystone, sacrifice, and, endowing the word with a lay and humanized significance, recover respect for that free gift that, demanding nothing in return, kneads and molds the giver and makes him a man among men. A shortsighted psychology may lead many of our contemporaries to believe that the world, in its revolutions and its wars, is led by interest in the guise of 'economic causes.' A man who had, with few scruples, led many men through many wars, Napoleon himself, knew better when he admitted: 'Interest is the key to vulgar actions alone.' Saint-Exupéry, in his turn, in the very last message he sent to his American friends, formulated his creed as follows:

> Whatever I was paid for my work at the rate of a pilot's pay was never important . . . My work, even while it furnished me food and shelter, would have been of no value whatever if it had not made me one *of* something — pilot *of* the line, gardener *of* the garden, builder *of* the cathedral, soldier *of* France. The airline laid out by us, who were its first pilots, enriched us by virtue of the gifts it forced us to make — the line was born of our gifts. Once it was born, it bore us, made us men. Two weeks ago one of my fellow pilots of that line

turned up in New York. 'Do you remember . . .' we said to each other. And we discovered that those had been marvelous years; for, having been woven together out of the common strands of our gifts, we were fellows, and we loved one another.

On July 31, 1944, Saint-Exupéry left Bastia, in Corsica, for a flight over Savoy. His plane mysteriously disappeared. His wife [6] and his friends hoped against hope that a miracle would once again save him. They waited. The war ended some months later. The flier was not among those who returned from prison camps. He had clearly met with the kind of death he had courted so often and would have chosen for himself if, as was Rilke's constant dream, men could elect the mode of dying most fitting to what their life had been. But his name lives on. He will not rank among the giants of the French novel; he has not made any new discoveries in man's psychological secrets or created a new style of writing. But he ranks high among those moralists who are to this day one of the most valuable contributions of France to world literature. Not only as a pioneer who has annexed the virgin domain of aviation to letters, but as a thoughtful writer who formulated anew, with force and beauty, some of the baffling problems facing man, he has won an enduring place among the champions of the true civilization, that of the soul.[7]

BIBLIOGRAPHICAL NOTES

A very great deal has already been written on Saint-Exupéry in many languages. A bibliography by John R. Miller and Eliot G. Fay in the *French Review* (XIX, 5, March 1946, pp. 299–309) covered the book reviews and essays published during the author's lifetime. Two later articles by Philip Wadsworth, 'Saint-Exupéry, Artist and Humanist' (*Modern Language Quarterly*, XII, 1, March 1951, pp. 96–107) and by Léon Wencélius on *Citadelle* in *Modern Language Notes* (LXVI, 5, May 1951, pp. 289–95) are valuable. Wencélius is to publish a detailed

6. Consuela de Saint-Exupéry, who is of Central-American origin, published a light and pleasant volume relating her life in France during the early months of German occupation, *Oppède* (Brentano's, New York, 1945) for which her husband was to write a preface.

7. *Citadelle* (Gallimard, 1948, *The Wisdom of the Sands*), a bulky collection of oracular utterances, grave maxims, mystical aphorisms, and meditations on man, is much admired by some followers of Saint-Exupéry; to others, with whom we align ourselves, it was a disappointing publication of a sadly unfinished work. In any case, it is a long series of allegories and parables, which occasionally elucidates Saint-Exupéry's thought but is of little concern to our point of view here, that of an interpreter of Saint-Exupéry's novels.

commentary on *Citadelle*. Jean-Claude Ibert already organized and treated Saint-Exupéry's philosophical and moral thoughts around a few themes (Editions Universitaires, 1953).

Among the volumes on Saint-Exupéry, we shall mention one by a Swiss, Daniel Anet (Corrêa, 1946) and one by a Belgian, André Gascht, *L'Humanisme cosmique de Saint-Exupéry* (Stainforth, Bruges, 1947); also R. M. Albérès, *Saint-Exupéry* (La Nouvelle Edition, 1947), Pierre Chevrier, *Saint-Exupéry* (Gallimard, 1950), Maria de Crisenoy, *Saint-Exupéry, poète et aviateur* (Spes, 1948). Pierre Delange et Léon Werth's *La Vie de Saint-Exupéry* (Editions du Seuil, 1948) is an excellent collective volume published in 1947 by *Confluences* as its numbers 12–14, and there is a tribute of raving admiration by Jules Roy in his *Passion de Saint-Exupéry* (Gallimard, 1951), in which the admired writer is compared to Pascal, to Leonardo da Vinci, and to an immense cathedral, whose growing shadow will end by covering the earth. Curious letters by Saint-Exupéry, notably to Mlle Decour, have been published in *Le Figaro littéraire* (July 8, 1950), and extracts from his *Carnets* in *La Nouvelle Nouvelle Revue Française* (July 1953). From England, where much attention is being paid to Saint-Exupéry, came, in 1953, *The Winged Life* (Weidenfeld and Nicolson, London), by Richard Rumbold and Lady Margaret Stewart.

VII

ANDRÉ MALRAUX

T HE DETACHED OBSERVER, who is able to look at the contemporary European novel without being dazzled by its prestige or its temporary appeal, may well decide that until 1930 or 1940 it proved deficient in audacity. For a while, it toyed with technical innovations: reversed the slavery to time, shifted the storyteller's point of view; and penetrated into the interior monologue. But it failed to renovate the very substance of fiction. Although the French and English novel of the last decades has thrown some light on individual psychology and patiently unwound the mechanism of falling in and out of love, it has usually kept to a narrowly monotonous setting.

Meanwhile, the man of the twentieth century has been gradually engulfed by metaphysical and social preoccupations that have scarcely found expression in the novels of 1910–30, not even in those of Proust, Joyce, and Mann. The originality of our age lies in a tragic conception of philosophy, and Pascal, Kierkegaard, Nietzsche, Unamuno, Sorel, and Heidegger (to cite men of very unequal stature) are its most influential exponents. It has dawned on many of us, in the course of two world wars, that revolution, intense and chaotic action, violence, torture, and sadism are the climate of modern man, a climate to be found, for those who had lived through some of the horrors of the years 1936–45, in the novels of Balzac, Dostoevski, and Faulkner.

In France, Céline and Bernanos are often mentioned by their admirers as writers who have recaptured the tone of *The Brothers Karamazov*. These writers cannot be ranked among the truly great, for what is false within becomes apparent after their sarcasm and their declamatory hysteria and their struggle with the Devil have lost their first appeal of novelty. It is doubtful whether they will have lasting or universal significance. André Malraux, however, reaches higher. Even in his partisan years, he never limited his vision to a few characters advocating the return to medieval saint-liness or considered the destruction of the Jews as the sole salvation for the modern world. He broadened the setting as well as the spirit of French fiction and boldly assailed the enigmas of man's fate.

Malraux is not a clear and easy author. His writing spurns the conventional storytelling technique, with its continuous narrative leading to a climax and a denouement and its gradual presentation of characters with the focusing of interest on a few of them. He avoids the description of scenery and seldom deigns to enlighten his reader on the complex historical and political background of his many-sided plots. His style is elliptical and jerky, rich in apho-risms and in imperious utterances on the meaning (or the meaning-lessness) of life, some of which will appear to many readers as bril-liant *non sequiturs*. 'All art rests on a system of ellipses,' Malraux once posited as an assertion essential to him. His own elliptical art demands much from the reader and allows no nonchalant dream-ing.

Malraux's themes are universal; his tone is one of metaphysical anguish, which has become the new *mal du siècle* of our neo-romantics; the stress of an intense personal suffering underlies his stories of violence. Malraux is obviously not an Anatole France smiling with detachment at man's insoluble contradictions nor a jesting Pilate amused by the diverse follies of human puppets under exotic skies. He is engaged in the struggle that he depicts. He has, in Pascal's terms, gambled his whole life on the causes for which he successively fought. But he has never failed to do justice to his adversaries, and his novels have the artistic irony that en-visages the two opposite sides as impelled by noble and meta-physical motives. The acrimonious partisanship of the Catholic Bernanos or the Communist Aragon or that of many former and disillusioned communists turned propagandists is never present in Malraux as an imaginative writer. He has turned to political action and to art criticism since 1941. Many regret it. But it was a sign of unusual courage in a writer who, emerging as a hero from the war and the resistance and surrounded by the admiration of the youth as Gide and Barrès had been in their day, might have attempted to repeat his earlier literary achievement and would perhaps have been only a shadow of himself. This constant seeker after fraternity has once more preferred solitude.

This explorer of remote lands and champion of Asia in turmoil was born in Paris. This fighter for revolutionary causes came from the bourgeoisie and apparently from a family that enjoyed financial ease. His studies at the Lycée Condorcet, which Proust had attended some thirty years earlier, were chiefly humanistic in character. Art and archaeology soon fascinated him, and his ambitious *Psychology of Art* is the outcome of long observation and reflection. As a very young man, Malraux, whose brilliant intellect dazzled his elders in a country wont to admire intelligence and conversational talent, edited some little-known texts by Charles Baudelaire, Édouard Corbière, and Jules Laforgue and, in 1920, wrote a brief article on the origins of Cubist poetry (Max Jacob, Pierre Reverdy, and Blaise Cendrars) in a magazine entitled *La Connaissance*. His earliest imaginative attempts were two strange fantasies in poetical prose, which already pointed to some of the constants in his future work and to a fascination with wars, cruelty, and tragedy: *Royaume Farfelu* (1920) and *Lunes en papier* (1921).

Except for these very brief essays, Malraux did not rush into print, as many young men were then doing in the literary upheaval that shook Paris as soon as the Treaty of Versailles had been signed. Malraux wisely chose to gain some experience of the world in time and space before composing a novel. He sensed the peril of beginning a novelist's career by the usual introspective volume.

In 1923, the young archaeologist left for Asia. He undertook excavations in Indo-China, which soon brought him into conflict with the French Department of Antiquities in Hanoï and with the scrupulous bureaucracy of colonial administration. It was widely rumored that the young archaeologist was more an adventurer than a legally minded museum curator and that he was impatient to appropriate some of his finds. He was, in any case, accused of carrying off some of the Khmerian sculpture that he had been instrumental in discovering and was probably sentenced to imprisonment. His wife, a German woman, Clara Goldschmidt, from whom he was to separate in the thirties, called upon Malraux's Parisian friends to stand guarantors for his integrity, and he was released — not without some fear of imprisonment, which he lent to several of his characters. In 1925, Malraux seems to have gone to China to work with the revolutionary committee of the Kuomintang. He acquired prominence in organizing conspiracies and in directing revolutionary propaganda. His exact whereabouts has not been ascertained by his biographers, and he prefers to be surrounded by a mysterious halo of legend rather than to provide inquisitive historians with facts and dates.

The account adopted by journalists and critics has it that Malraux soon became prominent in revolutionary circles in China and that he was, in 1926, one of the twelve leaders entrusted with organizing an uprising in Canton. When, in 1927, Chiang Kai-shek brutally turned against his communist allies, Malraux left the Kuomintang and seems to have gone back briefly to archaeology. In 1934, he was reported to be flying over Arabia, in the hope of discovering ancient ruins from the air (some said, the palace of the Queen of Sheba). But he had by then made a name in literature.

Europe had meanwhile become ready for revolutions. With the advent of Hitler to power in 1933, the era of postwar bourgeois complacency was clearly over. A showdown between fascism and communism seemed inevitable. Malraux apparently never belonged to the Communist party, but he had sided with communism and defended Dimitrov at the Berlin trial which followed the Nazi-fomented Reichstag fire. The Bolshevik authorities looked askance at a writer who showed little regard for Marxist orthodoxy and must have appeared temperamentally closer to Trotsky than to any other communist leader. The French Communist party avoided making too much of Malraux; the French right did not attack him as venomously as they did other leftists. The liberal Catholic philosopher Maritain spoke with respect, in 1936, of the 'tragic feeling and of the spiritual quality of Malraux's work,' and Mauriac, the following year, in his *Journal* II looked with both fascination and envy at the ardent novelist then campaigning in Spain.

Malraux's service with the republicans in Spain was outstanding. He commanded the squadron *España* in the Republican air force, rallied faltering energies, and exerted himself to teach the ill-united forces fighting for Madrid and Barcelona the value of organization. He stayed in the war until the fall of Málaga. Injured in service, he then came to America, in February 1937, and attempted to collect funds for the republican cause and to explain 'the value to literature of active political careers by its creators.' Engagement was not yet the fashionable motto for men of letters, but Malraux was campaigning for it and asking American intellectuals to leap forward to a heroic life or death. 'If they lived,' said he, according to *Time* (November 7, 1938), 'their writing would be better for the experience gained in the fight; if they died, their deaths would make more living documents than anything they could write if they remained in ivory towers.'[1]

The republican cause was doomed by the indifference of the democracies, the perverse blindness of many Catholics and conservatives, and the Spanish lack of aptitude for disciplined and united fighting; and the course of history was changed thereby. But some artists and writers had proved more foresighted than diplomats and professional strategists. 'The bloody manoeuvers preceding the European war had begun,' noted Malraux in *Espoir*. While he wrote that feverish book, literally on the battlefield, he made a film, also on the spot, which is a document charged with emotion.

His Spanish experience was to haunt Malraux. If revolution still appeared to him as the myth of the modern world, for he is not one to subscribe to any established order, he became aware of the usual aftermath of revolutions: one tyranny is replaced by another one, perhaps worse. No revolution can be effected without the great dynamic hope called by him the 'apocalypse.' But no revolution can survive without rushing into organization and order, police, and a repressive bureaucracy. Thus comes the crystallization, or perhaps the strangulation, of the revolutionary impetus. Malraux began to appear suspect to many orthodox communists.

When the war actually broke out in Europe in 1939, Malraux was not to be found among those European writers who elected to live in New York, California, or Mexico so that, as they put it, some of the torchbearers of European culture might survive. Along with former antimilitarists like Louis Aragon and André Chamson, he volunteered for the hardest missions. He fought in 1940 in the tank corps and was taken prisoner in the French debacle. He was able to escape before the Germans, who had reason to fear the author of *Le Temps du mépris*, had recognized him. He worked for a while in Roquebrune, on the Mediterranean coast, on his

1. See also Malraux, 'Forging Man's Fate in Spain,' *The Nation*, CXLIV, March 20, 1937.

volumes on art and on a life of T. E. Lawrence, whose personality seems to have impressed him powerfully. He saw his war novel, *Les Noyers de l'Altenburg,* through its first edition in Switzerland. The Germans occupied the whole of France in 1942, and Malraux then plunged into the underground movement. Under the name of Berger, he commanded a group of partisans in central-western France with the rank of lieutenant colonel. He maintained a close liaison with the British fliers who parachuted arms to the French guerillas.

Once again, wounded in the leg, he was captured by the Germans, and it is said that he paraded as a British officer to avoid being summarily shot. The French partisans raided the Saint-Michel prison in Toulouse, where the Gestapo held him, and set him free. He soon resumed fighting and became a colonel in the Alsace-Lorraine brigade, which he had helped organize. He served in Alsace during the hard winter of 1944–5 and answered his many admirers who wished him back in Paris at that time, 'I am fighting for my ideas as I have always done, and I shall not write one line until Fascist and Nazi methods are annihilated.'

After the German army surrendered, Malraux found himself estranged from his former revolutionary friends. The death of his second wife in a railroad accident on the very day of the liberation, and the death of his own brother in the war had grievously affected him. He subsequently married his brother's widow. De Gaulle and he were drawn to each other by some similarity in their views and a common conviction that they were both men of destiny, impersonating forces doomed to triumph in the general decadence of politics around them. De Gaulle appointed Malraux as his minister of information in the short-lived cabinet that he constituted after the elections of October 1945. In January 1946, De Gaulle resigned abruptly to meditate on the reform of the party system and of the constitution, which he hoped to propose to France. Malraux became one of the directors of his propaganda. His gifts of intelligence and of nervous, staccato eloquence fascinate audiences, but they convert few. Malraux's eventual success in politics is doubtful. He did not choose to try for election in the 1951 elections and he may still go back to the continuation of the *Lutte avec l'ange,* the trilogy that he had left interrupted after the first volume, *Les Noyers de l'Altenburg,* had failed to satisfy him as a novel.

Malraux will never be a systematic or a very rational thinker; but he gained much from the mental discipline provided by his study of oriental languages and of archaeology. His reasoning will not always be logical or deductive; but it will not tolerate vagueness and pathos. His tone will be romantic, because he will be concerned with the past and impatient to act upon the future. His style will owe nothing to the preponderance of form over substance, which marked Chateaubriand, Hugo, and even Balzac. Stendhal is closer to his heart. The secret preoccupation of the postwar youth that, in 1920, had survived the great slaughter was death. The presence of death alone seemed capable of enhancing man's determination to live with purposeful intensity. And the contemplation of history, of old stones and mysterious inscriptions, and of civilizations that had been mortal, as Western civilization seemed, pathetically, in 1920, filled young men with a strange ardor to seek a means of defense against omnivorous Death.

Malraux is not the traditional or the conventional novelist, not any more than Proust or Kafka. He does not describe places or manners; he does not build love plots or tell a smooth story; he does not weave his intense tragic crises into one dramatic conflict. Yet Malraux is primarily a novelist, and even his volumes on art, perhaps lauded to excess, are those of an imaginative creator who molds reality anew rather than those of a historian or a philosopher. He overflows with ideas. But he does not invent puppets to exemplify them. He is not superior to his characters, but at one with them. He preaches no doctrine. He obviously could not linger long in communism, which became intolerant of any literature and art not at the service of the party line. He courageously pointed out, in 1935, the weakness of modern Russian literature, which had, after Dostoevski, failed to be both psychological and pathetic. The year before, in a speech delivered in Moscow and published in *Commune* (September–October 1934), he had warned the communists of the disappointment of all their friends who failed to find power and truth in Soviet letters:

> Beware, comrades, of assuming that one necessarily creates a powerful literature because one expresses a powerful civilization; do not readily believe that, from the photographing of a great age, there will automatically spring a great literature . . . Art is not a submission but a conquest: a conquest of sentiments and of the ways of expressing them . . . a conquest over the unconscious, almost always; over logic, very often. Marxism is the consciousness of the social; culture is the consciousness of the psychological . . . The cultural motto of Communism must be that of Marx: 'More consciousness.'

Such an avidity for an increased consciousness sets Malraux's characters outside and above ordinary humanity. They seek neither money nor property nor do they, like Stendhal's, set out every morning hunting for happiness. Their quest is metaphysical and moral. At the very moment when they raise their arm to kill with a dagger, or are blown up by a bomb, they seize in a flash the essential meaning of life. The 'fraternity of death' lays bare to them the purpose for which they were living. The highest form of love is, to Kyo and May in *La Condition humaine,* to lure the loved one into death. Malraux rejects the static introspection of many French novelists. 'Man is an unknown animal,' he wrote, reviewing Matveev's *Les Traqués,* 'who thought he could know himself in quietude. Let drama intervene and he discovers his powers of dream, his specific madness.'

But Malraux's man does not surrender to the forces that would engulf his lucidity and his will power. He directs them and unceasingly ponders over the moral issues raised by tragic life: How can, how must man guide his fate? Of what is he capable? One recognizes Nietzschean questions, carried over to an age that has unfortunately fulfilled some of Nietzsche's prophecies. To them, Malraux adds another preoccupation, which has become that of a whole generation deprived of God and unable to bear its loss: Is it possible for a man who thinks and who has the will to act to escape from the implacable solitude of tragic heroes? Can he reach solidarity with his fellow beings, whom he wants to love and serve?

Along with Nietzsche, who permeated his thought and influenced even his style, Dostoevski is obviously the master whom Malraux recalls. But he has never discussed and probably never studied his Russian predecessor with especial concentration; his technique owes little to him. Trotsky's powerful intellect held Malraux under its spell when orthodox communist literature repelled him. Trotsky was indeed one of the few who praised Malraux's first novel as having dared to seize the great modern theme, revolution. As an artist, however, Malraux must be placed in the French tradition, which he pursues while transforming and extending it.

He voiced his distaste for Flaubert's rhythmic prose and carefully balanced novels. Flaubert's fiction appeared to him, perhaps wrongly, as imprisoning and debasing man. Malraux wants to exalt man, through his challenge of the mediocrity of life. He has no affinities with Zola, although some literary historians, strangely misled by their partiality for labels, have occasionally classified *La*

Condition humaine as 'a proletarian novel.' Masses do not appear in Malraux's scenes of conspiracy. Stendhal is clearly the novelist most dear to him. He was the first, Malraux remarked, 'to see that the most powerful means of expression of the novelist lay in the ordering of facts.' He drew a similar lesson from the American novelists whom he has admired most: William Faulkner, of course, but also John Steinbeck and especially Dashiell Hammett. He borrowed nothing from their technique. But he was attracted by the melodramatic violence of their stories, by their disregard of regular arrangement of material, and by their graphic rendering of gestures, attitudes, and objects. In one of his few pronouncements on his own literary views, Malraux, who had set out in life as an explorer of Asia, prophesied the development of an Atlantic culture, as distinct from the former great Mediterranean heritage. He hailed the achievement of American fiction, more concerned with the fundamental man than the English, and observed shrewdly: 'To my mind, the essential characteristic of contemporary American writing is that it is the only literature whose creators are not intellectuals . . . The great problem for that literature is to intellectualize itself without losing its direct approach.'

Malraux's first significant work is not a novel but a brilliant ideological debate between two lobes of his brain and between two poles of modern thought and sensibility. The title itself, *La Tentation de l'Occident* (1926), is ambiguous, since it designates both the temptation of the West for some Easterners, and the far more potent attraction, after World War I, of the East to Western men. It came out at a time when Europe, led by a defeated Germany, which saw in her collapse the metaphysical portent of the collapse of Western civilization, was taking stock of those elements in the West that could withstand the Eastern invasion and an inner disintegration. To many Frenchmen, the East included Bolshevist Russia and extended as far as the Rhine; the phrase coined by Jules Michelet to designate Germany, which he admired, 'the India of Europe,' had enjoyed a great fortune. Hermann Keyserling was at that time interpreting the wisdom of Asia, as his facile mind had absorbed it during his travels; Morand, Giraudoux, Huxley, and other literary travelers were toying with the opposition of East and West. Romain Rolland led the discouraged band of those who, despairing of the West doomed to mechanization and to warfare, turned longingly toward

Asia.[2] Of all these men, Malraux proved the least partisan and the least superficial.

La Tentation de l'Occident is a series of letters supposed to have been exchanged by a Frenchman living in China and a Chinese visiting France. The Frenchman refrains from generalizations and is content with sketching a few vignettes of Eastern scenery and Chinese life, vividly expressed. The Chinese visitor to Europe is less easily carried away by what he sees. His letters constitute an unflinching diagnosis of the sickness that afflicts Europeans. Cities, museums, machines, hygiene, and books hardly concern him. He sets out to analyze a more subtle element — European sensibility. Europeans appear to him as weary of themselves and weary of their crumbling individualism, having built their lives upon a structure of negations. They act feverishly, often heroically. Their 'soul's joy lies in doing' and in rushing to generous self-sacrifice. But they do not find underlying reasons for their activity. Boredom is their constant fear. They must resort to pastimes to escape it. Art is one of these and eroticism is another.

Malraux's Oriental mouthpiece ponders, in Malraux's disconnected, enigmatic fashion, on eroticism, as the characters in the novels will repeatedly do. The closing scene of *La Voie royale*, the episode in *La Condition humaine* in which the banker Ferral is humiliated by Valerie and vexes her in revenge, the latent drama of Kyo and May, tormenting each other in their love, which they had imagined to be above conventions and above sentimentality, reveal in sudden flashes the significance of the theme in Malraux's virile universe. Here is clearly one of the keys to the understanding of Malraux's psychology; but the author's reflections on the subject are too fragmentary to allow any construction that would substitute a systematic view for his occasional pronouncements. It is to be hoped that some day Malraux may express himself more fully on the subject than he has done in his essay on Laclos and in his five-page preface to the French translation of *Lady Chatterley's Lover*.

Malraux's conception of love stands at the opposite pole from D. H. Lawrence's, for it stresses the cerebral aspect of love more than the physical. It is Proustian in the sense that it is imprisoned in subjectivity. 'One only possesses what one loves,' says a character

2. We have mentioned other features of that debate in a brief article on 'East and West in Contemporary French Literature' (*The Dial*, LXXXIV, 5, May 1928).

in *La Voie royale;* and again in *La Condition humaine:* 'One possesses of another being only what one changes in that being.' Appeasement of their senses or of their mental anguish seldom follows the brief and usually venal sexual experiences of Malraux's characters. They remain desperately alien to the woman whom they have just caressed. Of all of them it could be said, as it is of Ferral: 'He never slept with anyone but himself.' They will only be aroused by feeling some opposition in their partner, by a conquest to be made. 'There is eroticism as soon as to the notion of pleasure is added that of coercion,' declared Malraux. He stresses the eroticism of men who want to humble the woman, to treat her as an object, to demand gratitude for the pleasure she has received and the shame she may have experienced. But they are no conquering Don Juans. Their eroticism exists almost independently of the person loved or desired, and their pleasure springs more from their tortured brain than from any physical fulfillment, from imagining themselves in the place of their partner. Their inner solitude is in no way alleviated by their ecstasies, which ignore tenderness, humiliation of male pride, and affection.

The Chinese observing the West, who prefigures Malraux's characters in the novels, is haunted by two other themes: the absurdity of life, and death. The life of the Western man is absurd, for he pursues goals he does not enjoy reaching. The loss of Christianity's hold upon the European man appears to Malraux as irretrievable. God is dead, as Zarathustra had shouted in his bitter exultation; but now man also is dead, and we seek his successor whom we might entrust with his legacy. Malraux will, in his last novel and his volumes on art, attempt to reconstruct the basis on which a renewed concept of Western man might be established. In his first volume, he was intoxicated with the wild despair of his youthful negations.

Upon all our joys the prospect of ultimate death sits as a curse. It impels Malraux's characters to seek violent action, to seize power, to rush to pleasure or to lose themselves in the creation of art, as if they were thus averting the sting of death. They will cherish death when fearing it most. In thus projecting his own obsession into his heroes, Malraux is voicing one of the preoccupations of many modern minds faced with a huge void inside and around them and powerless to fill it.

In order to destroy God, and after destroying Him, the European mind has annihilated all that could be opposed to man:

having reached the goal of his efforts, like Rancé [3] in the presence of his mistress' body, he finds nothing but death . . . Never was discovery more disquieting.

Les Conquérants (1928) is a very different book. It is less finished in structure and less polished in style than its predecessor and therefore more promising, for in it Malraux no longer recalls poetical masters of prose, such as Barrès or Gide. He is elaborating a technique of his own, which is purposely disconcerting to the usual fiction reader. The characters are plunged into action and reflect only as they act.

Again the title is ambiguous. It may designate revolutionary agitators plotting against European imperialism, or Asia in ferment and one day enabled to turn against Europe, or the strong men who galvanize the masses, or even disease and death, the ultimate conquerors of men of action. There is hardly any unity to the book, little progression, and no organized plot. Malraux, one of the first among the writers of the present time, wants to utilize and rival a journalistic technique. Dispatches are flashed in the text, and events are reported as they happen, with the suspense of a still uncertain outcome, not embraced and weighed by the comprehensive eye of the novelist who controls their unfolding. The scene is laid in China, but not in the picturesque China described from the outside by travelers or by thrillers. There is no description of nature, no evocation of swarming crowds, no respite from the jerky, feverish action. The reader is plunged into a confused turmoil and shown a few episodes as disconnected as scenes in a newsreel. Whether such a method leaves the reader with a stronger impression of reality faithfully rendered is doubtful; there is even more artifice in the author's effort not to organize and not to intervene in his abrupt chapters than in the traditional device that, grasping the reader's interest, allows the author to be forgotten behind his narrative.

The setting is in Canton, where the Chinese, incited by Russian

3. Rancé is the famous seventeenth century Frenchman who, after a not very edifying youth, reformed the monastery of La Trappe. Hearing that his mistress, the Duchess of Montbazon, had just died, he rushed to her house to see (so the story goes) that the men come to bury her, unable to fit the body into too short a coffin, had sawed the head off and placed it in the oblong box alongside the body. Chateaubriand related Rancé's career in a small volume, in 1844. A study should be undertaken on the theme of death as it pervades much of modern literature between 1920 and 1950: Rilke's *Notebooks* and his poems, Thomas Mann, Malraux, Charles Morgan, the *Overtures to Death* of Cecil Day Lewis, and others.

agitators, have decreed a general strike. The danger of insurrection threatens Hong Kong. Malraux has not attempted to exploit the epic possibilities of such a theme: East against West and the rise of communists against Europeans. He has focused the light on the different factions and methods among the revolutionaries, and on the leaders, almost excluding the masses. The protagonists are not men of the East; there are practically none of them in Malraux's fiction. They are European adventurers, to whom the author has liberally lent his own problems: How turn the absurdity of life into meaningfulness? How challenge disease and death through action? How reconcile what is most precious in individualism with the exigencies of a collective task that requires the sacrifice of the present and of the nuances dear to the intellectual? How accept the means required in order that the end imposed by the anonymous party line be ruthlessly achieved?

One of the characters, Borodin, borrowed from history, is a man of action, determined to devote all else to the obedience demanded by his party. He welcomes fanaticism, without which the order of tomorrow would never dawn. Garin, who stands in contrast to him, is more complex and more like his creator, though Malraux is too much of an artist ever to paint only in black and white. Garin was born in Geneva of a Swiss father and a Russian mother. He was molded by French ideas, deserted from the Foreign Legion, and mixed cynicism and idealism in his attitude. He never subscribed to any body of ideas, not even to Marxism in which he saw only a powerful incitement to the tension of the will. He is enough of an individualist to be repelled by what he terms 'the doctrinal farrago' of Bolshevism. He is less concerned with the lack of justice in society than with his deep anarchy. 'I am a-social as I am an atheist, and in the same fashion.' He is ready to devote his life to the cause of the people, but he has no love for them; and he hates the middle class, from which he sprang, even more. Those who possess defend their possessions with such stupid principles that they deserve no respect.

That strange, semi-Nietzschean revolutionary is an organizing genius. He helped Chiang Kai-shek reform the military academy, and he organized a good deal of communist propaganda in China; but he has not abdicated his individual intelligence. Sooner or later, he will be liquidated by the very cause whose triumph he will have furthered. He cares little. For years he has been afflicted with paludism and dysentery. He hardly condescends to cure his sickness. A strange exaltation comes over him, when he contemplates the absurdity of any social order and of all that is human. Revolution had provided a means of escaping temporarily from that absurdity; for it had afforded some men a little more hope, and 'man's hope is his reason for living, and for dying.' Garin-Malraux has found one of the themes of all his meditations: 'No strength, no true life without the certainty and the obsession of the vanity of the world . . . The only defence is in creating.'

Les Conquérants, with its contempt for the ordinary devices of storytelling and of character presentation, with its bitter, if constructive, pessimism, was not likely to be a popular novel. It suffered from obvious faults. Its imperious dialogues, formulating the essential preoccupations of the author, were not skillfully merged into the action. The protagonist was analyzed independently of the plot. The characters tended to be types. The style was too elliptic in its incisiveness. But these were original and promising faults, asserting a haughty temperament, too rich to be tamed too soon by any readily accepted order.

La Voie royale, which followed in 1930, is in some respects more conventional. It is the smoothest of Malraux's novels, with a dramatic build-up of the reader's curiosity and several thrilling moments. The characters are again intellectuals. They are characterized with greater individuality than in the earlier novel; and their language is less uniformly that of their creator.

The title alludes to the unexplored expanse of the Indo-Chinese jungle, where old tombs and stupendous sculptures have been overgrown by the vegetation of several centuries. Claude, a young archaeologist with many features of the author, has long hoped to discover these carved stones, both for the aesthetic thrill of it and for the profit of trading them. The French institute in Hanoï, suspecting his purpose, refuses to lend him any assistance in his dangerous expedition, which will take him through the area of savage tribes. A Danish adventurer, Perken, whom he met on the boat, will be his companion.

Perken would be a Byronic hero but for the cynical bluntness of his talk, which contrasts with the affectation of Byron's mysterious and ever-eloquent corsairs. He fascinates Claude by his scorn for established values and by his passion for action, linked with his conviction that action, like everything else, is vain. Both are obsessed with death and convinced that courting it with a lover's zeal sets them above other mortals, who cling to a life they do not know how to enjoy. Old age is to them the worst calamity that can befall man, for it represents to them cowardice and semi-impotence. But suicide is a fallacy; he who kills himself runs after a complacent image of himself. These lovers of death are most avid for life, and Perken voices Malraux's favorite views in neat aphorisms: 'I have staked my life on a gamble greater than myself.' 'I think of death in order, not to die, but to live.' 'The exaltation which springs from the absurdity of life when you face it as you face an undressed woman.'

The two men, exchanging such formulas in their daily conversation, set out in their expedition. They succeed in reaching the Royal Way and in loading enormous sculptured stones on their ox-drawn chariots. But their guides betray them when they announce their determination to pursue their way to a remote village where Perken hopes to find a former comrade, Grabot. Grabot, a gambler against fate, had also fled from the conventionality of European life. He had sold arms in Thailand, dreamed of erotic experiences with native women, of power over the unruly tribes. But the man who would be king had ended as a wretched slave. The natives had blinded him and tied him to a treadmill; like a camel or a donkey, he turned round and round in a narrow cabin, covered with dirt, a bell dangling around his neck. He had not even lost his reason in the process. When, after a long search, the two explorers discover their compatriot in that abject decay, he could only utter one discouraged word — 'nothing.'

After elaborate negotiations with irate tribesmen, the Frenchmen succeed in buying back their companion. Their march amid dangers is told like a thriller. Malraux could indeed have become a writer of lurid stories of violence. But adventures in themselves do not interest him long — only as a means of showing how low man can sink when afflicted with suffering and how intense can be the lucidity gained when death is felt to be near. Perken, while returning, has been wounded by the poisoned splinters planted by the natives on their warpath. He knows that he is doomed. He will enjoy a last experience of physical love, coolly and precisely described, and then accept his end.

La Voie royale showed Malraux's growing mastery over the mold of the novel. But he would not repeat that easy success. *La Condition humaine,* which followed in 1933, is a more ambitious work. It is one of the striking novels written in any language during the fourth decade of the present century. The atmosphere is still that of Malraux's earlier works, but his tenseness is somewhat relaxed. There are philosophical conversations, sections that verge on tenderness but just miss it at the last minute, and even scenes of comedy when Clappique, the tragic and farcical mythomaniac, appears. After the first few pages, the reader accepts Malraux's world unquestioningly, and this is the most telling tribute one can pay a novelist. The characters, all probing the mystery of death for the significance it can give men's meaningless lives, no longer appear as impossible revolutionists and philosophers waylaid in a world of action. They survive in one's memory for years. Indeed, in the second half of the twentieth century, which is likely to be dominated by events taking place in Asia, many observers will more than once be reliving scenes from Malraux's novels.

La Condition humaine is not a novel of ideas, although it forces one to think. It is even less a novel of propaganda. The Chinese revolution in Shanghai provides it with its general theme, but it is in no way dependent upon a historical framework for its major interest. Balzac would have described the city of Shanghai, its geography and appearance, its motley crowd of natives and foreign traders, its smells, and some of its shops and houses. Tolstoy might have written at length of the great and small causes that had brought about the revolt and of the way in which events had been determined. Malraux's method, like that of most moderns, makes greater demands on the reader's brain. Nowhere is the confused skein of factions and assassinations and plots unraveled for his benefit. The irrational disorder of history is scrupulously respected. Malraux relates the struggle as an actor in those events and not as an omniscient and reflective spectator. The contemporary public, which has lived through one or more wars and is learning daily, through the press and the radio, how disconnected and futile are most of the events in which they are forced to take an interest, do not balk at the efforts they are asked to make. They know too well that men are not heroes curbing fate at will and that betrayals, contradictions, and dissonances are the common occurrence of any war, civil or foreign.

It takes no great subtlety to discern a pattern and a structure in the novel and the seven parts or sections into which it is unevenly divided. The revolution is the center. It is first prepared by Ch'en securing the weapons, Kyo and Katow, the other chief actors, getting psychologically attuned to the gigantic event, and Gisors, more remote, and Clappique, theatrical, looming in the background. In sections two, three, and four, the revolution appears as it strikes diverse characters: Ch'en the terrorist and Ferral the banker; Kyo the leader confronted, during a trip to Hankow.

by the dilemma of political expediency imposed by higher orders as against individual action. The attempt to bomb Chiang Kai-shek, whose betrayal the revolutionaries foresee, fails. Ch'en dies in the process at the end of Part Four. Meanwhile, the individual struggles within each of the main characters have been presented: Gisors, while fearful for the fate of his son, extracts the philosophical and social significance of the fight; Ferral's sexual frustrations parallel his financial and unscrupulous deals; Hemmelrich is pitifully enslaved to a poor, ailing family; Kyo, Gisors's son, and his wife May torment each other through honesty, shyness, nobleness, and because it is difficult for human beings to seek happiness with a simple soul.

The descent from the climax begins with Part Five. Clappique's weakness causes Kyo to be captured by Chiang Kai-shek's police. Torture will follow for him and for Katow. Death triumphs in Part Six, and yet virile fraternity vanquishes death's horror. A brief final chapter adds a note of irony, with Ferral's attempt to receive his financial reward in Paris, and of tenderness, with May's devotion to the memory of Kyo. All through the varied episodes, the themes of revolution, death, eroticism, fraternity, and the fate meted out to man, as well as that which he can control and make for himself, recur as the unifying themes of the book.

The old unities of tragedy are respected, after a fashion, in that comprehensive and often baffling volume. All the action, or almost all, takes place in Shanghai. It is concentrated within a very few days, grouped around March, then April, 1927. At first, Chiang Kai-shek is still the ally of the communists. The general strike is declared; the movement spreads; it may fulfill its unbounded hopes, free the country from foreign domination, and initiate agrarian reforms. Then failure threatens. Chiang Kai-shek, bought by European finance, betrays his communist allies; he escapes the bomb. The higher revolutionary authorities, inspired by Moscow, do not support a revolution they judge to be premature. The organizers of the revolt are thrown alive into the fireboxes of locomotives; labor unions are dissolved; liberation is indefinitely postponed. But the abortive revolution has served one of its purposes: it has woven together individual lives and provided the violence necessary for intense thought.

It would have been an artistic fault of the author to weld the varied scenes and episodes of his book into an organic whole at the expense of the impression of jerky, scattered, and futile truth, which he wanted to produce. The real unity of the novel lies in the parallel but always separate preoccupations of the characters. More than any other motive, the consciousness of their implacable solitude drives them to common action. Those reckless revolutionaries constitute a motley gallery of tragic heroes, not without affinities with Saint-Just, Robespierre, or Lenin, eagerly molding a new world in Asia and haunted by the ultimate vanity of power, of greatness, even of all action. Ch'en, the first to appear on the scene, is the most pathetic. He is not fit for his role of murderer, and his determination to plunge his dagger into the sleeping man, with the city lights flooding the room and a cat weirdly observing him, is that of a diffident intellectual steeling his weak nerves for action. A sense of sin lingers in him, from his upbringing in a Lutheran environment; he is deeply insecure, doomed to solitude even in his loves, dissatisfied by the collapse of his childhood faith. Killing is to him an atrocious means of reaching a certainty, almost a substitute for a wild merging of his whole self in sexual passion. The opening scene of Ch'en's murder of the sleeping man, then his descent in the elevator in a state of trance, then his two vain attempts to bomb Chiang Kai-shek, and, finally, his desperate suicide are unforgettable scenes in the book.

The end of another conspirator, Katow, is no less superbly handled. He had already faced torture and death as a Russian revolutionary under the czars and had served a term in Siberian jails. He cannot forget or forgive. When the revolution is betrayed and crushed, and while Kyo dies by his side, he meets death by swallowing the cyanide he always carried in his belt. Two other prisoners lie beside him, young men who tremble before the end that awaits them in the fireboxes of the locomotives. Katow soon resolves to make the supreme sacrifice. He cuts his poison in half, hands it to the two young men, depriving himself. Their hands drop it clumsily; then, groping for the treasure that will shorten their pain, they grasp Katow's hand. A soft feeling of fraternity comes over him at that handshake. Death alone could provide 'that absolute friendship.' 'It is easy to die when one does not die alone.'

Kyo is the third hero of the book. He is the son, by a Japanese woman, of Gisors, an opium addict, a meditative dreamer, and a professor of sociology, who has powerfully influenced his disciples and even Ferral. To Gisors, Malraux has lent several of his favorite thoughts and he alone is loosely linked to the action, though essential to a novel that turns about man's difficulty in bearing his human fate. Kyo is no philosopher himself. A half-caste, he has early been wounded in his pride, and revolution is partly his revenge. But he is made for action; in it alone he can forget his solitude. May, his wife, has thwarted his desire for tenderness and feminine understanding and hurt him. He is not just the terrorist, like Ch'en, who concentrates on his immediate action. He believes in the revolution as a great cause, which alone can instill a sense of their own dignity into the millions of Chinese now perishing from slow starvation. 'There is no possible dignity, there is no true life for a man who toils twelve hours a day without knowing what he is toiling for.' When the chief of Chiang Kai-shek's police, the former German König, questions his prisoner Kyo, the latter will not jeopardize his dignity as a revolutionary idealist to save himself from torture and death. 'What would have been the value of a life for which he would not have been ready to die? . . . Dying could be an exalted act, the supreme expression of a life to which this death bore a strong resemblance.' Since the Renaissance heroes intoxicated with Roman Stoicism and at times by their own eloquent histrionics, few characters in literature have sung such hymns to meaningful death.

> The stroke of death is as a lover's pinch,
> Which hurts, and is desired,

whispered Shakespeare's Egyptian queen, kissing the asp. Malraux's heroes had looked in vain for those proud mutual caresses through which other tragic lovers boasted of 'standing up peerless' against challenges of fate and of death. Except for May, the women who gave a fleeting sense of companionship to these men were venal or semivenal professionals of love. Unable to learn humility or tenderness, these feverish rebels were only thrown back, unappeased, upon their own desolate solitude. Thus Malraux's universe, once again, recalls Pascal, but without God and without charity. Men forever pursue a diversion that will intoxicate them and make life bearable until the potion that soothes once for all is quaffed. Gisors explained his disillusioned view to Ferral: 'China has opium, Islam has hashish, the West has women . . . Perhaps love is chiefly the means by which the Western man tries to shake himself free from man's fate.'

  La Condition humaine won a resounding success. It was one of the few truly good choices of the Goncourt Academy, the best, perhaps, since the crowning of Proust in 1919. The critics from all parties hailed it. Abroad, where French literary prizes have very little influence on opinion, the book was praised as one of the more cosmopolitan and universal French novels. If devoid of superficial charm and undoubtedly a difficult book, indeed one calculated to repel the conventional woman reader as publishers unfairly picture her to their authors, it had meat, vitality, and boldness in it. The world, torn between the American depression, the ominous rise of Hitlerism, and the abject appeasement policy of the Western democracies, was realizing in 1934 that the time for effete entertaining literature and an ostrichlike fear of fear would have to come to an end. Malraux loomed as the prophet of the new era.

But he was a prophet for the few, for the middle classes, whom he treated scornfully, and the literati, whose circles he had fled. The working classes, as they are called, seldom opened his novels. They would have been puzzled by the difficulty of the style, by the lack of apparent continuity and traditionally lighted focus, and by the pitiless soul-searching to which the characters yield in the midst of action. Malraux's communists may well be found to have stood closer to reality than any others depicted thus far in fiction, much as their cynical egotism and their ruthlessness may have dismayed the idealistic admirers of communism in the thirties. At a time when *Coriolanus,* performed at the *Comédie Française,* almost provoked a revolution in Paris, René Lalou aptly quoted the words of Brutus, which seem especially fitting to Malraux and to most of the revolutionaries in *La Condition humaine:*

> You speak of the people
> As if you were a god to punish, not
> A man of their infirmity . . .

Malraux's next novel was much less detached from the fate of the common man, far more vitally 'engaged,' as the word now goes. Between 1933 and 1935, the crisis had deepened in Europe. The question was no longer that of winning part of Asia to the revolutionary cause, but whether western Europe itself could withstand the counterrevolution. 'Revolution! All that is not revolution is worse,' had exclaimed Malraux in *Les Conquérants.* It now had to be defended at home. *Le Temps du mépris,* translated as *Days of Wrath,* showed both an increased fervor in Malraux's faith and an original attempt at renovating his technique instead of repeating some of the devices that had succeeded brilliantly in *La Condition humaine.*

The book is less ambitious than any other work by the same author, more condensed, simpler, moved by feverish anger but tempered by humanity and even by pity. It is practically the novel of one single character, Kassner, engaged in one action for which even the name 'plot' would be a misnomer. A leader of communist trade unions in Germany when Hitler has come into power, Kassner falls into a trap set by the Gestapo. He chews and swallows the revealing list of his party comrades, which the Nazis had hoped to seize, and he steels his will to resist torture and the weakness of the flesh, which might lead him to speak. The first part of the novel is a vivid and subtly contrived picture of the prisoner's mind. The guards torment him, question him harrowingly, starve him. He emerges from a daze into dim childhood memories, flashes of his past career as a communist soldier in Russia, and disconnected and lurid nightmares.[4] The threat to his reason frightens him. He would rather, as his last lucid act of will, commit suicide and rest assured that the silence of death would save his comrades from being betrayed.

But the first act of the closely knit novel, swift and ardent as a tragedy, closes when Kassner is saved from his solitude and his vagrant sick mind. He hears knocking at the wall of his cell. He is aroused from his preying loneliness and, after hard mental effort, he deciphers an alphabet in the unequal knocks. 'Comrade, take courage' are the words he has time to spell before the guard discovers his neighbor's device. The message binds him to another man. He emerges from the slough of despondency. Then, as in a tragedy, a surprising vicissitude occurs. Another communist, judging Kassner's life to be essential to the cause of the party, gives himself up as Kassner, and the real Kassner is freed. Another comrade agrees to fly him, in bad weather and before the Nazis discover their mistake, to Czechoslovakia.

The danger is over, the storm is vanquished. The released prisoner reaches Prague and meets his wife. Unlike Malraux's other characters, he behaves toward her with simplicity, directness, and a tender consciousness of the anxious strain to which his revolutionary activity condemns her. She has not a word of reproach, and, hinting at his next mission, she comforts him implicitly by the fortitude with which she will bear her fate. The drama is resolved with a serene restraint rare in Malraux. Malraux refrained from political dialogues and reflections on life's significance in the face

4. An acute and very ingenious analysis of the book and of its technique has been done by W. M. Frohock in *The Romanic Review* (XXXIX, 2, April 1948, pp. 130–39).

of annihilation. He stripped the book bare to a long short story
and reserved the message with which he wanted to accompany it
for a separate preface.

The preface, apparently written after the novel had appeared
serially, is the most important text penned by Malraux on his
faith and on his artistic intentions. In it, Malraux defined (neither
geometrically nor logically) his conception of tragic fiction, reduced, like ancient tragedy, to a very few characters: man, the
crowd, the elements, woman, and destiny. He took issue with the
nineteenth-century conception of fiction and opposed to it his
own, thus strikingly formulated: 'One may wish the word Art to
mean an attempt to give men a consciousness of their own hidden
greatness.'

Art, for Malraux, was never equated with propaganda and never
was assigned the purpose of demonstrating anything. But, says
the author in his fervent preface, it can also impoverish itself by
systematically ignoring or belittling the brotherhood of man, or by
that contempt for one's fellow-beings which is the surest mark of
a fascist mentality. In noble language, Malraux added a few elliptical but pregnant sentences, which clear much of the misunderstanding raised by the imperious Nietzscheism of his earlier novels:

> The individual stands in opposition to society, but he is
> nourished by it, and it is far less important to know what dif-
> ferentiates him than what nourishes him. All psychological life
> is an interchange; the basic problem for the living individual
> is to know upon what he intends to feed . . . It is difficult
> to be a man. But it is more difficult to become one by enrich-
> ing one's fellowship with other men than by cultivating one's
> individual peculiarities. The former nourishes with at least as
> much force as the latter that which makes man human, which
> enables him to surpass himself, to create, invent or realize him-
> self.[5]

L'Espoir (1937, translated in America as *Man's Hope,* in Great
Britain as *Days of Hope*) comes near to being a great book on a
great theme; but we would not be ready to agree with Malraux
who declared to Ralph Bates that he thought it his best book.[6]
The novel is instinct with a warm quality of sympathy for men

5. The translation is, but for very slight changes, that of Haakon M. Chevalier,
   quoted through the courtesy of Random House (*Days of Wrath*, New York,
   1936, pp. 6–8).
6. *The New Republic,* November 16, 1938.

of all parties and with a welcome gift for personifying philosophical views in living and moving characters. Malraux no longer seems to look upon revolution as a personal opportunity to live tragically and escape from dull, prosaic pursuits. His own faith is deep and sincere. The style itself has sloughed off some of its flashy brilliance; it occasionally submits to reposeful dialogues and relates some incidents with patience and humble fidelity to events as observed. *L'Espoir* stands as a powerful work inspired by the most productive (on the literary plane) of recent wars — the civil war in Spain; and it deserves the preference granted it by most critics and students over *For Whom the Bell Tolls*. Yet we doubt whether any but a very few scenes and the characters actually remain impressed upon the reader's memory. Malraux purposely played against several self-imposed difficulties. It is not certain that he won.

For one thing, the volume is very close to the events it describes. It respects their confusion, takes us alternately to Barcelona, Madrid, Toledo, Guadalajara, and multiplies scattered scenes of fighting and of cruelty, interspersing them with conversations now humorous, now enigmatic and perhaps profound. While reality may indeed have been irrational and disorderly, as Malraux depicts it, and while it is true that the republican cause in the Spanish war counted an unusually large number of intellectuals and thoughtful debaters among its defenders, it may be questioned whether Malraux did not violate some conventions of the art of fiction, only to be punished for his transgression. Even Stendhal's celebrated Waterloo episode and Tolstoy's admirable war diary of Sevastopol respected a pattern of unity more than does *L'Espoir,* and they had fewer pages. The very variety that Malraux wanted to embrace in his several scenes turns into monotony when the reader perceives that they all bear the imprint of the author's vision and style. The reader expects a sense of progression of interest, which the novelist refuses to satisfy.

Such a criticism may seem unfair since it tends to take an author to task for not having achieved what he deliberately refused to undertake. But the question recurs again and again to the mind of the reader: Is not Malraux clinging to a musical composition or, as it might rather be termed, to cinematic devices of disconnected scenes through some deficiency of his imaginative power? Is he not naïve in his sophisticated attempt to respect literal truth and to reject the synthetizing power of invention, co-ordinating the scattered debris of reality into a living order? The sparkling exchanges of ideas in which all those exceptional soldiers indulge might have become superfluous if Malraux had made his characters live those truths in action and had refrained from voicing their reflections in his own words. The novelist's task is to make us believe in truths that need not be translated into neat formulas.

Malraux similarly defied the conventions of the novelist's art when he refused to focus the interest on one or more heroes. He valiantly attempted to violate our expectation that a novel must be enacted by a few outstanding characters who will engross our attention. It is true that the Republican cause in Spain did not create or find its representative men, its Mirabeau, its Lenin, or its Bela Kun. But the reasons for this failure, the psychological dramas within some of the individuals tormented by the gulf separating reality from their ideal, would have been worthy of concentrated exploration. Malraux preferred the divergent novel in which centrifugal forces constantly move away from an elusive center. His novel consequently demands from the reader that he reconstruct in his own imaginative memory the scattered data laid before him. For that exceptional reader alone does the book take on full significance.

L'Espoir is an intellectual epic, critical and lyrical at the same time, on the great hope of the revolution. Seldom has a revolutionary creed been more alien to materialistic aims. Other leaders have held out promises of more comfort, more justice, better hygiene, and less poverty. Malraux's revolutionary fighters are all alike in this, but their hope in the victory of their cause does not preclude understanding their adversaries and realizing that the same men who shoot at each other could, in different circumstances, have been comrades at arms. They are not sentimentalists. Malraux never was squeamish about scenes of cruelty, and some of his episodes of horror are worthy of Goya's brush. 'The highest duty of the soldiers,' one of the characters remarks, 'is to do one's utmost so that shreds of iron will riddle human flesh.' But those fighters are also intellectuals, bent on absorbing with their sensibilities and analyzing with their minds a momentous experience. Malraux, fighting in Castile, is a true son of Montaigne, Descartes, and Stendhal when he coins some of those formulas that sum up and guide a life. 'Tell me, Major, what is, in your opinion, the best thing a man can do with his life? — To transform as wide as possible an experience into consciousness.'

The true tragedy in *L'Espoir* is indeed of an intellectual order. The implicit unity of the novel lies in the anguished questions it poses about the revolution as it was envisaged and enacted by men of thought. These strange fighters flocked to Spain from several countries, after being trained in art and books, after pursuing the nuances that make truth complex and fascinating. They plunged suddenly into the world of action. They realized that 'action is Manichean, and pays a tribute to the devil.' The most dearly cherished part of their being had to be offered in sacrifice on the altar of a better world, in which their hope seemed at times rather dim. They had to learn action, fanaticism, and organization.

There lies the rub. Revolutions, to be sure, are a poetical myth or, as Malraux prefers to say, an apocalypse. They exalt men above the present, in an *élan* comparable to the Messianic hope of the Jewish people or to the religious aspirations of the early Christians. 'Men will only die for what does not exist,' that is, for sublime but half-fallacious hope never to be fulfilled. And there will never be any dearth of youths eager to risk their lives for an abstract cause. In fact, all modern wars are fought for abstract causes (democracy, a way of life, the cause of peace) and no longer to capture or recapture a province or a colonial island or to protect one's trade.

But the willingness to die is not enough. Malraux soon learned in Spain that intellectual anarchists may provide martyrs and warriors but that Spain needed men who would fight first and then organize their victory. Revolution and war cannot be justified by the fact that they afford an opportunity for intense living and meaningful dying. The word 'organize,' dampening as it is to the rash hopes of mystics of the revolution, becomes the burden of Malraux's mournful song. 'Courage is a thing which must be organized; it has to be kept in good condition, like a rifle'; or 'A popular movement, a revolution or even a rebellion, can hold on to its victory only by methods directly opposed to those which gave it victory — sometimes even opposed to the feelings from which it sprang.'

Hence the unresolved and insolvable conflict in the book and in Malraux's soul. In the past, the man of thought or the artist could afford to stay aloof and to avoid or ignore practical politics. He prepared action in undisturbed meditation; he observed it detachedly, meted out praise and blame, and retained unsullied an ideal of pure justice. He was the cleric who did not betray.

But during and after World War I, the world changed. New political leaders claimed to control the minds and the souls of their subjects — subjects who had often willingly and in mass hysteria elected them to uncontrolled power. At the same time, military service claimed all men, even those intellectuals who once were left

alone provided they celebrated the beauties of war and the greatness of the sovereign's conquest. Hence the revenge taken by the
war literature of Erich Maria Remarque and Henri Barbusse, of
John Horne Burns, Norman Mailer, and James Jones. A thinker or
an artist was no longer left free to reap the benefits of a social order
in which and for which he took no risks and which he often scorned
as impure. He had to take sides in a Pascalian wager.

And as sincerity had meanwhile become part of his ethics as a
writer, Malraux had to realize that, as Goethe expressed it in
Wilhelm Meister, to think is easy, to act is less easy, but to act according to one's thought is the most difficult thing in the world.
The whole twelfth chapter of Part two, Section two in *L'Espoir* is
concerned with that crucial problem. The intellectual plunged
into war and revolution must consent to the hardest sacrifice for
him — *il sacrifizio dell' intelletto.* He is constantly faced with a
dichotomy. Malraux has sketched it more than once. There are
two types of revolutionaries: the individualist or the anarchist,
who will not renounce his freedom of thought and lives intensely
in the present (Garin, Tchen, Scali, and the Negus in *L'Espoir*),
and the organizer who accepts and imposes discipline, silences his
scruples, and suppresses all else for the sake of a better future
(Borodin, Kyo, Kassner, and in *L'Espoir* Garcia and Manuel). Between the two, Malraux, deep down, has never made the final
choice. As much as Gide though less complacently, he is *un être de
dialogue.* His present political alignment may not be his last.

The very dilemma in which he writhes is that of his age. Around
him in many lands, men are wavering between the revolutionary
apocalypse and the inevitable and ruthless organization of the
apocalypse; between the nuances necessary to thought and Manichean action; the sanctity of the individual and the inevitable
sacrifice of the most precious in him to the collective good. The international revolutionaries whom Malraux has gathered on the
Spanish battlefield symbolize the tragedy of modern man at his
crossroad. Their dialogues can hardly sound natural, under the
buzz of airplanes. But they voice the hope and also the forebodings
of the modern man, willing to help the advent of a future he hopes
may prove brighter, yet conscious of all that is irreplaceable in the
art and culture of the past. 'For a man who thinks, revolution is
tragic,' says Garcia. 'But for such a man, life, too, is tragic . . .
There may be such a thing as a just war, but there is no such thing
as a just army . . . There is a politics of justice, but there is no
just party.'

L'Espoir revolves around another dilemma, still, no less tragic for the twentieth-century revolutionary who can no longer believe that an uprising of the people and the raising of barricades will bring about the triumph of a generous cause. The republican forces in Spain had met with defeat because they were not assisted from outside, but also because they had not found leaders. Malraux soon observed it, and understood that any popular movement that fails to evolve leadership is doomed. Power corrupts or intoxicates; most revolutions have been known to end in a stronger centralized authority, a more repressive police, a more rigid bureaucracy than had the regime they overturned. But, unless leaders emerge from the masses, a rebellion will soon flounder into anarchy; and a reactionary and militaristic tyranny will replace it.

Malraux's novel does not give a glowing picture of the leader whom he sees as indispensable. His dialogues comment sadly upon the solitude of the chiefs, whom authority and efficiency make daily more alien to the men whom they command. *Misereor super duces* could be one of his mottoes. For the task of a chief is exacting. He must be loved because he is just and efficient but not because he courts popularity. 'An officer must never seduce . . . To be loved without seducing is one of the highest feats of man.' And again: 'There is more nobleness in being a leader than in being an individual: it is more difficult.'

The role of the chief, who is himself condemned to solitude, is to develop 'virile fraternity' in his men. The phrase is among the most striking coined by Malraux; the passage in his books where characters reach that fraternity, when threatened by death, are the summits of his art as a novelist. In *L'Espoir,* the Spanish peasants carry down the mountain paths the stretchers of wounded airmen. In both the book and the film, the scene is rendered with a sobriety and an emotion not often achieved by Malraux. Without any unanimist theory, without any of the moralizing that tempted Saint-Exupéry, without the reasoning about their all-embracing responsibility indulged in by some existentialists, Malraux makes fraternity a living and moving force.

Soon after *L'Espoir* appeared, the Munich crisis, then World War II burst upon Europe; and the novelist's prophecies of a world in which sadistic cruelty and mass brutality would reign were fulfilled. Malraux had even foreseen that, parallel to wars between nations striving for power and impelled by hatred, implacable rivalries between ideologies and parties would henceforth rend nations internally. Malraux was much read and often quoted in the years 1940–44. The scene in which Kyo refused to betray his cause and his honor before the chief of police was often re-enacted in the underground movement and before the Gestapo. 'Human dignity . . . is the contrary of humiliation.'

Malraux did not then capitalize on the timeliness that his ideas and his writings had assumed. He acted, and wrote little. He avoided publicity. He published only one novel in Switzerland, in a limited printing of fifteen hundred copies, in 1943: *Les Noyers de L'Altenburg*, as the first part of a longer work with the title, evidently an allusion to Jacob's struggle in Genesis, *La Lutte avec l'ange*. As an artistic achievement, the book is not satisfying. Its long ideological discussion is badly integrated into the plot, and there is hardly any semblance of a plot. The characters are too clearly the mouthpieces of the author's own anxiety. Yet several passages rise perhaps higher than anything Malraux had previously written; and they are free from the obsession with lurid violence and with death, which harried Malraux in his earlier novels. Edmund Wilson was right, at the time, when, in a thoughtful critique, he called the novel 'the most impressive and the most exciting piece of literature . . . inspired by the war.' [7]

Les Noyers de l'Altenburg derives its title from the peaceful setting of an old abbey in Alsace, shaded by walnut trees. The novel is made up of three parts of unequal length and purposely disjointed, but in each the same question is asked. The hero in the first part is a young French Alsatian, Vincent Berger, who, in the battle of France in 1940, was taken prisoner by the Germans and thrown with thousands of other captives into the nave of the Cathedral of Chartres. The naïve hopes of his fellow prisoners and their bewilderment are rendered with human pity and with power. The young Alsatian, in the next part, then meditates upon his father's experiences, which he has pieced together from a set of notes found after his father's death. The bulk of the volume is devoted to that tale of the elder Berger's career and to philosophical meditations connected with it.

Berger's father, whose life was lived mostly before 1918, was of German nationality. He combined intense scholarly curiosity and adventurous action. The East lured him. He had served with the German mission in Turkey, dreamed of a movement uniting all the people of Turkish origin, and had been disillusioned after a stay in Afghanistan. He then took part in the serene Altenburg

7. *The New Yorker*, September 8, 1945.

colloquies in his native Alsace. There, immense problems were stirred up by a few thinkers: Nietzscheism, Hegelianism, Pan-Germanism, and anthropological observation of primitive people. Nietzsche's shadow hovers above the talks, and his madness is depicted in vivid pages by the narrator's great-uncle, who had been a friend of the philosopher. Malraux's criterion for a great work, to which he has himself frantically tried to live up, is Nietzschean: a work is great through its ability incessantly to question the validity of the world, *par son aptitude à remettre le monde en question.*

During World War I, the elder Berger took part in an attack against the Russian lines, in which the Germans experimented with poison gas. The scene is reminiscent of Malraux's most violent and dramatic moments. The German soldiers, following up their gas shells, stand horrified at their own murderous success. They rush to help their dying enemies and feel seized with revulsion against the modern methods of warfare. In the last part of the book, the scene shifts to World War II and to young Berger fighting with the French and defeated. He relives in his memory his last fight before he was captured. He was, like Malraux, serving in the tank corps. While he was leading his tank against the Germans, it fell into a trap where death was a certainty. He waited for it, horror-struck. Miraculously, the German shells missed him. He and his crew crawled out of their ditch, reached a village, and escaped from the jaws of death into the rediscovery of life.

If *Les Noyers de l'Altenburg* probably does not succeed as a novel, even in Malraux's own opinion, it reveals much about its author, in an earnest and passionate tone. His youthful obsession with hatred, eroticism, and action for the sake of action has disappeared. His early rhetoric and his Byronism have been transformed and raised to a plane of universality. This war book, completed while the French were fighting the occupying German forces in the underground, is devoid of partisanship. The very choice of heroes of Alsatian origin, with a name as much German as French, is significant. In the middle of the most atrocious fight, the wish of one of the characters is that of the author and many of his countrymen during World War II: 'Ah! May victory come to those who have fought the war without loving it.'

For the true subject is not war, but man's fate, his struggle against it and his acceptance of it. Repeatedly, and more than ever in his books on art, Malraux has played striking variations on the theme of fate and paraphrased, never clearly, the significance of the word.

The word holds for him an undying fascination. 'It owes its special accent,' he says, 'to the fact that it expresses our dependence, and the mortal lot of all that imposes upon man the consciousness of his nothingness, and first of all of his solitude.' Thus, in his third volume on art, Malraux continued his search for a world intermediate between the absolute world of God, which he considers dead, and the ephemeral world of men, which fails to satisfy his anguish. Malraux's heroes, and all men as he sees and pictures them, are creatures conditioned by the privilege that has been bestowed upon them; man is 'the only animal which knows that it must die.' [8] His joys are poisoned at the source by the realization that he is not to be immortal. But the awareness of death awaiting him urges man to action. He seeks beauty in a frail world in which his stay will be brief, or creates beauty in order to triumph over death, the ephemeral, and the relative. After looking death straight in the face, the characters in *Les Noyers de l'Altenburg* find 'Life more inexhaustible than Death.' Malraux the negator does not look for an easy refuge against the contemplation of man's weakness; he remains a tragic pessimist, as Nietzsche and Pascal, and the Greeks before them, had been. But there is hope indeed in his fight against the angel, or against the gods. In one of his most Pascalian sentences, he exclaims in his last novel: 'The greatest mystery is not that we should have been thrown here below at random between the profusion of matter and the profusion of the stars, but that, from our prison, we should draw from our own selves images powerful enough to negate our own nothingness.'

'What is man capable of?' was one of the Nietzschean interrogations, which echoed in Malraux's earlier work. In action and adventure, in eroticism and an anguished but vain quest for identification with his partners in love, in shaking audiences and political parties to the depths through his nervous eloquence, and in courting and vanquishing death, Malraux had attempted to push further the boundaries of man's capabilities and of his self-knowledge. With *Les Noyers de l'Altenburg* and his subsequent books on art, his tone has ceased to be one of jerky and passionate questioning. A positive faith is formulated. It rests on the central issue raised by Malraux's studies in ethnology and anthropology, as well as by his confrontation of East and West, past and present. On what basis can the notion of man be founded? Are there unity and continuity

8. The remark was a commonplace of eighteenth-century philosophy. Rousseau defines man, in his *Discourse on unequality,* as outgrowing the animal condition when he begins to know that he must die.

in men's successive and isolated efforts to challenge fate? Is the experience of men cumulative or do cultures appear and die as detached cycles, all doomed to tragic failure and leaving nothing but a few sculptured stones around which 'the lone and level sands stretch far away,' as around Ozymandias's shattered visage?

The colloquy in *Les Noyers de l'Altenburg,* and even more the contemplation of the serene and aged walnut trees shading the house in which facile thinkers exchanged ideas always born from other ideas and not originating in facts, already showed Malraux as transformed by his experience of revolution and war. Fraternity is a noble ideal, though a difficult one to live by in everyday existence; our affection for our fellow-beings has to withstand severe jolts when daily confronted with men's greed, cowardice, and superstition. But the realm of art provides Malraux not with an escape but with the means of a transfiguration. For if the pre-eminent role given to interrogation constituted the best in Western civilization, art, with Leonardo and Rembrandt, with Cézanne and Picasso is, or has turned into, 'an interrogation of the world.'

Malraux's works on art, collected in a one-volume edition, reorganized and somewhat clarified, as *Les Voix du silence* may well remain his greatest achievement and one of the significant books of our century. They negate history and disregard the filiation of schools and of ideas. They are hardly concerned with technical discussion of the pictorial elements in painting. They force upon the reader a broadening of his Greco-Roman-western European perspective by letting African masks, Oceanic idols, and Chinese and Indian temples and sculptures intrude incessantly upon his secure, narrowed vision. Malraux's attempt to redefine man reflects his concern and that of the moderns; unless the Asiatic and the African men are integrated into, but not summarily merged into, our broadened concept of man, modern Western humanism is a ludicrously complacent fallacy. The 'museum without walls' has made such an integration possible. Photography enables us to familiarize ourselves with the art of all times and of all nations, and the juxtaposition of heterogeneous works of art in modern galleries allows us to compare and to set up new systems of relations or of metaphors in the original sense of constant 'carrying over' from one culture to another. Parallel examples drawn from many lands and forty centuries converge around a few lessons, which Malraux lived in his own fiction before he rediscovered them in the great creators of the past — who all assume the mask of Malraux's characters. Every artist is a lonely hero, set by his genius at a wide distance from ordinary mortals. He is a rebel against fate, a living revolt against history. He is more sensitive to his own universe, the universe of art, than to that of other men, into which he happens to be thrown. He is driven to painting or to sculpture by an inner daemon that impels him to oppose, to works of art that their predecessors had created, new or future works of art that they must create in their turn, as rivals of nature and not transcribers of it. Borrowing, probably without knowing it, a notion Croce had once developed, Malraux proposes a pattern to which he submits every style and every individual artist. According to that pattern, every creator begins by imitating former artists; then he breaks away from his early models and turns ungratefully against them. Writers and artists regularly started from other writers and artists, never or seldom from nature. Their own originality is, in terms dear to Malraux, an annexation of the achievement of others and an imperious conquest.

Thus is some continuity in our civilization established, and some degree of universality, underlying varied cultures and different continents, asserted. Modern times have, according to Malraux, witnessed the end of the absolute. Religion survives with undoubted fervor in many of us. But it has lost the character of an unchallenged belief in another world, which it once possessed; it no longer conditions our daily lives, as it did in the Middle Ages. In his essay on European youth, written in 1927, Malraux had remarked that Christianity is like a scar imprinted deeply in our very flesh, and we, who are no longer Christians, are still forced to perceive and to decipher the world through a Christian code. Nostalgia for a new absolute plaintively breathes through the pages of Malraux's volumes on art; it may well some day bring the former Nietzschean negator to a religious conversion. He cannot rest content with the acceptance of the relative and the worship of history, which, since the late seventeenth century and even more since Hegelianism, have expelled the absolute from our philosophies. He is concerned about the dissatisfaction and the anxious despair that are reflected in modern art. But he unstintedly admires the modern artists who struggle against fate, as El Greco and Tintoretto once did, and are not content with adorning and prettifying life. 'Civilization is not sweetness, but consciousness and mastery of man.' In the very last sentence of his long excursus through the art of several continents, Malraux lyrically exclaims: 'O scattered world, ephemeral and eternal world which, to survive itself instead of repeating itself, stands in such need of men.'

Malraux's message, like that of Giraudoux, of Giono, of Gide, and of Cocteau, is a message of humanism. To have become a man without the help of the gods, such is, to Malraux, man's chief claim to greatness. Such humanism is superficially antireligious. But it voices one of the most eloquent protests against the debasing of man, which has been systematically practiced in our century by internecine wars, ideological hatreds, tyrannies of the mind, and much literary obsession with all that is low. Malraux's fiction answers in the affirmative one of the most tragic questions asked by Nietzsche: *Ist Veredlung möglich?* Is it possible to ennoble man?

BIBLIOGRAPHICAL NOTES

The following novels by Malraux have appeared in English translation: *The Conquerors,* translated by Winifred Stephens Whale (Harcourt, Brace & Co., 1929; Jonathan Cape, London, 1929); *The Royal Way,* translated by Stuart Gilbert (Smith and Haas, New York, 1935); *Man's Fate,* translated by Haakon M. Chevalier (Smith and Haas, New York, 1935; *Storm in Shanghai,* Methuen, London, 1934); *Days of Wrath,* translated by Haakon M. Chevalier (Random House, New York, 1936; Gollancz, London, 1936); *Man's Hope,* translated by Stuart Gilbert and Alastair Macdonald (Random House, New York, 1939; *Days of Hope,* Routledge, London, 1939). The three volumes on art have been published in New York by Pantheon Books as *The Psychology of Art,* translated by Stuart Gilbert, and *The Voices of Silence* was published in 1953 by Doubleday and Company, New York.

Other writings by Malraux not available in English and very revealing of his philosophy of life and of his attitude to the art of fiction are 'D'une Jeunesse européenne' (*Ecrits,* Grasset, 1927, pp. 129–54), *La Tentation de l'occident* (Grasset, Paris, 1926), a penetrating essay on Laclos's *Les Liaisons dangereuses* in *Tableau de la Littérature française* (Gallimard, Paris, 1939), and several book reviews in which Malraux expressed himself apropos of the author discussed. The most valuable ones, all in the *Nouvelle Revue Française,* deal with Marcel Arland's *Où le coeur se partage* (1928), Keyserling's travel diary (June 1929), Faulkner's *Sanctuary* (November 1933), Matveev's *Les Traqués* (June 1934), Gide's *Nouvelles Nourritures* (December 1935), and a novel by Ehrenburg, which inspired Malraux with interesting considerations on Stendhal (November 1935). See also Malraux's *Esquisse d'une psychologie du cinéma* (Gallimard, 1946) and his very curious declarations in *Horizon* (XII, 70, October 1945, pp. 236–42), originally published in *Fontaine,* as well as his lecture at the Sorbonne of 1947 in the collective volume *Conférences de l'Unesco* (Fontaine, 1947).

Malraux has received more attention from critics than most other contemporary French novelists. Two books of very high excellence have been written on him: W. M. Frohock's *André Malraux and the Tragic Imagination* (University of Stanford Press, Stanford, California, 1952), on which we have commented in the *Romanic Review* (XLIV, 3 November 1953, pp. 229–31) and Gaëtan Picon's second book on him, *Malraux par lui-même* (Editions du Seuil, Paris, 1953), with enlightening remarks by Malraux himself, on his conception of the novel in particular. Gaëtan Picon's earlier and more youthful volume, *André Malraux* (Gallimard, 1945), remains superior to the brief monographs by Marcel Savane (1946), Claude Mauriac (1946), and Pierre de Boisdeffre (1952). One may also consult Roger Stéphane's *Portrait de l'aventurier* (Sagittaire, 1950) and good book reviews of Malraux's work on art, notably by Joseph C. Sloane in *The Art Bulletin* (December 1952). A whole number of *Esprit* (October 1948) was devoted to Malraux. Pierre de Boisdeffre published a small book on Malraux in his collection, *Classiques du XXᵉ siècle* (1952). Janet Flanner had two well informed articles in *The New Yorker*, November 6 and 13, 1954.

VIII

EXISTENTIALISM AND FRENCH

LITERATURE

JEAN-PAUL SARTRE'S NOVELS

EXISTENTIALISM is a metaphysics, an ethics, a psychology, and a sociology of literature. There are several existentialist systems, fighting each other but encroaching upon each other and not always clearly distinguishable; for the notions of essence, of existence, and nothingness, of which they make so much, have seldom been precisely defined by the thinkers and polemists of existentialism. Even the easy distinction between Christian existentialism (that of Karl Jaspers and Gabriel Marcel, for instance) and atheistic existentialism (that of Martin Heidegger, at least in his works published before 1945, and, with many a difference, that of Sartre and his followers) is not as clear-cut as it might seem. On several essential points, the theses of different existentialist philosophers of the same sect are at variance. But while they vary so widely that no significant common thesis can be found, existentialist theories have had valuable effects. Out of them have come a wealth of ingenious analyses of concrete cases and an *Erlebnis,* a lived experience of subjectivity.

But one point may be stated clearly at the outset. Existentialism, as it has come to the fore in France since 1942 or so, has been seriously misunderstood in America, and many of the commentaries published in our general magazines have been misinformed, distorted, uncritical, and blind. This is in part excusable; for, while Sartre's *L'Etre et le néant* was not translated into English, *Existentialism Is a Humanism,* which was published in translation, is a very elementary and superficial summary, which fails to do justice to Sartre's real gifts. Much of the journalistic information that reached this country about the disheveled bohemians of the *Café de Flore* stressed chiefly eccentricities, which accompany any literary movement, and the selling devices that French literary publicity uses even more provokingly than does American salesmanship.

But the many eccentric, cheap, or coarse aspects of existentialism need no dwelling upon. Any system, as Leibnitz and Renan liked to assert, is false in what it negates, true in what it asserts. The negative and superficial aspects of existentialism may be dismissed without delay. Its positive contribution alone deserves our attention. And the positive or credit side of existentialism, as a perspective of ten years establishes it for us, is considerable. Existentialism is important not as one or several systems but as a philosophical mood characteristic of our times. It is at least as significant today as Bergsonism was in 1900–14, and as pragmatism from William James to John Dewey may have been in America.[1] It is, in our opinion, important as a psychology, and Sartre's psychological analyses of the *café* waiter and of the caress are classic models already. It is, or is trying to become, a system of ethics, with Simone de Beauvoir's *Ethics of Ambiguity,* Sartre's admirable *Réflexions sur la question juive (Portrait of the Anti-Semite)* and his long-awaited treatise on ethics, fragments only of which, on evil, have been published to date. But it is especially considerable as literature. And this chapter is concerned with existentialism in its relation to literature. While with Husserl and Heidegger, both greater philosophers than Sartre, phenomenology and *existentiale* philosophy (which Heideg-

1. Sartre has not always been fair to Bergson, whose view on the 'deeper self' and the 'superficial self' is not far remote from the existentialist distinction between the authentic and the unauthentic in us. One of the best French philosophers of our generation, Jean Hyppolite, marked the relative position of the two systems in an able article, 'Du bergsonisme à l'existentialisme' (*Mercure de France,* July 1948, pp. 403–16). Merleau-Ponty inserted a sympathetic and luminous brief discussion of some aspects of Bergsonism in his inaugural lecture at the Collège de France (*Eloge de la philosophie,* Gallimard, Paris, 1953).

ger distinguishes sedulously from *Existenz* philosophy) [2] remained enclosed in university seminars and in abstruse volumes, which hardly touched literature and consequently the outside world, with the French the movement of ideas derived from those German predecessors soon made a momentous commotion, shaking the novel, the drama, criticism, politics, fashion, and the daily lives of thousands of responsive individuals. Again, as with Bergsonism, as with the Age of Enlightenment, and earlier with Cartesianism, France seems to have wed philosophy and literature with equal gains to both. Philosophy has sprung to life, pursued the study of the individual, and attempted, in the apt definition of Simone de Beauvoir, to understand the abstract concretely. It has projected itself into the future, which alone endows the past and the present with meaning. It coincides with life, fulfilling the wish formulated by the true father of existentialism, Sören Kierkegaard, when he complained that 'we live forward, but we understand backward.' This coincidence between life and philosophy was a boon to literature. It was no longer content with being mere ornament superadded to life, a pleasing garland of imagery and music. It faced the anguish of modern man and the tragedy of man's fate. It questioned everything anew, displaying what the poet Henri Michaux has termed the most precious asset of Western man — 'irrespect.' It refused to dally on the surface of life but was determined to be radical, in the sense in which Marx uses the word in his critique of Hegel's philosophy: going to the roots. And, Marx added, the root of everything is in man himself.

It seems futile to try to define a 'true' existentialist and to decide who belongs or does not belong to the group. Surrealism had proceeded with pontifical solemnity to a vigilant excommunication of members of the sect who refused to subscribe to one of the creeds imposed by André Breton. Not so with existentialism, which is not a closed chapel but a mood. Albert Camus refused repeatedly to be labeled an existentialist. But for all practical purposes he is one, at least in his philosophy of the absurd, in his constructive and

---

2. In French, Heidegger's philosophy is called *existentiale* as opposed to *existentielle* and especially to Jaspers. Heidegger has taken great care to separate his own doctrine from *Existentialisme,* as he calls, using the French substantive, the French movement, in which he sees and deplores a dualism as radical as that of Descartes. He wishes to erase such an excessive differentiation between the object and the subject and to restore a link between the two. His own concern is with existence, in what is, and as he says, using the Latin plural, in *Existentialia.* Jaspers' doctrine, which stresses anguish, is in German *Existenzphilosophie.*

moral pessimism, in his portrayal of the alienated man in *L'Etranger* (*The Stranger*), and in his plays. Simone de Beauvoir is the high priestess of existentialist altars. Maurice Merleau-Ponty is the leading French phenomenologist, an understanding but not a servile friend of Sartre on whom he wrote an excellent essay in his *Sens et non-sens,* and the chief political thinker of the group in his attempt to substitute existentialism for Marxism as a philosophy for the proletariat. Francis Jeanson and Jean Pouillon are penetrating existentialist essayists. Poets, dramatists, and novelists have rallied around the leadership of Jean-Paul Sartre, though the master has never tried to imprison them in his views or to propose his technique to them. He is too intelligent not to be aware of the danger of epigoni, who would soon degrade his most successful artistic devices by turning them into mere tricks. His review, *Les Temps Modernes,* has been a disappointment, for it has signally failed to include novelists, poets, and critics of the quality and range that the prewar *Nouvelle Revue Française* had grouped in the twenties. But in a period of French letters that is as conspicuous for its experimenting as for its achievement, Sartre stands out, 'above the rest proudly eminent' as an extraordinary intelligence and as an essayist, a psychologist, a playwright, a novelist, and a storyteller of the first order. Voltaire himself did not unite so many diverse gifts in one person.

Some hasty commentators have thought they could discredit existentialism, which they did not want to take the trouble to understand, by stating that it was nothing but the postwar philosophy of a sick continent and Europe's escape from its political and economic problems into philosophical, or perhaps logomachic, speculation. It is true that the postwar mood of western Europe must have been conducive to some pessimism. But pessimism is not discouragement; it is often the very opposite. We believe we have shown elsewhere that the pessimism found in the French existentialists is courageous and constructive and that their philosophical attitude is one of faith in man's freedom and in man's responsibility for changing his fate.

It is natural and legitimate for postwar Europe to evolve a philosophy that takes into account its recent experience, the failure of earlier systems and faiths to account for the tragedies of wars, revolutions, and concentration camps, and the present reign of fear and insecurity. 'Insecurity, that is what sets men thinking,' remarked Camus. Existentialism was not, in point of fact, the result of World War II. The influence of Kierkegaard and Nietzsche, from whom much of this philosophy is derived, was considerable as early as 1930, and even before. And Sartre's psychology, Camus's *Noces,* and the first version of *Caligula* antedate the outbreak of the conflict of 1939. But existentialism met, or created, its public after 1941, when the overthrow of all secure and normal conditions of life and the constant threat of bombings, shootings, and slow death in German camps invited men and women to find new reasons for dying and for living.

If in existentialist literature there is brutality and delight in pointing out the absurdity of our lives, it must be borne in mind that brutality was unleashed everywhere and absurdity was rampant in the decade 1940–50, and that a literature that would have closed its eyes to it and smiled with humor or with sarcasm at an evil world, or taken refuge in a new *préciosité* would have been false and truly discouraged in its cowardice. Our culture is faced with anxious questions, indeed with the possibility of sudden annihilation. Modern man witnesses violence, uncertainty, the collapse of many of his values, and is fascinated by abysses opening before his steps. Psychological contradictions and Kierkegaardian paradoxes laugh him in the face as soon as he observes his fellow beings, his social institutions, his ethics, and his religion. A Nietzschean and pathetic questioning is the normal mood of the thinking man of this mid-century. A literature that teaches that man is solidary with all other men and that human life truly begins the other side of despair has much to commend itself to a generation that must transvaluate all values in order to find new ones or to test which of the older ones are worthy to survive.

The balance of talent has clearly been with atheistic existentialism as opposed to Christian existentialism, the latter having inspired no good novels and only the mediocre plays of Gabriel Marcel. Hence existentialism is here taken as being that of Sartre and of his friends. It must not be inferred, obviously, that Christian writers have disappeared from modern France: they have never been more numerous or more gifted. Simone Weil's posthumous influence today outdoes that of Maritain and rivals that of Sartre. The Catholic periodicals — from *Dieu Vivant* and *La Vie Intellectuelle* to *Etudes* and the mildly religious *Table Ronde* — are the best published in French. The very best books on Heidegger and on Merleau-Ponty are those of the Louvain philosopher, A. de Waehlens. Indeed, Catholic thought owes not a little to the challenge that atheistic existentialism has thrown to it; and, since

Camus has rejected the advances of Catholics, Sartre may perhaps some day be favored with authentic stigmata and be received into the bosom of the Church.

The first notion stressed by existentialism is that of nothingness. That notion was discarded by most philosophers, and lately by Bergson, as unthinkable. But the existentialists stress it, at least negatively, and, outdoing or contradicting Pascal, they establish a colloquy with the absence of God. Why do I exist? Why does anything exist? Why is there not just nothingness? If the idea of nothingness does not lend itself to analysis, it can at least be experienced in fear and trembling. The *Angst* or anguish, of which Kierkegaard made so much, is the starting point of a personal philosophical reflection.

Man facing nothingness has the revelation of the absurd: thus the second tenet of existentialism is man's thirst for rationality, and he finds irrationality prevailing. He has in him a 'wild need for clarity,' as Camus calls it, and is confronted with confusion and darkness. He wishes happiness, and the conditions of life hardly make happiness obtainable. He would like a presence to watch over him and warn him of perils, but the heavens and their 'eternal silence' fill him with dread. Existentialists stress that absurdity that invades their stomachs and their brains with nausea. They undergo the temptation of the one truly philosophical gesture, as Novalis calls it — suicide. But suicide would only amount to the suppression of the one element, rational, courageous, and capable of clarity, that protests against the absurd irrationality of a blind universe. Camus rejects suicide, as Schopenhauer had done. He welcomes the paradoxes that Kierkegaard, in his *Journal* for the year 1838, lauded as the true privilege of intellectual life and the hallmark of great thinkers, the ability to proclaim the truths of tomorrow. Existentialism also practices a leap, not the leap of faith, striding over reason to reach 'the absolute Paradox, Christianity' (Kierkegaard), but a transcendence toward other men.

Atheism is the third postulate. It cannot be demonstrated, for no negative proposition can be. But existentialists merely assume that everything takes place as if God did not exist, and they draw the consequences implied in Nietzsche's famous 'death of God.' They spurn the easy solaces of deism and pantheism. Too often, according to these modern negators, God becomes merely a convenient symbol to whom to transfer the burden of our problems and thus evade solving them. Let us transcend ourselves toward men, horizontally and not vertically, and assume our human condition and, most difficult of all, our freedom.

There is thus more stoicism and optimism in existentialism than there is apathy or flippancy. Indeed, these moralists have again and again stressed their difference from Dostoevski's character, Kirilov, who cries in *The Possessed:* 'If God does not exist, everything is allowed.' To them, on the contrary, man must fully assume his duties to himself and to others and set himself up in the place of an absent or silent God. He must create his own essence and accept his total freedom.

The fourth credo of the existentialists is the well-known assertion that existence precedes essence. Man was not created according to a pre-existing mold or pattern, like a table or a knife. He is not just one sample of a general entity called 'human nature.' He is not a shadow in Plato's cave, aspiring to the noble and stable Idea. He was thrown into the world, a derelict; he exists. And the only essence that is conceivable for him is the one that he can progressively create himself, by living. He does not have to fulfill, on this earth, some pre-established plan. Only as he is, here and now, does something begin for him. Man exists; he chooses himself and thereby he chooses other men, too. He creates his own values, indeed his own human nature, through living and especially through projecting himself, transcending the past and the present by throwing himself into the future. 'One is nothing else but one's own life.'

Subjectivity is clearly the starting point for such a philosophy, and here again Kierkegaard is the ancestor. *Sum,* in the famous Cartesian formula, becomes the foe of *cogito.* The Danish thinker said: 'A thinker cannot prove his existence through thought, for insofar as he thinks abstractly, he forgets exactly this: that he exists.' *Sum, ergo cogito.* Man is a subject with a self to acquire, and not an object to be known. The literature of existentialism does not proceed through generalities about man, nature, passions, and the world. It attempts to seize man in the quick, to grasp him in the irreducible uniqueness of his existence. Man is described *en situation,* and in certain conditions that happen to constitute the framework of his existence, and in his 'project.' He fulfills himself, through living, in a world and with a consciousness inextricably welded to each other. *Sein ist Zeit* for him.

The fifth postulate is man's freedom, as fundamental as it is unproved. Man has the freedom of becoming free. He chooses and projects himself toward his choice. This freedom, which man does not want, is a heavy burden and fills with dread the creature who has realized its momentousness. But it is also the greatest single asset of man. For this freedom entails involvement, or *littérature engagée;* it entails the duty of bringing a similar consciousness of man's potential freedom to others, through literary works and political and journalistic action. This freedom must always be reconquered, for it is incessantly in danger of being lost. Existentialist freedom is the basis for responsibility and for a new categorical imperative. Not only must the free person avoid being frozen by an earlier choice and becoming the mere captive of former decisions, for the irreplaceable quality of individual existence would then be dried up, but the existentialist hero must also extend his responsibility to the awakening of placid unprivileged mortals who have not yet assumed the burden of their freedom. One of the favorite existentialist maxims is the declaration of *The Brothers Karamazov:* 'Everyone is responsible for everything before everybody.' [3]

It is clear that the demands made by atheistic existentialism upon the average man are exacting. But existentialist dramas and novels have not yet presented many of the lofty moralists who might personify the ethical ideals of the existentialists, unless it be Orestes in *Les Mouches (The Flies).* Existentialist literature, however, cannot remain a literature of passivity and of the acceptance of one's lower depths. Complacent as it may be at times toward the paludean stretches in which inverts, weaklings, idle drinkers, and sex-obsessed men and women like to wallow, it usually becomes a literature that transcends the baser sides of human nature and advocates the resolute assumption of man's duties to himself and to others. A few declarations by Sartre in his very important and inspiring volume *Qu'est-ce que la littérature? (What Is Literature?)* will some day find a place in anthologies of moral sayings of our century.

> There is no such thing as a given freedom. One must conquer oneself over passions, race, class, nation, and one must conquer other men along with oneself.

3. These postulates of freedom and responsibility raise a multitude of questions and objections, which we are not attempting to enumerate here. Sartre will doubtless answer some of them in his book on ethics. For does man choose the good? And what is the good? Sartre has defined evil as a pure luxury, a gratuitous activity, which presupposes much vigilance and a perpetual inventiveness akin to genius. But his dramatic embodiment of Evil in his play *Le Diable et le Bon Dieu* (Gallimard, 1951) is mechanically contrived and unconvincing.

Every one of our acts has, as its stake, the meaning of the world and the place of man in the universe. Through each of them, whether we wish it or not, we set up a scale of values which is universal. And one would want us not to experience dread and anguish in the face of such a momentous responsibility!

The literary artist in Sartre is not a mere adjunct to the philosopher; his dramas and novels are not artificial arrangements designed to fit into a preordained pattern or to prove a thesis. We even believe that plays like *Les Mains sales* and *Le Diable et le Bon Dieu* and stories like *Intimité* may be enjoyed more keenly and understood more deeply by readers who do not seek in them the expression of any existentialist secrets.

Sartre, like many other thinkers and writers, in spite of his uncanny virtuosity, is probably a living embodiment of an internal contradiction. His conscious desire is to raise man above his nausea and to direct him, through his own free choice, toward heroism; but attaining heroism, as Sartre has acknowledged, is no easy affair. The pages that Sartre seems to have written with the greatest gusto and that come easiest to him are woefully devoid of conventional beauty, though not of the poetry of evil: in the mournful scene in *Le Sursis* (*The Reprieve*), which draws together two pitiful disabled beings amid foul smells, in *L'Enfance d'un chef,* in the obsession with abortion, and in the indigestible complacence with which he analyzed Jean Genet, Sartre has expressed an almost Jansenist and relentless obstinacy in depicting the irretrievable defilement of man. Even if one takes into account the implied existentialist contention that life has constantly to be lived under the threat of disintegration, one may regret Sartre's unprotesting acceptance of all that is viscous, moist, and lush, and his assimilation of human flesh to crawling slugs. Malraux, Saint-Exupéry, and Camus himself have proved more responsive to the deeper message voiced by Nietzsche in his beautiful avowal: 'In man, there is matter, fragment, excess, clay, mud, folly, chaos; but in man there is also a creator, a sculptor, the hardness of the hammer and the divine contemplation of the seventh day.'

Sartre's nausea, however, is, or should be, a temporary *ascesis,* an inverted mystical experience or a visitation from outside objects, which upsets the selfish quietude of a life and forces the mind to start abruptly again *ex nihilo* and to revise all its values. It is not unlike Descartes' methodical doubt. The veneer of falsehood, which concealed authenticity in things and persons, is scraped off. From mere existence, the victim, who is also the victor, of the nausea passes on to being and reaches toward his own essence.

La Nausée (*The Nausea* in the American translation and *The Diary of Antoine Roquentin* in the British version, which preceded the American) is a remarkable novel — one of the masterpieces of the twentieth century. When it appeared in the summer of 1938, some of the less conventional French critics hailed it at once as a resounding literary debut. It has the fresh impetuousness of a youthful or an early novel, the joy of an amused, yet savage, revolt against the sham values of one's environment, the audacious mingling of philosophy and fiction, and more poetry of its kind than perhaps any other work by Sartre.

The novel is the diary of Antoine Roquentin, in Bouville (le Havre), a scholar-thinker, whose achievement thus far has been disappointing. He is thirty, has some money of his own, is red-haired and rather ugly, has never married, and has a capricious and tenderly scornful mistress, Annie, whom he visits in Paris at the end of the novel. She has a passion for playing at transfiguring life around her and reaching 'perfect moments' by ignoring or altering the data of the real and sticky world. Like not a few excellent novels, *La Nausée* is an ironical work. It includes a virtuoso's satire of Proustian privileged moments, of the personal novel and the journal à la Gide, and even of classical funeral orations and of the pompous gallery of ancestors' pictures in Hugo's *Hernani*. All the parts are harmonized in an impeccably composed novel. Indeed, more justly than the Proustian novel, it could be compared to a symphony, with unforgettable scenes, such as the Sunday-afternoon walk of the Bouville inhabitants, and the epic tour of the provincial museum climaxing in the now famous cry: 'Farewell, beautiful lilies, elegantly enshrined in your painted sanctuaries, good-by, lovely lilies, our pride and our reason for living! Good-by, you bastards [*salauds*]!" Several of the more concrete scenes, such as the meditation on the bluish suspenders of the *café* waiter, the pompous and fake strutting of the self-taught man in the local library, the personality of the dreary provincial boulevard, all setting off the unauthentic bad faith in which one is bogged down, are equal to anything in Flaubert and Zola.

Little happens outwardly and little need happen. Roquentin is working on a historical biography in which he never seems to become engrossed; he sleeps with the coarse woman who owns his favorite *café;* he meets in the library the self-taught man, a farcical creature, who is a cruel caricature not only of Flaubert's Pécuchet but of any scholar who has been professionally deformed to the extent of never entertaining a single idea that is his own and of resting content only if it has already been expressed before by some revered name. He acquires culture voraciously, through asking for all the books in the library, one after the other in alphabetical order. In the end, his grotesque comedy is exploded: he is discovered by the Corsican employee, who has all along resented handing down the books to him, to be a pederast, making advances to young visitors of the sanctum of dead knowledge.

But the drama lies in Roquentin's sudden experience of nausea. A sickening feeling takes hold of him when a new aspect of objects is suddenly unveiled for him: their opaque, absurd existence. He realizes that we cannot receive any consciousness of the outside world except as a projection of our own minds. He is oppressed by the slimy viscosity of things, of people, of his own flesh reflected in a mirror, of his eyes, like fish scales, of all that is like a repellent polyp in him. The veil that seemed to prettify things has been torn open. Everything now seems meaningless, in the way, gratuitous, *de trop.* He, too, is *de trop.* He, and all that is, appears contingent, superfluous. His own irreversible past stretches as a mere disconnected succession of events. He is seized, not with fear of objects, but with the anguish with which his immense responsibility overwhelms him. Blessed with such an inverted 'mystical' ecstasy, he returns to the world of men as if he were alienated from him, like a crab or some crawling beast. He knows the meaning of existence.

> I too wanted to be. I wanted nothing else. I now see clearly through the apparent disorder of my life. At bottom . . . I only wished to banish existence out of me, . . . Then the pitiful fellow that I was has understood and opened his eyes . . . He thought: I am a fool. Just then, on the other side of existence, in that other world which one can see from afar but never come close to, a little melody ('Some of these days, you're gonna miss me, honey') began to dance and sing: 'You must be like me; you must suffer in tune.'

Sartre's next volume, though of more limited range and closer to phenomenological description than to any metaphysical revelation, is also a masterpiece of storytelling and of humor. For, contrary to what blind or prejudiced critics of Sartre have contended, he is no exception to the saying that no great intelligence is devoid of the comic spirit. The five stories that make up the volume *Le Mur* (*The Wall*) have become classics, collected (with a few expurgations) in college anthologies.

The most moving is 'La Chambre,' which concretely displays the bad faith of Pierre, the husband, who went a few steps further than Roquentin and voluntarily deluded himself into perceiving things in a way different from that of 'normal' people. He is crazy. He lives with his favorite visions in a room; and his wife, Eve, though aware that Pierre in no way needs her, insists upon playing up to him and sharing his schizophrenic existence.

'Le Mur' is a masterly treatment, achieved in a dry, restrained, Hemingway-like manner, of the attitude of man toward death, a theme that is one of Sartre's concerns in his philosophical *Summa*. A Basque, captured by the Spanish soldiers of Franco, does not analyze himself or meditate when faced with execution. He knows no big words like immortality, regret, suffering. In a graphic manner, he witnesses and describes the future that is being obliterated, the essential absurdity of everything. He does not try to behave heroically but, playing a trick on his torturers, he gives them a false lead, which ironically proves to be true and brings about the arrest of his companion, for whom they were hunting.

'Intimité' is probably the most successful and the most entertaining interior monologue in French literature. Lulu, an empty-headed Parisian girl, married to an impotent but good-looking husband, quarrels pathetically with him, leaves him, on the advice of a girl friend, who insists upon making her heroic, to join a lover, becomes remorseful and, as far as she is capable of it, anguished, and returns to her weak and pompous husband. All of the characters are glaring illustrations of bad faith: the husband because he will not accept himself for what he is; Lulu because she vacillates and will not confess that an impotent husband is, to her (half Lesbian), more restful and safer than a possessive and carnal lover; the lover because he is a bourgeois at heart and dares not confess that he would be bored were he to elope with Lulu and break with the safe routine of life with his mother and father.

There is more strain and some artificiality in 'Erostrate,' the story of a weakling who tries to become a gratuitous criminal in order to live in the memories of men, like the ancient who, to attain glory, set fire to the temple in Ephesus.

There is more crudity, but an unrivaled satirical gift in 'L'Enfance d'un chef,' a mock biography of an ambitious and vain middle-class character, who espouses all the literary fashions and all the vices of the years 1920–40. Unlike Roquentin, he flees his own nonexistence and joins anti-Semitic and fascist groups in order to delude himself that 'he belongs' and that there is more in him than gelatinous amorphousness.

Three volumes of *Les Chemins de la liberté* (*The Roads to Freedom*) have appeared, the first two, *L'Age de raison* and *Le Sursis*, in French in 1945, the third, *Le Mort dans l'âme*, in 1949. They have all been translated, the first two by Eric Sutton [4] and the third by Gerard Hopkins [5] under the title *Troubled Sleep*. While they met with considerable success, especially in Europe, it is our conviction that the superb skill of the author and their immense significance as sheer literary works have been underrated by many hasty or hostile reviewers. Two easy escapes were offered to critics, who could not remain unaware of Sartre's immense importance in world letters: one was to brand him as immoral and pessimistic, whereas no great writer has perhaps been more concerned with the formulation of moral values. His outlook on life has been called, by a very lucid critic, Oleg Koefoed, from a Protestant, earnest, and 'bourgeois' country, Denmark, 'the most rashly optimistic humanism which our generation has produced.' The other was to acknowledge Sartre's triumph as a dramatist (and it is indeed dazzling),[6] but to add in the same breath that, as a novelist, he was a failure. Our conviction is that not only *La Nausée* but *Les Chemins de la liberté* (*The Roads to Freedom*) tower above most European fiction of the years 1935–55.

Even in his hatred of the flesh and in his cruder pages, Sartre has remained a moralist and, as the French say, *un grand timide*, whose psychoanalysis would doubtless reveal him as an unusually

4. Alfred A. Knopf, New York, 1947.
5. Alfred A. Knopf, New York, 1951.
6. Even so, a great many cultured American readers and students, admitting that the two early dramas by Sartre were great achievements, will treat with condescension *Morts sans sépulture*, which is in no sense a sensational melodrama but a masterly study of pride, as one of the masks of bad faith, in the tortured resistance fighters. They pour out their scorn upon *La Putain respectueuse*, in which the Americans, who, since Tocqueville remarked upon it, have always been mortified at being misunderstood in Europe, have insisted in seeing a crude treatment of the Negro problem. Sartre intended nothing of the kind. The prostitute, Lizzie, and the innocent Negro are, in the eyes of the author, the true villains of the play. They lack the courage to revolt, to assume their responsibilities. They bow to prejudices through sentimentality, inadequate intellectual force, and the same fear of freedom that crushed Electra's early passionate revolt in *Les Mouches*.

sensitive orphan, hurt, like Baudelaire and Hamlet, by his mother's second marriage and wounded in his early idealization of women by his lack of facile grace and of superficial 'good looks.' The sound and the fury raised by some outraged Pharisees about Sartre's unromantic delineation of love have too easily blinded some readers to the highly perspicacious analysis of love and of sexuality in his works. The pages on love, desire, hatred, and sadism (pages 431 and following) in *L'Etre et le néant* go very deep and take for granted the truth that man is originally and fundamentally a sexual being, and aware of it, just as he is the only animal with the awareness that he will die (or so we claim). Love must be free, that is, without tyranny or sadism. The lover cries:

> My existence is, because it is called for. In so far as I assume it, it becomes pure generosity. I am because I give myself lavishly . . . Instead of feeling ourselves as superfluous [*de trop*], we now experience that our existence is prolonged and willed in its slightest details by an absolute freedom that, at the same time, it conditions, and that we want to deserve through our own freedom. In this lies the deepest element of our joy in loving, when it exists: that we feel justified in existing.

It is well-nigh impossible to summarize Sartre's novel, because its center is to be found neither in the plot or plots nor in the characters in the traditional sense. The protagonist is, once again, a professor, as was the case in the very early story written and published by Sartre at the age of eighteen, 'L'Ange du morbide.' Ever since he had broken a beautiful ancient vase at the age of seven as a gesture toward freedom and then, upon reading Spinoza at twenty-one, had decided to be in nature 'not like a subject, but like an empire within an empire,' reversing Spinoza's formula, Mathieu had been yearning for freedom. But he is no man of action or of determination. He has little will power, and he analyzes and ponders every problem, displaying his own flabbiness pitilessly. The others, however, respect him and cannot conceal their awe in the presence of a philosophy teacher who attends all their parties, lives unconventionally like them, but all the while pursues elusive freedom.

He has had a mistress, Marcelle, for several years. She appears in the book as not particularly attractive and as unusually sedate and weak-willed. She is now pregnant and, having few illusions about her lover's passion for remaining unattached, free from responsibility, and available for the visitation of freedom devoutly wished for by him, she is hardly surprised when he advises her to have an abortion. Mathieu, however, is disturbed by his act and by the little creature whom he will thus keep from ever existing. He silences his scruples and gets the money needed for a first-class clandestine 'operation' from his disciple Boris, who steals it from his mistress. But he is nonplussed when a friend of his, Daniel, offers to marry Marcelle and father the child.

Mathieu wallows in bad faith and unauthenticity, merely enjoying a mockery of freedom. Daniel lives in worse falsehood still: he is a homosexual who has not been able to accept himself for what he is. A concealed shame, hence a tormenting hatred for himself and for others, rules his every act. He is the ideal sado-masochist, who looks in vain for his own redemption in his 'generous' offer to Marcelle, who cowardly accepts it. Lola, a singer, a passionate and tragic woman whose mellow ripeness fills her with a desperate fear of losing her very young lover, Boris, and Ilich, also of Russian origins, an intelligent, peevish, unpredictable girl, not far remote from Xavière in Simone de Beauvoir's *L'Invitée* (*She Came to Stay*), are the other women portrayed. Mathieu feels attracted by Ilich, emulates her semimystical and masochistic gesture when, at a party, she pierces her hand with a knife, and is fascinated by her adolescent coldness, yet he refuses her when at last she offers herself to him. Boris, Ilich's brother, an admiring student of Mathieu, is a caricature of the disciple, like the famulus of Goethe's *Faust*, but a caricature delineated with warmth by Sartre; he has more ebullience and more naturalness than most of the other characters in the volume.

The actors in the dramatic fresco of *L'Age de raison* (*The Age of Reason*) seem to wade hopelessly through the marshes of the prewar world. Only one of them, the communist Brunet, has resolutely decided for *engagement,* for abdication of any further choice through affiliation with the Communist party and support of the Spanish republicans. Mathieu, as he himself confesses, sedulously tills the inner garden of his freedom, mistaking availability to any future whatever for freedom, awaiting, like Orestes in *Les Mouches* (*The Flies*), the ideal free act, his own freely elected deed, which would dispel his dreary complacence in his wasted Parisian years. He is now thirty-four; he has kept shy of political ties, of ideological affiliations, of patriotic *élans,* of any velleities of reforming the world, and of course of marriage. But, as Dr. Johnson said long ago and as Kafka has echoed, if marriage has many pains, celibacy has few joys. Mathieu is aware of his own desiccation, and, having read Hegel on the unhappy conscience, he has diagnosed the gnawing worms in him: bad faith and cowardice.

Le Sursis, which displayed Sartre's virtuosity in handling, better than John Dos Passos himself, the simultaneous technique of *Manhattan Transfer* and *U.S.A.,* is astonishingly clever. The reader wonders whether Sartre, like Picasso — Sartre and he have the same cool mastery in handling the new and the unpredictable, the same tantalizing knack for carrying off successfully tightrope acrobatics — has not starved his genius to feed his talent and his greed for experimenting. But Sartre's attempt was not that of the effete traditional novelist, laboriously building up characters whose dreary continuity seems unaffected by the momentous events in which they are immersed. He has vehemently repudiated the convenient faith in a stable, universal human nature, entertained by the classical writers of France, and has stressed man's perpetually fluid behavior.

His purpose was to embrace the variegated and discordant unity of Western Europe in the tragic week of September 1938, which preceded the surrender of Chamberlain and Daladier at Munich. Few of those who lived through those days and nights of anxiety and shame and saw the abject intellectual dishonesty of men who deluded themselves into believing they had achieved peace in our time will refuse to proclaim the truth and the power of Sartre's portrayal. Unanimism is at play here, far more felicitously than anywhere in Romains's works; the actors or the puppets in the tragicomedy of Europe are delineated with a concrete vigor and a skill in vivid dialogue that make many of the pretentiously symbolic and cerebral novels of the present time appear unreal and sham.

Daniel has hardly changed since the crisis in the first volume in which he attempted to drown his cats before his contemplated suicide, then toyed with the idea of mutilating himself so as to be free forever from his pederastic urges, and finally justified himself in his own eyes through playing the archangel for Marcelle. He will emerge fully in the third volume, when the reign of evil has spread over France with the defeat. And heroism may well save him, too, when, in the fourth volume, Sartre portrays the resistance to the German occupiers. Charles, a paralytic from Berck, evacuated under gruesome conditions with a whole trainload of invalids, 'rising' to a disgusting and yet pathetic copulation with another human wreck, is a bold and powerful character.

The adolescent, Philippe, even Mathieu's sister-in-law at Juan les Pins, and other episodic characters compel belief, as do the boisterously comic adventures of the illiterate shepherd from Prades, Jean-Louis. The humble fellow will never understand what the mobilization was all about or why he was buffeted by a fate personified by malicious men, greedy prostitutes, and the blind machinery of the army. But he rings truer than any heroes of Maupassant or of Courteline, and he provides the proof, if one were needed, that Sartre can depict people far removed from professors, phenomenological introspectives, and idlers of Montparnasse *cafés*.

The hydra of war reaching over men, aghast and powerless, enables Mathieu to cast a backward glance, ironically bitter, at his vain search for a false freedom. He had thought he could treasure up his leisure, his comfort, and his refusal of all family, party, and other social bonds. But, like a sponge, life had perfidiously absorbed the slimy semblance of freedom he had cultivated. In a classical meditation on the Pont-Neuf, at the end of *Le Sursis*, he realizes his error. His liberty had been there all along, at hand; he was *it*. It does not descend upon one like an illumination of delight, a tongue of fire. Freedom does not come laden with comforting presents; it is grave and massive, 'a plenitude.' 'Freedom is exile and I am condemned to be free.'

War is only delayed by the reprieve of Munich, and, when it comes, Mathieu will not turn overnight into a flamboyant warrior. The path to freedom and perhaps to heroism is an arduous one. (Sartre, remembering Gide's and Mauriac's warnings about the impossibility of portraying noble feelings and saints, must be pondering lengthily his fourth volume, now overdue.) *La Mort dans l'âme* still resorts to the devices of simultaneity bewilderingly used in *Le Sursis*. But there is more continuity within each chapter, and more concessions are thus made to the reader's laziness. Moreover, while Munich impressed western Europeans as Sartre depicts it, as a senseless shake-up of all illusions, in which placid and selfish beings like Mathieu were nothing but peas suddenly mashed up in the crushing of a big can, the defeat of France stressed again the barriers behind which countries sought to convince themselves that the wretched fate of France could in no case be theirs. A Spanish republican in New York, who represents the attitude of some of the European refugees in America, is aware that the events of June 1940 meant defeat for all liberals and for civilization, yet he sees in the oppression of France a punishment for her betrayal of the Spanish republicans and the Czechs. Boris has become a determined fighter. Mathieu has witnessed, as a participant, the disorderly retreat. He now stirs up other French soldiers to re-organize and to shoot the approaching Germans. It will be of no avail and he knows it; the armistice is then being signed. But through the ordeal of fire he will emerge a new man.

Sartre has been accused of lacking warmth and sensibility. But sensibility need not be declamatory and does not necessarily lie at the opposite pole to the superb intelligence, one of the broadest since Goethe and Renan, which marks the existentialist leader. Though cold and insensitive, the man who wrote 'La République du silence,' 'Paris sous l'occupation' in the third volume of *Situations*, the impassioned evocations of torture and injustice in *Qu'est-ce que la littérature?*, and the chapters in the third volume of *Les Chemins de la liberté*, devoted to the communist Brunet, bolstering up the morale of his companions in a German prison camp, has produced some of the most moving passages in modern fiction. (Sartre had a firsthand acquaintance with prison camps in 1940–41, until he was released because of his deficient eyesight; he then engaged in the resistance movement.) We do not believe there is anything more telling, more restrained and, since the word must be used in spite of Sartre's *pudeur*, more noble in spirit in the abundant literature devoted by the French to the ordeal of captivity.

Sartre's fiction is original on many counts. First of all, his mastery of the language is extraordinary. And few significant works of our age, since Joyce and Mallarmé, can afford to ignore the problems and the pitfalls of language. The flashes of poetry in prose, which illuminate the novels of Malraux and of Giono, are absent from Sartrian fiction. Metaphors are scarce, but they are precise, convincing, and sharply delineated. Sheer adornments are spurned by him, as well as the music of prose. But the great moments when the characters, suddenly aware of their existence or of their nascent freedom, seem to be favored with a gift of second sight are impregnated with a severe and precise beauty, not unlike that of Stendhal, without his fondness for dreams. Above all, Sartre's mastery is conspicuous in some of his dialogues, in an interior monologue purified of much of the irrelevancy and insignificance of the genre, and in his unorthodox use of the spoken language. With less artificiality than Céline or than Queneau, Sartre has successfully broken with the romantic illusion that interposes a pretty screen of words between the reader and the scene represented. His language welcomes slang, profanity, and obscenity. It catches up with the least conventional spoken language, as written words had not done for a whole century, in spite of Wordsworth's rebellion against poetic diction and of Hugo's *mettant un bonnet rouge au vieux dictionnaire.* Not only does it thus translate an individual, specific, and concrete reality without betraying it and without imprisoning it in abstract categories, it revivifies French through integrating into the written style all the fluid and picturesque, or malodorous, wealth of the language of the common people.

Then, in spite of many assertions to the contrary, Sartrian fiction avoids most of the dangers of philosophical literature, and it gains, in our opinion, far more than it loses, in paralleling an arresting philosophy. Sartre's early novel, *Défaite,* written in his teens and destroyed for lack of a publisher, his early story, 'L'Ange du morbide,' and even *La Nausée* seem to indicate that he was, even in terms of chronology, a literary artist before he was a philosopher. Whatever philosophy there is in his fiction and in his plays is not artificially and didactically placed there, as might be said to have been the case with Balzac and Tolstoy, and even more so with Bourget and Romains. He creates and endows with autonomous life his own universe. The main postulates of Sartre's philosophy are to a certain extent present in his fiction. But they are no longer assertions dialectically presented; they are lived situations. There are no essences, and therefore no types, no general categories, no universal human nature, no harmonious consistency in man. There is no determinism, and man is not to be 'explained' ponderously by all the shackles that bind him to his environment and to his past. Freedom alone, slowly and painfully conquered, can constitute an exit from a world that would otherwise be a purposeless, loveless, derelict abode of viscousness and cowardice.

The novels of Sartre thus stand in reaction both to naturalism and to intellectual analysis. Existentialism as conceived by Sartre, despite some superficial similarities with the stories of men adrift, dear to Zola and the early Huysmans, despite the dreary humiliation of sex lengthily described by the same writers in *Pot-Bouille* and elsewhere, is a revulsion from the materialistic and deterministic novel of Zola, Maupassant, Dreiser, even of Hardy and Heinrich Mann, to the extent that they might be called naturalists. For Sartre, man is not determined by heredity and environment, and only to a very limited extent by his past. He himself is his own Prometheus, as Michelet would have put it. He always remains unpredictable, free to break with what he has been and to elect a new path. Within each of Sartre's characters there is indeterminacy and the possibility of accomplishing a new action, which will stand totally unconnected with previous actions and inconsistent with other features of the characters as they had previously appeared. In a revealing interview, granted on November 24, 1945, to Mme Dominique Aury and published in *Les Lettres Françaises*, Sartre declared:

> Every one of my characters, after having done anything may still do anything whatever . . . I never calculate whether the act is credible according to previous ones, but I take the situation and a freedom chained in situation . . . In Zola, everything obeys the strictest determinism. His books are written in the past, while my characters have a future . . . With Mathieu, for example, the situation which he slowly created for himself is of consequence. He is bound hand and foot by his mistress and by his culture. He himself forged his own links. He is much too clearsighted for psychoanalysis to be of any usefulness to him; this is moreover true for all intellectuals . . . He is still waiting for God, I mean for something outside him to beckon to him. But he will only have the cause which he will have decided to be his own.

Proustian analysis is treated with no less severity, and Mauriac's technique of leading his heroes by a leash to God come up for even harsher criticism. Such analysis appears to Sartre as the luxury of a select leisure class, trained in self-contemplation and cherishing every nuance of its enjoyment of nature, of food, of art and of the delicious 'reciprocal torture' of love. It went as far as it could go with Proust, Joyce, and Mann; it perhaps even became lost in a blind alley. But this analytical literature no longer fully answered the demands of a new and less cultured public and of a generation that had endured the material and spiritual agonies of World War II and German concentration camps. Many young men discovered that Dostoevski, Malraux, and Faulkner had a truer ring for them. The French, who had hitherto constituted the ideal audience for the novel of analysis, went over to the side of the unanalytical novel of action and violence translated from the American. Sartre proclaimed how significant to him and to his generation the discovery of Dos Passos, Hemingway, and Faulkner had proved.[7] His own novels tend to set off the truths that man per-

7. *The Atlantic Monthly*, August 1946.

ceives when he least expects them and when a new quality in objects is suddenly revealed to him.[8]

Lastly, much has been written, often glibly, on the pessimism of existentialist fiction. There is far more pessimism in Thomas Mann's stories of decrepitude and of the inevitable unbalance of genius, in Cesare Pavese's and in Alberto Moravia's novels, indeed in almost all modern Italian literature, and in three-fourths of American letters, Mark Twain and John Dos Passos not excepted, and William Faulkner himself included in spite of his official speeches, than there is in recent French literature. There was infinitely more obsession with decadence and death in Flaubert and his contemporaries, between 1850 and 1870, than there has been in our own age.

To be sure, some form of pessimism is rampant around us today. But it is, we believe, a very different pessimism from that of the nineteen-twenties, much less cynical and complacent, more courageous and more constructive. The men and women of 1920–30 had tried to forget a war they considered as a huge mistake and to resume, freed from all remnants of Puritanism and from bourgeois morality, a search for happiness, often conceived as mere pleasure, once hampered and then interrupted. Their literature refused *engagement* and closed its eyes to tragedy. It took the American depression, the advent of Hitler in Germany, the vogue of Russia as the new land of promise, and the threat of an impending new war to arouse the writers of the early thirties out of the shallow optimism of the preceding years. The Spanish civil war and the defeat and occupation of France were then the two great creative events in thought and literature. Catastrophes had not been forestalled. They had to be lived through.

Existentialism does not ignore despair. But it attempts to lead away from it after having drunk from its cup to the dregs. 'The gravest form of despair,' said Kierkegaard, 'is not to be desperate, not to be aware of one's despair.' Faith in a divine providence is rejected. Faith in progress is rejected likewise, or at least critically re-examined. Faith in the innate goodness of man has been ex-

8. Similarly, in a remarkable manifesto, 'Forgers of Myths: the Young Playwrights of France' (*Theatre Arts,* June 1946), Sartre declared that, for the existentialist dramatists, 'man is not to be defined as a "reasoning animal" or as a "social" one, but as a free being, entirely indeterminate, who must choose his own being when confronted with certain necessities . . . we wish to put on the stage certain situations which throw light on the main aspects of the condition of man and to have the spectators participate in the free choice which man makes in these situations.'

ploded by the spectacle of wars, of concentration camps, of man's
inhumanity to man. Fear is with us, and it has spread to the New
World, once immune from it. Like the conscience in existentialist
doctrines, it gnaws like a worm in the fruit, at our unequaled
prosperity and at our worship of science, education, and good
neighborliness.

The usefulness of existentialist literature, regardless of its aesthetic value, is in its rejection of the delusions through which
modern man often attempts to forget the duties he must assume.
It is deliberately modern, and, as Sartre put it in a famous manifesto, one must write for one's own time. It thus spurns the easy
escape of many scholars who, heirs to a nineteenth-century tradition, seek the explanation of the present in the past and of modern
man in the study of primitive societies — the matriarchate among
the Polynesians, incest among the Amazon tribes, or the swaddling
clothes of Russian babies. Existentialism is a socially conscious
literature, which fights with equal ardor communism on its left
and the middle class on its right; the one has abdicated critical
spirit and freedom, the other suffers from a Hegelian bad conscience and dares not face the future; it is pitiful in its good will
and in its maze of contradictions, but it is sterile. 'The freedom
to write,' Sartre asserts in his remarkable *Qu'est-ce que la littérature?*, 'presupposes the freedom of the citizen. One does not write
for slaves. Prose-writing is bound up in solidarity with the only
regime in which prose retains a meaning: democracy . . . To
write is another way of wanting freedom.' Marxist materialism
has been dealt grievous blows by Sartre and Merleau-Ponty, for the
existentialists reject the acrobatics through which good and evil
play off against each other in the dialectical pursuit of the synthesis. But they stand equally firm against the easy solace of religion or the comfort of philosophical idealism, for which evil is
merely a shadow necessarily accompanying the good. If elsewhere
Sartre may be charged with excessive *virtuosité* and even with
sophistry, he has written, in *Qu'est-ce que la littérature?* and in
Réflexions sur la question juive, some of the most moving and
most definitive pages of our age. Better than any other French
writer since Bergson, or earlier still, since Renan and Voltaire,
he has combined clarity and depth, a tragic feeling for life and
the conviction that man has not yet said his last word. Through
revolting against God, or against one of the successive conceptions
of God that man has made for himself, the modern hero who has
plumbed the depths of absurdity and of anxiety and discarded the

illusions of mechanical progress teaches and practices self-reliance and holds out a beacon in the night, which threatens, or lures, us today.

In words that aptly render the moral attitude that is Sartre's as well as his own, Camus has stated the existentialist position, deprived of all philosophical subtleties and expressed with forthrightness and nobleness:

> We refuse to despair of man. Without having any exaggerated ambition to save him, we hold at least to the idea of serving him . . . To the last we shall reject a divine charity that would deprive men of the justice which is their due.

And elsewhere, after defining his position:

> Is this pessimism? No. This is an honest effort to determine what is wanted, what is unwanted . . . We, young Frenchmen, label as pessimists those who say that all goes well and that nothing changes human nature. We call them pessimists, because they are among those from whom nothing can be expected. *They* will be to blame if the world indeed never changes. But there are among us enough men of decision pledged to do all that is within their power to cure the world and themselves of their present sickness.

BIBLIOGRAPHICAL NOTES

Kenneth Douglas has published an extremely useful critical bibliography of French existentialism (Yale French Studies Monographs, No. 1, 1950) to which we may conveniently refer the reader. The number of articles and books on Sartre and on existentialism, in a dozen languages at least, is already prodigious. The best works, from a philosophical angle, are the essays of Jean Beaufret and A. de Waehlens mentioned in Douglas's bibliography, the book by Robert Campbell, *Sartre ou une littérature philosophique* (Ardent, 1945), and Francis Jeanson, *Le Problème moral et la pensée de Sartre* (Myrte, 1947).

In English, James Collins, *The Existentialists: A Critical Study* (Henry Regnery, Chicago, 1952), is a solid volume from a Catholic viewpoint. Oreste Pucciani's article, 'Existentialism,' in *Modern Language Forum* (XXXV, 1–2, March 1950, pp. 1–13), is wise and well informed. The first number of *Yale French Studies* (1948) entirely devoted to existentialism, has lost little of its value. Margaret Walker has a good article 'The Nausea of Sartre' in the *Yale Review* (XLII, 2, winter 1953), and Marjorie Grene wrote a penetrating volume, *Dreadful Freedom: A Critique of Existentialism* (University of Chicago Press, Chicago, 1948).

The Italians have written prolifically on Sartre. A partial bibliography of Italian works is appended to a well-informed book by Carlo Falconi, J. P. *Sartre* (Guarda, Modena, 1948). So have religious writers and theologians: Roger Troisfontaines, *Le Choix de Sartre* (Aubier, 1945) and two Benedictines, H. Paissac, *Le Dieu de Sartre* (Arthaud, Grenoble, 1950), and Benoit Pruche, *L'Homme de Sartre* (Arthaud, Grenoble, 1949).

One of the most valuable of all studies is by the Dane, Oleg Koefoed, 'L'Oeuvre littéraire de Sartre' (*Orbis Litterarum*, VI, 1948, pp. 209–72 and VII, 1949, pp. 61–141). The slim volume by R. M. Albères, *Sartre* (Editions Universitaires, Paris, 1953), is an intelligent introduction.

From the literary angle, some of the best French essays are those by Maurice Blanchot, 'Les Romans de Sartre' (*L'Arche*, October 1945, and in *La Part du Feu*, Gallimard, 1949, pp. 195–211); Claude-Edmonde Magny in *Esprit* (March 1945, pp. 564–80 and April 1945, pp. 708–24), in *Poésie* 46 (No. 29, January 1946, pp. 58–67), and in her book *Les Sandales d'Empédocle* (La Baconnière, Neuchâtel, 1945, pp. 105–172); Gaëtan Picon, in *Confluences* (V, 8, October 1945, pp. 883–90); and Claude Roy in *Poésie* 47 (VIII, 38, March 1947, pp. 35–49).

ALBERT CAMUS AND SIMONE

DE BEAUVOIR

THE POSITION of Albert Camus in modern French letters is still a controversial one. None of his books has been a recognized masterpiece; his plays have been moderately successful but reproved for not being dramatic in the usual manner; and his philosophical thinking has been criticized, not altogether unjustly, for being loose, unoriginal, and sentimental. Yet his success, which has aroused not a little envy in several quarters, has been immense. Within the ten years after *L'Etranger,* which first revealed Camus's talent in 1942, its author had won more admirers among the youth of France and of other countries than any other French writer except Malraux. The French, always gratified when they can stress their divisions, have rejoiced in opposing Camus to Sartre and in siding with the one or the other.

Camus was born in 1913 in or near Algiers. There are a number of Africans in contemporary French literature, as there once were in Latin letters (Amrouche, Mouloudji, and Memmi), and Camus has voiced the hopes and the social aspirations of those young men who have grown up around the harbors of Algiers and Oran, intoxicated with sunlight and the Mediterranean sea, accepting the pleasures of the flesh with pagan simplicity. There is mixed blood in their veins: Arab, Berber or Jewish, Spanish, Italian or French. Camus's mother was Spanish, and his father, whose death in World War I made his childhood difficult, was a man of humble condition, whose grandparents had emigrated to Algeria from Alsace after 1871.

Noces, first published in 1939, is a romantic hymn to life, to joy, and to pagan beauty. It celebrates the wedding of the sun and the sea, vigorous young bodies swimming voluptuously in the clear blue water, the embrace of feminine flesh. 'Except the sun, kisses and wild perfumes, all seems futile to us . . . There is but one love in this world. To embrace a woman's body is also to hold close to oneself that strange joy which descends from the sky to the sea . . . There is no shame in being happy.' The style of the young writer has already reached sonorous cadences and a poetical finish, with none of the luxuriance or crudity in which Giono indulges. A lyrical meditation at Fiesole, in the last section of *Noces,* ranks among the finest French pages that have been inspired by the Italian landscape. But, in the land where Giotto and Fra Angelico painted, Camus spurns the worship of death and the 'amiable jokes,' as he terms them, of paradise and hell. 'There is only one sin against life,' he exclaims, 'that is not so much to despair of it as to set one's hopes on another life and to blind oneself to the implacable greatness of this one.' With the intransigence of youth, he spurns all the lies and disguises with which we cover up death. Death is horrible, but he wishes to retain his horror of it and to exalt life, even at the cost of thus increasing life's absurdity. In his play *Caligula,* the first version of which, prefiguring Hitler's monstrosities, antedated World War II, he lent to his protagonist the complaint that will set the mad emperor on his furious course: 'Men die, and they are not happy.'

The concept of absurdity became essential to Camus. A robust, athletic young man, successful in his studies (he specialized in philosophy at the University of Algiers), confident in the future, Camus was suddenly diagnosed as tubercular, and most of his hopes were blighted. Soon after, came Munich; then the European war and the collapse of France occurred. The young man in his late twenties was confronted with a wall of the absurd. To him, this constituted the starting point of all meditation, the *tabula rasa* that must precede any clear-sighted reconstruction. Man wants rationality, and he is faced everywhere by the irrational. He is impelled by the will to control and steer his fate, but he is chained by blind and evil forces. He is athirst for freedom, fraternity, soli-

darity, and everywhere he encounters a selfish social order, a
dried-up bureaucracy, a mechanized world readied for the imper-
sonal slaughter of modern war. Man waits for a voice from Heaven
but receives only the answer of eternal silence. He feels dissonant
in this cruel world (dissonance is the original meaning of absurdity), *de trop,* unwanted and insignificant, and the temptation of
suicide follows fast upon the realization of such all-pervading absurdity. 'There is but one truly serious philosophical problem:
that of suicide.' Thus opens Camus's philosophical essay, *Le Mythe
de Sisyphe* (1942).

Like Schopenhauer, who had pondered the same problem and
concluded that suicide would merely play into the hands of the
perfidious will to live, Camus decides against such an inane gesture. For self-slaughter merely cancels the conscious revolt and
silences the voice that protests against injustice and senselessness;
it actually consents to absurdity. Revolt, not suicide, is the one
courageous protest against the absurd; and the revolt of the
thinker and of the artist is the most disinterested of all. 'Art and
nothing but art,' said Nietzsche in an aphorism that Camus likes
to quote. 'We have art in order not to die from truth.'

Camus, however, is far remote from the glorification of art for
the sake of art. He is a moralist to the core, far more than a philosopher. The moralist in him seeks clear-sightedness amid confusion,
and an *ascesis* in a work of art, which seems gratuitous. Literature
enables author and reader alike 'to conquer their ghosts and to
come a little closer to their naked reality.' Sisyphus, king of Cor-
inth, had been sentenced to roll eternally a big stone up the mountain, only to see it tumble down again as soon as the summit had
been reached. Sisyphus, for Camus, is invested with the same nobleness as was Oedipus who, unjustly criminal, having undergone his
gruesome punishment, proclaimed in the end that all was well.
He negates the gods, he is superior to his fate because he has retained conscience and the ability to surmount his fate through
scorn and forbearance. Sisyphus follows his stone rolling downhill.
But 'the very struggle toward the top is enough to fill the heart of
a man. We must imagine Sisyphus as happy.'

World War II was to demonstrate that Camus could live up to
his ideas and that his ethics, based on the postulate that God is
absent from the world, was worthy of the loftiest demands of the
sternest among the pagan moralists. 'Even the men without the
Gospel have their Mount of Olives,' he had proudly declared, rejecting the Christian solution as too easy and often as cowardly.

'On theirs also, one may not go to sleep . . . Everything starts from clear-sighted indifference.' The French Catholics have repeatedly voiced their respectful esteem for the anti-Christian Camus. With him and other writers more or less directly affected by existentialism,[1] the tragic feeling for life, anguish, a tone of burning sincerity, and an exacting moral code seem to have been taken over from the Christians. They seem to constitute the modern progeny of Pascal, more so than many churchgoers. Camus fought against tuberculosis, without ever accepting withdrawal from active life. The threat is still with him, but it has proved a spur to action and creation. He also fought against the German occupation; founded, directed, indeed distributed at the peril of his life the underground newspaper *Combat,* and continued to write editorials of the highest quality in it during the years following the liberation of France.[2] He has since been a crusader for several generous causes: among others, the abolition of capital punishment, the revolt against communist tyranny, the denunciation of the Pharisaic inequalities of our social order.

L'Etranger (The Stranger, less happily entitled *The Outsider* in the British translation, for which Cyril Connolly wrote a preface) provides not the demonstration but the feel of the absurd as Camus conceives it. This brief novel, whose technique reminds one both of Hemingway and of Kafka, has had a strong impact upon young readers of two continents. Many veterans of World War II and their successors, who fear they may be the participants in World War III, have recognized themselves in the unheroic hero. Seldom have the detached tone and the apparent lack of emotion reached such intensity in fiction. Seldom has the calm art of understatement succeeded in being so explosive.

Meursault, a clerk in a commercial establishment in Algiers, leads the uneventful, drab life led by most characters in naturalist

---

1. We have already noted that Camus never belonged to the existentialist 'sect' and did not subscribe to the (undefined) creed of the group. But, in fact, he matured in the same ideological climate, hailed the same masters (Nietzsche, Kafka, Kierkegaard, and Husserl), shared the same general assumptions: the death of God, unconcern for essence and stress upon existence, the absurd, humanism in the sense that the man freed from belief in God must love and serve men all the better, and so forth.

2. Several of these articles have been collected in the volume *Actuelles* (Gallimard, 1950 and 1954). Camus also wrote for an underground publication his splendid *Letters to a German Friend,* reprinted in 1945, perhaps the noblest pages of prose inspired in any language by World War II.

fiction. His mother dies — in a home for the aged where he had placed her three years before, because, he says, they had nothing more to say to each other. He attends the burial, unable to shed a tear or even to feel any emotion or to translate his experience into words. He goes swimming the next day, meets a girl Marie, goes to the movies, and then goes to bed with her. He sees her again the following week end, and at lunch time she asks him if he loves her. The question was meaningless to him, and he could only answer that he supposed not; but when she asks if he will marry her, he answers yes, with indifference. He then goes out with a not-too-respectable neighbor to a friend's bungalow on the beach. They eat a big lunch. After lunch, he takes a walk with his friends and they get into a brawl with some Arabs. The sun and the sand are hot and dazzling. Meursault, in the course of the brawl, sees the glint of the Arab's knife and pulls the trigger of the revolver, which his friend had asked him to carry. He kills the Arab, for no reason whatsoever, except the glare of the sun or because he did not care enough not to do it.

He is thrown into prison, and the usual investigations are started about his private life. The investigators are antagonistic, for the Stranger has consistently failed to show normal social reactions. It is brought up against him that he showed no grief after his mother's death. When the examining magistrate asks him if he loved his mother, his only answer is, 'Yes, like everybody else.' He is a man of few words and of slow reactions, and he can only state the actual fact dryly, while others seem to live in a world of conventional patterns of emotion and according to myths. He has never believed in God or in any values except living. His defense is as direct, naïve, and unskillful as can be, and he succeeds in antagonizing the jury. The verdict is soon issued. He will be guillotined as guilty of premeditated murder.

Then, back in his prison cell, his thoughts seem to reach a little deeper, and, in his replies to the chaplain who visits him, he bursts into anger against the conventional solace of religion. He cries out his love for this life as he had known it and his total unconcern about the other and about God. 'Nothing was important, and I knew why.' He is ready for the execution and hopes there will be a huge crowd of spectators when it takes place, so that he will feel less lonely.

It is superfluous to stress the symbolic meanings that may be read into the story. Man is a stranger in an alien world, and a stranger to himself. It takes only momentary detachment from our

usual passive sharing in conventional values for us to be struck
with the meaninglessness of it all. It is, as Sartre suggested, like
watching dancers from behind a glass door or a man gesticulating
and laughing in a telephone booth. The Stranger has taken nothing very seriously in this world and he has implicitly rejected any
ethics that stakes everything on another life. This life does not
have to be transcended, but it has to be lived. Camus, it need
hardly be pointed out, does not uphold the Stranger as an exemplary hero. Society is more hypocritical and more unjust than he
is guilty. But he is a caricature of the absurd hero, observed and
described behavioristically, and in no way an inartistic attempt
to prove or to propose a model. Sartre underlined the absence of
a thesis in the novel, and Camus, in one of his later pronouncements (*Atlantic Monthly,* June 1953), had to protest that a man's
work is almost never autobiographical and that he and his French
contemporaries had never stood for a literature of despair. 'In the
lower depths of our nihilism, I have searched only for reasons to
transcend it.'

Indeed, *L'Etranger* is especially conspicuous as a feat of skill by
a young author who has superbly mastered the technique of
Hemingway and has poured more content into it than the author
of *The Sun Also Rises* had been willing or able to do. Meursault
rises to tragic stature, without his creator's ever lifting his voice
to a pitch of eloquence or poetry, without any naïve stress on
symbolism (except the sweltering heat of two summers and the
glare of the sun), and without the intrusion of an analysis of his
mind or of commentary on his behavior. There was bound to be
some trickery in the author's stacking all the cards of fate against
Meursault and emptying him of will power, of anger, of passion,
even of psychological density. Such a protagonist is almost as
elementary as some of the puppets adopted by Steinbeck and Caldwell as their heroes. The condemnation of society, shocked at a
man who, unlike most gangsters and criminals, shares none of its
moral reactions, not even to the extent of recognizing them in
the breach by distorting or defying them, is a trifle too facile. But
the style is well-nigh infallible, and Camus displays the resources
of a classical master who has already tamed the romantic exuberance of *Noces.* There are hardly any subordinate clauses or con-
junctions linking one sentence to another. The compound tense
to denote the past is used throughout, to render the senseless
bursting of air bubbles on the surface of a stream and the lack of
any real past surviving in the protagonist's consciousness. Nothing

is said or hinted about Meursault's childhood, education, training, and parents. The narrative is carefully calculated not to endow the recorded events with any significance; this is contrary to most fiction, which, depicting the world or a world, necessarily rebuilds it and hence explains it. Seldom has utter aimlessness in a character been suggested with such originality.

La Peste (*The Plague*, 1947), Camus's only other novel to date, ranks among the most admirable attempts by French authors to write a work of fiction divested of all that normally makes fiction attractive to readers (imaginative escape, love adventures, seductive women characters, and surprise in the invention of incidents). The book is marked at the outset by severity and a haughty nobleness. It is no mean compliment to French readers that it won great acclaim from the critics and the public. It sold upward of one hundred and twenty thousand copies within a few months of its publication. It has stood the test of rereading and of classroom dissection and has reached audiences in various languages. Indeed, critics have been almost too uniformly impressed by the merits of the book. Only one of the most gifted among the French appraisers of contemporary literature, Gaëtan Picon, granted *La Peste* the tribute of a serious and at times faultfinding critique, in the magazine *Fontaine* (No. 61).

The style of the volume is deliberate and restrained. If sincerity in writing has any meaning, Camus's sincere, that is spontaneous, manner of expression would be the poetical and overeloquent one we commonly attribute to some Mediterranean peoples. (A case could be made for certain Spanish features in the personality of Camus, who is partly of Spanish descent.) But Camus undertook, very early, to curb all that was high-sounding, hyperbolical, or even metaphorical in his style. In his eyes, the French novel is entrusted with a special mission, which sets it apart from the other great fictional literatures of Europe. That mission is, thanks to a very limited number of situations, to express and illustrate a certain conception of man. The primary role belongs to intelligence, which rules over the conception of such a novel and imposes upon it 'a marvellous economy and a kind of passionate monotony . . . To be classical means to repeat oneself and to know how to repeat oneself.' [3] The texture of the novel indeed strives after monotony. There are hardly any touches of humor, no ad-

3. A. Camus, 'L'Intelligence et l'échafaud,' in *Problèmes du Roman*, Jean Prévost, ed. Confluences, Lyon et Paris, 1943, p. 220.

jectives for adornment, and very few evocations of scenery to appeal to our dreams; all takes place in the dullest of provincial cities, with no lurid scenes of horror, which the subject might easily have seemed to call for.

Camus has likewise curbed his imagination in his approach to the subject. There are celebrated evocations of the plague in literature, in Thucydides and Lucretius, in Gregory of Tours and Boccaccio, which come to us dressed in awesome magnificence. Camus chose to place his under the aegis of the barest, dryest of them all: Daniel Defoe's *Journal of the Plague Year*. His own narrative is an impassioned matter-of-fact diary of the plague at Oran, kept by Dr. Rieux, Camus's mouthpiece, or one of them, for Camus knows better than to point out an obvious moral in his tale. But it is clear from the outset that the epidemic that struck an average and unaesthetic Algerian city is an allegory. To his French readers, the allusions to the plague clearly referred to Europe under the German occupation. War, with the separations and prison camps, the cowardice of some, the deliberate heroism of others, and the feeling of solidarity that it fostered, was clearly designated. And, under the permanence of those age-old evils like plague and war, the problem was no other than man's fate. The question may, however, be asked whether Camus's classical restraint did not clip the wings of an allegory that, as *Moby-Dick, Ulysses,* or *The Trial,* should have been expanded into a myth.

La Peste is like a classical tragedy in the sense that a given situation (the epidemic afflicting the city of Oran) is powerfully depicted in the opening scenes. The question then turns on the reactions of the characters to the plague, their inner torments stemming from their obstinate will to rest their actions upon some moral justification. There are those whom Camus ridicules or pities, who establish themselves in the abnormal conditions and even rejoice at them, because, like Cottard, they can thus take refuge from some past misdeed and, in the midst of the exceptional, escape the attention of the police. Likewise, some, during the war, basked in the dealings of the black market. There are also the seekers of 'diversion,' such as those that Pascal condemned, who concentrate all their misplaced energy on the endless repetition of some meaningless gesture. One spits from his balcony on cats, every day at the same hour. Another has adopted as his hobby railroad timetables and imaginary traveling. A third crazily hopes to write, and polishes up the same sentence year after year, adding, then erasing, an adjective or refining a cadence. Men, as Pascal, and Vigny after him, used to say (the two names often occur in the minds of Camus's reader), are prisoners sentenced to death who weave straw in the courtyard of their prison in order to forget.

The Christian attitude (or perhaps a caricature of it) is illustrated by a learned Jesuit, Father Paneloux. He has devoted his life to archaeological research. The catastrophe moves him to address packed Sunday audiences in two notable sermons. The dilemma posed by the plague is, for the Christian, that of justifying the catastrophe through transcending it; of negating the absurdity and the injustice of evil through appealing to a higher significance. Can a Kierkegaardian leap do away with the harrying doubt raised by the epidemic? Paneloux's first answer is that which was heard in some French cathedrals under the Pétain regime: the catastrophe was willed by God as a punishment for the sins of men. The plague is the just penance meted out for some concrete sins or misdeeds. But Paneloux, leaving his scholarly pursuits, watches the concrete suffering in the city of Oran and particularly the most revolting of all deaths, the death of innocent little children. The Slaughter of the Innocents, Paneloux reminds his audience, is commemorated by the Church calendar. Such a criminal absurdity cannot be overlooked. In his second sermon, the Jesuit takes the 'leap': we must will the suffering of children since God wills it. 'One must either believe all or deny all. Who among you would dare deny everything?' The ultimate logic of his position brings him to reject the assistance of a doctor and to refuse to alleviate evil, just as the Church, two centuries before, had banned vaccination. Camus rightly remarked to an interviewer that *La Peste* was more anti-Christian than his earlier volumes. The harsh logic of Father Paneloux becomes a distortion of the Christian attitude. But Camus's own position is unequivocal: he will not consent to a view of creation that accepts and seems to condone the slaughter of the innocent ones. One will fight against evil more deliberately if one does not believe in God.

Rambert, the journalist who was caught by the plague in Oran, felt that he did not belong there; he was a mere temporary visitor, the plague was none of his business. He could remain an isolationist or a neutralist in the presence of the scourge. He would at first use all the means he could to escape from the besieged city and join the woman he loved. Another absolute, that of love, was his concern. But when all was ready for his flight, he reversed his decision and chose to remain and fight against the evil, along with

Tarrou and Rieux. He discovered that solidarity extended to strangers, to foreigners, and to all human beings.

The two protagonists, both embodying elements of their creator's personality, are Tarrou, who kept notebooks and recorded his tragic moral concern during the plague, and Dr. Rieux, who is revealed at the very end as being the narrator. Camus, who is chary of publicity and of interviewers, consented to give a few declarations to an interviewer from *Le Monde*, Claudine Chonez, soon after his novel came out.

> For Paneloux, I feel some sort of sympathy, necessarily, for
> the men who have a vocation are not so very numerous . . .
> But note that, when he dies, the words 'a doubtful case' will
> be written in his file, and this is not unintentional. In a sense,
> this book is more anti-Christian than my earlier ones. For
> above the 'scandal' in the Kierkegaard or in the Paneloux
> sense, and also above holiness without God as Tarrou con-
> ceives it, it opens up another human possibility, the one that
> Rieux is seeking . . . The closest to myself is not Tarrou
> the saint, but Rieux the doctor.

Tarrou had been profoundly impressed by his youthful experience as the son of a prosecutor general. He had heard his father request the death of an accused man, obviously guilty. But the son had watched the hunted and frightened criminal, listened with horror to his father's passionate rhetoric indicting him in the name of society, and had become obsessed by the thought of his father's rising early the following morning to watch, as was his duty, the execution. From then on, he felt alienated in a social order that rested on legalized murder. He knew one thing alone for certain: There are on this earth plagues, tormentors, and executioners on one side, and, on another side, victims; and he knew that he would never align himself with the former. Can one be a saint without God? That, for him, is the only urgent question. Tarrou dies from the plague, against which he had organized the fight — without hope and without illusion, as he had lived.

As he was watching Tarrou's last breath, Dr. Rieux received the news that his wife, whom he had sent to a nursing home in the country early in the story, had died. His own mother, a shriveled old woman of few words and of patient devotion, had helped him through the fight against the disease. With admirable modesty, Rieux refused to resort to notions or words like charity or saintliness or heroism, which have been dragged into the service of too many unworthy causes. 'Honesty' is the one word he will tolerate, or 'sympathy,' to denote the devotion he has unstintingly given to the care of the sick.

Rieux does not intend to invent another ideal of saintliness, parallel to, and rivaling, that of religion. He is a rationalist, who knows that reason is not all-powerful but that the abdication of reason, granting free rein to fanaticism and stupidity, is immeasurably worse. He will spurn rewards and honors after the plague has finally been vanquished. He has fought against the plague empirically, efficiently, as a medical man, and as one who will reserve all his affection for men and transcend himself only toward other men and for them. 'There are in men more things to be admired than things to be scorned,' he declares, when joy again enters the city liberated from the evil, for he is content with that severe and modest reward granted to 'those for whom man and his poor and terrible love suffice.'

The ethics implicit in *La Peste* is not presented by the author as universal or as constructive. Camus has refused to play the part of a prophet, uttering moral advice on all the problems of the hour and sermonizing on his favorite mottoes: honesty and revolt. The courage to declare that one does not know is a virtue that the man of letters in France seems most reluctant to borrow from the scientist. Camus would readily admit that the very subject of *La Peste* stressed the combat against a physical and collective scourge. It is relatively easy to rally men's energies against war, invasion, foreign occupation, a flood, and so forth. But could social oppression, involving our more perfidious prejudices about property, free enterprise, and the privileges of a workers' union, be cured, as the plague in Oran was cured in the end? Could spiritual tyranny, racism, and nationalism be opposed with the same means? Efficiency, which can be a worthy criterion for a businessman or for a physician, can turn out to be the most odious of all criteria for a man of thought and even for a politician. Camus, who witnessed some of the results of German efficiency, imitated or rivaled in other lands, is, like most western Europeans today, bitterly suspicious of the word and of the thing. He has written a book, which we find unconvincing, *L'Homme révolté*, on the attempt to found a positive ethics upon the notion of revolt. Only in and through other imaginative works of fiction may he perhaps succeed in giving the world a new powerful formulation of his views.

Camus rightly insisted that he and his contemporaries in France were idealists and optimists. 'An optimist on the value of man and a pessimist on his destiny': thus he defined himself in a talk to the Dominicans, reported in *La Vie Intellectuelle* (April 1949). He refuses the present order, which Christianity, he insists, has too placidly accepted; he declares the universe, as it is, to be unacceptable. Justice, liberty, and sincerity are the three cardinal virtues or values that he will not forsake. Let the Christians fight for them in their own way. In an elegant reply to Mauriac, first published in *Combat* (January 11, 1945) and reprinted in *Actuelles*, Camus made his position as a 'humanist' unambiguous.

I believe I entertain a just notion of the greatness of Christianity. But there are some of us in this persecuted world who feel that if Christ died for certain men, He did not die for us. And at the same time we refuse to despair of man . . . If we consent to do without God and hope, we are not so easily resigned to do without man.

This noble and modest cult of man he had opposed to the German attempt at dehumanization. He opposes it today to all forms of oppression and of mechanical and administrative efficiency, which grind down man's *élans* toward more freedom of the spirit.

Official history has always been the story of great murderers. It is not today that Cain is killing Abel. But it is only today that Cain is killing Abel in the name of logic and then claiming the ribbon of the Legion of Honor . . . Men can only live on the basis that they have something in common on which they can always get together.[4]

Since women's education became generalized or even since the age of the salons, France has until lately counted relatively few women writers of towering eminence. Even George Sand and Colette pale when ranked beside the dozen women novelists who have contributed to English fiction since Jane Austen. French fiction of 1910–30 does not seem to boast the equivalent of Willa Cather, of Virginia Woolf, or even of Rosamond Lehmann. Male critics, with their usual patronizing complacence, have remained

4. Camus, 'The Artist as Witness of Freedom,' *Commentary*, December 1949.

tempted to pronounce the words 'charm,' 'deftness,' or 'graceful elegance' in the presence of many *ouvrages de dames*. They resort, not too fairly, to irony toward women who have the courage to think and to invade the literature of knowledge as well as the literature of power.

Simone de Beauvoir has not been daunted by that male conspiracy. Feminine charm has not been denied her; her intuition can be as piercing and her touch as delicate as those of women writers who never mastered Spinoza or Hegel. With *Le Deuxième Sexe* (*The Second Sex*), she has achieved, however, in spite of some needless display of pedantry and crudeness, the most formidable vindication of woman's rights since Mary Wollstonecraft, and she has, in her *Ethics of Ambiguity,* given the best exposition to date of existentialist ethics. She ranks, with Merleau-Ponty and Sartre, as one of the three best philosophers of French atheistic existentialism. And two of her novels are among the finest fictional accomplishments of that militant group that has invaded the drama, the short story, and critical and polemical writing, as well as the novel and philosophy. The third, *Tous les hommes sont mortels,* is an artistic failure such as the most intelligent writer will sometimes perpetrate, and needs no mention here, except as a reminder of the author's dangerous bent, in which her qualities melt into faults: too clear an awareness of her purpose and too obstinate a zeal in building a work of fiction around an idea.

L'Invitée (*She Came to Stay*), published in 1943, was, along with *L'Etranger,* the most penetrating revelation of the war years in the domain of French fiction. The epigraph from Hegel boldly advanced the claim of transposing a philosopher's notion into a concrete situation: 'Every conscience seeks the death of the other.' But the first pages arouse the reader's curiosity in the old-fashioned manner of novelists (What will happen? How? Why?) and strike him with the novelty of the psychological analysis. Every object or person perceived by us is a reminder that there is more than ourselves in the world. The experience of otherness, or as the French existentialists call it, of *altérité,* comes first as a shock. A fine page in the sixth chapter, which anthologies of the future will certainly collect, describes the first impression of solitude and of anguish experienced by the heroine as a little girl, when, alone in the house, she gazed with earnest sympathy at an old coat thrown on the back of a chair. The worn coat could not complain, could not even notice her, it existed and was not aware of it, and she could not identify herself with it, translate its sadness, speak for it. For others, each of us is often likewise a limited, alien, cold object. We dread to accept as valid the vision that others, and especially spiteful or envious rivals, may entertain of us. We may be driven to the extermination of such a vision.

The heroine, Françoise, is thirty and is proud of the mature wisdom and of the directness that set her apart from some of the women around her, either younger and girlishly coquettish in their devious calculations or frustrated in their life and loves, unstable, and lying to themselves. When the story begins, she looks wistfully at Gerbert, a rather inarticulate young man, handsome and awkward, who has worked all evening with her at their theater. She feels an urge to tempt his naïve and admiring youthfulness, but she resists the temptation easily.

For several years, Françoise and Pierre have lived a model liaison; they share every thought, they esteem, respect, and love each other. Pierre would confess to her, and thus justify in her eyes, a passing whim for another woman, which sometimes waylaid his imperious nature. She feels secure in her conviction that he would, of himself, always return to the almost virile and fraternal comradeship he had formed with her eight years before. Pierre, the director and leading actor of a Parisian theater, a Dullin or a Jouvet, is returning that night from an absence. Their company will then rehearse and produce *Julius Caesar*. Françoise watches the theater lobbies and, backstage, the dressing rooms, deserted and unused that night. Through her, these objects and places assume an existence. She reflects, interprets, and thinks the sweetness of that lovely hour.

Pierre and Françoise have invited Xavière, a girl whom they met in Rouen, to come to Paris, stay at their expense in the hotel where they live, and find her way into some career. Xavière's dream was to act, but she conceived of the theater romantically and was disappointed when she saw Françoise and Pierre, producers at the head of a vanguard stage, living regularly and prosaically, succeeding by dint of hard work, and observing effortlessly a code of mutual loyalty. Xavière is lazy, unable to organize her life, totally ignorant of punctuality, capricious, and nervous. How the older couple could bear with her after a few weeks astonishes all their friends, and the reader. She obviously takes a malicious pleasure in filling the function Claudel attributes to women, that of complicating life incessantly.

Françoise, like most human beings, has the instinct of a teacher. She wanted to train and to mold Xavière and to launch her into

Parisian life, imagining her at first more manageable than the little provincial girl turns out to be. She would thus satisfy some instinct for domineering in herself. Xavière held little interest for Pierre until he, accustomed to being the admired and obeyed boss, never questioning the assumptions on which his life rested, and serene in the security of his union with Françoise, suddenly discovers, in Xavière, 'the other.' Her petulance, her unpredictability, and her blunt questioning of the placid semimarital order of his life with Françoise amuse him at first. He becomes interested in Xavière, eager to instruct the inexperienced girl in literature and acting and in the mysteries of Parisian night life. In the presence of that other one, whose values upset theirs, whose youthful vision is fresher, Françoise witnesses the sudden collapse of the artificial world that she and Pierre had thought they were building on authenticity and a freely accepted order. Jealousy, which she had imagined banished from her life (for she has a direct and virile nobleness of soul, akin to Corneille's Pauline), now stings her venomously. She is ill for some weeks, and, during her absence in a clinic, Pierre is drawn closer to Xavière. The 'other' couple becomes crystallized, and Françoise is a stranger to it.

Heroically, she tries to maintain remnants of her dream. Pierre, who is a little callous in matters of sentiment and does not realize how cruel telling the truth that hurts can be, does not conceal from Françoise that he now loves Xavière. Generously, Françoise tries to integrate her into a trio. Her very nobleness humiliates Xavière, who delights in inflicting suffering upon Pierre. The girl gives herself to young Gerbert after a drinking orgy, is peeved at her own conduct, hates Françoise for still sharing the thoughts and the professional interests of Pierre, and blames herself morbidly amid scenes of sulking in her room and of insulting Françoise. The war breaks out. Pierre is mobilized. The two women attempt to patch up their differences. Françoise has done her best to live truly and frankly, avoiding the banality of the usual adulterous trio, maintaining seriousness and loyalty above all other values. She has failed. Neither Pierre's sentimental seduction and physical possession nor the more subtle fascination that Françoise, as an older woman, with moral and intellectual qualities, exercised on the young girl, proved successful in achieving the impossible: knowing and controlling the consciousness of the other one. Françoise, in the end, is reduced to contemplate, aghast, the picture that Xavière has of her, that of a domineering, mean woman, prosaically jealous of a younger person, lying to herself in spite of all her claims to utter sincerity. She turns on the gas in the room where Xavière is asleep and thus achieves the death of the other one.

The novel suffers from one fault: it is too long, too leisurely in its pace, and too tolerant of sinuous ups and downs, which are no longer necessary once the atmosphere has been created and the central issues formulated. But it is in other respects a remarkably incisive psychological portrayal of the conflict opposing, as in a classical tragedy, three characters whom a fatal logic sets apart. The life of a Paris theater, the meetings and excited conversations in the *cafés* and *dancings* of Montparnasse, the sense of the preciousness of every hour in the face of the threat of World War II, and the parting of Pierre from Françoise, when he dons his uniform and leaves for the *Gare de l'Est,* are rendered with superb mastery. The triumph of the author is not only in the new nuances of psychology she renders but also in very expert dialogue, never wordy, abstract, or unnatural, and in the impressionistic touches through which the unceasing change in the consciousness of the characters is faithfully revealed. *L'Invitée* is a philosophical novel made fully concrete.

It is also one of the ablest delineations of women attempted by a woman novelist. *Jeunes filles* have become a rarity in contemporary French fiction; and very few of them, certainly neither Montherlant's, who exist only for and through the man, nor Giraudoux's, too idealized and too sweetly reasonable, attain the convincingness of selfish, capricious, fierce little Xavière. Rare are the women novelists who have depicted women as other than passionate and sensuous, enthroning love as the cynosure of their lives. Françoise, fully feminine and somewhat maternal, embodies reasonableness, straightforward loyalty, devotion to a professional task lucidly undertaken and intelligently pursued, and tender affection, which are seldom portrayed in literature and frequent in actual life. 'The friendship of women is far superior to their love,' decreed Balzac. The heroine of *L'Invitée* is a woman capable of friendship. Her final crime is gradually and subtly made to appear inevitable and almost justified. At the same time, both she and Xavière and episodic women in the book are feminine to their fingertips and are portrayed smoothing their hair, concealing or betraying the drawn weariness of their features, expert in making up their complexions or their eyes, analyzing mercilessly the blouses, the tailored suits, or the gait of other women, and piercing cruelly the mask of steady composure under which their sex conceals their fear of aging and of loneliness.

Le Sang des autres (*The Blood of Others*), published in 1945, is not unequal to *L'Invitée*. It has less classical concentration on the inner life of a very few characters and it offers more variety as a fresco of the moods and problems of French youth before and during World War I. It, too, incarnates a philosophy and illustrates a problem, but with no lack of concreteness and restrained emotion. The emphasis in Simone de Beauvoir's thinking is twofold: on ethics rather than on metaphysics, and on the peculiar situation of women in the world and especially in the world of literary creation. On ethics, she expressed herself fully and clearly in her volume *The Ethics of Ambiguity* (published in translation by the Philosophical Library, New York, in 1948, one year after its appearance in French). Ambiguity is the inevitable condition of man, and the disbelief in God, which existentialists take for granted, only serves to make that ambiguity more tragic and a courageous way out of it more necessary. Man tries to expand and enrich his life, to act as if an indefinite future were assured for him, but he knows that there is one end to it and that is death.[5] Man is conscious of a world yet part of that world, confronted and oppressed at times by the consciousness of others. Man is a subject and also, for others, an object. Freedom is his one safe privilege. But he can only make that freedom meaningful if he outgrows the attitude of children as yet unaware of it, the despicable attitude of slaves abdicating it, the conventional cowardice of the 'serious man' preferring security, and the domineering passion of those who want to possess and control others and do not respect their freedom. Engagement is inevitable but hedged around with pitfalls, which *Le Sang des autres* conjures up vividly.

The position of a woman of letters is especially arduous. She enters a world fashioned by man and has to meet standards set by him. She has to live imaginatively in an artistic and literary universe created by man to complete, replace, or interpret the real one. She tends to be restricted to one domain: that of woman's

5. Simone de Beauvoir treated the subject of action, adventure, and projecting oneself incessantly into the future in an essay of intelligent popularization, *Pyrrhus et Cinéas* (Gallimard, 1944). Her long novel, *Tous les Hommes sont mortels* (Gallimard, 1947), revolves around the theme of death as giving value to life. Immortality, far from constituting a desirable goal as it does to the Christian, would deprive immortal men of the privilege of giving their life to a cause and of loving someone or something *usque ad mortem*.

existence, where the search for love and for man's caresses, for the family comfort of children, a home and a tenderly tilled garden, and refuge in childhood memories are the main themes. Simone de Beauvoir is determined to meet successfully the challenge often thrown by male critics to female letters and to pass from the particular truth of women, which they alone can express in their subjectivity, to a universal truth. From the desolate solitude of a consciousness set apart from others, she passes on to the interaction of several conscious beings upon one another, hence to the eventualities of responsibility, risk, and guilt faced by the characters in *Le Sang des autres*.

An epigraph from *The Brothers Karamazov* has been popularized by existentialist literature: 'Everyone is responsible for everything before everybody.' It stresses the claim of existentialist ethics to rival the Christian ideal of charity and solidarity and to evolve a communion of saints and sinners, in its own way. There is no escape into solitary contemplation or forbearance from participating in political and social action, which lured the writers of the symbolist and postsymbolist era, from Mallarmé to Valéry, who dreamed of Axel's castle. Through the mere fact that we exist, we act upon other people. We had better face our interdependence and our far-reaching responsibility unflinchingly from the start. 'Live — our servants can well do that for us,' exclaimed the author of *Axel*. The protagonist of *Le Sang des autres*, sixty years or so later, strikes another tune, closer to Voltaire and Diderot: 'We exist only if we act.'

Jean Blomart was born in a comfortable middle-class family. His father, the owner of a big printing establishment acquired solely through his own merits, embodies the conventionality and unimaginativeness, but also the honesty, the frugality, the assiduous and conscientious virtues of the middle class. But Jean suffers from scruples that keep him from enjoying his privileged position in society. He is attracted to workmen and to revolutionary action in their ranks. It is difficult, in continental western Europe, as Sartre and other well-meaning intellectuals have found out, to 'go to the people' without also going to communism; and communist workers eye with suspicion a bourgeois who joins their party and obviously does not want his own liberation, as every one of the workers thinks he does, but theirs. A friend of Jean Blomart remarked to him: 'There will always be a gulf between a workingman and you; you choose freely a condition which he did not choose and has to endure.' Jean, however, soon becomes a leader in the trade-union movement and in syndicalist agitation. He has drawn to the cause a friend and admirer of his, Jacques. In one of the riots between Communists and royalist agitators, which preceded World War II, Jacques, to whom Jean had lent a pistol, is killed.

Jean is harried by remorse and by the sense of his responsibility. He will henceforth renounce direct action and refrain from influencing others and limit himself to supporting only the professional claims of the unions. A girl, Hélène, engaged to a workman, Paul, who is a friend of Jean Blomart and a colleague of his in the trade-union movement, meets Jean, in an entertaining scene, described with much freshness, in which she has tried to involve the men in the theft of a bicycle. She falls in love with Jean, who treats her like the peevish, romantic, and fickle young girl she is and refuses to listen to her declarations. He is not interested in her. He is solely concerned with his self-assigned mission, and he will remain loyal to his friendship for Paul.

Hélène is stubborn. She breaks with her fiancé and, vexed by Jean's spurning of her advances, gives herself, in one night of desolation, to an unworthy and unscrupulous man. She becomes pregnant and must arrange for an abortion. She asks Jean to lend her his room for the very night when the gruesome operation is to take place. Jean, taken aback, consents, assists her timidly and clumsily, takes pity upon her, and gradually feels for her a tenderness akin to love. We are responsible also for those who love us.

The great tragedy of Europe in 1937–9 now engulfs the more limited drama in which Jean is an unwilling but inextricably involved actor. The Spanish republicans are being crushed, and Jean had contended that the French working classes could do nothing for them. Austria and Czechoslovakia are invaded. It dawns upon Jean Blomart that he may have erred in avoiding his responsibility to others, to the whole world. 'I have not created the world. But I re-create it through my very presence at every minute. And all that happens to it seems to happen through me.' The war comes to France, and Jean is mobilized. Hélène tries desperately to have him withdrawn from dangerous positions. She defies army regulations, suspicions which mistake her for a spy, and her own weariness to visit him in the village where he is stationed. The scene, related in Chapter Eight, is one of the most vivid narratives of World War II. But Paris falls. Hélène at first, ranking Jean's life and her own happiness with him above all else, comes near to collaborating with the Germans. But Jean has worked out the problem of his responsibility to others. He joins the resistance movement, and

Hélène freely follows him. The choice entails Cornelian dilemmas. Blowing up trains and shooting a few German officers in dark streets may appear as vain gestures and will surely cause the deaths of many innocent French hostages. Yet it must be accomplished; for only through the ruthless German retaliation on French civilians will the French patriotic conscience be aroused and the fight against the invaders be resumed some day.

Jean now truly loves Hélène, and they are fighters in a common cause. The sight of little Jewish children carried away by the Germans moves her to the depths. She is now ready to face death, as Jean had explained to her, so that life may retain a meaning. She joins the resistance network directed by Jean. Once again he, as the chief, sends others to risk their lives, while he stays relatively secure, organizing the fight. Hélène, lucidly, volunteers for a perilous mission and is gravely wounded. She dies and has only words of gratitude and solace for Jean. One must pay with the blood of others, heart-rending though it may be. Jean embraces her as she dies, while his comrades are pressing him to give the signal for the next attack by the *maquis*. Without any outburst of emotion or of eloquence, Jean moves on to the battle, silencing his sorrow and his scruples. He knows that responsibility can never be eluded and that he has fought all along for 'that good which saves every man from all others and from himself: freedom.'

It would be neither correct nor fair to maintain that *Le Sang des autres* is the demonstration of a thesis or the imparting of a message. The artistic and technical merits of the novel are in no way subservient to the moral thinking that informs the tale. The characters are concretely and unpredictably alive. Hélène, at first selfish and light and girlishly immature, then determined to win the man whom she fails to understand but admires and loves because she *wants* to love him, is a very true person. So is Mme Blomart, the distressed mother who, torn and powerless, watches her son standing against his father, rejecting the bourgeois order he was to inherit and preserve, living on a workman's wages, and then courting death in the resistance. The atmosphere of the strikes of 1936, of the political debates, then of the awareness of the national peril overshadowing the social struggle, and the unfolding of the gradual growth of the moral conscience in the French people, at first dazed by their defeat, are rendered with more simplicity and naturalness than in perhaps any other French novel since 1944. The past is merged with the present without any technical jugglery. Blomart is at the bedside of Hélène, who is dying, and relives his past life. He moralizes occasionally, but that is in keeping with his character and with the situation in which he finds himself, anguished at the deaths he has caused by paying with the blood of others, desperately seeking a moral justification for his acts.

Simone de Beauvoir does not cultivate emotional effects and does not utilize the violence, the coarseness, or the surprise that have been frequent in recent fiction. She also shuns the relative facility (for French authors steeped in that tradition) of the psychological novel in the first person singular. Although everything is seen and related by Jean Blomart, it is not colored by his own spectacles, and events are never a pretext for introspective delving. The forte of the author, indeed, is dialogue. Through their earnest desire to face each other with full frankness, the characters lay bare and discover what is truest in them, in brief, clashing sentences. They talk too well, to be sure, and with a neat firmness of phrasing that is part of the stylization of the novel. One never quite forgets the author, who has planned and governed every incident with a lucid intellect and an inflexible will. There is more mystery and less docile obedience in the truly living and haunting characters molded by the very great masters of fiction.

Still, both *L'Invitée* and *Le Sang des autres* deserve to rank among the important novels of the decade 1940–50. Existentialism as a philosophical and moral message embodied in fiction offers little that is revolutionary. And that little should have appealed particularly to American audiences, which have been disappointingly slow in hailing the very creed by which they have been living all along, while paying lip service to traditional religion.[6] But the phenomenological psychology that underlies the novels of Simone de Beauvoir is far more original, when transposed into imaginative literature. It is indeed no mean tribute to her and to other novelists in France since 1935–40 to remark that they have succeeded in breaking free from the examples of Proust and Joyce, which might

6. Simone de Beauvoir, like other leading existentialists is fascinated by America, even while sharply criticizing much that she has encountered here and often very hastily misinterpreted. In a very able exposition of her philosophy for American readers (*The New York Times Magazine*, May 25, 1947), she stressed the chief pragmatist elements in her creed, which many Americans might feel they have been living by all along: 'Man is man only by his refusal to be passive, by the urge which throws him from the present toward the future, which thrusts him toward things with the aim of dominating and shaping them; for him, to exist is to remake existence, to live is to will to live.' Man's freedom is only real if it strives to effect some change in the world. One should judge a man not by what he is but by what he does. Man fulfills himself by his will to realization, by his project in the world.

well have proved overpowering, and, in applying the lessons learned from American writers, have renovated the psychological content and technique of the French novel.

BIBLIOGRAPHICAL NOTES

The two novels by Camus, *The Stranger* and *The Plague,* have appeared in translations published by Alfred A. Knopf, as has *The Rebel* (1954), but not *Le Mythe de Sisyphe.* The two slim volumes on Camus by de Luppé and Thoorens, listed below, are disappointing, and the more substantial criticism on him has been in the form of articles. The following articles by Camus will be found especially helpful to the understanding of his thought and art:

Interview with Dominique Arban, in *Opéra,* October 17, 1945.
'Non, je ne suis pas existentialiste,' *Les Nouvelles Littéraires,* November 15, 1945.
'L'Intelligence et l'échafaud,' in *Problèmes du Roman,* Jean Prévost, ed., Confluences, Lyon et Paris, 1943, pp. 218–23
'L'Exil d'Hélène,' *Cahiers du Sud,* special number on *Permanence de la Grèce,* 1948, pp. 381–6.
'Le Meurtre et l'absurde,' *Empédocle* I, i, April 1949, pp. 19–27.
'The Artist as Witness of Freedom,' *Commentary,* VIII, 6, December 1949, pp. 534–8.
'What a Writer Seeks,' *The Atlantic Monthly,* June 1953, pp. 72–3.

On Camus, excluding the articles dealing with his plays or with *L'Homme révolté:*

Ayer, A. J., 'Albert Camus,' *Horizon,* XIII, 75, March 1946, pp. 155–68.
Bataille, Georges, 'La Peste,' *Critique,* Nos. 13–14, July 1947, pp. 3–15.
Bespaloff, Rachel, 'Le Monde du condamné à mort,' *Esprit,* No. 163, January 1950, pp. 1–26.
Bieber, Konrad, *l'Allemagne vue par les écrivains de la résistance française,* with a preface by Camus, Droz, Geneva, 1954.
Blanchot, Maurice, 'Le Mythe de Sisyphe,' and 'Le Roman de l'Etranger,' in *Faux-Pas,* Gallimard, Paris, 1943, pp. 70–76 and 256–61.
Blin, Georges, 'Camus ou le sens de l'absurde,' *Fontaine,* No. 30, 1943, pp. 553–62, and 'Camus et l'idée de révolte,' *Fontaine,* No. 53, 1948, pp. 109–17.
Boudot, M., 'L'Absurde et le bonheur dans l'oeuvre de Camus,' *Cahiers du Sud,* No. 315, 1953, pp. 291–305.
Brée, Germaine, 'Introduction to Albert Camus,' *French Studies* (Oxford), IV, No. 1, January 1950, pp. 27–37, and 'Albert Camus and The Plague,' *Yale French Studies,* No. 8, 1951, pp. 93–100.
Brombert, Victor, 'Camus and the Novel of the Absurd,' *Yale French Studies,* No. 1, 1948, pp. 119–23.
D'Astorg, Bertrand, 'La Peste,' *Esprit,* X, October 1947, pp. 615–21.
Desgranges, Pierre, 'Sur A. Camus,' *Poésie* 47, No. 37, pp. 115–25.

Duron, Jacques, 'Un nouveau mal du siècle,' *Renaissances*, No. 16, November 1945, pp. 62–68.

Guérard, Albert, Jr., 'A. Camus,' *Foreground* I, winter 1946, pp. 45–9.

Grubbs, H. A., 'Camus and Graham Greene,' *Modern Language Quarterly*, X, No. 1, March 1949, pp. 33–42.

Hell, Henri, 'L'Etranger,' *Fontaine*, No. 23.

Jagger, George, 'La Peste,' *Yale French Studies*, No. 1, 1948, pp. 124–27.

Luppe, Robert de, *Camus*, Editions du Temps Présent, 1951.

Magny, Claude-Edmonde, 'La Littérature française depuis 1940: Camus,' *La France libre*, IX, 52, February 15, 1945, pp. 292–304.

Mason, H. A., 'Camus and the Tragic Hero,' *Scrutiny*, December 1946, pp. 82–9.

Mohrt, Michel, 'Ethic and Poetry in the Work of Camus,' *Yale French Studies*, No. 1, 1948, pp. 113–18.

Mounier, Emmanuel, 'Camus ou l'appel des humiliés,' *Esprit*, No. 163, January 1950, pp. 27–66.

Ollivier, Albert, 'Camus ou le refus de l'éternel,' *L'Arche*, No. 6, October–November 1944, pp. 158–63.

Picon, Gaëtan, 'Remarques sur La Peste,' *Fontaine*, No. 61, September 1947, pp. 453–60.

Rochefort, Henry, 'L'Etranger,' *Renaissances*, 7 bis, November 25, 1944, pp. 206–208.

Roustu, Jean du, 'Un Pascal sans Christ: A. Camus,' *Études*, October and November 1945, pp. 48–65 and 165–77.

Roynet, L., 'Camus chez les Chrétiens,' *La Vie Intellectuelle*, April 1949, pp. 336–51.

Sartre, J.-P., 'Explication de *l'Étranger*,' in *Situations* I, Gallimard, Paris, 1947, pp. 99–121.

Simon, P. H., *L'Homme en procès*, La Baconnière, Neuchâtel, 1950, and *Les Témoins de l'homme: De Proust à Camus*, A. Colin, Paris, 1951.

Thoorens, Léon, *A la rencontre de Camus*, La Sixaine, Brussels, 1947.

Simone de Beauvoir's *The Ethics of Ambiguity* (The Philosophical Library, New York, 1948) and *The Second Sex* (Alfred A. Knopf, New York, 1953) have appeared in translation, as well as *The Blood of Others* (Alfred A. Knopf, New York, 1948). *L'Invitée* was translated in English as *She Came To Stay* (Secker and Warburg, London, 1949; The World Pub. Co., New York, 1954). Her article, 'An Existentialist Looks at Americans,' appeared in *The New York Times Magazine* (May 25, 1947).

There is little valuable criticism of the novels of Simone de Beauvoir. The best is to be found in 'Ethics and Art,' by Gwendolyn Bays (*Yale French Studies*, I, i, 1948, pp. 106–12); Georges Blin's essay in *Fontaine* (No. 45, October 1945, pp. 716–30), Claudine Chonez, 'Avec Simone de Beauvoir' (*Le Monde*, March 20, 1948), and, above all, Maurice Merleau-Ponty, 'Le Roman et la métaphysique' (in his volume *Sens et non-sens*, Nagel, Paris, 1948, pp. 51–82).

X

THE IMPACT OF THE AMERICAN

NOVEL

O NE OF THE striking phenomena of world literature in the years 1930–50 has been the emergence of modern American literature as the more important of the two literatures in the English language. The drama and the poetry, but chiefly the novel, of America have risen to a position of prestige and of influence abroad seldom equaled in history. Three out of every four translations from the English language currently published in France — and in Italy, Russia, and South America — are from American works. *Traduit de l'américain* has become a magical phrase in Paris and a quick-selling device for book publishers.

This vogue of American letters abroad is all the more remarkable as it stands in sharp contrast to the failure of other American artistic means of expression to establish themselves in Europe. In spite of determined, though perhaps ill-conceived, attempts made after 1944, exhibitions of American paintings in London and Paris have met with marked lack of interest. American composers have been played abroad before polite but frigid audiences. Architecture arouses greater admiration. Frank Lloyd Wright is revered as a legendary figure; but American buildings, in part for obvious reasons, have not been imitated to any marked extent. As to the movies, the time is gone when European intellectuals composed subtle essays on the profundity and the genius of American actors, except for the three names revered by all European aesthetes: Charlie Chaplin, John Ford, and Orson Welles. Never has the stock of Hollywood stood so low among European (and, indeed, American) audiences.

This extraordinary prestige of American letters came at an opportune moment, when several of the traditionally great literatures of Europe seemed to be undergoing a crisis. Modern Russia has not had the first-rate novel that alone would have explained the country's revolutionary era to millions of foreign readers. Kafka, who has been dead since 1924, and Rilke, whom death silenced in 1926, are the German literary forces most keenly felt abroad. (The influence of the Mann brothers on literature has been slight.) Little of modern Italian, Spanish, and South American letters has been able to win large audiences; and Italy, with Cesare Pavese especially, but also with Carlo Coccioli and Elio Vittorini, responded enthusiastically to the modern American novel. France alone, with Malraux, Giono, Saint-Exupéry, the existentialists, and her war poets, proved a great international force through and since World War II. And not a little of the revived energy and of the appeal of French fiction has been due to its assimilation of American influence.

As to Great Britain, the ordeal of the war strained her energies to the breaking point, without affording her the opportunity of creating literature that the resistance and the temptation to flout the invader through 'artistic superiority' gave the French. English literature has been so continuously rich for three hundred years or more that the recent eclipse can be counted only temporary. But, since the passing of Lawrence, Joyce, and even Virginia Woolf, the English novel has lacked power to renew itself. E. M. Forster, acclaimed by many as the chief English novelist alive, cannot rank with the giants. Graham Greene has more forcefulness, but he and Christopher Fry have perhaps been acclaimed too loudly too soon. Richard Hillary, had he lived, might have risen high. Maugham, Huxley, Waugh, Isherwood, even Joyce Cary, Patrick Hamilton, and relative newcomers, such as Angus Wilson and Geoffrey Cotterell, seem pale compared with the ebullient energy of their American contemporaries. The drama of England can boast of no O'Neill. Even her finest poets of the thirties, Auden, Spender, Day Lewis, MacNeice, have lately disappointed us. Time will soon tell if, as we personally believe, T. S. Eliot's *Four Quartets* has been ri-

diculously overpraised. Dylan Thomas had striking originality, but
he reminds the French of their own surrealists. Two exceptions,
however, should be mentioned. Malcolm Lowry, with his powerful
though overworked novel about a man pursued by alcohol,[1] and
Walter Baxter, with his tragic novel,[2] have had a powerful impact
upon French critics. Many British intellectuals, at a time when
liberated Europe, grateful to the England of the R.A.F., expected
a new message from them, were found either to have taken refuge
in America or to have been seized with a new 'failure of nerve' and
to have resorted to Buddhism or Catholicism. English critics and
readers have also been swayed by the vitality, at first only grudg-
ingly acknowledged, which seems to radiate from American literature.

   This focusing of attention on American books is not, contrary to
the too diffident explanations offered by American journalists, a
mere consequence of the war and a reflection of the accrued respect given the all-powerful country, which owns the secret of the
future. For Russian arms enjoyed immense prestige in 1942–45,
and the prestige did not automatically extend to their culture. We
are faced with a purely literary phenomenon, which, indeed, was
already noticeable five or ten years before Pearl Harbor. The wave
of enthusiasm for American books began at the very time when
the United States had isolated itself from Europe and when its
power seemed sapped by the great depression. Indeed, American
material prosperity and American power, complacence, and nationalism are conspicuously absent from American books read abroad
and do not seem to have ever intoxicated Steinbeck, Dos Passos,
O'Neill, or Robinson Jeffers.

   What is more, this vogue of American writers has been in no way
fostered by the renowned advertising methods of American business or by the official representatives of America in foreign lands.
Americans have had one successful traveling salesman of American
culture, Waldo Frank, and they have treated him with great reserve. As to professors of American literature, they have done their
best to dampen or deride the European enthusiasm for Hart Crane,
Sinclair Lewis, Faulkner, and — understandably — Henry Miller.
Representatives of American publishers abroad have frowned for
other reasons upon the success of novels unsponsored by book clubs
and have feared that such novels might convey an unfavorable picture of American civilization. They have tried to divert the en-

1. *Under the Volcano*, Reynal and Hitchcock, New York, 1947.
2. *Look Down in Mercy*, G. P. Putnam's Sons, New York, 1951.

thusiasm of Europeans to Henry James, to the delicate craftsmanship of Willa Cather, and to volumes on American history. Their success has been scant. We have, in fact, since 1945, read and met several Frenchmen whose fondest dream is to cross the Atlantic some day to see the land of Faulkner or Caldwell; who are haunted by the vision of California Steinbeck or Jeffers gave them; and who enjoy the thrill of recognition when they read, on actual signs, the magical words *Main Street* or *Manhattan Transfer.*

Classical American literature has received a share of the present French curiosity. Whitman has been praised anew, notably by Gide and Giono. Several new translations of Melville (*Benito Cereno, Billy Budd, Moby-Dick,* and *Pierre*) have appeared since 1939. Indeed, the present cult of Melville has had no more ardent prophets than some Europeans like D. H. Lawrence, who, as early as 1923, proclaimed *Moby-Dick* 'an epic of the sea such as no man has equalled, and a book of esoteric symbolism of profound significance.' Hawthorne, long read in Europe, has been recently retranslated. His obsession with crime and with 'Freudian' repressions, as well as his pagan aspiration to joy, have made him appear as the ancestor of the present-day American novel. But in psychology and technique he brings little that is radically novel to the successors of Proust, Mauriac, and Julien Green.

Henry James is respected by all, read by a very few, and considered a classic, but without living influence. Proust was content to know him by name only; Forster has been severe on him; Gide, indoctrinated by his Jamesian friend Charles Du Bos, tried in vain to read him. The French, apparently, find that they have the equivalent of James in their own analytical novelists, who are legion, and find his psychology too static and devious, his pace too slow, his content too remote from common life.

American writers whom one might group as traditional, or even as genteel, have little attraction. They include excellent craftsmen, usually women, like Ellen Glasgow and Willa Cather, even Pearl Buck, although she has enjoyed greater success, and Margaret Mitchell, who became a best seller on the black market during the German occupation but exercised no influence on the writers themselves. Some short stories of Eudora Welty and Katherine Ann Porter have recently been rendered into French, and their skill may help revive an art that has not received brilliant treatment from French hands for forty years. The less 'genteel' authors of *Forever Amber* and, with the literati, of *The Heart Is a Lonely Hunter* have been far more appreciated in France. J. P. Marquand

and Louis Bromfield, the latter in spite of his long familiarity with
the French scene, which should have endeared him to the French,
lack the power, perhaps the brutality, that the world seems to
expect from American literature.

As to naturalism, which is one of the living currents in American fiction, it seems to stem from the French school of Flaubert,
Maupassant, and Zola and has, therefore, little novelty for the
French readers of today, who have turned their back on their own
realism. William Dean Howells, Stephen Crane, even Upton Sinclair, once read for the documentary value of their works, are
now but names in Europe (except, in the case of Sinclair, for Russia). Theodore Dreiser, with all the undeniable power of his earlier
works, appears melodramatic and crude. Sinclair Lewis has long
descended from the place of eminence won with *Main Street* and
Babbitt. Most of his later works have belonged to the most ephemeral of all types of literature, the literature on social problems. For,
as even Ibsen and Shaw have experienced, nothing is deader than
a play or a novel on a social problem that has been solved. There
seems to be a deep-seated incompatibility between Thomas Wolfe
and Latin minds, which find that, even in fiction, the most formless of arts, Wolfe's deluge of words and of reminiscences is too
unrestrained, and they do not discern the inner tragedy of the man
underlying his long, verbose, and solitary quest.

The great names of American fiction are, in French eyes, Hemingway, Steinbeck, Dos Passos, and Faulkner. Scott Fitzgerald has
only lately (1948–53) been revealed as the precursor of that group.
Erskine Caldwell is occasionally added to the American quartet,
with a little hesitation caused by the marked inequality between
his best and his worst books. These novelists are read and discussed
wherever French is spoken, and they are acclaimed by all those
who in the Near East, in South America, and even in Russia are
inclined to subscribe to French literary fashions. Their heroes
and heroines have become familiar accessories of French life.
Crossword puzzles have been devised, made up entirely of titles
and characters of American fiction. Elaborate critical disquisitions
by the best critics of the day (Sartre, Claude-Edmonde Magny, and
Maurice Blanchot) have analyzed the secret intentions of Faulkner
and Dos Passos, the philosophy of Steinbeck, and the technique of
Hemingway. Until a very few years ago, these novelists had not
met with such thorough criticism in their own country.

After 1948–50, the French have naturally devoured all the
younger American novelists, in whom they were hoping to find

the worthy successors to the giants revealed in the thirties. They have voiced their disappointment, due in part to unreasonable expectations. Tennessee Williams, very successful on the Paris stage, has bitterly disappointed the readers of *The Roman Spring of Mrs. Stone,* understandably enough. *La Harpe d'herbes (The Grass Harp)* has not been judged to be quite so naïvely poetical as enthusiasts of Truman Capote in America had professed to find it. Gore Vidal has aroused little admiration. Paul Bowles offered little novelty to French readers, who have long had a chance to read more authentic novels on the lure of Arab life for Western ladies. The reception given to *From Here to Eternity* and to *Lie Down in Darkness* (translated in 1953 as *Un Lit de ténèbres*) has been favorable, but cooled by the inordinate length of these novels. *On meurt toujours seul (The Gallery),* Norman Mailer's *Les Nus et les morts (The Naked and the Dead),*[3] and Salinger's superb story of adolescence, *The Catcher in the Rye,* have been singled out as the best American novels of the postwar era.

Whether well informed or naïve, misguided or penetrating, the outcome of a passing vogue or a more deeply rooted reaction, the unprecedented success of American literature abroad is a sociological as well as an aesthetic phenomenon of striking significance. It deserves not only describing but analyzing and perhaps explaining and appraising.

Geographically, the region of the United States that is brought to the fore is no longer New England, once the abode of culture in the New World. It is not even New York. The literary map of America, as pictured in the minds of millions of foreign readers, draws, in sharp outlines, the country of Steinbeck, the California of James Cain, the setting of *Desire under the Elms,* and the proud solitude of Carmel and Point Sur, dear to Robinson Jeffers. It also emphasizes the importance of the Middle West, from which have sprung Sherwood Anderson and Hart Crane (Ohio), Vachel Lindsay, Carl Sandburg, Edgar Lee Masters, and Archibald MacLeish (Illinois), T. S. Eliot and Marianne Moore (both from St. Louis, Missouri).

But the most original American works have since 1930 been inspired by the South. The most active critics have been linked with the Southern periodicals: the now-defunct *Southern Review,* the *Virginia Quarterly Review,* the *Sewanee Review,* occasionally the

3. The second novels by both John Horne Burns, *Le Diable au collège (Lucifer with a Book),* and by Norman Mailer, *Rivage de Barbarie (Barbary Shore),* proved, as is to be expected, disappointing.

Southwest Review. Allen Tate, John Crowe Ransom, and Robert Penn Warren had even dreamed of building up in the South a new economy as the basis for a better-balanced culture, and French periodicals have occasionally treated that movement of 'the Fugitives.' James Branch Cabell, Ellen Glasgow, and Willa Cather were Virginians. Thomas Wolfe and Margaret Mitchell have popularized other parts of the South, which they love. William Goyen, Truman Capote, and half a dozen other writers of note, since 1945, also came from the Deep South. Negro writers, at least two of whom have been warmly admired in France, the novelist Richard Wright and the fine poet Langston Hughes, have added to the poetical prestige of the South. Above all, Erskine Caldwell in Georgia and William Faulkner in his Yoknapatawpha County in northern Mississippi have done for those states what Thomas Hardy had done for Wessex and Walter Scott for Scotland, Giono for Provence and Mauriac for the French Bordelais. They have annexed new provinces to literary geography and won for their native districts an epic glamor, which is already attracting pilgrims.

Such is the magic of literary creation. The South, vanquished in the Civil War, left behind in the economic struggle, the depressed area of the United States in the eyes of many Americans, has had its revenge; it has won the literary battle of America. Through the South, the immense continent seems to have gained a consciousness of tradition and a sense of history. Through the South also, it has acquired a sense of tragedy, which haunts Southern novelists (Wolfe in *You Can't Go Home Again* and Faulkner in 'A Rose for Emily') like a curse; but this sense of history and of tragedy was probably necessary to the growth of American literature, since its expansion beyond Concord and Boston and Baltimore. Faulkner, like Hardy in England and Mauriac in France, has tapped the richest source of fictional themes for a novelist: the excessive concentration of life in a restricted provincial environment, the jealous spying of family upon family, the bitter struggle between dispossessed traditional heirs and brutal newcomers. Above all this, he has conjured up the ghost of slavery, which hovers over his novels and for which the South must still atone. The fascination of the American South has proved so great for several younger writers of France who have never crossed the Atlantic that they have unwittingly transplanted that setting into their own novels of French life; one hears Negro spirituals in the Pyrenees or drinks Jamaica rum in Burgundy to exorcise ancestral spirits, the fields are planted with cotton or with corn, and the smell of sassafras perfumes the countryside. Thus the mechanical imitation of much-admired American novels has played upon some French writers the same literary trick of which American poets had been victims in the early nineteenth century, when they conscientiously composed hymns to skylarks and odes to nightingales without ever having heard or seen those European birds.[4]

Strangely enough, the natural scenery of America, which now populates the imagination of European readers, is no longer that of Mayne Reid or Fenimore Cooper, not even that of Jack London's stories. It is seldom that of New England or of the Midwestern plains, for neither Robert Frost's verse nor evocations of *American Beauty* attempted by Edna Ferber or LeGrand Cannon, neither Ruth Suckow's descriptions of Iowa nor Willa Cather's Nebraska scenery in *One of Ours* have succeeded in bringing those sections of America vividly to foreign eyes. The Far West and its colorful canyons, the splendors of Nevada, Arizona, and Colorado, and the bays and mountains of Washington and Oregon have had thus far little or no place in American literature; the superb rivers and trees, unequaled on the European continent, have apparently beggared description or daunted the powers of writer and painter alike. As a result, the most familiar local color for readers of American works is the dreary expanse of Georgia or Mississippi, humanized by deeply rooted traditions and apparently better attuned to the tragic sensibility of literary creators.

The second feature that marks the American novels selected by the French for translation is their violence. The day now seems remote indeed when Flaubert and Zola were deemed too brutal for English-speaking readers! The compatriots of Proust and Céline apparently find their own literature too tame, for they plunge with the delight of exotic discovery into the improbable scenes of American letters. Desertion occurs in almost every war novel, in Dos Passos's remarkable *Three Soldiers* and in Hemingway's *Farewell to Arms* for instance. Rape, next to incest, might be judged, from several of these novels, to be a favorite pastime of Americans. O'Neill, Jeffers, even Faulkner seem haunted by incest. Only homosexuality seemed, again judging from literature, to find more favor with the French than with the Americans, until a new generation

4. Indeed, it is seriously advanced that the widespread reading of Southern writers has led the French agronomists to turn the Rhone Delta, the once-arid Camargue, into rice fields, and the region south of Montpellier, once exclusively planted with vines, into a cotton-growing district. Some success seemed to have crowned their efforts, which the development of irrigation financed by the Marshall plan helped also.

of American novelists rose to redress that 'defect' in their national heritage. John W. Aldridge, in his *After the Lost Generation,* listed a number of novels touching on that burning theme. Some recent French plays even take place in an American setting, so as to enjoy, one suspects, the advantage of a dramatic lynching scene.

But the amusement and amazement of French readers have been especially aroused by the drinking and loving habits that they find described in American fiction, heightened, of course, by the intensity or the conventionality of art. Heroes of *The Sun Also Rises,* of *The Iceman Cometh,* of Salinger, Hammett, and others seem endowed with a superhuman capacity for imbibing, at which the French marvel all the more as they would inevitably have to pay for such orgies with liver troubles and dreary Vichy 'cures.'

As to sex, the French feel vaguely humiliated by the descriptions of American fiction, which are throwing many of their own love stories into the tepid category of Sunday-school reading! Hemingway's evocations of love as the most glamorous of sports next to bull-fighting, Caldwell's *Journeyman* and *God's Little Acre,* and Steinbeck's *Wayward Bus* are a veritable orgy of love. Edmund Wilson's *Hecate County* has not ravished French critics. But the greatest uproar was caused in 1946–47 by Henry Miller. This disciple of Céline and Lawrence found himself the cynosure of literary life in 1946. Critics, reporters, and moralists aligned themselves for or against him; his books were deemed so perilous to virtue that they were brought to trial, while admirers of *Tropic of Cancer* and *Tropic of Capricorn* compared their hero to Christ flagellated by jealous or narrow-minded Pharisees! Sober commentators remarked that it had taken an American (long steeped in the most malodorous aspects of Parisian life, to be sure) to make Céline appear more innocent than a choirboy and Casanova an impotent weakling.

The entertainment derived from the debauchery of violence in American fiction is accompanied by some feeling of silly complacence among the inheritors of an old culture who like to think of North America as populated by young barbarians. The interest taken by Europeans in the United States has not ceased, since the *Jesuit Relations* and Rousseau, to be an aspect of their taste for primitivism. Few Frenchmen, however, are naïve enough to take the murders, the sexual prowess, and the drinking bouts of American fiction as a faithful copy of American life. Rather do they admire in that violence a healthy, if brutal, reaction against the monotony and standardization of conditions prevailing in America. Many of them heave a sigh of relief, after imagining American life as an 'air-conditioned nightmare,' in which cleanliness reigns supreme, efficiency crushes individuals, and conformity is the law, when they discover that there are also the itinerant destitutes of *The Grapes of Wrath,* the noncon-formists of *Tortilla Flat,* the human waifs of *Tobacco Road,* and the idiot, whose masterly monologue in *The Sound and the Fury* is already a *locus classicus* of French criticism.

Their esteem for America is in no way impaired by contempla-tion of the seamy side of things. Only Nazi Germany (and perhaps Stalinist Russia) has insisted upon displaying in their literature nothing but the clean, efficient, moral — and lifeless — face of their country. They left the world unconvinced. Robust and adult nations like the United States and France know fully well that there is more to their civilization than the Champs Elysées and the Riviera hotels, than Fifth Avenue and Miami Beach. They are not afraid to emphasize the uncomely sights of their country in their plays and novels. Only a few superficial observers will see in this a proof of French corruption or American brutality. Behind unusual aspects of the United States, the French readers of American works seek something deeper, of which they are in dire need: a message of vitality and a freshness of vision, which raise violence and vice to the stature of the epic.

The literature of Europe, however expert in technique and subtle in psychological dissection, lacks vigor and knows it. Kafka and Proust, Huxley and Gide, Auden and Rilke are supremely endowed with intelligence and sensitiveness; but they lack im-aginative power to re-create life, that is, an intense grasp on the concrete. They are unequaled in self-conscious delineation of moods of frustration and repression, in polished irony, and even in searching exploration of the recesses of the ego. But their readers detect signs of excessive maturity in their overrefined works and yearn for the uncouth youthfulness that Steinbeck, Heming-way, and Caldwell seem to have in abundance. The splendid promise of American letters, to be sure, is seldom fulfilled; the last touches that would assure true greatness, the tranquil recollection that might sublimate and prolong the shock of immediacy, and the depth of thought that has seldom marred good novels are often lacking. But Europeans who dip into *Sanctuary, God's Little Acre,* even *The Big Money* are relieved to discover characters who take hold of them and plots in which the authors seem to have earnestly believed. We may imagine their thrill of discovery, after having lived too long in the rarefied atmosphere of Proust and become weary of the effete irony of Maurois or E. M. Forster, the unconvincing and laborious synthesis of Jules Romains, the impalpable halo into which Virginia Woolf dissolves her heroines, and the elaborate philosophical discourses of Thomas Mann's mouthpieces.

The ambition of the novel has been, since Balzac and Tolstoy, to take the place left vacant by the disappearance of the epic. An element of willful intensification of life has always been necessary to the epic. The power to move heroes through ordeals and battles and to relate adventures with convincingness have been attributes of the epic creator. In this sense, the American novel of today, at its best, comes near to the epic. Dos Passos in *U.S.A.*, Steinbeck in his admirable *In Dubious Battle,* which is a greater achievement artistically than *The Grapes of Wrath,* and Faulkner in *As I Lay Dying* rank among the epic novelists of our age.

Jean-Paul Sartre, whose prestige is second to none with the contemporary French public, said aptly: 'What we looked for above all in the American novel was something quite different from its crudities and its violence.' [5] It was nothing less than a renewal of the setting, the subject matter, and the technique of the traditional French novel. The recent vogue of American letters was excessive; some of its manifestations were at times ludicrous and will pass away, as the waves of enthusiasm for Byron, Poe, and Dostoevski ebbed away. But they left French and other European literatures profoundly transformed.

The French are the unchallenged masters of the *roman d'analyse*. From *La Princesse de Clèves* to Marivaux and Laclos in the eighteenth century, then from Benjamin Constant's *Adolphe* and Stendhal to Proust and Mauriac, their vocation in fiction has been to probe searchingly into the workings of man's mind and soul, to bring to light the hidden motives of actions and the complex nuances of feelings. Proust has gone as far as seems humanly possible in that direction. Nothing was left for French novelists to do, after him, but to break away from an introspection that was becoming static and artificial. Since 1925 or 1930, French fiction, led by Malraux, Saint-Exupéry, and Giono, has aimed at capturing the mysteries of man in action and not at rest, at substituting a synthetic perception of human nature for an analytical dissection. While they were seeking new paths away from a valuable but exhausted French tradition, they hit upon Faulkner and Dos

5. *The Atlantic Monthly,* August 1946.

Passos and even upon Dashiell Hammett, Damon Runyon, Raymond Chandler, and writers who were lesser artists than themselves but from whom they were ready to learn. In an important interview given in January 1945, to the English review *Horizon*, Malraux declared: 'To my mind the essential characteristic of contemporary American writing is that it is the only literature whose creators are not intellectuals . . . They are obsessed with fundamental man . . . The great problem of this literature is now to intellectualize itself without losing its direct approach.'

Malraux converted elder writers like Gide, who, himself more gifted in abstract analysis of man than in concrete evocation of man's behavior, had nevertheless felt the need of more 'raw meat' in French literature, which was addicted to dressing and softening its fare. Gide went so far as to proclaim his admiration for the superior detective stories of Dashiell Hammett (*The Thin Man, The Maltese Falcon,* and *The Red Harvest*). The most refined of French novelists then discovered with eagerness *Miss Lonelyhearts,* the cruel and very able story by Nathaniel West, whose untimely death at thirty-six is one of the gravest losses of modern American literature; John O'Hara's skillful rendering of the atmosphere of the twenties in *Appointment in Samara;* James Cain, Horace McCoy, Damon Runyon, and other 'poets of the tabloid murder,' as Edmund Wilson once called these novelists of the hard-boiled school.

This is not only contagion of literary fashion. The French have realized lately that their excessively analytical literature was too narrowly addressed to an 'unhappy few': the few thousands in any country who are capable of introspection and enjoy the leisure required by such soul-searching. Millions of other potential readers, untrained in such examinations of conscience and often inarticulate, were never reached by the traditional novel of analysis. These readers had to resort to the coarser type of murder stories. Why not do for them what Poe and the author of *Crime and Punishment* had already done, cater to their legitimate craving for sensation and the thrill of violent action, while fulfilling many of the requisites of art?

This taste for synthetic as against analytical psychology, for sensations powerfully evoked as against elaborate disquisitions on hidden motives, has been apparent in France since Malraux, Giono, and Saint-Exupéry succeeded Proust and Gide in popularity, in 1930 or thereabouts. It became more marked with the war years. The vision of brutality and swift, cruel, illogical action presented

by American novels then became an all-too-real nightmare in the
countries invaded by Germany. Any attempt to understand rationally a baffling apocalypse or to philosophize about events
seemed ludicrous. For the men and women summarily arrested
by the Gestapo, huddled together into concentration camps, and
for the youth exposed to the hazards of the *maquis,* American
books assumed a prophetic character. They proved to be the ones
best attuned to a tragic era of incomprehensible violence and
brutal sadism.

To be sure, the French readers, when some semblance of nor-
mality was again enjoyed, could not fail to be sensitive to the
lack of art, which characterizes much American literature. Very
soon the most gifted followers of Dos Passos, such as Sartre, of
Hemingway, such as Camus, and of Faulkner, such as Mouloudji,
Desforets, and Magnane, were much more preoccupied than their
models by the problem of discovering a form for their functional
attempts. But the form will be a richer one for having known a
few variations from the older, and outworn, French mold. The
writers of the New World have taught the French a refreshing
disregard for composition, a total detachment from such rules as
unity of plot, a youthful freedom from artistic restraint. Theirs was
a type of writing that aimed neither at pure art nor at eternal
values and that cared little for posterity or even for survival. To
compatriots of Flaubert and Mallarmé, whose sin was to deify
literature, the contrast was salutary.

The best among modern French writers are not content with
imitating their American models. Camus, in *La Peste,* and Sartre,
in *Le Sursis,* have beaten Hemingway and Dos Passos at their
own game. Elsewhere they have out-Faulknered Faulkner. With
more art than their masters, they have used their devices: Faulkner's reversibility of time, Dos Passos's simultaneous action, the
'punch' of Caldwell's dialogue, Steinbeck's vivid narrative, and
Hemingway's 'eye on the object.' The coarseness and orgy of sex
and lust, which entertained the French public for a time, will
soon be forgotten; but the lessons of concreteness and effectiveness,
learned from American writing and substituted, in the canon of
literary qualities, for abstractness and beauty, are likely to remain.
American fiction has brought to European artists a new accumulation of materials.

Another characteristic of modern American books fitted them
peculiarly to the days of wrath through which Europe had been

living. Their implicit philosophy is one of pessimism. Their pessimism may be a constant and deep-seated feature of the literature of America, for, with the exception of Emerson and possibly
Whitman, it has characterized most of the important writers of
the 'young country': Mark Twain, Poe, Hawthorne, Melville,
Emily Dickinson, Henry James, Stephen Crane, Edgar Lee Masters,
Theodore Dreiser, and all our contemporaries, including Ameri-
can-born Julien Green, the gloomiest of present-day French authors. The most disillusioned books about World War I came from
the writers of the country that was physically least affected by it:
The Enormous Room, Three Soldiers, What Price Glory, and
A Farewell to Arms. The sharpest revulsion against mechanical
civilization, the bitterest satire of businessmen and of ladies' clubs,
of the good fellowship of Rotarians and of standardized religion
have been expressed by O'Neill and Steinbeck, by the authors of
Elmer Gantry and of *Journeyman,* even by James Branch Cabell
and the Thornton Wilder of *Heaven's My Destination.*

But America need not blush at this literature of despair. Its
pessimism is not the sterile mockery of cynics nor the decadent
need to soil the beauty of the world. It is the expression of sincere idealism, of lucid faith. It asserts with eloquence that all is
not well with the world, but that, by facing realities boldly, we
could make life more worthy of being lived. If American literature today has scaled epic heights more courageously than any
other, it has also plumbed the depths of tragedy. André Malraux,
as early as 1933, prefacing the French translation of *Sanctuary,*
called Faulkner's book 'the intrusion of Greek tragedy into the detective novel.' [6] Few writers, since Emily Brontë and Thomas
Hardy, have a more just claim to being continuators of Sophocles
than has Faulkner.

The reasons for this tragic pessimism of American writing are
complex. They are in part social and reflect the isolation of the
artist in a society in which money values are paramount, which
esteems him no more than a flute player. They are in part religious,
for the fatality of original sin haunts Faulkner as it did his truest
predecessor, Hawthorne. O'Neill revives the Catholic doctrine of
man's guilt, and Jeffers the wailing of the Jewish prophets about
the vanity of everything under the sun. The greatest American

6. That important text by Malraux, which in 1933 assured Faulkner's glory in
   Europe, appeared in English translation in *Yale French Studies,* No. 10,
   1952.

poet of the century, Hart Crane, was driven to suicide. Henry Miller, with all his obscene eroticism, is far remote from any cheerful enjoyment of life; his torrent of words hardly conceals an abyss of inner emptiness.

But this tragic pessimism of American writers is to be explained chiefly by their acute perception of the gulf that divides man's power to transform the world through science and technology and his powerlessness to change himself. A similar gulf lies gaping between man's proud assertion of his freedom and his bondage to the fatalities that flesh is heir to. His official philosophy bids the American citizen practice the pursuit of happiness, and as soon as he stops working, he is oppressed by boredom and must drink a few cocktails so as to endure his leisure hours. He claims to live without tragedy, and he is driven to seek substitutes for tragedy in drinks, sex, or murder stories. He stares several times a day at advertisements that proclaim that women are lovely, pink-cheeked creatures, with immaculately waved hair and alluring stockings, intent upon welcoming husbands in the cleanest of modern homes — and no literature is more deeply obsessed than his by misunderstanding and antagonism between the sexes. Seldom has woman been hated and love reviled, in fiction or drama, as it has been in *Desire under the Elms, Tamar, Men without Women,* and *Miss Lonelyhearts.*

But this pessimism is virile. It is probably the deep manifestation of the influence that movies have had upon American letters. Through the shallow conventionality of its films, their sickening happy endings, and their fear of the realities of life, Hollywood has driven many of the best American writers to emphasize what the screen has left unsaid: the seamy but authentic and robust aspects of modern life. In so doing, American novelists have provided their countrymen with a healthy psychological outlet. They have been led to eschew sentimentality and to reach for great subjects. Their pessimism and violence conceal a virile quality of warm humanity. Foreign observers have seen it perhaps more acutely than many Americans. The critic of a French weekly, *Action,* wrote, on October 6, 1944: 'The American novel is well suited to teach us the road to a healthy, powerful literature which finds, in a broad contact with the world, essential reasons for faith in itself.' Others lauded plays drawn from American novels and acted with phenomenal success in Paris — *Of Mice and Men* and *As I Lay Dying* — because their humanity had helped the French live through the darkest days of the war and the postwar years. Sartre, who is the influential prophet of a new French generation, paid a debt of gratitude when he declared in 1946:

> The greatest literary development in France between 1929 and 1939 was the discovery of Faulkner, Dos Passos, Hemingway, Caldwell, Steinbeck . . . To writers of my generation, the publication of *The 42nd Parallel*, *Light in August*, *A Farewell to Arms* effected a revolution similar to the one produced fifteen years earlier in Europe by the *Ulysses* of Joyce.

BIBLIOGRAPHICAL NOTES

Out of the huge mass of articles on the modern American novel that has appeared in France (or in Great Britain), a very few essential titles are mentioned here.

L'Age Nouveau, Visages des Etats-Unis, Nos. 74, 75 and 76 in one volume, June–August 1952.

Arnavon, Cyrille, *Histoire littéraire des Etats-Unis*, Hachette, 1953.

Coindreau, Maurice-E., *Aperçus de littérature américaine*, Gallimard, 1946.

Cunliffe, Marcus, *The Literature of the United States*, Penguin Books, London and Baltimore, 1954.

'The Fallacy of Experience,' *The Times Literary Supplement*, May 15, 1953.

Fontaine, Ecrivains et Poètes des Etats-Unis, Nos. 27 and 28, August 1943. *Yale French Studies*, French-American Literary Relationships, No. 10, 1952.

Frohock, W. M., *The Novel of Violence in America*, Southern Methodist Press, Dallas, Texas, 1951.

Magny, Claude-Edmonde, *L'Age du roman américain*, Editions du Seuil, 1948.

Russell, Bertrand, and others, *The Impact of America on European Culture*, The Beacon Press, Boston, 1951.

Sartre, J.-P., 'American Novelists in French Eyes,' *The Atlantic Monthly*, CLXXVIII, 2, August 1946, pp. 114–18.

——, 'A propos de *Le Bruit et la fureur:* la temporalité chez Faulkner,' *Nouvelle Revue Française*, XXVII, 309, July 1939, pp. 1,057–61, and XXVIII, 310, pp. 145–51, reprinted in *Situations*, 70–81.

——, 'A propos de Dos Passos,' *Nouvelle Revue Française*, XXVI, 299, August 1938, pp. 292–301, reprinted in *Situations*, pp. 14–25.

——, '*Sartoris* par W. Faulkner,' *Nouvelle Revue Française*, XXVI, 293, February 1938, pp. 323–28, translated in *Yale French Studies*, No. 10, reprinted in *Situations*, 7–13.

XI

THE PRESENT TEMPER IN FRANCE

JUDGED THROUGH FRENCH

LITERATURE

T HE PURPOSE of this volume has been to offer a comprehensive
view of the chief novelists and of the main trends of the
novel in France since 1930 and, more particularly, since Proust
and Gide. Comprehensiveness, however, is not synonymous with
inclusiveness. Every reader could probably mention one or two
of his favorite writers, who might have deserved treatment in a
separate chapter or section. A similar claim might be made for
half a dozen novelists of different age groups, who count a number of devotees — Colette, Céline, Bernanos, Green, Queneau,
Aymé — and for three others — Cocteau, Giraudoux, and Montherlant — whose achievement as novelists pales, in our opinion,
when compared with their far more original accomplishment as
dramatists or as moralists. It is our conviction that special treatment is not justified even for Céline and Bernanos. Granting our
inveterate lack of sympathy, we cannot bring ourselves to declare,
with honesty, as critics must often do: 'I do not like him, but he
is very great.' Brief mention in an enumerative appendix would

give a truer measure of our moderate admiration; it would be fairer to Céline and Bernanos and to our readers to leave to other students of modern fiction a more enthusiastic appreciation of two visionary giants with clay feet, addicted to orgies of words.[1]

We are reluctant, however, to bring our fairly comprehensive treatment of the French novel to a close with Sartre, Camus, and Simone de Beauvoir. High as our esteem of these writers is and significant as existentialism appears to us in retrospect to have been in the decade 1940–50, French fiction did not stop with Sartre, and it certainly was not summed up in him. No one may presume to decide which of the younger French novelists are, once for all, to be set apart as 'great' (and there are, of course, many ways of being 'great,' with new ones being invented every year). Some who were very promising at thirty-five may be diverted to other media; others may not choose to write a second novel, or may repeat their past performances without instilling new energy into their later works. The participants in the race against oblivion among the recent French novelists are many. We have repeatedly asserted that a critic must take his stand and, if he has any discernment, it must be applied to the elucidation of contemporary works, as well as to values already classified. This we are doing in an Appendix, which lists nearly one hundred modern French novelists, all or almost all born since 1900; in it we venture a succinct appreciation of their achievement and promise. We believe that such a reader's guide may be of service to many a person who, not frightened by some exploration into uncharted lands, wishes to go beyond Nobel Prize winners and glamorous existentialists. Publishers translate French novels avidly, and not a few of these recent works of fiction may soon appear in an English version. Clearly, a critical listing of immediately contemporary books lays no claim to finality. We do not even attempt to anticipate the judgment of posterity, which may have hardly more finality than that of discriminating contemporaries. We take our stand, arbitrarily, no doubt, but in honesty and humility. A choice must be made, and we propose ours in the spirit defined by Bergson in the first chapter of *La Pensée et le mouvant*:

We transmit to future generations what interests us, what our attention considers and even sketches in the light of our past

1. Albert Béguin and Gaëtan Picon, two very acute critics, have written with warmth on Bernanos as a novelist and as a pamphleteer. Germaine Brée is soon to publish a volume on French novelists in which Céline and Bernanos will be treated with sympathy.

evolution, but not what the future will have made interesting for them through the creation of a new interest, through a new bent given to their own attention.

Much of this volume and the attention given in our final chapter and in our Appendix to the present writers who may win real eminence tomorrow have rested upon our reasoned conviction that the French novel of today continues to be rich, varied, and significant — indeed, second in quality to no other comparable period of French literature. It is true that much wailing is heard among Frenchmen, and much negative and surly frowning at recent novels is indulged in by weary or crabbed academic critics. Complaints that we hear today have been uttered in the past and may, indeed, inspire us with healthy optimism. At all times, not excepting the times of Proust, Zola, Balzac, and Rousseau, critics and readers have deplored the formlessness, the lack of refinement, and the immorality of the novels then being written. Yet after a few decades, the literature thus condemned, disengaged from more ephemeral attempts, has outlived the lamentations of the critics. Sainte-Beuve, Nisard, Montégut, Brunetière, and a score of others who opposed a genteel and moral literature to the more energetic works, which repelled their 'good' taste, have been regularly proven timid or ridiculously blind by later consensus of opinion. So few critics are honestly sympathetic to younger talents that we would rather err on the side of generosity than on the side of systematic disparagement. The latter is often an easy pretext for not attempting to read the new works or not venturing to form an opinion about them. The critics who are now in their fifties or sixties are fond of repeating that the French novel of 1940–55 lacks the brilliance and the audacity of the fiction that entranced their younger days, when, between 1920 and 1935, the discovery of Dostoevski, then of Joyce, Proust, Gide, and Mann spurred literature to renew both its themes and its technique. It is true that literature proper attracted more talents and monopolized the attention of the public after World War I, when a dozen important periodicals were devoted to it. Since then, philosophy and, to a lesser extent, social and economic speculation have vied with literature in liveliness and in force. The atmosphere of the 'forties and 'fifties is darker, the sense of tragedy more oppressive; poetry and fiction have had to discard any air of irresponsibility and often a sense of humor and playful nonchalance. Yet, except for Proust who has had no equal in our time, we doubt that the talents of 1935–55, starting with Malraux, Green, Giono, Montherlant, Sartre, and Camus, and continuing with Bazin, Beckett, Blanchot, Brincourt, Cabanis, Gadenne, Genet, Nimier, Roblès, and Thomas (to name ten of the most promising novelists of the present time), are inferior to those who fired the enthusiasm of the youth after World War I: Bernanos, Cocteau, Duhamel, Durtain, Lacretelle, Larbaud, Mauriac, and Maurois. The critical articles of the years 1920–35 echoed with the same lamentations on the dearth of new talents and on the invasion of immorality as we read today.

In one respect at least, a new force is at work in contemporary French literature, which gives the years after 1940 a clear advantage over the earlier postwar era: the number and eminence of women writers.

French feminine literature can boast a long and glorious tradition. Marie de France, Louise Labé, Mme de Sévigné, and the creator of the psychological novel, Mme de la Fayette, long had no equals in Europe. Strangely enough, with the advent of the nineteenth century, women writers, after Mme de Staël and George Sand, almost disappeared from the front rank of letters in France. Yet the invasion of poetry by the lyrical and elegiac muses, the vogue of the personal novel and of confessions and memoirs, even the observant eye directed at manners and at the setting of life should have favored women writers, for more women than ever before had acquired literacy and culture. In the first half of the twentieth century, Colette became an institution for many literary connoisseurs. That she was the finest French prose writer alive was an unchallenged opinion. Expert as she is as a stylist, exquisite as her chiseling of words and images can be at times, we believe that her prose is too ornate and too remote from the naturalness and simplicity of the very great works of art for her to rank with the truly eminent masters of French prose. Her mannerisms soon pall on the fastidious reader. Her characters are too monotonous and they wander complacently in an atmosphere of venal loves, carnal concerns, and gigolos, without rising to the stature of Proustian lovers or Toulouse-Lautrec's mournful seekers of joy. The men whom she depicts, including weak-willed Chéri and a number of vain Don Juans more often jilted than jilting, seldom come to life. They certainly never attempt to reach toward their partner's or their own inner life or to attain heroism. Love, with Colette as in the early work of Paul Bourget and in Anatole

France's faded *Lys rouge,* inevitably means lies. 'There is a pleasure in being devoted to those who deceive us, who wear their lie like a finely adorned gown and open it only through the voluptuous pleasure of showing themselves nude.' Thus wrote Colette in *La Retraite sentimentale.* This woman, who went deep into the bitter abyss of sensation and whose many volumes endlessly illustrate Paul Valéry's celebrated epigram ('The deepest part of man is his skin'), failed to create solid works of fiction or characters likely to live in the memories of generations of readers. Her prestige discouraged French women writers for several decades. Today, however, she appears almost prehistoric, with her 1900 atmosphere of boudoirs and calculating demi-mondaines. A revolution has thrown her back into the era of an old regime.

The liberation of women between the two world wars was a considerable event, the consequences of which have not yet been fully assessed. The sudden conquest of political and social rights seemed at first to embarrass women, as a similar victory had left men uncertain and timorous after the French Revolution and after their first social gains. In France, women leaped to the fore in many professions, proved brilliantly audacious in the resistance and in social work, won an influence second to none as philosophers (Simone Weil and Simone de Beauvoir), as critics (Claude-Edmonde Magny), and as journalists. Yet neither women nor men may become fully aware of the implications of the 'redemption of women out of these incredible folds and webs of silliness and millinery' (Walt Whitman) until women novelists universalize their experience in powerful works of fiction and hold the mirror up to men, creating male characters in whom men are forced to recognize themselves.

The task is arduous, and until recent years it had been more successfully assumed by British and American women novelists. More often than the French, perhaps, they had what Virginia Woolf has defined as the prerequisite for a thinking and writing woman, 'a room of one's own,' and could achieve the intense concentration that makes up half of genius. More freely than most French women, Anglo-Saxon writers could, perhaps, disregard concern with the company of man and the tributes of male gallantry and achieve the addition of madness to talent, a condition by which Simone de Beauvoir defines genius. A few women, in the years preceding World War II, had however, in contrast with Colette's sensuous pursuits of 'those pleasures which are too lightly called physical,' attempted the grave and fervent theme of woman's solitude. Marcelle Sauvageot's *Commentaire,* in the 'thirties, was a searching self-analysis of a young woman, raised in comfort and happiness and crowned with every grace, who became tubercular and was condemned to a sanatorium. She wished to live for the sake of being loved. She awaited an avowal of love from a man whose reserve she ascribed to shyness. One day, a fateful letter arrived, selfishly and cowardly masculine. 'I am going to marry . . . but our friendship will remain.' The young woman was to die soon after, but her lucidity never deserted her. In 1933, another lonely woman, afflicted with a physical deformity, Paule Régnier, published one of the finest feminine novels in French, *L'Abbaye d'Evolayne.* A struggle between religion and love, in a woman reminiscent of Corneille's Pauline, whose husband had suddenly become a convert and a monk, ended in the defeat of religion. Paule Régnier's tragedy was fully revealed when her *Journal* appeared posthumously in 1953. She had loved a young writer of promise, Paul Drouot, the author of *Eurydice deux fois perdue,* a long prose poem of lasting beauty. He was killed in battle in 1915. Much later, after his dying mother had entrusted the soldier's papers to Paule Régnier, she discovered that he would never have answered her love and had only been kind to the superior intelligence and the hunchback that she was. All along he had loved another. For years she lived on, writing, in the bitterness of her heart, to deaden her pain, until in 1950 she took her own life.

The solitude of the single woman or of the aging married woman, of the woman whom conventions prevent from declaring her passion or of the woman plunged into the 'well of loneliness' is one of the themes that women novelists will explore in the coming decades. The woman as mother, and especially the tragedy of a vicious and cruel childhood as watched by the powerless mother, is a second theme that has been too little exploited. Social questions, even metaphysical ones, and, of course, the dismal picture of heinous families in which Mauriac and Green have specialized, followed by at least one successful woman novelist, Lucie Marchal in *La Mèche,* lie within the reach of the new feminine literature. Célia Bertin, one of the most able of the newcomers, has ventured into the field in a striking novel, *La Dernière innocence* (1953). To women we owe some of the finest storytellers' tales of recent years (Elsa Triolet, Nicole Vedrès, Zoé Oldenbourg, all Russian born or part Russian); the finest psychological reconstruction of an ancient character attempted since Walter Pater,

Memoires d'Hadrien, by Marguerite Yourcenar; the most conspicuously successful novel in the tradition of Laclos, *Le Rempart des Béguines,* by Françoise Mallet; one of the few good poetical novels since Giraudoux, *Eve la Blonde* by Lise Deharme; an airy fairy tale steeped in Breton folklore, *Jabadao,* by Anne de Tourville, and some fiercely 'masculine' and thoughtful fictional works by Simone de Beauvoir, Marguerite Duras, and Beatrix Beck.

Simone de Beauvoir, in her huge *Summa* on the second sex, stole all the weapons in the arsenals of male philosophers, anthropologists, and psychoanalysts and threw the gauntlet to her sex, heretofore too shy in its ambitions. Feminine literature has indeed, in the past, limited itself to a small number of provinces: escape to a world of dreams, the beautification of daily life through graceful art and the tenderness of a sentimental presence, and, more generally, concern with the question of happiness and with feminine subjectivity. The most touching gift of a loving woman is that of her past, of her jealously preserved treasure of childhood memories and of the world of purity and of dreams in which she grew up; she wishes her lover to share it with her and to recapture the lost paradise. Such an expression of happiness — the banished theme of modern letters — is not lightly to be cast aside. The French, who have not lost their zest for happiness through the ordeals of two world wars, have for all practical purposes exiled this theme from their literature, most of all from the comedy of Anouilh, Aymé, and others. It would be a noble achievement for women writers to restore the word and the subject to their rightful estate, in a frail and threatened world. All literature rests on a system of conventions and, as André Gide once said, an individual, a people, and a civilization are best revealed by the parts of their physical and moral beings that they conceal.

But the nature of literature demands that it be laden with more intensity and more energy than is normal life, hence that it grant a large place to passion and violence. Feminine fiction in France has seldom, in the past, hit what would seem to be a just note when treating the relations between the sexes. It has either lost itself in half shades and in a graceful modesty, which kept too shy of risk and dwelt complacently in 'the envelopment of the body by the soul,' the Nietzschean definition of *pudeur;* or else, from George Sand to Mme de Noailles and, more recently, to Dominique Rolin, the author of *Moi qui ne suis qu'amour,* it has thrown chastity and shame to the winds. The claims of women, during the two decades following World War II, to the unreserved rights to love, to know happiness, and to enjoy pleasure in love, and to dispose of their bodies, as well as of their cultivated and self-asserting minds, shook many men from their complacence. These claims may explain, in part, the concentrated attacks against romantic love, which fill the literature of these years. Never, indeed, has the age-old battle between the sexes raged more furiously than in the pages of Proust, Gide, Mauriac, Jouhandeau, Green, Malraux, Montherlant, and their successors, even more outspoken in their arrogant treatment of women as tools (Roger Nimier, Raymond Guérin, Hervé Bazin, and Roger Vailland) or in their proclaimed preference for homosexual loves. Catholic writers themselves, from Paul Claudel down, who paid women the tribute of believing them dangerous as vessels of sin, saw in them baits laid by God to bring men back to divine love after human passions had sufficiently disappointed their quest for a total fulfillment, which their earthly life regularly frustrates.

Woman thus became exiled from a vast section of literature, in France as in America. She was feared more often than loved, and hated because man saw a judge and a witness in her. She cuts a sorry figure in the most typical of the American novels inspired by World War II (*The Gallery, The Young Lions, The Naked and the Dead, From Here to Eternity, The End of My Life, The Sheltering Sky,* and *Lie Down in Darkness*). Men seem systematically to be bent upon avenging themselves upon her for the respect they have to show to her in American life. The French manner of throwing woman off her pedestal is to attack the myth of love and replace it with eroticism. Roger Vailland has formulated the theory and suggested the methods, after Malraux and Montherlant had paved the way. French literature of the third and fourth decades of this century truly became a desert of love, and many a humorist proposed a mournful epitaph to inscribe on the grave of the theme that once enraptured poet and novelist: 'Love, an invention of the thirteenth century, deceased in the twentieth.'

Women writers have gained from the unvarnishing of the worn-out theme, conventionally treated in too rapturous a fashion. They do not ask for any condescension from men critics and they refuse to be restricted to a literature of romance and gently embroidered falsehood. No subject is forbidden them, and Lesbianism has been squarely set at the center of several recent feminine novels, by Célia Bertin and Françoise Mallet, for instance. Even more difficult, however, are the simpler theme of the position of the modern woman in the family, in society, and in professional work, and the theme of her insistence on not forsaking, in love, her clear-sightedness and her sincerity. Such are the vindications formu-lated by recent women writers in France and made good by several of their works of fiction. Through them, the prophecies of Rilke in his *Letters to a Young Poet* and of D. H. Lawrence in his letters, that love is a difficult fulfillment, reached only through much suffering and a patient quest, after 'a journey towards the other soul, not away from it,' may come true; or the even more startling wish formulated by Rimbaud at the age of seventeen in his Seer's letter that 'when the infinite serfdom of woman is broken, when she lives for and by herself, . . . she too will be a poet. She will find the unknown, strange, unfathomable, repulsive, delicious things . . .'

Next to the accession of women writers, who constitute one-fifth or one-sixth of the number of novelists worthy of note today in France, the enrichment of French literature by another group, whose autonomous character is geographical, has drawn some com-ment in our Appendix (see under Mammeri): the North Africans, mostly of mixed blood. A growing originality distinguishes their work, far more markedly than, in British literature, that of the Australians or the New Zealanders. The North Africans have contributed the robustness of newcomers to culture, the deep roots they seem to cherish in their mountains or plains, a Mediterranean paganism, which has been opposed by Camus to the northern worship of death, less introspective refinement than one finds in authors of metropolitan France, and a more powerful impulse toward heroic transcendence.[2]

The youth or the early manhood of most of the writers whose ages range from thirty to fifty, was indelibly impressed by one momentous event: the defeat of 1940 and the subsequent under-ground struggle or the alignment with the German occupants. The impact of this war of volunteers, in which ideological and ethical problems were primary and in which each had to take a stand and engage in a Pascalian, or existentialist, wager, has marked the adolescents and the young men and women who lived through it far more than World War I had touched their eld-ers, even more than the impact of the Spanish civil war upon Western intellectuals. Some of the thrilling dramas of the re-

2. See, in the Appendix, comments on Albert Memmi, Emmanuel Roblès, and Jules Roy.

sistance struggle were exploited early, in memoirs or in novels. The more profound aspects have only more recently been the themes of novels going beyond the ironical and healthy 'debunking' attempted by Roger Vailland, Jean-Louis Curtis, José Cabanis, and others.[3] A laudable *pudeur*, which explains, in part, the coarseness of some of the contemporary letters in France, has kept many of the writers who had fought with courage in the underground from utilizing their experience as a theme, from André Malraux and André Chamson to J.-P. Sartre and Albert Camus, even to Vercors (Jean Bruller) and Emmanuel Roblès. It may be prophesied that, for years to come, the moral issues raised by the resistance, as well as by the lamentable collapse, after 1945, and the hopes aroused during the underground struggle will echo in French literature. The experience of the concentration camps is too horrifying a nightmare to be, as yet, utilized for literary purposes. David Rousset's grim analysis of the 'concentrationary universe' hardly belongs to fiction, and one would be ashamed to treat it as such. But even the novels about the military prisoners of war, or by them, have been few and disappointing. The best is probably Sartre's *La Mort dans l'âme;* next to it, a condensed and moving story first published in the clandestine Editions de Minuit by Mortagne (that is, the Communist Claude Morgan), *La Marque de l'homme,* a masterpiece of its kind; and then paler novels by conscientious intellectuals, *Les Grandes Vacances* by Francis Ambrière,[4] or *Le Millième Jour* by Raymond Las Vergnas.[5]

The year 1950 and those following have witnessed an offensive return of former collaborators with Germany, who had been condemned to, or awed into, silence after 1945. There was and there still is obstinacy among intellectuals who want to try and prove (a common French sin) that they were right because they lost out and that the future, with the incipient German-American-western European crusade against Russia, will prove that the Germans and their few French admirers who advocated a holy war against communism were but the harbingers of the 'rollback' policy now heralded by new prophets. It seems beyond question to us that a bad conscience lingers among those who now justify themselves overeloquently and even among those who, once the admirers of Charles Maurras, like Pierre Gaxotte and Thierry-

---

3. See the Appendix for further discussion of these writers and other young French novelists mentioned in this chapter.
4. A Goncourt Prize winner. Éditions de la nouvelle France, Paris, 1946.
5. A. Michel, Paris, 1951.

Maulnier, sensed the trend of events shrewdly enough to forsake an ill-smelling cause and become honorable pillars of the French Academy or of its antechamber. A relentless obduracy characterizes the French intellectuals who belong to what we have to call 'the Right'; one of them, Montherlant, declared cynically in 1953 that civil wars are the most splendidly and ardently fought of all wars, because they are the only ones in which one knows what one is fighting for, or perhaps against. In several of the younger writers (Raymond Abellio, Roger Nimier, Pierre de Boisdeffre, Michel Mohrt, Lucien Rebatet, and others) it is easy to detect undertones of their regret for the past and their scorn for an ill-governed and vulgarly democratic France. Talent abounds among these men. They were and are intelligent and passionate; they have a highly cultured sense of style and that gift for invective that makes French polemics lively, and they have long nurtured in themselves what Molière's Alceste calls 'vigorous hatreds.'

The French novel of the last two decades is not remarkable for originality of technique or of structure. The initiators in this province were several masters from other countries whose example, which fascinated the French, was at times very successfully imitated by them: Dostoevski first of all, whose influence began to ebb after 1930, then Joyce, particularly his interior monologue, Kafka, and Dos Passos. Joyce, himself, has waned now in the admiration of the French, and the more dramatic models of interior monologue provided by the author of *The Sound and the Fury* have held the younger French generation under their sway. Yet not only Romains and Mauriac, who attacked the interior monologue as nonselective, untrue to life, and unauthentic, but the novelists of 1940–50 who have resorted to it (Raymond Guérin, Louis Pauwels, Marguerite Duras, and Nathalie Sarraute) have avoided taking it overseriously and using it, as it were, pure and unadulterated. Such a monologue, as the earlier examples of Valéry Larbaud and of Édouard Dujardin prove, can become a very tricky and wearying device.

Most of the other innovations, which professors of literature like to stress and to teach, have been treated with irreverence by the very novelists who used them: reversibility of time and kaleidoscopic action, in the manner of John Dos Passos; irony, after the fashion of Thomas Mann; multiplicity of plots eventually woven together by the author, who gapes naïvely at his own mastery; use of recurring motives, like the Proustian 'little phrase,' and so

forth. Indeed, the detachment toward all the recipes that should
be relegated to the back kitchens but that, since Flaubert, Henry
James, and the once-fashionable diaries kept by novelists concocting their novels, had gained undue prominence, is one of the most
refreshing features of the younger group of French novelists. The
sacrosanct phrases of modern pedants, 'levels of meaning,' 'formal
patterns,' 'symbols' and, worst of all, 'myth,' which have marred
much German and American fiction [6] seem to have left not only
critics but, more fortunately, novelists in France untainted. Few
of them would probably disagree with the following typical answer
made by one of the most expert craftsmen of fiction, Louis Guilloux, to an interviewer, in *Les Nouvelles Littéraires* of December
21, 1935:

> There is no technique of the novel properly speaking. There
> is a technique appropriate to each novel and it is not trans-
> missible. The novelist must incessantly invent his technique,
> and this means that the work he has just completed teaches
> him, as a rule, very little about the way in which he will write
> the next. The novelist is a man who is obsessed: What are the
> means of making the objects of his obsessions visible? . . .
> If there existed a technique of fiction, the writing of novels
> could be taught.

The bulky and very rich volume compiled by *Confluences* in 1943
under the editorship of Jean Prévost, which contained some sixty
essays under the title *Problèmes du roman,* paid hardly any attention to technique. No wonder Flaubert seems remote and totally
inactuel to the Frenchmen of today! Unashamedly and senti-
mentally, they prefer to state, as did Paul Gadenne in the same
volume: 'Faire acte de romancier, c'est faire acte d'amour.' And,
unlike their fathers or forefathers, who delighted in Colette and
Pierre Louÿs, young Frenchmen no longer seem inclined to agree
that technique, in love, is of very great moment.

Two trends seem discernible in the artistic preoccupations of
novelists today. One is the obstinate meditation on language. This
can be traced back to Mallarmé, and more immediately to the
man who, though not an imaginative storyteller himself, has exercised a very great influence upon younger writers and who is like
the archbishop *in partibus* — an impious and mischievous one,

6. Malcolm Cowley has, not unfairly, lashed out against such jargon in 'The
New Critics and the New Fiction,' *The Saturday Review,* July 25, 1953.

capable of the most baffling about-faces — of Parisian literature: Jean Paulhan. Maurice Blanchot, a far deeper critic than Paulhan, has centered all his critical meditations and, in part, his novels around the problem of language. Raymond Queneau and a number of other novelists have undertaken to instill new life into the written style by bringing it sharply into line with colloquial spoken language. This very deep concern is not merely a formal one; it translates the fundamental anguish of the modern creator, which will be touched upon below: the anguish of his solitude, of the inability of human beings to communicate.

The second general trend is that which has caused us repeatedly to use the word 'poetry' when trying to characterize certain contemporaries and to trace lingering influences of surrealism on them. The surrealist novel itself, in our opinion, has been a consistent failure, from the novels of Breton to those of Julien Gracq and Maurice Fourré.[7] This is probably because of the ponderous theoretical baggage of surrealist doctrinaires and their painfully pedestrian endeavors to grow wings and to restore magic to the world. Yet surrealism assisted in the liberation of French minds, of authors and readers alike, from the constraints of social realism, from orderly plots and rational and progressive development of characters. An atmosphere of fairy tale, an unceasing *chassé-croisé* between reality and dream, and the splendidly capricious behavior of girls free of original sin and apparently unafflicted by the weight of our 'too, too solid flesh' make up half the charm of the fiction by Henri Thomas, André Dhôtel, Anne de Tourville, André Pieyre de Mandiargues, and Jacques Perry.

One is also struck by the dwindling role, perhaps a consequence of surrealism, played in recent fiction by eloquence, pure narrative, and ambitious attempts to portray whole groups, professions, or classes. The disappearance of eloquence hardly needs elaborating upon. It has yielded to either poetry or ruthless irony. But verbal inflation, such as was conspicuous in Céline, in Bernanos, especially in his polemical or political writings, and in the early Giono has ceased to afflict French fiction. Southern Frenchmen are even more careful to avoid it than those from other regions; indeed the craving for a stripped and terse prose has become most noticeable in Italian letters, where the style of Gabriele D'Annun-

7. The contrary opinion is held, and brilliantly expounded, by a novelist-critic, Armand Hoog, in 'The Surrealist Novel,' an essay in *What's Novel in the Novel*, Yale French Studies, No. 8, 1951.

zio and Giuseppe Borgese has given way to the precise and restrained aridity of Alberto Moravia, Carlo Levi, and Elio Vittorini,
or to the discreet and timidly but hauntingly poetical manner of
Carlo Coccioli and Cesare Pavese.

Pure narrative still abounds; Elsa Triolet at her best, Guy
Dumur, Roger Nimier, Jean Dutourd, José Cabanis, Noël Devaulx,
and Hervé Bazin excel in it, or could excel in it if they really cared.
But these young novelists refuse to take it seriously and throw in
irony as a reminder of the author's momentary condescension to
the simple art of storytelling or to suggest that he is not wholly
deaf to the anguish and the misery of his fellow beings, buffeted
by wars, hatreds, and vices. We have become horribly puritanical
or utilitarian, even in Latin countries, and the chances are that
after reading a story by Maupassant, Chekhov, or Boccaccio, many
a reader, even the youngest ones, would at once pout their lips
into the damning phrase 'Et après? So what?' Even those ersatz for
literature, the comics, have to point up a message in our moral,
or morality-intoxicated, era.

As to the marriage between literature and sociology, fervently
wished for, first by Zola and his school, then by the practitioners
of sociology, and by many earnest teachers who accept fiction only
when it is justified as a social document, it has been one of the
piercing disillusionments of our century. Two types of social novels
alone seem to have met with success, and neither is original: the
Bildungsroman, or the study of the childhood, adolescence, and
early manhood of one character growing up in a variety of environments; and the portrayal of a family, invariably of the decadence of that family. Lacretelle, Maurois, Troyat, Kessel, Plis-
nier, Druon and many others have attempted the family novel,
with moderate effectiveness. It is one aspect of the theme of
disintegration, as dear to the moderns as it was to Balzac and Zola.
Such novels, with very rare exceptions, of which Thomas Mann's
Buddenbrooks is the most conspicuous, seldom avoid monotony
and dreariness. Yet whole worlds could be observed and re-created
by novelists, although they seldom venture into them. The professions of many men, for only aviators and a few professors have
written movingly of their métier — doctors, bankers, speculators,
engineers, and priests, for example — offer a rich mass of fictional
material. Using this material, the novelist could avoid the too
often inefficient attempt to depict a whole class and might concentrate upon representative individuals. Politics, 'the tragedy of our
times,' a saying of Napoleon I, dear to Malraux, has scarcely

tempted French novelists; yet few characters could provide such possibilities for ideological and emotional conflicts, such a display of ambition and ruthlessness as some of the men of affairs and of politics today. They deserve better than the paltry and belittling treatment thus far meted out to them by novelists. The fiction about the poorer classes, attempted by Eugène Dabit, Maxime Van der Meersch, and André Stil, has been similarly devoid of inventiveness. Misery and factory work may indeed prove too drab a picture to offer escapist readers, and western Europeans would not easily tolerate such naïve, made-to-order idealization of the five-year plan as has invaded Russian writing, or the description of lovers wandering hand in hand between wheat fields in some kolkhoz, tenderly commenting upon the prospects of the crop and the efficiency of tractors. But there were in 1936, again in 1945, and there are in the middle fifties profound revolutionary surges among French workmen, countless problems of adaptation of Spanish republicans or Italian immigrants on French farms and of conflicts of generations among peasants, which lack reality for most of us because novelists have shied away from them.

Two hundred years of attempts to direct literature toward the study and portrayal of conditions, professions, classes, and collective problems, for Diderot, the Encyclopedists, Lessing, and the authors of bourgeois drama, were the first to enter these new paths, have apparently proved ineffectual. The individual still reigns supreme in poetry, drama, and fiction. Moreover, if one may take literature as a reliable mirror, never has the individual felt more desperately lonely than in our age of mass media, of speedy and universal communication, and of education directed toward life in common and toward 'fitting in.' The solitude of man is probably the anthem most frequently chanted in the literature that has followed Kafka, Joyce, and Proust, Thomas Mann's *Doctor Faustus* and André Malraux's *Man's Fate*.

Man is alone, especially in the midst of 'the lonely crowd,' even in friendship, even in love — indeed never more so than in love. Once again, as in the romantic era, writers carry their hearts in a sling and recognize in themselves and in their characters, because of their cultivation of a feeling of solitude and their sadness at carrying such a burden, the new elect. 'Sadness' is a weak word. It may have accurately described the old *mal du siècle* of 1830, which was termed, sixty years earlier, 'spleen.' It seems too weak a word to be applied to *le mal du demi-siècle,* as the new melancholy or despondency of the youth of 1951 and the years following has been called.[8] 'Anguish' is the new key word.

Explanations for this display of anxiety in recent literature can claim to be no more than very tentative approximations. Some bring forward the breakup of community patterns of living, the weakening of the family, the decreased fear of, or respect for, the father. However, it is doubtful whether the break between the individual and a social group is any sharper now than it was in France in 1900, 1850, or even in 1790. The claim of our age that we live in circumstances radically different from all those that have preceded us is a most dubious one. Others adduce, as a plausible cause of our anguish, the weakening of religious beliefs. But, among novelists and the characters they create, such a weakening is far from manifest. Indeed, there is far deeper faith in François Mauriac, Julien Green, Luc Estang, Georges Bernanos, Jean Cayrol, Noël Devaulx, Marcel Guersant, in the writers of nonfiction such as Simone Weil, Albert Béguin, Gabriel Marcel, and in a score of thinkers, poets, and critics, than there has been at any time in France since the waning of the Middle Ages. The religion of these writers is not necessarily placid or soothing. It envies the disquietude of the nonbeliever. It heaps contempt upon the orthodox and complacent churchgoer who is a mere conformist, devoid of social conscience. It attempts to go to the people and to steal more than a few pages from the books of the communists. It revels in conjuring up the Devil as the tempter perpetually lying in wait, and is occasionally perilously tainted with Manichaeism.[9] Still others would argue that philosophy, having become, among many of its practitioners, an elaborate private game, endlessly pursuing the puzzles lurking behind words and rivaling algebra, fails to be an outlet for philosophical sensibilities. These sensibilities are thrown back to literature, which has inherited the philosophical anxiety rejected by the professional logicians. It has been enriched by this anxiety, as it has also been by the sensuousness and the remorseless eroticism that have been banished

8. See the inquiry into the mood of the newer French generation by two critics, Robert Kanters and Gilbert Sigaux, *Vingt Ans en 1951, Enquête sur la jeunesse française,* Julliard, Paris, 1951, and our essay on the romantic features of this recent literature in *The Modern Language Quarterly,* spring 1954.

9. The most recent work, and the most elaborate (five volumes are promised), written from an orthodox Catholic viewpoint on this subject is that of Charles Moeller, *Littérature du xxe siècle et christianisme,* Casterman, Paris et Tournai, 1953. The author remonstrates sternly with the devotees of the Manichaean heretic Simone Weil.

from abstract painting to make room for subconscious urges and pedantically suggestive squares and circles.

It is our opinion that such pseudo-explanations, ingenious to the point of being ingenuous, are hardly apposite. At any rate, while loneliness and anxiety, inherited in part from Kierkegaard and Rousseau, or confirmed by their prestige, are the two moods prevailingly indulged in today by the writers of five or six literatures, their expression has, in France, assumed a certain hue and color that are autochthonous. French literature, French fiction in particular, is not unrelated to the mood of the country in which it has its roots and in which it arouses echoes. There is a malady, in the second half of our century, which is particularly French, and the attitude adopted by French writers when facing their despair and attempting to rise above it is also peculiarly French. Can it be described more precisely, without falling into some of the brash generalizations of those who read literature for its 'social value'?

First, the French writer consciously strives to be the interpreter of his times and of his country, and even the prophet ushering in a new age, through his pen. Sartre, in his powerful manifesto *What Is Literature?* has recalled that every French writer, especially at the present time, claims to be the heir of his eighteenth-century ancestors, who prepared the French Revolution, or of the nineteenth-century novelists, who forged myths: the myth of the bourgeois, the Napoleonic legend, the myth of adultery restored to its high estate of courtly love, the *idée-force* of *revanche,* and so on.[10]

Next came the acceptance of defeat by what was at first (1940–42) a large majority of the dazed and demoralized French people, and the eagerness of a number of intellectuals and some members of the ruling classes to collaborate with Germany. Excuses for their

10. Any deduction that works backward from literature to life must, to be valid, remain prudent, undogmatic, open to nuance, and ready to temper its own rashness with gentle irony. A mere glance at some of the dissertations perpetrated by social interpreters of literature would be enough to inspire one with modesty. Books by professionals are not more reassuring. As an example, see *America in Fiction,* by Otis W. Coan and Richard Lillard, Stanford University Press, Stanford, California, 1941. *Manhattan Transfer* is characterized there as 'good on new folkways.' *Of Mice and Men* is presented as 'discussing the problem of migratory ranch workers.' The untranslatable phrase *idée-force,* coined by the philosopher Alfred Fouillée, designates a dynamic myth, a powerful idea, which drives groups to action. *Revanche,* which is not 'revenge,' but the French patriotic desire, after 1871, to have a chance to vanquish Prussia in their turn, is equally hard to translate.

behavior are many, and we are in no way here claiming to set ourselves up as judges. But, behind the very profuse insistence with which some of those former collaborators have lately justified themselves and derided the 'vain' martyrdom of resistance fighters, it is easy to discover a troubled conscience. A social psychoanalyst might easily read into the French temper since the liberation a disturbing guilt complex. This complex has, as is usual, either taken refuge in philosophical escapism and in farfetched theories, which seem to some, retroactively, to justify their abstention or the wrong course they had adopted, or it has assumed the appearance of a sickly superiority complex, pouring scorn on the new barbarians of America and Russia, who were incapable of understanding the 'Greece of the modern world.'

The resistance movement, however, cannot be belittled, nor can the eagerness with which the French soldiers, in Libya, North Africa, Italy, Normandy, and the Vosges, fought after 1940, as if to wash away the shame of their early disaster. The years 1941–4 witnessed not only heroism but also a splendid moral and spiritual fermentation, which aroused unbounded hopes in all observers of France. For the French, the war of 1941–4 was a war of volunteers and of civilians who, after a harassing crisis of conscience, decided to forsake comfort, the peace of family life, their work, and their loves to jeopardize their future and to risk, not death alone, which every soldier half expects, but the tortures of Buchenwald and Dachau. Normal wars mow down indiscriminately cowards and the brave. Concentration camps inflicted their calculated slow deaths upon some two hundred and fifty thousand men and women who had given evidence just shortly before of their being the true elite of the country; in character, fortitude, willingness to accept risks, and unselfish devotion, they would have constituted the nucleus indispensable to the rebuilding of a rejuvenated France.

Hopes raised by the resistance movement were immense. Catholics and communists, scions of old families and unskilled workers fought side by side and experienced a new feeling of fraternity. Farmers and city dwellers who had taken to the bush relinquished their mutual diffidence or their prejudices. A vast resistance literature, printed and distributed at the risk of one's life, planned for Utopian reforms in the structure of the country. It should be studied some day; it will be found to have been far better than mere naïve and apocalyptic dreams. Many of the elements required for a spiritual, political, and administrative renaissance of the country are to be found in it. A government that knew how to draw on these elements of rejuvenation would, at that time, have been supported by popular enthusiasm in laying the groundwork of a revolution equal to that of the Consulate, from which nineteenth-century France had stemmed.

Most of these hopes were woefully disappointed. It would take an involved, and perhaps a partial, historical and political discussion of postwar France to assess responsibilities. Not one man, not one party deserves the blame. All Frenchmen feel collectively guilty. A brooding sense of frustration hangs over the former members of the resistance, over the advocates of social and political reform, and over the intellectuals in general, and recent French fiction betrays this feeling. The French failure in 1940 — and this is what most irks a country that prides itself on its intelligence — was in great part a failure of the intellect, as it had been in 1870. An old, honest, and lucid novelist and essayist, Jean Schlumberger, meditating upon the catastrophe that had befallen his country in 1940, reopened Renan's *Réforme intellectuelle et morale* and quoted approvingly: 'In the struggle which has just taken place, France's inferiority was mainly intellectual: the head, and not the heart, is what proved deficient in us.'

The mistakes committed in 1945 and since that date have been many, while the achievement has proved far from negligible, but one problem has eclipsed or controlled all the others — continued inflation. We are very far from claiming that economics is primary in a world that has consistently belied Marx's prophecies on this score. But it would be equally Pharisaic, for a student of letters, to ignore the fact that writers are human beings who have to earn a living and who expect a moderate degree of stability. French writers used to enjoy prestige and were granted, with relative ease, posts as library curators, keepers of archives, and even, like Stendhal, positions as consular officers abroad. Some even had fixed incomes as *rentiers,* and Flaubert, Proust, and Gide might not have polished their prose or wandered in lost time without such an advantage. But ever since 1918, and far more gravely since 1945, the fundamental factor in French life has been the infernal circle of inflation. It has precluded any stability, economic, political, or psychological. It has molded the present temper of the nation far more than have the political crises that stem from it, which mystified foreign observers take as one more sign of French levity.

French education persists to this day in ignoring economics and finance and in favoring law and literature. The political leaders of the country thus lack the minimum of knowledge required for handling economic problems, and the insight gained from such knowledge. Late in 1944, when the government in liberated Paris was faced with the liquidation of the past, it had to curb inflation wilfully encouraged by the Germans, who had exacted a daily levy from the occupied country. It had to punish, as everyone expected it to do, producers and tradesmen who had made exorbitant gains on the black market and in dealing with the enemy, and it had to withdraw from circulation the accumulated paper money. Not a few Frenchmen perceived and pointed out the road that should have been taken. Moral indignation against profiteers and eagerness to return to economic and social health were such that the country would have been ready to follow Mendès-France, when he advocated stern deflationary measures. Instead, the government upheld Pleven's policy of raising wages inordinately and of thus launching France upon the path of price increases, devaluations, and insecurity, while seeming to approve the ill-acquired wealth. Mendès-France resigned in March 1945. Years of economic and social uneasiness ensued. Psychological conditions in France were such that she was the only country to remain unaffected by decreases in world prices, hence her protectionist policy, which failed to raise productivity and which maintained agricultural and even industrial prices so high that workmen's wages proved inadequate. As a result, the anger of the working classes mounted to a prevolutionary temper, and the middle classes, from which the majority of writers stem, were ruined. It is hardly to be wondered at if frustration, which exists in effect, even if the word is not used, insecurity, and despondency are the moods of many a novelist in France; or if a large proportion of writers must depend upon another profession, usually that of teaching; or if sex manners have become relaxed in a world where few women can count upon eking out a decent living by their work alone. The loss of dignity of the franc, until 1918 the symbol of French stability and of French thrift, while the dollar, and even the German mark, and the Belgian and Swiss franc command respect, gnaws deeply at French pride. Literature does not ignore this.

During the political crisis of May 1953, which proved to be a profound crisis of the French conscience as well, a veteran statesman, Herriot, lamented the decay of politics of France, reduced to begging from the United States and to bargaining with or to blackmailing its benefactor in order to meet its engagements. A candidate for the premiership, Mendès-France, announced to his countrymen that they had to face the 'cruel fact' of the decline of

France. There are other signs of an imminent change in the French temper at the time of this writing (late 1953) and of the close of the post World War II period in literature, a period we have been trying to interpret through its writers. These signs point to the closing, between 1953 and probably 1955, of an era. Once again, the premonitory signs were first read by the group of men whose sensitiveness is most acute, whose intelligence is most alert, and whose very profession inclines them to probe the unexpressed mood of the youth through whom they hope their work may retain its timeliness — the writers.

French writers and philosophers have not turned parochial in their interests, solely engrossed by some of the economic and social evils particular to their country, which we have just tried to describe. They have not lost the knack of raising their problems to a level of universality. If their protests against the decline of western Europe and the subservience of once-free countries to American subsidies are often more vociferous and more acrimonious than those of their neighbors, it may well be that they are less obsequious than some peoples who can only be rehabilitated and defended through American favors, less cynical than others among our former enemies of World War II, and less inclined to compromise than the British or the citizens of the Low Countries. Their fear of a different way of life, moreover, has deeper roots. It is clear to many Frenchmen that only greater productivity, hence mass production, the 'strangling' of a million or so outmoded artisans and little shopkeepers, who are today an obstacle to economic progress, in a word, the resolute acceptance of American industrial methods and American merchandizing and salesmanship can modernize French business and enable it to compete abroad and thus survive. But the sentimental resistance to such a deliberate break with the past is strong; the fear of Americanization is widespread; the longing for the charms of the past haunts French memories. There is a radical opposition between those for whom production, steady work, and money-making (often for unselfish purposes, in order to assist their country or the rest of the world) are primary, and the French and other Europeans for whom such activity is tolerable only if it eventually brings leisure and the refined enjoyment of the material or spiritual goods so arduously acquired. An American officer whose open and cordial manners and courageous role at the time of the Berlin airlift won the hearts of many Europeans, General Frank L. Howley, expressed it thus in his book *Your War for Peace:* [11] 'We need France to teach us how to enjoy the peace when we have it.'

The pessimism that has been traced in recent French literature finds its source, and perhaps its justification, in the French situation. A glorious past cannot be forgotten overnight; the lofty hopes of the war years, when anything appeared possible in a Europe freed from Nazi tyranny, have been shattered, and such disillusionment is not accepted lightheartedly. French politicians are bogged down in the same quagmires in which their predecessors had too often stagnated; and the policies of the great power overseas, upon which the task of guiding the free world has perforce been thrust, fail to rally the French unreservedly. But this French pessimism is voicing the secret concerns of the whole civilized world, as it enters the second half of a century threatened by an Armageddon. If the audience that French literature finds abroad has in no way decreased since the ascendancy of America and the spread of English as a world language, if French books still sell as actively as ever and are widely translated into other tongues, it must be that French authors have victoriously maintained their claim to universality.

We have tried to state in the course of this volume some of the universal problems of our time, which have been powerfully felt as well as thought, and transmitted through the vehicle of fiction by Malraux, Saint-Exupéry, Sartre, Camus and their successors. Viewed in this light, Malraux, in his volumes on art, as well as in his tragic novels, has expressed, far more movingly than Spengler did in his day, the fears and hopes of our contemporaries, based on the twilight of an absolute, the end of the myth of progress, the collapse of our unlimited faith in science, the refusal of a large part of the world to subscribe to the American concept of happiness, and the tragically waning conviction of Americans themselves that their own concept of happiness is still tenable. Existentialism cannot be equated with nihilism; indeed, it is the opposite. And it is far more than a passing vogue. It has provided postwar generations with courage, faith, and hope. The literature now in the process of maturing, which has to be evaluated chiefly on its promises (few novelists are fully themselves before the age of forty-five, and the artistic achievement of the present writers has been delayed by the war years), bids fair to be worthy of that of its elders. Malraux, Montherlant, Saint-Exupéry, Paulhan (for special reasons rather than for his books), Sartre, Camus, and perhaps Giraudoux are its main inspirers.

11. Henry Holt & Co., New York, 1952.

The merits we perceive in these men and in the younger ones to whom we have pointed as the most promising talents of tomorrow, could be, as a conclusion to our long journey, defined under three headings.

The first is clear-sightedness. If the French today appear at times to lack enthusiasm and to shrink in horror from uncritical acclaim of a cause or a leader, if they continue to stress their diversity to the point of risking anarchy, we cannot forget that they grew up at the time of Mussolini's speeches, applauded (so long as he was victorious) by over three-fourths of his countrymen, in the days of the hideous Nuremberg conventions; that they themselves were not immune from the cult of a marshal and of a general and are now slightly ashamed of it; that even in the firmest of democracies, a priest from Michigan, a senator from Louisiana, and a senator from Wisconsin have sobered our fond delusion that 'it can't happen here.' Mass hysteria is a standing peril in our century. Moving back the clock is neither possible nor desirable. Enlightenment, which should stress intelligence and a critical spirit, is the only path open to us.

It is a source of comfort to the student of French literature of the last two decades to come across a number of attempts to revaluate the word 'intelligence.' Schlumberger, in his *Nouveaux Jalons*, recalled to the disheartened French people, oppressed by their enemies and their own feeble regime, in 1943, that intelligence is in no way opposed to vitality, character, and moral virtues. Montherlant, who has often enough indulged in flippancy and showmanship, has never wavered on this point.[12] From the Catholics grouped around *Esprit* to the communists, several of whom have, strangely enough, been the warmest in their praise of Laclos, Sade, Stendhal, and the French classical masters,[13] there seems to be a French consensus to uphold the benefits of clear-sightedness.

The second rock to which the French seem to cling in the midst of many upheavals and in a rebellious literature, which has not

12. In *Service inutile* (Grasset, Paris, 1935), Montherlant upbraided those who denounced the critical spirit. 'Whenever they attack the critical spirit, their true target is intelligence. But we shall never lay down our intelligence, frail and relaxed as it may be. We simply cannot do it.' In a less admirable volume, *Textes sous une occupation,* he added in 1953: 'All the harm done on earth is done by those who are convinced and ambitious. The skeptic devoid of ambition is the one harmless being.'

13. Claude Roy, a communist intellectual, proclaimed in *Le Commerce des classiques* (Gallimard, Paris, 1953) that he ranks highest 'the masters of a precise style placed at the service of a dry vision: Racine, Retz, Laclos, Constant, Stendhal, men with no illusion.'

left many idols standing, is sincerity. The word is ambiguous, and it is well established that sincerity alone does not endow a writer with talent or intelligence, still less with imagination. But, in a world in which governments, candidates for office, radio orators, and salesmen lavishly dispense lies or half-truths, and in which many of us, afraid of seeing ourselves as we are, unable to bear our own liberty and our own solitude, escape from freedom, huddle together herdlike, gleefully worship collective and monotonous thinking and conventional living, the man of letters in France has assigned himself the task of upholding seriousness and total honesty to oneself. He has done away with most of the old taboos, even the sexual ones. He has ruthlessly scanned the old beliefs and flouted the bourgeois conventions. But, from Gide to Sartre, from Montherlant to Anouilh, from Proust to the very youngest novelists, Cabanis, Guérin, and Rossi, French writers have left one value unattacked: good faith or authenticity. They have hunted out selfishness, hypocrisy, and vanity more relentlessly than even the moralists of the seventeenth century had done. Upon this impregnable fortress of truth to oneself, a new ethics is being raised, and a valuable literature has arisen.

But, if modern books wail the loneliness of man as they do, their authors are well aware that man today is more avid than he has ever been of transcending himself, if not vertically toward God, at least horizontally, toward other men. 'I am a pessimist where man's fate is concerned,' declared Camus, 'but an optimist where man himself is concerned.' The line is a most tenuous one to draw and Camus, who admires clarity, it not always the clearest of thinkers. However, the cry echoes through all his books, and it concludes the gravest of them, *The Plague.* 'We refuse to despair of men.' 'To live is not to be resigned.' The doctrine of universal engagement of the existentialists and their assertion that man incurs an unlimited responsibility have aroused many a skeptic's smile. Nevertheless, existentialism was formulating a creed concerning the significance and the duties of the man who thinks and writes, a creed that challenged the parallel nostalgic longing for engagement among communists and among Catholics. For we cannot avoid the fact that parallel, if not exactly similar, preoccupations move the three families of minds around which French authors are grouped today: Christians (with a fervent sense of their duty toward the people), communists, and existentialists. All of them have wanted to 'go to the people'; and since the workers, among the people, are of communist allegiance, the priests them-

selves have had to emulate communism in carrying their message
to the most unprivileged workers, and the existentialists have attempted to outwit Marxism in dialectical dexterity.

When John Keats undertook, in his twenty-fifth year, to revise
his unfinished 'Hyperion,' he described a temple and an altar
watched over by Moneta, a goddess of the fallen race of the Titans.
The admonishing voice warned off those men of letters who were
content with artistic isolation and who disregarded the human
misery that surrounded them.

> *'None can usurp this height' returned that shade,*
> *But those to whom the miseries of the world*
> *Are misery, and will not let them rest.*

A great many faults have been found with contemporary French
literature, and no branch of this literature is more wearying to
study than the novel; for it is woefully true that a great many of
these novels were composed hastily, with no inner compulsion in
the writer, with little weight of pregnant experience to impart, and
with scant originality in workmanship. But only a cantankerous
critic could long dally with that part of literary production that
is content with being ephemeral or entertaining or is a preliminary
stage in the acquiring of a skill. Behind the deceptive screen of
surface impressions, a deeper conviction soon appears to the reader
of modern French fiction. It is deadly earnest about essentials.
Elegant skepticism and urbane irony, which once delighted the
readers of Anatole France or of the early Aldous Huxley, are today
the exception, and sound out of place. The sheer humiliation of
man's efforts to rise above his condition and to escape from his
fatalities, such as filled the surly naturalist fiction, is gone too.
French literature, in Bernanos, Green, Malraux, Sartre, Camus,
Guilloux, and Beckett, is deeply serious. It usurps the roles once
played by religion and philosophy, while it avoids the stifling
peril of too much abstraction; and writers remember that a novel
must primarily impose a presence and not propose ideas, give
reality to a world and not dissect it dryly.

This modern fiction takes evil seriously, and Sartre has told us
why, in his analysis of the role of literature today. History forced
the hunted men of the resistance to live with the knowledge that
'torture was a daily occurrence' and that absurdity was not an
empty word but a threatening monster. But the writer tempered
his courage in those ordeals. He refused indifference, as Sartre
puts it, and, convinced that the miseries of the world were indeed

miseries to him, he attempted to formulate anew an ideal of fraternity and of transcendence through pity for his fellow sufferers and alleviation of their sorrows.

Behind this modern novel, with the frequent disappointments it brings to readers who expect too much from it, behind the France of today, often woefully inadequate to the extravagant demands made upon it by the rest of the world, it is easy to see that one passion survives: love of life. And a second one smoulders, at times concealed by argumentative zest and by the cold insistence upon lucidity: love of literature, as the last bulwark of diversity, of intellectual freedom, and of the noble humanist and Christian ideal of fraternity. The eloquent essay in which Camus has presented the artist as the witness of freedom may be quoted from as our most fitting conclusion. Retorting to politicians, ideological fanatics, propagandists for all causes, and so-called practical men intent upon selling their own way of life, Camus voiced the reply that the writer or the artist is entitled to make to the cynical blackmailer who wants him to be the servant of a cause.

> The misery of the world? I am not adding anything to it. Which of you can say as much? . . . There is ample justification in practicing a profession which, in the midst of a world withered by hate, enables every one of us to say in all peace of mind that he is no man's mortal enemy . . . True artists are on the side of life, not of death . . . Artists bear witness to that in man which refuses to die.[14]

14. 'Le Témoin de la liberté' is the last text in Albert Camus's *Actuelles, Chroniques 1944–48* (Gallimard, Paris, 1950). It has been translated as 'The Artist as Witness of Freedom' in *Commentary*, VIII, 6, December 1949, pp. 534–8.

Panorama of PRESENT-DAY NOVELISTS

The reader will find grouped in this appendix, in alphabetical order, the names of young French novelists who have been conspicuously successful or promising since 1945 or thereabouts and are likely to be the authors of significance through the nineteen-fifties and sixties. Succinct information about their works and a candid and summary judgment of their merits, as they appear to us, are presented in each case.

ABELLIO, Raymond (b. 1907). The author who writes under this pseudonym came to literature after World War II, after a varied and stormy career that compromised him into collaboration with the Germans and landed him in exile in Switzerland. There was a great deal of publicity about his position and the strangeness of his books, which are full of political digressions and mystical interpretations of the Old Testament. They can be called 'novels' only through a painful stretch of the mind or of the definition of a novel. *Heureux les pacifiques* (Le Portulan, 1946) is a tortuous intellectual autobiography of a man who, between 1934 and 1944, embraced, successively, opposite parties, as well as several women. *Les Yeux d'Ezéchiel sont ouverts* (Gallimard, 1950) is an even more disorderly and pretentious book. The main events, violently dramatic, take place in December 1945 and are told with undeniable vividness. An undercurrent of prophetic mysticism runs through the book. A Spanish priest, whom the protagonist had helped during the Spanish civil war, repays him with endless prophecies supposedly interpreting the Bible. (Abellio is also the author of *La Bible document chiffré*.) The gist of it all is that murder, evil, and bloodshed are a prerequisite for our salvation and that a chosen band of a few superior persons, depositories of spiritual energy and technocratic secrets, will alone save a world sunk deep in evil. The author writes with occasional power. He may some day either become a literary figure of mark or end in an orgy of unreason.

AUCLAIR, Georges (b. 1920) wrote a very promising first novel about a young Frenchman serving in occupied Germany in 1945–6 and falling in love with a young woman, a former Nazi. The atmosphere of ruined and demoralized Germany and of obsequiousness and self-pity in the German middle classes is ably rendered, and the narrative is speedy and natural. After *Un Amour allemand* (Gallimard, 1951), the author's second book, *Une Vie barrée* (Gallimard, 1953), proved disappointing. It is the diary, strained, morbidly introspective, and totally unexciting, of a young man intent upon suicide, who drives a young woman to suicide and fails to kill himself *in extremis*.

AYMÉ, Marcel (b. 1902) has scored some triumphs on the stage since 1945. He composed some excellent short stories during World War II (*Le Passe-muraille*, Gallimard, 1945) and a bitter satire of the mores of a small town during the years of German occupation, in which Aymé's political distrust of enthusiasm and of reforming impulses is translated into boisterous comedy in *Uranus* (Gallimard, 1948; *The Barkeep of Blemont*, Harper and Brothers, New York, 1950). *Le Confort intellectuel* (Flammarion, 1949) is ponderous, and its characters are papery puppets, mocking the literary vogues of the day. His best work since 1939 is, in our opinion, *La Belle Image* (Gallimard, 1941; *The Second Face*, Harper and Brothers, New York, 1952), whose fantasy and use of the supernatural win admiration. But, as is often the case in such tales, credibility is smoothly achieved in the first hundred pages but not long sustained. The claims of some of his admirers, who see in Marcel Aymé an unacknowledged genius, seem to us unfounded. He approaches power, but somehow, in his novels at least, he misses it, and he does not reject facile or cheap effects.

BARBEY, Bernard (b. 1900), a Swiss author of several colorless novels after World War I, wrote, in 1951, a solid work on a hero who married the daughter whom his mistress had had by her husband, a general. The young wife, who had known about the liaison before she accepted marriage to him, suddenly commits suicide. The title is *Chevaux abandonnés sur le champ de bataille* (Julliard, 1951). It received the *Prix du Roman* of the French Academy.

BAZIN, Hervé (b. 1917) made a resounding entry into the literary world with *Vipère au poing* (Grasset, 1948; *Viper in the Fist*, Prentice-Hall, New York, 1951), then with *La Tête contre les murs* (Grasset, 1949; *Head against the Wall*, Prentice-Hall, New York, 1952), *La Mort du petit cheval* (Grasset, 1950), and *Lève-toi et marche* (Grasset, 1952). His success was due in part to his being the scion of a very conservative family of western France, nurtured in the strictest Catholic traditions, who stood up in revolt against his class and exploited a relatively untouched subject, the hatred of one's mother. But the literary merits of the young writer were obvious: he had a lively style, handled cruelty and sarcasm with elegance, and did not fall in with the vogue of philosophical anguish or of ponderous self-pity. He told a bitter story and sketched characters or caricatures mercilessly. His second book was hardly a novel, and it shunned emotion and even naturalness to the point of artificiality. It was a pamphlet against French mental hospitals, close to journalistic reporting. *La Mort du petit cheval* followed and turned out to be a better book, full of dash and of calculated nonchalance, on the subject of family hatreds and of son against mother, a subject that began to wear thin, however. Bazin, who has been hitherto a French equivalent to Evelyn Waugh or an acrid successor to Jules Renard, changed his tune in *Lève-toi et marche*. The heroine is a paralytic young woman whose family has been killed in a bombardment. She frets against her enforced idleness and her worsening malady, and she tries to help friends and neighbors. But her own bitterness and the venom that rankles under her impulse toward goodness bring about woeful results. The total impact of the book is uncertain, but the intelligence, the gift of vivid characterization, and the stylistic verve of the author are beyond doubt. He may become an important novelist. *L'Huile sur le feu* (Grasset, 1954) contains some of the best writing done by Hervé Bazin. It is less voluntary and strained, less consistently hostile to all feelings of family affection than his earlier books. The strange character of the father, a wounded veteran of the war, cruelly treated by his wife and admired by his daughter, who turns into a maniacal arsonist and ends in suicide amid the fire that he has lighted, is skillfully delineated. His daughter is the first convincing woman in Hervé Bazin's fiction. The tone of the book is more natural.

BECK, Béatrix (b. 1914) has written two novels (*Barny*, Gallimard, 1950, and *Une Mort irrégulière*, Gallimard, 1951) superior in many respects to her winner of the Goncourt Prize of 1952, *Léon Morin, prêtre* (Gallimard, 1952). The author was the daughter of one of Gide's friends, had served as the secretary of the aging writer, and learned from him how to prune and omit, and even how to banish sentiment and rhetoric. *Barny* is one of the very few good, imaginary autobiographies of a little girl. Her second novel told of the early days of the war and of the suicide of her Jewish husband, who was serving in the Foreign Legion. *Léon Morin, prêtre* is the sketch of a city occupied by the Germans and a description of the increasing attraction of religious faith for the heroine. Not Christ, however, but a handsome, courageous, at times slightly vulgar priest, Léon Morin, is the conqueror of Barny's atheism. The priest, sensing the peril of that violent and rebellious convert, who is more than half in love with him, is transferred elsewhere. Béatrix Beck, a rather arid and strained storyteller, strangely lacks the tenderness and the poetry commonly associated with feminine literature. She does not seem to us destined to a much higher fame than she has now achieved. Her next volume, *Des Accommodements avec le ciel*, published in the *Revue de Paris* in July and August 1954, shows no renewal of her manner and no deepening of her talent.

BECKETT, Samuel (b. 1906), an Irishman, has become a French

writer, like Julien Green or the Hungarian Dormandi. He sprang to glory with *Molloy* (Editions de Minuit, 1951), which attracted readers to his earlier *Murphy* (Bordas, 1947) and to *Malone meurt* (Editions de Minuit, 1951). Beckett's play, *En attendant Godot,* which is remarkable, was a signal success in the spring of 1953. While he is very much of an Irishman and deeply marked by Joyce (as well as by Kafka), Beckett 'belongs' to the French literary climate: the total absurdity of everything, the worthlessness of love, of life, and especially of literature and language, ludicrously vain representations of a meaningless world, are his themes. Humor abounds, but it is bitter and 'black.' *Molloy* is an epic of nothingness about an ill man, whose memory has been destroyed and who rides on a bicycle to visit his dying mother. He will never reach his goal, like Kafka's surveyor. He gets lost in a forest, falls into a ditch, and stays there, mumbling to himself. Meanwhile, a man and his son have been asked to go after Molloy, of whom they had never heard. Both become afflicted by paralysis, are separated, involved in a murder, and reduced to the lowest level of degradation. The voluntary obscurity of the novel has spurred commentators to ingenious exegeses. The underlying assertion, if one may use such a term for a literature of total negation, seems to be that everything and everybody is in a state of disintegration and that yielding to some abject nirvana is perhaps the only relief from anguish and absurdity that man can seek. Beckett writes only for the unhappy few, and too much fashionable literary despair entered into his success. But his force is undeniable.

BLANCHOT, Maurice (b. 1907), one of the three or four acute critics in France today, is also the author of several difficult works of fiction, in which a few philosophical readers see one of the deepest symbolic portrayals of our age. One cannot summarize Blanchot's novels, for in them he unequivocally rejects imitation of life and reality; he rejects all that is not ambiguous and allegorical. The themes that obsess Blanchot, as novelist as well as critic, are the loneliness of man, the even greater solitude of the artist who must communicate through language and begin by making language over again so that it will be authentic, and death, which is the beginning and the end of all meditation for Blanchot. The very data of his creation force a rarefied and unreal atmosphere upon the novelist, as in *L'Arrêt de mort* (Gallimard, 1948), where 'death pauses,' somewhat as in the myth of Orpheus. There are monotonous, yet inevitable, repetitions in the novel. The name Kafka has often been pronounced in connection with Blanchot, but he is in truth far closer to a Mallarmé who might have translated into fictional form his aspiration toward silence, his denial of gods, and his weird fantasy. *Thomas l'obscur* (Gallimard, 1941) is the most accessible of Blanchot's novels, *Le Très-Haut* (Gallimard, 1948) the most esoteric, and *Aminadab* (Gallimard, Paris, 1942) probably the least successful. Blanchot is not a critic or a philosopher who has turned novelist. Fiction is to him the fittest means of expression, or rather of the dissolution into an imaginary form, of all the details that normally obstruct our perception. He will never be read by more than a few, but those few prize his gifts of imagination and style as singularly original.

BLOCH-MICHEL, Jean (b. 1912) wrote a concise analysis of the bad conscience of a young man who, having acted twice like a coward, cannot silence his belated scruples, an approximation to a more analytical *Lord Jim*. He relates his own failures unflinchingly and becomes his own witness. After this first and very effective *récit*, entitled *Le Témoin* (Gallimard, 1949; *The Witness*, Pantheon Books, New York, 1949), and a colorless collection of essays (*Les Grandes Circonstances*, 1949), the author's second novel, about a family carried away in the debacle, *La Fuite en Egypte* (Gallimard, 1952), appears unconvincing.

BOISDEFFRE, Pierre de (b. 1926), an impetuous young critic, attempted the novel of collaboration (a theme that is likely to be long exploited) with *Les Fins dernières* (Table ronde, 1952). His hero has been sentenced for siding with the enemy and relates everything retrospectively before his imminent execution. He blames the society that has made him what he is (he came from a family of officers, worshipped Maurras, and so forth) as much as himself. The book is thin, in every sense, and declamatory, but does not preclude more genuine fictional writing by the author, misled in part by his admiration for Stendhal, announced in the epigraph.

BORY, Jean-Louis (b. 1919) won the Goncourt Prize in 1945 with a pitifully mediocre story of the German occupation, *Mon Village à l'heure allemande* (Flammarion, 1945). *Fragile ou le panier d'oeufs* (Flammarion, 1950) has a little more sprightliness and humor and lauds moderate, everyday happiness, an uncommon theme today. Still the future of the writer, a professor, as are many recent writers, seems doubtful as a novelist.

BOSCO, Henri (b. 1888) started publishing as early as 1924. His early work, written while he taught Italian in southern France, was gracefully poetical and fragrant with the herbs of Provence. The author was then transferred to a teaching position in Morocco, from where his novels *Hyacinthe* (Gallimard, 1940) and *Le Mas Théotime* (Charlot, Alger, 1945) won sudden and wide fame. His subsequent works, *Monsieur Carre-Benoit à la campagne* (Charlot, Alger, 1947), *Malicroix* (Gallimard, 1948), *Un Rameau de la nuit* (Flammarion, 1950), and *Antonin* (Gallimard, 1952), betrayed some monotony and he creates an atmosphere that is not without artificiality. In our opinion, *Le Mas Théotime* is both the most successful and the most typical of Bosco's novels. The plot owes much to detective stories, but the mystery is unnaturally kept up through an abnormal capacity for silence displayed by the narrator, a cultured farmer named Pascal. He welcomes into his house, without a single question, his cousin Geneviève, whom he loves in silence. She has left her husband who, by mistake, killed a neighbor with whom he was on bad terms, instead of killing Pascal, as he had probably intended to do. Through some unexplained confusion, Pascal inherits the estate of the murdered man. The whole novel hinges on the obstinacy of the characters in keeping their lips sealed and in coming and going mysteriously and mutely. Such behavior is not a little surprising in normally garrulous farmers from southern France, but it is necessary to the frail and artificial plot, whose assumptions would collapse at once if the characters ever explained themselves to one another. The one undeniable gift of the author is that of poetry, especially of nature and of animals, but he deserts logic and credibility to a point where few readers will be willing to suspend their disbelief to follow him.

BOUTRON, Michel (b. 1912) wrote a story of a German prisoner in a French village who wins the esteem and the respect of the farmers who employ him, *Hans* (S.E.G.E.P., 1950, translated in England under the same title, Verschoyle, 1952). The volume, while immature, shows a rich gift of human sympathy and of artistic condensation, which the collection of tales which followed it, *Juliette des Montagnes* (Bonne, 1952), did not belie. *Les Enfants du matin* (Julliard, 1952), which takes place in America, is a little too obviously didactic.

BRASILLACH, Robert (b. 1908, d. 1945). His prewar novels barely missed the Goncourt Prize twice and deserved some esteem, but they were unduly overpraised by the author's fanatic friends of the extreme right. He was subsequently executed for collaboration with the enemy, and some of his followers have tried to present him as a martyr. His posthumous works include mediocre poems and a novel, *Six Heures à perdre* (Plon, 1953), which is his freshest and most human book. A French officer released by the Germans from his prison camp describes wartime Paris, as he finds it and relates the life of a young woman who, once married to a brutal husband, killed him point-blank during the confused and thrilling years of the black market and of universal conspiracy.

BRINCOURT, André (b. 1920) is one of the most promising among the rising talents. His *Vert Paradis* (Table ronde, 1950; *The Paradise below the Stairs,* Duell, Sloan and Pearce, New York, 1952) ranks among the most revealing imaginative portrayals of the cruelty, viciousness, and essential naïveté and repressed sentimentality of adolescence. *La Farandole* (Table ronde, 1952) paints a more poetical and more analytical picture of love and friendship at odds within a man, who ends by preferring the friendship of his mistress's husband to her love. The novel, very deftly constructed and perfumed with the poetry of southern France, is also an attempt to dissociate sentiment and eroticism in love, along the lines indicated by the author's master, Laclos. It also presents a disturbing picture of the uneasy fear that love for a career woman, too lucid and too practical, stirs up in a male.

CABANIS, José (b. 1922) wrote one of the most mature and best integrated first novels of recent years, *L'Age ingrat* (Gallimard, 1952). There is no symbolic or philosophical message in it and no calculated obscurity. It reveals only the brilliant abilities of a storyteller and a dispassionate observer of bourgeois hypocrisy. The author combines the crudities of certain naturalists with a gift for pitiless and ironical dissection of human frailties, which marks him as another admirer of Stendhal and Laclos. The theme is the sensual education of an adolescent in a provincial city of the south of France, recorded without monotony and with a keen sense for comic situations and, incidentally, for the caricature of the pompous complacence of some of the supporters of Marshal Pétain. The novel, with its distrust of sentiment, pales a little in the second half. But it reveals technical mastery. Cabanis must be either a magistrate or a professor-author. (The protagonist becomes a teacher.) The second novel by Cabanis, *L'Auberge fameuse* (Gallimard, 1953), portraying two children exposed early to the vices of grownups and preferring death, heralded a more sympathetic understanding of life's tragedies.

CAYROL, Jean (b. 1911) has a voice and a tone that are distinctly his own and conjures up a misty, melancholy, and overlyrical, but authentic, fictional world. He is one of the sad southerners, more numerous than is commonly thought. He was born in Bordeaux, and, after courageous activity in the resistance, he spent three trying years in German concentration camps, from which he emerged a poet and a poetical novelist. He is the author of a trilogy, *Je vivrai l'amour des autres* (Editions du Seuil, 1947–50: 1. *On nous parle*, 2. *Les Premiers Jours*, 3. *Le Feu qui prend*), and of a smoother and more restrained story, *La Noire* (Editions du Seuil, 1949). The earnestness of the author, his profound pity for poverty, misery, and dereliction, and his attempts to picture the sudden invasion into daily life of a superreality, which is reminiscent of surrealist ambitions, arouse sympathetic emotion in the reader. Yet, and again in *Le Vent de la mémoire* (Editions du Seuil, 1952), Cayrol seems to drown his vision in a deluge of would-be poetical words and to lack the vividness and the sharpness of outline that might give more compelling reality to his evocations of a wretched Lazarus in our midst. The reader and perhaps the author himself, bogged down in the marshes of this *romanesque lazaréen*, seem to wait in vain for the advent of a resurrected Christ.

CESBRON, Gilbert (b. 1913), after several indifferent novels, reached a wide public and aroused much discussion with his book on the *prêtres-ouvriers*, *Les Saints vont en enfer* (Laffont, 1952). The picture of the misery, even more spiritual than physical, of the French and North-African communist workmen of the Paris suburbs and of the priests who endeavor, against heavy odds, to bring Christ's message to them is achieved with vigor. It does not seem, however, that either his technique and style or the quality of his vision and imagination promise Cesbron a great future as a novelist. Cesbron attempted another social novel, *Chiens perdus sans collier* (Robert Laffont, 1954) on the problem of juvenile delinquency. He succeeded in creating living individuals out of two adolescents who were not raised by a family and, yearning after a happiness they never knew, wandered through revolt before finally recovering confidence in men.

COLIN, Paul (b. 1920) was awarded the Goncourt Prize in 1950 for his one novel, *Les Jeux sauvages* (Gallimard, 1950; *Savage Play*, E. P. Dutton and Company, New York, 1953). The book is unequal. The first part, which describes, in the form of a diary, the wild and cruel play of three children in the Sologne region, has vivid freshness and beauty. The author sings hymns to nature and to woman's body, which are not often heard in recent fiction. The second part, in which the adolescents studying in Paris are unable to outgrow the splendor of their radiant childhood, seems strained and too long. The third ends in tragedy. Paul Colin is talented but inexpert as yet. But he has the romantic sense of wonder and the gift of profusion, which are of good omen in a young novelist.

CORDELIER, Jean (b. 1912), a Breton doctor who spent five years in a German prison camp, scored some success with *Les Yeux de la tête* (Editions du Seuil, 1953). His book, which describes, in a manner reminiscent of John Dos Passos, life in German cities as seen by a prisoner of war enjoying a good deal of freedom as a doctor, is much too long and too monotonous. But several scenes, depicting with extraordinary sympathy German women in love with war prisoners, are vividly written and very revealing as documents with only a veneer of fictional arrangement. The hero dies when he tries chivalrously to protect one of his German mistresses from rape by a Russian.

CURTIS, Jean-Louis (b. 1917), also a member of the teaching profession, has the gifts of lucid analysis, irony, even of irreverential take-off of his elders (in the clever pastiches of *Haute-École*, Julliard, 1950), but also those of a modest, patient teller of tales who avoids falling into the literary fashions. *Les Forêts de la nuit* (Julliard, 1947; *The Forest of the Night*, G. P. Putnam's Sons, New York, 1951) is one of the truest and most comprehensive pictures of a French province under German occupation. The author has kept clear both of emotional enthusiasm and literary heroism, and of the debunking of the resistance forces. His novel, told with discreet irony, is a valuable social and historical document. His next story, *Gibier de potence* (Julliard, 1949; *Lucifer's Dream*, G. P. Putnam's Sons, New York, 1953), shows no letdown after the success of the earlier one, which had been distinguished by the Goncourt award. It depicts the amoral and delinquent youth of postwar Paris, and its protagonist, the former inmate of an orphanage, groping toward purification through love for an innocent girl. J. L. Curtis may well mature into a novelist of true stature. He attempted with success an ambitious fresco of the youth of our time which eagerly embraces what it takes to be "just causes," rushes to fight, if necessary to die for them, and grows disillusioned with politics that divide men artificially. His story of four young Parisians thus divided by political ideas and by their background and training is a revealing document on modern France and a good comic and even picaresque novel: *Les Justes Causes* (Julliard, 1954).

DEHARME, Lise (b. 1902). Her novel *Eve la blonde* (Gallimard, 1952) shows a rising talent worth watching. It far outstrips her earlier *Cette Année-là* (Gallimard, 1945), an attempt at poetry, and *La Porte à côté* (Gallimard, Paris, 1950), an overwritten and unconvincing story of fabulous love. She writes as would one of Giraudoux's heroines — no mean compliment.

DEVAULX, Noël (b. 1905), fervently admired by a few, stands for the maintenance of a poetic tradition in the French novel, attracted since 1940 by philosophical and existential speculation. His short stories (for he has written no continuous novel as yet), collected as *L'Auberge Parpillon* (Gallimard, 1945) and *Le Pressoir mystique* (Editions du Seuil, 1948), give evidence of a graceful touch and an ability to feel and suggest mystery, which are worthy of Kafka. Like Blanchot and other moderns, Devaulx (who joined the Catholic Church in 1934) seems obsessed by the omnipresence and the significance of death, envisaged without morbidity but with visionary innocence. His *Sainte-Barbegrise* (Gallimard, 1952) was more strained than his earlier tales.

DHÔTEL, André (b. 1900), who teaches in a secondary school near Paris, at Coulommiers, and once wrote studies on the logic underlying the visions of his compatriot from the Ardennes, Rimbaud, became a very fecund novelist in the years 1948–52 when he published, in rapid succession, *Le Plateau de Mazagran* (Editions de Minuit, 1947); *David* (Editions de Minuit, 1948); *Les Chemins du long voyage* (Gallimard, 1949); *L'Homme de la scierie* (Gallimard, 1950); *Bernard le paresseux* (Gallimard, 1952). The surrealist adventure of the nineteen-twenties left him with a passion for mystery and for the marvelous inserted into daily life. He surrounds his half-real characters with a halo of poetry and an obstinate elusiveness, which bewilder most readers. There is no structure, no solidity whatever to his stories, no progression, only gratuitous fireworks of tender poetry amid rolling layers of clouds. *Bernard le paresseux* seems to have more psychological density, through the delineation of the bonds of unexplained hatred, stronger than love, between Bernard and a woman who finally is drowned with him in a frozen river. In our opinion, far too much has been made of Dhôtel's very moderate gifts as a novelist.

DRUON, Maurice (b. 1918) tried, with some robustness and workmanship, but with otherwise undistinguished gifts, to revive the portrayal of a French family, more or less decadent. His stories do not stand out among many others of the same kind, which have preceded them and which will doubtless follow. Their titles are *Les Grandes Familles* (Julliard, 1948), *La Chute des corps* (Juilliard, 1950) and *Rendez-vous aux enfers* (Julliard, 1951).

DUMUR, Guy (b. 1921) is, like Cabanis, Vailland, and not a few others, a spiritual son and an admirer of Laclos, Rétif, and Stendhal. His novel, *Les Petites Filles modèles* (Gallimard, 1949), relating the hesitations of a young man, loved by Annie but loving Joyce, going from one to the other of the two very 'knowing' and expert girls, constituted a very elegant literary debut. Is there enough in such dry clear-sightedness to make a novelist? 'No one can become a novelist who does not love his fellow-men,' said Cyril Connolly, who did not attempt to do either and who also revered the French eighteenth century.

DURAS, Marguerite (b. 1914) published a first and rather undistinguished tale, *Les Impudents,* in 1941, then a remarkable *récit* of country life in southwestern France, told in the first person by a girl naïvely attached to her brother and then to a friend of his, who loves her, *La Vie tranquille* (Gallimard, 1944). It has no plot, nothing but childish happenings, but it shows the nascent talent of an expert writer. *Un Barrage contre le Pacifique* (Gallimard, 1950; *The Sea Wall,* Pellegrini & Cudahy, New York, 1953) is written in the same objective jerky style but shows more ability to frame characters involved in the semblance of an action. It takes place in Indo-China and relates the pathetic and frustrated efforts of a destitute French woman to erect a wall against the ocean to protect her meager holding. The adventures of her daughter, courted by a wealthy but incredibly stupid young Frenchman, whom she rejects obstinately, and the behavior of her lazy and shrewdly simple-minded brother Joseph provide the comic element. The novel is clearly modeled after Steinbeck and especially after Caldwell and the action might almost have taken place among poor whites in America instead of poor whites in a French colony. It is not without flaws, but the author has a vigor that is not common among feminine novelists. *Les Petits Chevaux de Tarquinia* (Gallimard, 1953), entitled after a famous Etruscan fresco, which French tourists in Italy are expected to visit, is a very discreet and subtle novel about human relations and the obstacles to sincerity and to communication, even in love.

DUTOURD, Jean (b. 1920), after some early and pale attempts at the humorous novel (*Le Complexe de César, Le Déjeuner de lundi*), won a larger public with his entertaining and bitter story of a metamorphosis, *Une Tête de chien* (Gallimard, 1950; *A Dog's Head,* Simon & Schuster, New York, 1953). The sad plight of a boy born with a dog's head, his misfortunes in the army, then in love, his fortune, made on the stock market, and the sudden flattering advances made by men and women to a man of wealth, and his sorry end after he married a beautiful but crazy wife are told with incisive humor reminiscent of a Voltairian *conte.* *Au bon beurre* (Gallimard, 1952), the story of the social ascent of a butter-and-egg merchant, leans too heavily on Balzacian social description, but it has verve. The author promises to be one of the good minor talents of his generation and one of the rare entertaining writers of an age that prefers to wallow in its anguish rather than to laugh at it. His risqué treatise of seduction, *Le Petit Don Juan* (Laffont, 1950), is entertaining and healthy.

EMMANUEL, Pierre (b. 1916), better known as a poet and for his very outspoken, yet tactful, autobiography, *Qui est cet homme?* (Egloff, 1947), invaded the field of the novel with a very personal — at times embarrassingly so — love story, *Car enfin je vous aime* (Editions du Seuil,

1950). It is the poetical and rapturous record of a brief encounter in America, with the two partners soon recovering their clear-sightedness and knowing when and how to break off what might have degenerated into prosaic dullness. The book has occasional poetical beauty but shows little evidence of fictional mastery.

ESTANG, Luc (b. 1911) is commendable for his virtues of earnestness and steady zeal and his touchingly good intentions. Yet his first novel, *Les Stigmates* (Editions du Seuil, 1949), disturbed Catholic orthodoxy; it presented a man who, a prey to evil in all its forms, still drew some drops of grace from his sea of corruption and redeemed himself, after a fashion, through bringing the son of his mistress to religious faith. The same plunge into evil, fascinating to a Catholic novelist who, coming after Bernanos and Gide, must believe in the positive reality of the Devil, constitutes the substance of *Cherchant qui dévorer* (Editions du Seuil, 1951). The novel depicts a college for future priests who seem more 'devoured' by anguish and shame at the sins of their parents than inspired by faith. The book fails to spring to life.

ÉTIEMBLE, René (b. 1909), a university professor and an ebullient and bellicose critic, showed no mean courage in choosing the themes of his first novel, *L'Enfant de chœur*, published before his thirtieth year and reprinted by Gallimard in 1947. A note of venomous revenge against his mother (incest sprawls unashamedly in the book) and against his education and society is sounded throughout the novel, which is replete with vivid dialogue and caricatural sketches of human, and especially provincial, stupidity. The long novel on his youth and the Parisian circles in which he lived as a student, entitled *Peau de couleuvre* (Gallimard, 1948), did not fulfill the promises of the more compact, more spontaneous earlier book. It suffers from stuffy laboriousness. Polemics and combative criticism may be the author's most felicitous bent.

FONTAINE, Denise, died in 1932, leaving two volumes of high quality, *Geneviève Savigné* (Rieder, 1930) and *Rivages du néant* (Rieder, 1933), both among the most serious and virile attempts by a woman writer of her generation.

FOURRÉ, Maurice (b. 1877). In 1950, André Breton, starting a new collection called *Révélation,* cried up a baffling novel, *La Nuit du rose hôtel* (Gallimard, 1950), written by a seventy-three-year-old amateur from western France. A few obedient surrealists followed the master's dictum and acclaimed the new surrealist novel. There are indeed strangeness, innocence, even simple-mindedness in this novel, but we confess having not been struck by grace and having found it, above all, tawdry, meretricious, and woefully insignificant.

GADENNE, Paul (b. 1907) is another professor who, after taking his *agrégation* and starting teaching, was struck down by disease and had to live, a semirecluse, in the provincial cities first of Gap, then of Bayonne, in a more suitable climate than that of the north of France, where he comes from. A creeping sadness, some complacence in northern mists and in the barriers separating souls, even a bold but perilous challenge to tedium, in which tedium occasionally gets the better of author and reader, characterize his novels. Yet Gadenne occupies an original place among contemporary novelists: he is one of the least superficial of them, unconcerned with ephemeral vogues and publicity, and one of the most successful in evoking inner life. *Siloé* (Julliard, 1941), then *Le Vent noir* (Julliard, 1947) were tenacious explorations of the mysteries of individual life, by a novelist who had mastered the lessons of Thomas Mann and of Franz Kafka, without losing his originality. In *Le Vent noir* especially, the character of the protagonist, living passionately for the sake of a few meetings with the girl he loves, is reminiscent of the Proustian narrator, torturing himself through his insatiable search for knowledge and tormenting those whom he pursues with such intellectual passion. Gadenne's aspirations are for a spiritual, perhaps an inhuman, love. *L'Avenue* (Julliard, 1949) had a similar density; the hero, a sculptor driven by the war to southern France and exploring an avenue leading to a mysterious building, multiplies grave meditations on art and on all human effort. *La Plage de Scheveningen* (Gallimard, 1953), entitled after Jacob van Ruisdael's picture, is more concrete and revolves around a man's insistent pursuit of his past, of a former friend who had collaborated with the Germans and was shot, and of a woman, Irene, who has ceased loving the overintrospective narrator. Gadenne's novels are neither easy to read nor joyful; they grant too much to symbolism and to style, but they are important, and among the few truly deep novels of our age.

GARY, Romain (b. 1914) stands at the opposite pole to Gadenne. He is a novelist of action and adventure, the impetuous storyteller who lives in the concrete. He is half Russian, has traveled extensively, fought in the air force, and struck a resounding success with *Education européenne* (C. Lévy, 1945), a broken-up story of Polish partisans during World War II, in which certain scenes, alternately tender and brutal, are hard to forget. His next book, *Tulipe* (C. Lévy, 1946), is a pretentious and hollow allegory. *Le Grand Vestiaire* (C. Lévy, 1948) is a more acute study of adolescents in the demoralized and unbalanced war and postwar years, blending pity and comedy, satire and sentiment. *Les Couleurs du jour* (Gallimard, 1953; *The Colors of the Day*, Simon & Schuster, New York, 1953) is again of unequal and uncertain merit, hesitating as it does between satire and a deeper and more sympathetic attitude of the author toward his weak-willed movie actor. Gary has possibilities of growth and he should soon reach a genuine originality. His ultimate purpose is, as he defines it, to renovate the picaresque novel and, in the face of adverse literary vogues, to stand for adventure, movement, optimism, and laughter.

GASCAR, Pierre (b. 1916) won fame in 1953 when his two *récits* published in one volume, *Les Bêtes* and *Le Temps des morts* (Gallimard, 1953) were awarded the Goncourt Prize, an award which aroused less dissent than usual among French critics. The author drew on his experience as a prisoner of war in the disciplinary camp of Rawa-Ruska, called Brodno in the book. The hero is entrusted with the grim task of digging graves in a cemetery for the deceased prisoners. The tone is objective and documentary, but the effect is powerful without stressing the macabre. The stories which compose *Les Bêtes* are equally effective, especially the first about horses watched by a frightened soldier and escaping in a mad rush to freedom when starved during the early days of mobilization. The style of Pierre Gascar is at times needlessly pretentious and involved and his pessimism rings too familiar a note. But his talent is great.

GAUTIER, Jean-Jacques (b. 1908) has a vivacious talent, journalistic in the best sense of the word, although too often derogatory, sprightly, and ingenious. He is neither better nor worse than the average Goncourt Prize winner (he won it in 1946), and his *Histoire d'un fait-divers* (Julliard, 1946) shows skilled workmanship and some overworking of tenuously thin material. He followed it with *M'auriez-vous condamné* and *La Demoiselle du Pont aux Anes* (Julliard, 1951). The latter is an entertaining, though cruel, satire of theatrical manners and of an aging writer imprudent enough to fall in love with a dry-hearted candidate for the stage. Conviction, penetration, and emotional content seem to be too deficient in Gautier's stories for him ever to rise to the rank of a true 'creator.' He has shown insight and laudable severity as a dramatic critic.

GENET, Jean (b. 1909) is probably the most controversial writer to have risen to fame since 1940. The differences of opinion concerning him are attributable to considerations of morality and taste, but also to the permissible anger of broad-minded readers who will not be browbeaten by the contention of a few elect that only homosexuals have any literary talent. The atmosphere of coterie, which surrounds Genet, is regrettable, for his books are bought, if not read (for they are not easily digestible), on account of the legend surrounding their author. The publication of the *Oeuvres complètes* of Genet (the second and third volumes, the first being Sartre's unwieldy but profound exegetic *Summa*) by Gallimard (1952-3) may help dispel that aura. Whether Genet is a novelist or a poet is an idle question — his most magnificent gift, however, is that of poetic style. Next to this is his ability to conjure up a universe of 'evil' that compels our belief and to forge a new language. Last is Genet's success in extracting the universal significance of his stories of thieves, traitors, and sodomites. The outlaws and the hunted men of all ages are his subject. His 'transvaluation of all values' endows the wretched creatures who, with relentless monotony, people his world of prisoners and perverts with a weird, erotic, and saintly beauty.

GRACQ, Julien (b. 1910), whose real name is Louis Poirier, is a professor of geography who has been hailed by André Breton as the great hope of surrealist fiction. He writes beautifully, though with affectation and some pomp. He pursues Celtic mysteries through the modern world and is a devout worshipper of the Grail legend, whose multiple meanings lend themselves best, he feels, to the expression of our unquiet dreams. We must declare that his novels appear to us as unbearably pseudoromantic, as fake rehashings of Mrs. Radcliffe and Monk Lewis. *Au Château d'Argol,* first published on the eve of World War II, was reprinted by Corti in 1945, when the same publisher launched *Un Beau Ténébreux (A Dark Stranger,* New Directions, Norfolk, Connecticut, 1949). The latter, depicting a pretentious and handsome young man who transcends himself in death, through an ostentatious suicide after refusing the love of the beautiful Christel, is the least unconvincing of his novels. *Le Rivage des Syrtes* (Grasset, 1951) stirred up more attention, since, for the first time in French annals, its author was granted the Goncourt Prize against his will. It is a solemn allegory, which strains the reader's patience and brings him scant reward.

GREEN, Julien (b. 1900) had, with *Adrienne Mesurat* (Plon, 1927, translated as *The Closed Garden,* Harper and Bros., 1928) ranked with the three or four most authentic novelists of the generation of Malraux, Montherlant, and Giono. After a few other stories of violence and fear, he became obsessed with the visionary world, which he attempted to convey to his readers as more real than our familiar universe. *Le Visionnaire* (Plon, 1934) and especially *Minuit* (Plon, 1936) in its haunting first part came close to being the *Wuthering Heights* of the French novel, although the author seemed to be short of breath and seldom kept up the naturalness of tone and the simplicity of effects necessary to convey the extraordinary. Green, who had been born a Protestant (his father was English and his mother American) and had been brought up in the Catholic religion, returned to Catholicism in 1939. His conversion at first did not seem to have brought new vigor to his novels. *Varouna* (Plon, 1940, translated as *Then Shall the Dust Return,* Harper and Bros., 1941) and *Si j'étais vous* (Plon, 1947) are definitely unsuccessful in translating into fictional form the anguish and the aloneness of man, which are Green's main themes. With *Moira* (Plon, 1950; The Macmillan Company, New York, 1951), Green staged a brilliant comeback. The scene is laid in the American South, as is the scene of Green's first play, *Sud* (Gallimard, 1953). *Moira,* as Green confessed in his diary, is nothing but a long cry of hatred of instinct. It blends the violence associated with American novels with classical restraint, which enhances both its power and its credibility.

GROUSSARD, Serge (b. 1920), a widely read author, stands, in our opinion, just below the border line of what may be called literature. *La Femme sans passé* and *La Ville de joie* are hollow, conventional, and completely undistinguished.

GUÉRIN, Raymond (b. 1905) stormed French literature with a book so full of crudities and indeed obscenities that some lines had to be excised by the censor: *L'Apprenti* (Gallimard, 1946). The author, it is true, might have had his eroticism exasperated by four years of captivity in Germany. The strange hero of this epic of modern corruption is a servant in a low-class hotel, employed at washing dishes and perfunctorily cleaning bedrooms, who peeps through keyholes and seems fascinated by what he observes. But Guérin shows an immense power over words and of making his reader share in the unsavory atmosphere of his book. Had it been less morbidly weighted down with obscenity, L'Apprenti might have been a novel of true vigor. La Confession de Diogène (Gallimard, 1947) explores too slim a subject, the backstage activity of contemporary literature, and it failed to arouse interest. Parmi tant d'autres feux (Gallimard, 1950) is a volume of sprawling length — eight hundred pages — which could just as easily have gone on for two thousand more. A middle-aged man, after remembering at length his youth in Bordeaux in a corrupt circle of addicts to varied vices, marries. The loving bride, who had made advances to him, soon turns into a persecuting demon. Her death opportunely relieves him, and he may now relapse into his commonplace immorality. The volume evokes a dull boredom seldom equaled in literature, even by Sade or Henry Miller. Les Poulpes, the author's next venture, does not fulfill his promise.

GUERSANT, Marcel (b. 1913) was launched with some fracas in 1953 as the author of a bulky novel, Jean-Paul (Editions de Minuit). It is the story of a son of the upper bourgeoisie, severely educated, who discovers himself to be homosexual. He tries in vain to be won to the other sex, falls into the public pursuit of young men, is arrested and, having been gravely wounded by a bully who rejected his advances, he is hospitalized. An intern converts him to Catholicism. After some relapses, followed by remorse, confession, and a deeper faith, Jean-Paul is saved. The book, which is fearlessly crude in its first half, is presented as a moral and religious work likely to save sinners. The author is clearly a convinced Roman Catholic who poured too much too soon into a novel and could not resist moralizing inopportunely. He may grow into a really talented novelist.

GUILLOUX, Louis (b. 1889) had in 1935 stormed the literary world of Paris with Sang noir (Gallimard, 1935; Bitter Victory, Robert McBride, New York, 1836), a powerful delineation of a rebellious but weak intellectual, asphyxiated (hence the title) by his stifling Breton surroundings and by his own passionate anger. The book remains as one of the precursors of Sartre's La Nausée and of many novels of social and metaphysical revolt of the period following World War II. Unlike many other French novelists, but like Green, Guilloux is deeply concerned about his heroes and his inner world; his novels are not just intellectual pastimes and technical displays. His long and unwieldy Jeu de patience (Gallimard, 1949) is a purposely confused projection of many lives, with the distinction between the past and the present, what is actual and what is remembered by the characters, obliterated. It is also a unanimist record of the life of a small town through two world wars, with all social classes represented. The tone of social revolt and of revolutionary hope, which was heard in Guilloux's earlier work, has given way to gloomy acceptance of futility. The gruesome allegory of two Scandinavians vainly seeking an unhappy girl in Venice and remaining captives of some northern evil spirit, which Guilloux entitled *Parpagnacco ou la conjuration* (Gallimard, 1954) added little to the author's stature.

HOUGRON, Jean (b. 1923) is one of the novelists of adventurous life who have set themselves in determined opposition to the surfeit of symbolism, frustration, and nothingness, which they deplore in recent French fiction. He is also one of several who have discovered the opportunity of exploiting recent interest in Indo-China for imaginative literature. *Tu récolteras la tempête* (Domat, 1951; *Reap the Whirlwind,* Farrar, Strauss and Young, New York, 1953) is neither introspective nor elaborately constructed. It shows no conventional heroism and does not conceal the brutal murders that mark the war of ambush and treachery in the rice fields and jungle of Vietnam. The novel develops with impetuous energy, and the author is likely to become one of the popular successors of the adventure novelists of an earlier generation, Joseph Peyré, Roger Vercel, or even Henry de Monfreid. He can see and narrate breathlessly. The French Academy singled him out for its 1953 *Prix du Roman.* The next novel in Hougron's Indo-Chinese cycle, *Mort en fraude* (Domat, 1953), followed fast upon the previous one, itself to be followed by *Les Asiates.* In *Mort en fraude* the author deserted the world of traffickers and opium addicts of the European colony to attempt a powerful picture of the native villagers terrorized by the communists. The creation of atmosphere is very successfully achieved. The events of the 'fifties in Indo-China have brought forth other novels of note laid in that country: *Un Barrage contre le Pacifique,* by Marguerite Duras; *Les Chemins de la révolte,* by Nguyen-Tien-Lang (Amiot Dumont, 1953), an intelligent and peaceful Buddhist of Indo-China who suffered arrest and persecution at the hands of the Viet-Minh; *La Bataille dans la rizière,* by Jules Roy (Gallimard, 1953), a chivalrous flier and dauntless French patriot.

JOUHANDEAU, Marcel (b. 1888) has long been one of the unclassifiable outsiders of French letters. He emerged from the war years, during which he was far from heroic, with a limited but fervent circle of admirers, who tried to present him as Gide's successor and as one of the leading lights in the world of the novel. But Jouhandeau has a knack of disrupting all endeavors to raise him on a pedestal, through his own inordinate conceit and the tactless publicity around his books and his marital troubles, which he apparently condones. He has, since 1945, published far too much; he is repetitious and he has shown little attempt to deepen or renew his inspiration. Although he has remarkable introspective gifts, he has not succeeded in making his *Essai sur moi-même* (Marguerat, Lausanne, 1946) a probing autobiography. Nor has he found forcible expression for his sincere love of animals (*Animaux familiers,* Gallimard, 1947) and for his eleven-year-old pupils in a Catholic school in Paris, whom he has taught for years (*Ma Classe de sixième*, Editions de Flore, 1949). The best of Jouhandeau's work appeared around 1930, and little more can now be expected from him, except variations on his marital chronicles and perhaps, as death approaches, a more haunting obsession with the Devil and with the threats of hell. Claude Mauriac entitled his book on Jouhandeau *Introduction à une mystique de l'enfer* (Grasset, Paris, 1938). His chief works were a scathing picture of Chaminadour, an imaginary name for the small provincial town of Guéret, where Jouhandeau's father was a butcher; a bitter comedy of small-town life, *Les Pincengrain* (Gallimard, Paris, 1924), short stories that introduced the characters Véronique and Monsieur Godeau, who are Jouhandeau's truly great creation. His splendid economy of means, his incisive cruelty, and the Catholic undertones of his novels, in which God and the Devil are always struggling, have brought to Jouhandeau a few very warm admirers who, like the late Havelock Ellis, have hailed him as a modern Cervantes.

LAURENT, Jacques, began, like a few determined Frenchmen, with a huge novel of sprawling length (one thousand and sixty-eight pages), *Les Corps tranquilles* (J. Froissart, Paris, 1949), to prove to others and to himself that he had what is called a novelist's temperament. His potentialities are undeniable. There is imagination, verve, cynical and satirical portraiture, humor, a burlesque talent, and idea in his book, but there is also a deplorable confused accumulation of extraneous matter, which makes one pray for slender and selective *récits*. A few critics declared that their patience had been rewarded and that this first novel was a great book. We believe the author may indeed become an original novelist, especially in the humorous rendering of the foibles and inconsistencies of men.

LE CLEC'H, Guy (b. 1917) is a refined, introspective, and melancholy novelist, who is only gradually learning the technique of his trade but who has it in him to become one of the finest portrayers of inner life and of moral dilemmas. *Le Témoin silencieux* (Albin Michel, 1949) is a meditation on death, by a young man who, having just lost his father, examines and rejects the religious explanations or justifications for death and finally kills himself. (There is an epidemic of suicides in the contemporary novel.) The book offered promises that the author's second novel, *Le Visage des hommes* (Albin Michel, 1950), disappointed. *La Plaie et le couteau* (A. Michel, 1952), entitled after a line of Baudelaire and conjuring up a Dostoevskian atmosphere, is far more impressive. An exasperatingly weak, self-tormenting young man, Jacques, who likes to blame the 'out-of-joint' time in which he has to live for his own lack of will, becomes madly jealous of the happiness that a friend of his, Richard, has conquered for himself through loving and thus curing a paralytic young woman. He kills her and indirectly brings about the death of his friend. He regrets all the while, as we do with him, 'man's inability to kick himself in the pants.' *Le Défi* is to appear in 1955.

LEDUC, Violette (b. 1910) is the author of a strange and promising novel, *L'Affamée* (Gallimard, 1949), about an ugly woman who has long hated herself and the mirrored image that others seem to present to her of herself, but she finally discovers that love is a grace, which may still descend unexpectedly. This is a courageous 'feminine' novel, avoiding banality.

LEIRIS, Michel (b. 1901) cannot properly be called a novelist and seems to be more and more engrossed in his interests in anthropology and art. But *L'Age d'homme* (Gallimard, 1936; reprinted, 1946) is an extraordinarily sincere and revealing autobiography, which reads like one of the most probing *romans d'analyse*. It should be rendered into English.

LIMBOUR, Georges (b. 1902) wrote a story of charming and ingenuous fantasy, *Les Vanilliers* (Gallimard, 1938), followed seven years later by *L'Enfant polaire* (Fontaine, 1945). He seems thus far to have left undeveloped the clear promises of originality he had offered.

MALAQUAIS, Jean (b. 1908), a Pole by birth, was launched like many young novelists, by Gide's praise, lavished somewhat excessively on *Les Javanais* (Denoël, 1939; translated as *Men from Nowhere*, Fischer, New York, 1943). His *Planète sans visa* (Pré aux clercs, 1947; *World without Visa*, Doubleday and Company, New York, 1948) is a picture of the frustrated Europeans without a country awaiting an American visa. The two works have some solidity and weight, but, in our opinion, lack originality and even life. The author's next fictional attempt, *Le Gaffeur* (Corrêa, 1953) is a clever fantasy but too obviously in the manner of Kafka. It is less cruel than Aymé's satirical fiction, of which it is reminiscent.

MALLET, Françoise (b. 1930), a Belgian-born young woman, duplicated (as did Rossi) Radiguet's feat of writing before the age of twenty a novel of uncanny maturity and of impeccable workmanship: *Le Rempart des Béguines* (Julliard, 1951; *The Illusionist*, Farrar, Straus and Young, New York, 1952). Once again, the chief influence, discreetly but deeply felt, is that of Laclos. The daughter of an industrialist in Bruges visits her father's mistress and becomes her Lesbian lover. The story is never coarse or unpleasant; it is told with poetry as well as with cruelty, and with hardly a psychological or aesthetic flaw. If the author writes more than one adolescent book, she should have a successful future as a novelist.

MAMMÉRI, Mouloud, in *La Colline oubliée* (Plon, Paris, 1952), exploited the newly discovered subject and scene of North Africa and the conflict between ancestral traditions (Berber or Kabyl, in his case) and the breakup with which they are threatened by modern life and French culture. There are earnestness and concentrated power in the novel, which are of good omen. Mamméri is one of a number of French writers (often partly of Spanish descent, or wholly of Arab or Berber origin) born and trained in North Africa, who have lately brought new vigor into French fiction. The names of the best known among the others are:

Jean Amrouche, Albert Camus, René-Jean Clot, Mouloud Feraoun (author of *La Terre et le sang*, Editions du Seuil, 1953), Mohammed Dib (who received the Fénéon prize for *La Grande Maison* in 1952), Albert Memmi, Marcel Mouloudji, Robert Merle, Emmanuel Roblès, Jules Roy, and Michel Zéraffa. The influence of the American novel was especially strong on them.

MARCHAL, Lucie (b. 1902) struck success with *La Mèche* (Fortuny, 1948; *The Mesh*, Appleton-Century-Crofts, New York, 1949), a powerful story of family hatred, such as Mauriac wrote. The novel is well knit, vivid, and powerfully condensed. The author does not seem as yet to have followed it up with other books.

MARGERIT, Robert (b. 1910) impressed a few critics by the naïvely overstrained eroticism of his first novel, *Montdragon* (Gallimard, 1946), the story of a servant employed in a French castle to tame horses. He seduces the lady of the castle, then tries to pervert her daughter and her maid. He is finally killed by the daughter. Laclos (*lui, toujours!*) is obtrusively present here. He has not totally effaced himself in *Le Dieu nu* (Gallimard, 1951), the author's best novel, which celebrates the naked god of love. Many conventional elements encumber the novel. The characters ride on horseback around provincial chateaux, reminiscent of Victor Cherbuliez and Georges Ohnet, and they are restrained by family traditions and outmoded conventions. The beauty of the women always beggars description, and they all act unpredictably. Yet, to modernize his themes, Margerit has deftly added just a soupçon of Lesbianism and an even fainter one of a too-ardent attachment between brother and sister. The book is a novel of romantic passion that is frustrated to the end by the prejudices and the excessive prudence (or is it fear of love, or even lack of taste for the male sex?) of the beloved women. 'Ardent and chaste,' thus bracketed together, are the two key adjectives of the author. Margerit and Gracq, who sponsored him, Emmanuel, Brincourt, Dhôtel, and Gadenne seem to be the champions of a new romanticism in French fiction.

MEMMI, Albert (b. 1921) published, first in *Les Temps Modernes*, then at Corrêa, in 1953, an arresting novel, *La Statue de sel*, one of the five or six truly outstanding ones in a yearly production. It is a document rather than a cleverly arranged and elegantly adorned story. It rests upon an intensely personal experience of misery, injustice, and war. The hero is a Jewish boy of a poor family in Tunis. He is entranced by French culture, which was revealed to him at school, and he turns in revolt against his Jewish background, the rites of his religion, and even his half-illiterate parents. The war and the German occupation of Tunisia deprive him of his position and of his hopes for an academic career. He suffers from being a stranger everywhere, unwelcome to the French controlled by Vichy, hardly at one with the backward Arabs, distrusted by the orthodox Jews. He falls into stark despair, then decides to emigrate to Argentina. With earnestness and solidity, at times with some ponderousness, Memmi has hit upon and treated one of the significant problems of an age that has uprooted and alienated thousands of its most gifted men. The author is a teacher of philosophy.

MERLE, Robert (b. 1908) is another Algerian and another professor. His *Week-end à Zuydcoote* (Gallimard, 1949; *Week End at Dunkirk*, Alfred A. Knopf, New York, 1951) reveals his close acquaintance with the modern American novel. It was criticized as brutal, tough and artificial, but wrongly so in our estimation. It is one of the few true, convincing, and even moving novels written as yet on the catastrophe of 1940. The evacuation at Dunkirk had, as it happens, caught up with the violence of American novels, and the author conveys it truthfully. His next work of fiction, on a German bureaucratic torturer in concentration camps, *La Mort est mon métier* (Gallimard, 1953), on the contrary, sounds false from beginning to end and would be better forgotten. The author's most conspicuous gifts lie probably in the realm of the drama.

MOHRT, Michel (b. 1914) is a delicate, sensitive, and intelligent novelist, who began with a light but cheerful account, in Stendhalian fashion, of his war experience on the Italian front in 1940, *Le Répit* (Laffont, 1945). (There was, however, far more than nonchalant egotism in Stendhal the novelist, a fact that Stendhal's admirers often overlook.) The author touches upon the subject of collaboration (a subject on which many novels are likely to be written, as the events recede into the past) in *Mon Royaume pour un cheval* (Albin Michel, 1949) and reaches a more felicitous blending of lucid analysis and of poetry in *Les Nomades* (Albin Michel, 1951), which describes European exiles in America and the obstinate sentimental education of the protagonist. The novelist, thus far, seems to have fought shy of tragedy and of suffering, with a resulting thinness in his material. Perhaps, as he remarks in his third novel, 'the supreme sin is in failing to believe in one's passions.'

MOLAINE, Pierre (b. 1906), after pale earlier attempts, such as *De blanc vêtu*, impressed the public and the committee of the Renaudot prize, with *Les Orgues de l'enfer* (Corrêa, 1951; *Strange Laughter*, Roy Publishers, New York, 1953). The scene is laid in an insane asylum, whose inmates, buried alive, cry out their love of life and cherish in vain the dream of freedom. The wife of one of the patients persuades the doctor to admit her as a nurse. She and a former anarchist agitator, temporarily an inmate of the asylum, fall in love with each other but dare not betray the mad husband. The latter, after a hair-raising escape, is captured and confined once again. The events related in the novel have all the weirdness of a hallucination. The style is too labored and too rhythmic, but the classical structure of the novel contrasts felicitously with the disorderly minds of the madmen. Molaine succeeded honorably in this attempt, after courting many difficulties. His book is anything but commonplace.

MOULOUDJI, Marcel (b. 1922) was hailed as one of the revelations of the years 1944–5, when he received the *Prix de la Pléiade* for *Enrico*

(Gallimard, 1944) and soon after published *En souvenir de Barbarie* (Gallimard, 1945). The whole arsenal of tricks borrowed from American novelists is displayed in these two books. The young North African and itinerant actor clearly knew of no other literary tradition but the recent American one. The themes are as sordid as can be imagined: the repellent misery of the poorest eastern quarters of Paris, the squalor of stuffy rooms in which a whole family lives, sleeps, and raises rabbits, and a gruesome abortion, which the girl Barbarie undergoes. There is skill, but a derivative and imitative skill, in the broken-up narrative and the disjointed interior monologues. Mouloudji's talent has not developed since, and *La Grande Sortie* (Gallimard, 1951) may be dismissed as the most insipid of pretentious allegories (purporting to symbolize German occupation of France).

NELS, Jacques (b. 1901) hit upon a clever technique in his *Poussière du temps* (Bateau ivre, 1946), the retrospective story of a financier's life. His later books, *Les Enfants du désordre* (Presses de la Cité, 1950) and *Le Bal des victimes* (Corrêa, 1952), are only honest, colorless works of fiction.

NIMIER, Roger (b. 1925) clearly belongs to the family of minds of the French right, which has never lacked verve, robust use of hearty language, *élan,* and cynicism, and which, while claiming to be realistic, has also been fooled by its own slogans and has wistfully looked backward. He showed, in two volumes of essays, that he was no profound thinker. *Amour et néant* (Gallimard, 1951) is verbose and confused and succeeds in making most aspects of love, except perhaps jealousy, appear dull. *Le Grand d'Espagne* (Table ronde, 1950), which mentions Bernanos, is an organized attack against liberals, humanists, republicans and, most of all, Jacobins. It is full of zest and of wit, but negative and, as political thought, trite. Nimier the novelist happily knows how and when to throw the weight of ideas overboard. His early volume, *Perfide,* on fifteen-year-olds, is thin and cheaply cynical. *Le Hussard bleu* (Gallimard, 1950; *The Blue Hussar,* 1953, Julian Messner, New York, 1953) is a brilliant book. A French soldier serves in 1945 with the troops occupying Germany, maneuvers with skill among decrepit, vicious, or selfish officers, conquers a more than willing German lady for whose senses two French soldiers are hardly adequate fare. She kills one of them, however, at the behest of her brother, a Nazi without conviction. The nonchalance and the insolent dash of the book are its main charm. However, the author suffers from the serious sin that makes men attractive but novelists unconvincing: he never takes himself or his characters seriously and does not even lend any of them an individual style. Nimier can be exasperating, but he counts. Unfortunately he forced his talent in *Les Enfants tristes* (Gallimard, 1951), in which he tried his hand at the psychological analysis of the insipid amours of the modern fashionable youth.

ORIEUX, Jean (b. 1907) stands in contrast to Nimier; he is conservative, staid, and reassuringly old-fashioned. Hence the *Grand Prix* of the

French Academy was awarded to him in 1945 for the story of a provincial domain and its proprietors, *Fontagre* (Flammarion, 1945). *L'Aigle de fer* (Flammarion, 1949), which followed, is an honest effort to interpret the psychology of a German militarist family. *Cinq Filles et un fusil* (Flammarion, 1950) sketches the tribulations of a gentleman farmer who, like parsons in British novels of old, has six daughters to marry off. *Plus ça change . . .*

D'OTREMONT, Stanislas (b. 1899) is to be ranked among the conservative and even the conventional novelists. He recalls *Dominique,* the minor masterpiece of Eugène Fromentin and, what is worse, some of the effete stories of Victor Cherbuliez and Jules Sandeau. His *Thomas Quercy* (Gallimard, 1953) is a long canticle to love and purity. A young businessman, whom disease has induced to live in a country retreat and to analyze himself, falls in love with a radiant *jeune fille,* then, after her death, with her friend. Thanks to his romantic passion, he triumphs over disease and death. The author, a Belgian lawyer, has narrative gifts and stages a return to a well-built, romantic novel. Unfortunately, he spoils his best chapters through lengthy and unconvincing philosophical developments.

PAUWELS, Louis (b. 1920) published a superb *récit, Saint-Quelqu'un* (Editions du Seuil, 1946) on a clumsy workman, who bungles the happiness he should have enjoyed placidly with his wife and family and who involuntarily drives his wife and son to suicide. The gray, softly poetical style, the gentle sadness that suffuses the book, and the discreet religious implications of the title contribute to make a modest and moving work. The mysterious author seems to have remained silent after that striking debut, except for an essay, *Les Voies de petite communication* (Editions du Seuil, 1949). He contributed to *Gavroche,* then to *Combat* and *Arts.*

PERRET, Jacques (b. 1901) is not too remote from Nimier, though less youthful and less promising. After a brilliant war career as an escaped prisoner and a *maquisard,* he recorded or reimagined his experiences in a war book that is good but hardly of enduring worth, *Le Caporal épinglé* (Gallimard, 1948). His next novel, *Le Vent dans les voiles,* on nautical life, shows no deepening of his talent. *Bande à part* (Gallimard, 1952) is even more disappointing.

PERRY, Jacques (b. 1921) is not a man of action, like Perret, but an introspective writer, haunted by man's helplessness. The protagonist of his novel *L'Amour de rien* (Julliard, 1952) is determined upon suicide, and he casts a patient, backward glance at his lonely life. One hardly feels sorry about the oncoming death, for he had certainly failed to endow his life with significance. *Le Mouton noir,* published in *La Table ronde* in 1953, then by Julliard, is a very acute portrayal of a cruel childhood. A father, whose wife died of grief at the profound wickedness of her boy, spares no effort of devotion and comradeship to bring his son back to a decent life. An unexplained instinct for evil carries the boy away. The theme of the child irresistibly lured by evil is one of the most timidly approached themes in fiction. Here it is attacked frontally, and the novel, in spite of a few weaknesses, is effective, until the end, which ceases to carry conviction.

PEYREFITTE, Roger (b. 1907) is a genteel humanist, a devotee of pagan antiquity, and an elegant stylist who has not conspicuously succeeded in the novel, a genre for which he is poorly equipped in imagination and sensibility. His ironical *récit* of the death of his mother, *La Mort d'une mère* (Flammarion, 1950) was entertaining but very thin and strained. The author's travel books on his beloved Greece and Sicily show him at better advantage than his attempts, and failures, at fiction writing. But, in 1945, Peyrefitte encountered a subject on which he felt deeply and venomously, and which enabled him to tap his childhood memories and to portray the dubious and tender age of adolescence with heartfelt sympathy. *Les Amitiés particulières* (Vigneau, 1945; *Special Friendships*, Vanguard Press, New York, 1950) cannot be taken at its face value as a document on Catholic colleges or on the young men educated there, for the author depicts them as monsters of hypocrisy and deceit, unable to control their animal urges. But it is a very talented distortion and re-creation, and one more striking novel on the fashionable theme of pederasty.

PIEYRE DE MANDIARGUES, André (b. 1909) became known for his *Musée noir* (Laffont, 1946), a surrealist story under the influence of Lautréamont, and especially for his collection of fantastic tales, *Le Soleil des loups* (Laffont, 1951), which received the *Prix des Critiques*. The author is a man of wide culture, interested in archaeology, whose vast knowledge has not dried up a rich gift for inserting the marvelous into daily life. His tales are very skillfully contrived, but far more poetical than Maupassant's visionary stories, less crude in their effects than Poe's, far superior, in our opinion, to the *Contes de l'absurde* (Julliard, 1953) by Pierre Boulle (b. 1912), which are addressed to scientifically minded readers.

PONCHARDIER, Dominique (b. 1917) is likely to remain the author of one book, *Les Pavés de l'enfer* (Gallimard, 1950). He poured into it his thrilling experiences as one of the hardest fighters in the French resistance. Unlike Remy or Guillain de Benouville, Ponchardier, a former Navy officer, preferred to organize his recollections in the form of a novel. The tone is smooth and unemotional, the adventures related are hair-raising, and the sadness felt by the hero when faced by the collapse, after the war, of the lofty hopes cherished during the dark years for a renovation of the country are, without effort, imparted to his reader.

QUEFFÉLEC, Henri (b. 1910) is a professor. He began his literary career with a violent and cynical story in the fashion of the time, *Journal d'un salaud* (Stock, 1944). *Un Recteur de l'Ile de Sein* (Stock, 1945; *Island Priest*, E. P. Dutton & Co., New York, 1952), an indifferent novel, won acclaim in the movies as *God Needs Men*. The following stories by

Queffélec, notably that of a schoolmistress fighting against politics, administration, and pupils in a remote district of Brittany, *Au bout du monde* (Mercure de France, 1949), are not throbbing with life. *Tempête sur Douarnenez* (Mercure de France, 1951) is more moving and brushes aside much of the literary sentimentality about Breton fishermen. The author is not conspicuously adroit or poignant in creating living beings. But one character is alive and overpowers the book — the sea. *Un Homme d'Ouessant* (Mercure de France, 1954) shows Queffélec growing in stature as a creator of powerful characters. It is brief and tense, written with rare concreteness and evocative power. It takes place on a primitive island off the Brittany coast during the reign of Louis XVI and lends life to stubborn, superstitious yet magnificent fishermen, far different from Pierre Loti's sentimental Bretons, defying the law of their king and the teaching of the Church.

QUENEAU, Raymond (b. 1903) is perhaps not a great novelist but he is a great writer and an incomparable virtuoso of style. His chief concern seems to be re-creating language through effective use of colloquial speech, of slang and of many of the devices of rhetoric, entertainingly used. But he owes as much to Charlie Chaplin as he does to James Joyce. His *Pierrot mon ami* (Gallimard, 1942), which relates the hero's vicissitudes in an amusement park, in a truck in which he rides with apes, and his frustrated love affairs, is a masterpiece of hilarious comedy, as was his first and perhaps best novel, *Le Chiendent* (Gallimard, 1933). *Le Dimanche de la vie* (Gallimard, Paris, 1952) has excellent parts on naïve and winning fools at odds with wily women and escaping scot-free, like Chaplin or even like Dostoevski's idiot, from the ordeals of modern life. The stumbling blocks for Queneau are probably his immense store of knowledge, rivaling that of Joyce and occasionally intruding into the tale as pedantry, his total disregard of the structure of his novels, hence some monotony in the 'flat' comic characters, and an ending usually unequal to a brilliant beginning.

REBATET, Lucien (b. 1903), after a political career without honor as a collaborator of the Germans and a fierce anti-Semite, is putting his energy and his violent temperament to better use. He published a novel of inordinate length in two volumes of over five hundred pages each, *Les Deux Etendards* (Gallimard, 1951), from which politics is banished. It portrays a double religious vocation, in a young man and a young woman, who join the Jesuit order and a convent. A friend of the young man falls in love, in mystical exaltation, with the young woman who will soon be a nun. He fails to receive the gift of faith and elopes with the novice to whom the prosaic human love thus accepted will never bring spiritual peace. Rebatet's power is real but overabundantly displayed and, amid so many novels that lack substance and a theme, he has handled a tragic dilemma. Rebatet's next novel, *Les Epis mûrs* (Gallimard, 1954), is the story of an imaginary musical composer of genius, killed in World War I. It shows insight into artistic creation and avoids conventionality, so common in the fictional delineation of genius. The author stresses the obstacles in the path of genius which a vulgar democratic society, according to him, accumulates.

ROBLÈS, Emmanuel (b. 1914), the son of a mason in Oran, became one of the leaders of the brilliant literary group that, during World War II, gathered in North Africa. He published *Travail d'homme* (Charlot, Alger, 1942), *Nuits sur le monde* (Charlot, Alger, 1944), and *L'Action* (Charlot, Alger, 1946), three dramas of marked power. His one important novel is *Cela s'appelle l'aurore* (Editions du Seuil, 1952), from a sentence in Giraudoux's *Electra*. Its moral qualities have been warmly praised, because they stood out against the background of eroticism and of homosexual bad conscience in many contemporary novels. But the nobleness of the book is achieved through painful struggles against hypocrisy, narrow-mindedness, and cowardice. The book does not preach; but it implicitly revaluates true love and friendship. The hero is a doctor in Sardinia devoted to his wretched village and married to an insignificant wife. He falls in love with a superior woman, Clara. He struggles to maintain his loyalty to his wife and gives refuge to a murderer whom he knows to have acted madly out of grief for the loss of his own wife. The doctor's wife fails to understand him, while his mistress maintains her love for him and spurs him to his deeds of abnegation and devotion. Roblès, who was unsuccessful in weaving a novel out of North African resistance, *Les Hauteurs de la ville* (Charlot, 1948), has here composed one of the few haunting books of the early nineteen-fifties.

ROLIN, Dominique (b. 1913) was praised first as the author of *Les Marais* (Denoël, 1942), a debut whose promise, in our opinion, *Le Souffle* (Editions du Seuil, 1952) hardly fulfilled. She had failed also in attempting a story of half-mystical mists and undefined characters, *L'Ombre suit le corps* (Editions du Seuil, 1951). But *Moi qui ne suis qu'amour* (Denoël, 1949) is one of the most ardent novels of carnal and pagan love written by a woman, from the point of view of a woman who became, in adultery of course, 'the prey of Venus.'

ROSSI, Jean-Baptiste (b. 1931) is the author of one book, *Les Malpartis* (Laffont, Paris, 1950; *Awakening*, Harper and Brothers, New York, 1952), whose skill and discreet deftness in handling the most perilous of subjects were, in a lad of nineteen, literally disconcerting. An adolescent falls in love with a nun, ten or twelve years older. She defies her own scruples and her true purity, her convent and society in order to live a passion that fulfilled some claims of her maternal instinct but could only bring her grief and misery. The adolescent is soon taken away from her and placed in a religious school. Rossi was widely compared to Radiguet whom he has, in several respects, transcended in insight and narrative skill.

ROY, Jules (b. 1907) has at least two homonyms in contemporary letters, Claude Roy, an incisive and combative critic of communist affiliation (once a royalist) and Jean Henry Roy, an able reviewer in *Les Temps*

Modernes. Jules Roy, the son of a policeman and a peasant woman from Rovigo (North Africa), is, like Roblès his compatriot, one of the champions of loyalty to one's task, of fraternity, even of heroism. He gave brilliant service as a flier with the Royal Air Force, which his *Vallée heureuse* (Charlot, 1946) describes modestly. The euphemism, as is (or was) well known, designated the Ruhr Valley. It is hardly a novel, but it is one of the few good books devoted to aviation since Saint-Exupéry, whom Roy worships. The author, who had begun his literary career by writing poetry and delicate essays, published an essay, reminiscent of Vigny, *Le Métier des armes* (Gallimard, 1951), and attempted to master dramatic form with *Beau Sang* (Gallimard, 1952). The essay is probably a more fitting medium for him than imaginative creation.

SACHS, Maurice (b. 1906, d. 1944). The moot question of whether Sachs is a novelist should probably be answered negatively, if one excepts from fiction fairy tales, such as his *Abracadabra* (Gallimard, 1953), which is of mediocre quality in any case, and picaresque autobiography. *Le Sabbat* (Corrêa, 1946; *The Day of Wrath*, Barker, London, 1953), the first part of a meandering and entertaining autobiography of a youth who seems to have been killed by allied bombing while serving as a civilian in Germany, is brilliantly written. Its success was due in no small degree to its frankness in recording love experiences (chiefly, though not solely, of homosexual nature) and to its cruel portraits of well-known literary figures. The author was an insolent scoundrel, a shameless *arriviste,* an exhibitionist, and a pretentious rival of Rousseau in his urge for confessions, but nevertheless an entertaining, a brilliant, and, at times, a pathetic writer.

SAGAN, Françoise (1935), at the age of nineteen, scored the literary triumph of the year 1954 with her brief novel *Bonjour, tristesse* (Julliard, 1954). The title is drawn from a pretty poem by Paul Eluard, who has become a classic for the young generation. The story is that of a girl of seventeen, very naïve and very sophisticated at the same time, raised in a totally amoral way by her father who treats her as a friend and confides to her his feminine adventures. When he seems disposed to marry one of his mistresses, by whom his daughter is strangely fascinated as well as intimidated, the teen-age girl contrives a plot to break the marriage. The father's mistress seeks death in an automobile accident. His daughter has let sadness and a foretaste of the vanity of all pleasure creep into her life, up to then free from care. The plot is slim, but the technique is extraordinarily skillful; the style is restrained, almost abstract and classical in its purity. Françoise Sagan, a middle-class girl raised in a religious school, who lives a quiet life with her family, ranks with Raymond Radiguet, Jean-Baptiste Rossi and Françoise Mallet among the most surprising teen-agers of French literature. Will she become a new Colette?

SARRAUTE, Nathalie (b. 1902) was read by a sizable public chiefly because her second volume, *Portrait d'un inconnu* (Marin, 1948), was preceded by an important preface by Sartre. Her first volume, *Tropismes*

(Denoël, 1946), had passed unnoticed. We believe the second book a failure, though an interesting one. Sartre ranks it among the anti-novels, which he considers typical of our age; books that appear to be novels but undermine the genre, for they are novels of a novel that is never finished. Their value is the evidence they offer of the novel's keen self-awareness and of the novelist's impatience with his own bad faith, which lurks both inside and outside the characters. Mme Sarraute's novel appears as an honest, pedestrian, and fumbling search for authenticity. But good intentions count scantly in literature. *Martereau* (Gallimard, 1953), the author's third book, is not a much better performance and hinges again on the distorted vision that a sickly girl has of a rather simple old man.

SCHNEIDER, Marcel (b. 1913), a teacher in a Paris *lycée*, is a cultured, discreet, and highly polished teller of tales impregnated with the charm of Alsace and the poetry of childish loves. He has already written much, and his volumes emerge only faintly from an evanescent and glimmering light, which blurs all outlines and characters. His affinities seem to be with the authors who cannot resign themselves to outgrowing too splendid a childhood (like Alain-Fournier, Robert Francis, and Julien Gracq) and with the surrealists. *Cueillir le romarin* (Table ronde, 1949), his third novel, is a girl's confession, delicately portraying solitude and the intimate joy of suffering. *Le Chasseur vert* (Albin Michel, 1949) is a more robust evocation of a family in Alsace, whose most original member, dressed in green, shot but also loved and tamed birds. A half-humorous story of twins, *La Première Ile* (Albin Michel, 1950), struck us as strained and somewhat childish. *Le Sang léger*, which followed, played with the fantastic in narrating a New Year's Eve in Paris during which time became reversible, the two heroes were plunged backward through several centuries. Schneider has his devotees, who place him at the very top of the authors now writing fiction that is truly fictitious.

SPERBER, Manès (b. 1905) cannot legitimately be classified among French novelists, since he has, thus far at any rate, composed his books in German. His trilogy on political fanatics posed the tragic problems of communists painfully groping out of their illusions and discovering the dignity of being, as men, an end and not a means. Does the novel create characters and embody the ideas in compelling individuals? We doubt it.

STIL, André (b. 1921) may deserve mention, since communist novelists have been more scarce in France than communist painters and poets. He received the Stalin Prize in 1952 for his two-volume novel, *Le Premier Choc* (Editeurs français réunis, 1952), on the 'occupation' of a French port, presumably Bordeaux, by Americans in peacetime and on the wrath of French workmen in being humiliated by the 'imperialists' from overseas. The book plods conscientiously, portrays workmen's lives and feelings with honest application, but has neither insight nor life.

THOMAS, Henri (b. 1912) is one of the most original French writers today. He is a very delicate poet in verse and in prose, an admirer of

Melville and, above all, of Rimbaud. He, like several other French novelists of the years 1940–50, testifies implicitly to the profound impact of surrealism on French imagination. His heroes pursue a superhuman moment of exaltation, an invasion of the whole being with an ineffable joy and a sense of purity. Through such ecstasies, the anguish and the weight of solitude, which crushed these pilgrims of an *éternité retrouvée*, are swept away. *Le Seau à charbon* and *Le Précepteur* (Gallimard, 1940 and 1942) first revealed the extraordinary climate of purity and strangeness in which Thomas lived and plunged his creations. *Les Déserteurs* (Gallimard, 1951) is even more haunting. It has elements of a psychological detective story. An officer, after simulating accidental death, has started life again under a new name in Corsica. He is discovered through a doctor who had once known him and who leads toward him a young woman who is fascinated by his recognition of the metamorphosis that overwhelms human beings when, at thirty-five or so, they allow the energy accumulated in them to explode. The women in Thomas's novels are perhaps the purest and most mysterious in their unpredictable simplicity depicted in France since Giraudoux. Thomas creates his own universe.

TOURVILLE, Anne de (b. 1910), after a collection of colorless Breton stories (*Les Gens de par ici*, Stock, 1943), struck a richer vein with *Jabadao* (Stock, 1952; *Wedding Dance,* Farrar, Straus and Young, New York, 1953). There is some artificiality in her style, as in the imaginary backward and naïve Breton world she describes. But she has blended with great felicity folklore and tragedy, the supernatural and an airy, clean prose. The story is as good a children's story, or a story for those who like to recapture their childhood at will, as France has produced since 1940.

TRIOLET, Elsa (b. 1903), the Russian-born wife of Aragon, of whom he sang rapturously in his wartime poems, is a gifted storyteller whose best achievement remains her four stories on the French resistance entitled (after the mysterious phrase that signaled to the French in June 1944 that the Allies had landed and that the underground could unleash its full strength) *Le Premier Accroc coûte 200 francs* (Denoël, Paris, 1945). 'Les Amants d'Avignon,' which had already appeared in the clandestine *Editions de Minuit,* is the best of them. All of them are a little unreal, as many of the events described seemed to be, yet they convey the atmosphere of conspiracy and breathless confusion of Lyon during the war. Tender passion had its place among heroism and some cowardice in these adventures. Elsa Triolet's later books have proved very inferior to her vivid and attractive, if not profound, volume on an era that she lived and felt intensely.

TROYAT, Henri (b. 1911), also Russian born, also endowed with superb facility as a storyteller, has won several of the literary prizes of France. *L'Araigne* (Plon, 1938), which came after two earlier novels of some distinction, brought him a wide audience. The person whom Troyat compares to a venomous spider is a despicable intellectual who, out of spite and nihilistic wickedness, becomes the tormentor of his mother and his three sisters. (Europeans seem to depict tyrannical males, while Americans prefer domineering and stifling mothers.) Troyat's novel, however, lacks passion, psychological depth, and also renewal of the suspense presented too fully at the very beginning. His more ambitious trilogy, *Tant que la terre durera* (Table ronde, 1947–50; the first volume has been translated as *My Father's House,* Duell, Sloan and Pearce, New York, 1951), describing a boyhood in southern Russia, lengthy adventures through the Russian-Japanese war and anti-Tsarist riots, and finally exile after the Bolshevik victory, is eminently readable and smoothly told in a manner reminiscent of Gogol and Tolstoy; yet, when all is said, it suffers from its smooth facility and fails to move or to strike the reader. *La Neige en deuil* (Flammarion, 1952; *The Mountain,* Simon and Schuster, New York, 1953) is briefer, more concentrated, and built like a thriller. Two mountaineers search for a wrecked plane in the Alps, one out of greed, the other out of kindness and also because he was intimidated by his malicious younger brother. It is to be deplored that the author turned his vigorous story into a parable, with a beautiful lady from India, one of the travelers in the wrecked plane, symbolizing the rather obvious moral. Henri Troyat has consistently just missed satisfying those readers who want more from the novel than charm and escape, just as has another Russian-born writer of lesser talent, Kessel.

VAILLAND, Roger (b. 1907) was another of the literary talents revealed in the admirably rich period 1944–5. He had been much impressed by the surrealist clean sweep, then he became a Marxist and a courageous member of the resistance. He has portrayed himself, unfavorably, in Marat, the hero of *Drôle de jeu* (Corrêa, 1945), one of the earliest novels, and the best, on the French underground, a book full of destructive humor. Vailland diverged more and more from surrealist orthodoxy when he rejected the worship of love and insisted that, as another French novel has put it in its title, *l'amour n'est qu'un plaisir.* His three idols are Laclos, Sade, and Stendhal (the latter being, in our opinion, thus misrepresented as a cerebral sensualist). His subsequent novels never recaptured the vitality and the controlled frenzy of *Drôle de jeu. Les Mauvais Coups* (Corrêa, 1949) reads too much like a didactic debunking of *l'amour-passion* and like a story of demoralization in the Laclos vein. *Bon Pied, bon oeil* (Corrêa, 1950) is equally frank in its claims for a liberal and unsentimental ethics of sex, but naïve in its idealization of communists. *Une Jeune Homme seul* (Corrêa, 1951) is a poor novel but a clever demonstration of a social 'ascent,' contrasting with the one Paul Bourget used to depict. In Vailland's novel, a middle-class engineer, feeling unhappy and conscience-stricken among the bourgeoisie, chooses to go to the people and espouses communism. Vailland's promise was great, but it has not been matured by his cult for his desiccating master, Laclos, and by his communist orthodoxy. The question asked by Sartre when, in November 1938 he reviewed in the *Nouvelle Revue Française, La Conspiration,* the novel of a communist intellectual killed in 1940, Paul Nizan, is still a timely one: 'Can a Communist write a novel? I am not convinced that he can; he does not have the right to make himself the accomplice of his characters.'

VIAN, Boris (b. 1920) is one of the many *enfants terribles* of French existentialism. He has superbly assimilated and caricatured the tricks and the tone of the toughest American novel and is credited with the story of an American colored man hunted by the whites after he had committed a string of thefts, rapes, and murders: *J'irai cracher sur vos tombes* (signed Vernon Sullivan, Editions du Scorpion, 1946). His *L'Ecume des jours* (Gallimard, 1947) is entertaining, witty, and jocular, but it is decidedly unsubstantial and unconvincing.

VILMORIN, Louise de (b. 1906) maintains the light, graceful, and mundane traditions of the feminine novel. Her touch is poetical, her talent for contriving mysterious coincidences is expert, her artificiality almost appears natural. She lays no claim to importance as a novelist or to a revolution in the traditional picture of the second sex. Her best books are *Le Retour d'Erica* (Gallimard, 1948; *Erica's Return*, Random House, New York, 1948), *Julietta* (Gallimard, 1951; Julian Messner, 1953), and *Madame De* (Grasset, 1951; Julian Messner, 1953).

YOURCENAR, Marguerite stands in contrast with the feminine talent preceding her alphabetically in our list. She has an immense and solid culture, has written on Pindar, translated Henry James, and taught literature and art. After several volumes that had brought her the esteem of a limited circle, she won general attention with a novel that made no concession to fashions or to facility, the imaginary memoirs of Emperor Hadrian, *Mémoires d'Hadrien* (Plon, 1951). The aging ruler looks back over his career, records the lessons of his life for young Marcus Aurelius, and, having known the joys and sorrows of power and of passion, he faces death serenely. The book, impeccably documented, steers clear of all the pitfalls of this type of historical fiction. It is neither overwritten and anachronistic nor addicted to facile local color; it has more truth and more simplicity than *Salammbô* or *Marius the Epicurean*. It crowns worthily an author's career, which began twenty-five years ago.

ZÉRAFFA, Michel (b. 1918) was warmly praised for his first novel, *Le Temps des rencontres* (Albin Michel, 1948). It is a work of solid and ingenious craftsmanship, portraying five characters of varied backgrounds thrown together in a corner of the Alps, then following their fortunes through the resistance, collaboration, and the confusion of the war years. The author had not yet learned the art of omission and of going deeply into his chosen themes. *L'Ecume et le sel* (Albin Michel, 1950), which followed, deals with the scuttling of the French fleet in Toulon. It sets off the lurid and cruder sides of the people affected by the event and seems to seek brutality needlessly. *Le Commerce des hommes* (Albin Michel, 1952) shows progress in the author's portrayal of character and more naturalness in the invention of incident. A young man is desperately lonely (solitude is the obsession of all of Zéraffa's heroes) and remorseful after the murder of his brother in 1944. He watches with disgust his stepmother and her abject Russian lover, who, tired of the mother, makes love to her daughter as well and is shot by the jealous elder woman. The discouraged young man (a teacher, like the author) leaves for the New World. Zéraffa has more vigor than delicacy, and the behavior of his characters often lacks the inner compulsion that would make them truer to life or truer than life. But he has many of the gifts of a novelist of promise. (Zéraffa's first novel appeared in 1953 in New York as *The Living and the Lost;* Roy Publishers.)

Novels with Titles of ENGLISH TRANSLATIONS *

ARAGON, Louis. *Aurélien*, Fribourg: Egloff, 1944; *Aurelien* (Eithne Wilkins), London: Pilot Press, 1946; Duell, Sloan & Pearce, 1947. *Les Beaux Quartiers*, Denoël & Steele, 1936; *Residential Quarter* (Haakon Chevalier), Harcourt, Brace, 1938. *Les Cloches de Bâle*, Denoël & Steele, 1934; *The Bells of Basel* (Haakon Chevalier), Harcourt, Brace, 1936. *Les Voyageurs de l'impériale*, Gallimard, 1942; *The Century Was Young* (Hannah Josephson), Duell, Sloan & Pearce, 1941; also *Passengers of Destiny*, London: Pilot Press, 1947.

AYMÉ, Marcel. *Autres Contes du chat perché*, Gallimard, 1950; *The Magic Picture. More about the Wonderful Farm* (Norman Denny), Harper, 1954. *La Belle Image*, Gallimard, 1941; *The Second Face* (Norman Denny), Harper, 1952. *Le Chemin des écoliers*, Gallimard, 1946; *The Transient Hour* (Eric Sutton), A. A. Wyn, 1948. *Le Confort intellectuel*, Flammarion, 1949. *Contes du chat perché*, Gallimard, 1934; *The Wonderful Farm* (Norman Denny), Harper, 1951. *La Jument verte*, Gallimard, 1933. *Le Moulin de la Sourdine*, Gallimard, 1936; *The Secret Stream* (Norman Denny), Harper, 1953; London: The Bodley Head, 1953. *La Table aux crevés*, Gallimard, 1929; *The Hollow Field* (Helen Waddell), Dodd Mead & Co., 1933. *Travelingue*, Gallimard, 1941; *The Miraculous Barber* (Eric Sutton), Harper, 1951. *Uranus*, Gallimard, 1948; *The Barkeep of Blémont* (Norman Denny), Harper, 1950.

BAZIN, Hervé. *L'Huile sur le feu*, Grasset, 1954. *Lève-toi et marche*, Grasset, 1952. *La Mort du petit cheval*, Grasset, 1950. *La Tête contre les murs*, Grasset, 1949; *Head against the Wall* (W. J. Strachan), Prentice-Hall, 1952. *Vipère au poing*, Grasset, 1948; *Viper in the Fist* (W. J. Strachan), Prentice-Hall, 1951.

BEAUVOIR, Simone de. *L'Invitée*, Gallimard, 1943; *She Came To Stay* (Roger Senhouse & Yvonne Moyse), London: Secker & Warburg, 1949; Cleveland and New York: The World Publishing Co., 1954. *Le Sang des autres*, Gallimard, 1945; *The Blood of Others* (Roger Senhouse & Yvonne Moyse), Knopf, 1948. *Tous les hommes sont mortels*, Gallimard, 1946.

BECK, Béatrix. *Léon Morin, prêtre*, Gallimard, 1952; *The Passionate Heart* (Constantine Fitz Gibbon), J. Messner, 1953.

* Names of translators are enclosed in parentheses. Place of publication of the original books is Paris unless otherwise specified, and of translations New York unless otherwise specified. Also included here are the titles of recently published works not as yet translated but which are in the opinion of the author deserving of translation. N.t. means that no translator's name is given.

BERNANOS, Georges. *Un Crime*, Plon, 1935; *A Crime* (Anne Green), Dutton, 1936. *La Joie*, Plon, 1929; *Joy* (Louise Varese), Pantheon, 1946. *L'Imposture*, Plon, 1927. *Journal d'un curé de campagne*, Plon, 1936; *The Diary of a Country Priest* (Pamela Morris), Macmillan, 1937; London: Boriswood, 1937. *Monsieur Ouine*, Plon, 1946; *The Open Mind* (Geoffrey Dunlop), London: John Lane, 1945. *Sous le soleil de Satan*, Plon, 1926; *The Star of Satan* (Pamela Morris), Macmillan, 1940; also *Under the Sun of Satan* (Harry L. Binsse, Pantheon, 1949.

BLOCH-MICHEL, Jean. *Le Témoin*, Gallimard, 1948; *The Witness* (Eithne Wilkins), Pantheon, 1949.

BOSCO, Henri. *Malicroix*, Grasset, 1948. *Le Mas Théotime*, Charlot, 1945; *The Farm Theotime* (Mervyn Savill), London: Aldor, 1946; as *Farm in Provence*, Doubleday, 1947.

BOUTRON, Michel. *Hans* (Taken over by Editions André Bonne, 1951); *Hans* (Robin Graham), London: Verschoyle, 1952.

BRINCOURT, André. *La Farandole*, Table ronde, 1952. *Le Vert Paradis*, Table ronde, 1950; *The Paradise below the Stairs* (Herma Briffault), Duell, Sloan & Pearce, 1952.

CAMUS, Albert. *L'Etranger*, Gallimard, 1942; *The Stranger* (Stuart Gilbert), Knopf, 1946 (also Vintage Books, 1954); *The Outsider* (Stuart Gilbert), London: Hamilton, 1946. *L'Homme révolté*, Gallimard, 1951; *The Rebel* (Anthony Bower), Knopf, 1954. *La Peste*, Gallimard, 1947; *The Plague* (Stuart Gilbert), Knopf, 1948.

CÉLINE, Louis-Ferdinand. *Bagatelles pour un massacre*, Denoël, 1937. *La Bande de Guignol*, Denoël, 1944; *Guignol's Band* (Bernard Frechtman and Jack T. Nile), New Directions, 1954. *Mort à credit*, Denoël, 1936; *Death on the Installment Plan* (John Marks), Boston: Little, Brown, 1938; *New Directions*, 1947. *Voyage au bout de la nuit*, Denoël, 1932; *Journey to the End of the Night* (John Marks), Boston: Little, Brown, 1934; New Directions, 1949.

CESBRON, Gilbert. *Chiens perdus sans collier*, Laffont, 1954. *Les Innocents de Paris*, Corrêa, 1944; *The Innocents of Paris* (Marguerite Waldman), Boston: Houghton Mifflin, 1946; London: Collins, 1946. *Les Saints vont en enfer*, Laffont, 1952; *Saints in Hell* (John Russell), London: Secker and Warburg, 1953; Doubleday, 1954.

CHAMSON, André. *L'Année des vaincus*, Grasset, 1934. *L'Auberge de l'abîme*, Grasset, 1933; *The Mountain Tavern* (Edwin Granberry), Holt, 1933. *Le Crime des justes*, Grasset, 1928; *The Crime of the Just* (Van Wyck Brooks), Scribners, 1930. *Le Dernier Village*, Mercure de France, 1946. *La Galère*, Gallimard, 1939. *Les Hommes de la route*, Grasset, 1927; *The Road* (Van Wyck Brooks), Scribners, 1929. *Les Quatre Eléments*, Grasset, 1935; *A Mountain Boyhood* (John Rodker), London: J. Lehmann, 1947. *Roux le bandit*, Grasset, 1925; *Roux the Bandit* (Van Wyck Brooks), Scribners, 1929.

COCTEAU, Jean. *Les Enfants terribles*, Grasset, 1929; *Enfants terribles* (Samuel Putnam), Harcourt, Brace, 1930. *Le Grand Ecart*, Stock, 1923; *The Grand Ecart* (Lewis Galantière), New York and London: G. P. Putnam, 1925. *Thomas l'imposteur*, Gallimard, 1923; *Thomas the Impostor* (Lewis Galantière), Appleton, 1925.

COLETTE. *Le Blé en herbe*, Flammarion, 1923; *The Ripening* (Ida Zeitlin), Farrar & Rinehart, 1932. *La Chatte*, Grasset, 1933; *The Cat* (Morris Bentinck), Farrar & Rinehart, 1936. *Chéri*, Fayard, 1920; *Cheri* (Janet Flanner), Boni, 1929; London: Gollancz, 1930. *Duo*, Ferenczi, 1934; *Duo* (Frederick Blossom), Farrar &

Rinehart, 1935. *L'Entrave,* Librairie du livre, 1913 (subsequently Flammarion); *Recaptured* (Viola Garvin), London: Gollancz, 1931; Doubleday, 1932. *La Fin de Chéri,* Flammarion, 1926; *The Last of Cheri* (Viola Garvin), London: Gollancz, 1933; G. P. Putnam, 1932; also in *Cheri* and *The Last of Cheri* (Roger Senhouse), Farrar, Straus & Young, 1951. *Gigi,* Ferenczi, 1945; *Gigi, Julie de Carneilhan, Chance Acquaintances* (Roger Senhouse), Farrar, Straus & Young, 1952. *L'Ingénue libertine,* P. Ollendorf, 1909; *Gentle Libertine* (R.C.B.), Grosset & Dunlap, 1931. *La Naissance du jour,* Flammarion, 1928; *A Lesson in Love* (Rosemary Benét), Farrar & Rinehart, 1932. *Mitsou ou comment l'esprit vient aux filles,* Fayard, 1919; *Mitsou or How Girls Grow Wise* (Jane Terry), Boni, 1930.

COLIN, Paul. *Les Jeux sauvages,* Gallimard, 1950; *Savage Play* (Alfred van Ameyden van Duym), Dutton, 1953.

CURTIS, Jean Louis. *Les Forêts de la nuit,* Julliard, 1947; *The Forest of the Night* (Nora Wydenbruck), G. P. Putnam, 1951. *Gibier de Potence,* Julliard, 1949; *Lucifer's Dream* (Robin Chancellor), London: J. Lehmann, 1952; G. P. Putnam, 1953. *Les Justes Causes,* Julliard, 1954.

DUHAMEL, Georges. *La Chronique des Pasquiers:* (1) *Le Notaire du Havre,* Mercure de France, 1933. (2) *Le Jardin des bêtes sauvages,* Mercure de France, 1934. (3) *Vue de la terre promise,* Mercure de France, 1934. (4) *La Nuit de la Saint Jean,* Mercure de France, 1935. (5) *Le Désert de Bièvres,* Mercure de France, 1937. (6) *Les Maîtres,* Mercure de France, 1937. (7) *Cécile parmi nous,* Mercure de France, 1938. (8) *Le Combat contre les ombres,* Mercure de France, 1939. (9) *Suzanne et les jeunes hommes,* Mercure de France, 1940. (10) *La Passion de Joseph Pasquier,* Mercure de France, 1941; *The Fortunes of the Pasquiers* (Samuel Putnam), Harper, 1935, contains vols. 1, 2, 3; *The Pasquier Chronicles* (Beatrice de Holthoir), London: Dent, 1937; also Holt, 1937, contains: (1) *News from Havre* (also trans. as *Papa Pasquier,* Harper, 1934), (2) *Caged Beasts* (also trans. as *Young Pasquier,* London: Dent, 1936, as *Fortunes of the Pasquiers,* Harper, 1934), (3) *In Sight of the Promised Land* (included in *Fortunes of the Pasquiers,* Harper, 1934), (4) *St. John's Eve,* (5) *The House in the Desert. Cecile among the Pasquiers* (Beatrice de Holthoir), London: Dent, 1940 (American title *Cecile Pasquier,* same translator, Holt, 1940), contains: (6) *Pastors and Masters,* (7) *Cecile,* (8) *The Fight against the Shadows. Suzanne & Joseph Pasquier* (Beatrice de Holthoir), London: Dent, 1946 (American title *Suzanne and Joseph,* same translator, Holt, 1949), contains vols. 9 and 10.

Civilisation, Mercure de France, 1918; *Civilization* (E. S. Brooks), Century, 1919. *Vie des martyrs,* Mercure de France, 1917; *The New Book of Martyrs* (Florence Simmonds), Doran, 1918; London: Heinemann, 1918. *Vie et aventures de Salavin:* (1) *La Confession de minuit,* Mercure de France, 1920. (2) *Deux Hommes,* Mercure de France, 1924. (3) *Le Journal de Salavin,* Mercure de France, 1927. (4) *Le Club des Lyonnais,* Mercure de France, 1929, (5) *Tel qu'en lui même,* Mercure de France, 1932; *Salavin* (Gladys Billings), G. P. Putnam, 1936, contains: (1) *Confession at Midnight,* (2) *Salavin's Journal,* (3) *The Lyonnais Club,* (4) *End of Illusion. Le Voyage de Patrice Périot,* Mercure de France, 1951.

DURAS, Marguerite. *Un Barrage contre le pacifique,* Gallimard, 1950; *The Sea Wall* (Herma Briffault), Pellegrini & Cudahy, 1952.

DUTOURD, Jean. *Une Tête de chien,* Gallimard, 1950; *A Dog's Head* (Robin Chancellor), Simon & Schuster, 1953. *Au bon beurre,* Gallimard, 1952.

GARY, Romain. *Les Couleurs du jour,* Gallimard, 1952; *Colors of the Day*

(Stephen Becker), Simon & Schuster, 1953. *Education européenne*, C. Lévy, 1945; *Forest of Anger* (Viola Garvin), London: The Cresset Press, 1946. *Le Grand Vestiaire*, C. Lévy, 1948. *Tulipe*, C. Lévy, 1946.

GIDE, André. *Les Caves du Vatican*, Gallimard, 1914; *The Vatican Swindle* (Dorothy Bussy), Knopf, 1925. *Dostoievsky d'après sa correspondance*, Imprimerie Jean & Berger, n.d. (1908) (from an article in *La Grande Revue*, 25 May 1908, pp. 289–315) ; *Dostoevsky* (n.t.) , London: J. M. Dent, 1925; Secker & Warburg, 1949; Knopf, 1926; New Directions, 1949. *Les Faux Monnayeurs*, Gallimard, 1926; *The Counterfeiters* (Dorothy Bussy), Knopf, 1927; also The Modern Library; as *The Coiners*, London: Cassell & Co., 1927. *L'Immoraliste*, Mercure de France, 1902; *The Immoralist* (Dorothy Bussy), Knopf, 1930; also Vintage Books, 1954; London: Cassell & Co., 1930. *Isabelle*, Gallimard, 1911; *Isabelle* (Dorothy Bussy) in *Two Symphonies*, Knopf, 1931; London: Cassell & Co., 1931. *Les Nourritures terrestres*, Mercure de France, 1897; *Fruit of the Earth* (Dorothy Bussy), Knopf, 1949; London: Secker & Warburg, 1949. *Paludes*, Librairie de l'Art Indépendant, 1895; *Marshlands and Prometheus Misbound* (George D. Painter), New Directions, 1953; London: Secker & Warburg, 1953. *La Porte étroite*, Mercure de France, 1909; *Strait Is the Gate* (Dorothy Bussy), Knopf, 1924; London: Secker & Warburg, 1924. *La Symphonie pastorale*, Gallimard, 1919; *The Pastoral Symphony* in *Two Symphonies*. *Thesée*, Gallimard, 1946; Pantheon, 1946; *Theseus* (John Russell), London: Horizon, 1948; also in *Two Legends: Theseus* and *Oedipus*, Knopf, 1950; London: Secker & Warburg, 1950.

GIONO, Jean. *Batailles dans la montagne*, Gallimard, 1937. *Le Chant du monde*, Gallimard, 1934; *The Song of the World* (Henri Fluchère and Geoffrey Myers), Viking, 1937. *Colline*, Grasset, 1929; *Hill of Destiny* (Jacques LeClerq), Viking, 1929. *Le Grand Troupeau*, Gallimard, 1931. *Le Hussard sur le toit*, Gallimard, 1951; *The Horseman on the Roof* (Jonathan Griffin), Knopf, 1954. *Jean le Bleu*, Grasset, 1932; *Blue Boy* (Katherine A. Clarke), Viking, 1946. *Le Poids du ciel*, Gallimard, 1938. *Que ma joie demeure*, Gallimard, 1935; *Joy of Man's Desiring* (Katherine A. Clarke), Viking, 1940. *Regain*, Grasset, 1930; Harvest (Henri Fluchère and Geoffrey Myers), Viking, 1939. *Un de Baumugnes*, Gallimard, 1929; *Lovers Are Never Losers* (Jacques LeClerq), Viking, 1931. *Les Vraies Richesses*, Grasset, 1936.

GIRAUDOUX, Jean. *Bella*, Grasset, 1926; *Bella* (J. F. Scalan), Knopf, 1927. *Choix des Elues*, Grasset, 1939. *Siegfried et le Limousin*, Grasset, 1922; *My Friend from Limousin* (Louis C. Wilcox), Harper, 1923. *Simon le pathétique*, Grasset, 1918. *Suzanne et le Pacifique*, Emile-Paul, 1921; *Suzanne and the Pacific* (Ben Ray Redman), G. P. Putnam, 1923.

GRACQ, Julien. *Au Château d'Argol*, Corti, 1939; reprinted 1945; *The Castle of Argol* (Louise Varese), New Directions, 1951. *Un Beau Ténébreux*, J. Corti, 1945; *A Dark Stranger* (W. J. Strachan), New Directions, 1949. *Le Rivage des Syrtes*, Corti, 1952.

GREEN, Julien. *Adrienne Mesurat*, Plon, 1927; *The Closed Garden* (Henry L. Stuart), Harper, 1928. *Christine—suivi de Léviathan*, Editions des Cahiers libres, 1928; *Christine and Other Stories* (Courtney Bruerton), London: Heinemann, 1931, contains *Christine, Leviathan, The Keys of Death, The Pilgrim on the Earth*. *Léviathan*, Plon, 1929; *The Dark Journey* (Vyvyan Holland), Harper, 1929. *Minuit*, Plon, 1936; *Midnight* (Vyvyan Holland), Harper, 1936. *Moira* Plon, 1950; *Moira* (Denise Folliot), London: Heinemann; Macmillan, 1951. *Mont Cinère*, Plon, 1926; *Avarice House* (Marshall Best), Harper, 1927. *Si j'étais vous,*

Plon, 1947; *If I Were You* (J. H. P. McEwen), Harper, 1949. *Varouna*, Plon, 1940; *Then Shall the Dust Return* (James Whitall), Harper, 1941. *Le Visionnaire*, Plon, 1934; *The Dreamer* (Vyvyan Holland), Harper, 1934.

GUILLOUX, Louis. *Sang noir*, Gallimard, 1935; *Bitter Victory* (Samuel Putnam), McBride, 1936.

HOUGRON, Jean. *Soleil au ventre*, Domat, 1952; *Blaze of the Sun* (Mervyn Savill), Farrar, Straus & Young, 1954; London: Hurst & Blackett, 1954. *Tu récolteras la tempête*, Domat, 1950; *Reap the Whirlwind* (Mervyn Savill), Farrar, Straus & Young, 1953.

JOUHANDEAU, Marcel. *Chaminadour*, Gallimard, 1934. *Elise*, Gallimard, 1933; *Marcel and Elise* (Martin Turnell), Pantheon, 1953 (contains selections from several volumes by Jouhandeau). *Monsieur Godeau intime*, Gallimard, 1926. *Monsieur Godeau marié*, Gallimard, 1933.

LACRETELLE, Jacques de. *La Bonifas*, Gallimard, 1925; *Marie Bonifas* (Winifred S. Whale), G. P. Putnam, 1927. *Le Retour de Silbermann*, Gallimard, 1929. *Silbermann*, Gallimard, 1922; *Silbermann* (Brian Lunn), London: Benn, 1923.

LARBAUD, Valéry. *Amants, heureux amants*, Gallimard, 1923. *Fermina Marquez*, Plon, 1911.

MALAQUAIS, Jean. *Le Gaffeur*, Corrêa, 1953; *The Joker* (Herma Briffault), Doubleday, 1954. *Les Javanais*, Denoël, 1939; *Men from Nowhere* (n.t.), L. F. Fischer, 1943. *Planète sans visa*, Pré aux Clercs, 1937; *World without Visa* (Peter Grant), Doubleday, 1948.

MALLET, Françoise. *Le Rempart des Béguines*, Julliard, 1951; *The Illusionist* (Herma Briffault), Farrar, Strauss & Young, 1952.

MALRAUX, André. *La Condition humaine*, Gallimard, 1933; *Man's Fate* (Haakon M. Chevalier), H. Smith & R. Haas, 1934; also The Modern Library, 1934; *Storm in Shanghai* (Alastair MacDonald), London: Methuen, 1935. *Les Conquérants*, Grasset, 1928; *The Conquerors* (Winifred Stephens Whale), Harcourt, Brace, 1929. *L'Espoir*, Gallimard, 1938; *Man's Hope* (Stuart Gilbert and Alastair MacDonald), Random House, 1938; also The Modern Library, 1941; as *Days of Hope*, London: G. Routledge & Sons, 1938. *Les Noyers de l'Altenburg* (*Combat avec l'ange* I), Gallimard, 1945; *The Walnut Trees of Altenburg* (A. W. Fielding), London: J. Lehmann, 1952. *Le Temps du mépris*, Gallimard, 1935; *Days of Wrath* (Haakon M. Chevalier), Random House, 1936; as *Days of Contempt*, London: Gollancz, 1936. *La Voie royale*, Grasset, 1930; *The Royal Way* (Stuart Gilbert), H. Smith & R. Haas, 1935.

MARCHAL, Lucie. *La Mèche*, Fortuny, 1948; *The Mesh* (Virgilia Peterson), Appleton-Century-Crofts, 1949.

MARTIN DU GARD, Roger. *Jean Barois*, Gallimard, 1913; *Jean Barois* (Stuart Gilbert), Viking, 1949. *Les Thibault*, Gallimard, 1922–40, contains (1) *Le Cahier gris*, (2) *Le Pénitencier*, (3) *La Belle Saison*, (4) *La Consultation*, (5) *La Sorellina*, (6) *La Mort du père*, (7) *L'Eté 1914*, (8) *Epilogue*; *The Thibaults* includes Parts 1, 2, 3 (Madeleine Boyd), Boni & Liveright, 1926; *The Thibaults* includes Parts 1, 2, 3, 4, 5, 6 (Stuart Gilbert), Viking, 1939; *Summer 1914* includes Parts 7, 8 (Stuart Gilbert), Viking, 1941; *The World of the Thibaults*: I, *The Thibaults*; II, *Summer 1914* (Stuart Gilbert), Viking, 1941.

MAURIAC, François. *L'Agneau*, Flammarion, 1954. *Les Anges noirs*, Grasset, 1935; *The Mask of Innocence* (Gerard Hopkins), Farrar, Straus & Young, 1953. *Le Baiser au lépreux*, Grasset, 1922; *A Kiss to the Leper* (James Whitall), London: Heinemann, 1923, subsequently, *A Kiss for the Leper* (Gerard Hopkins),

London: Eyre & Spottiswoode, 1950, and also in *The Family*. *Le Désert de l'amour*, Grasset, 1925; *The Desert of Love* (Samuel Putnam), Covici-Friede, 1929; also (Gerard Hopkins), Pellegrini and Cudahy, 1951. *Destins*, Grasset, 1928; *Destinies* (Eric Sutton), Covici-Friede, 1929. *Dieu et Mammon*, Capitole, 1930; *God and Mammon* (n.t.), London: Sheed & Ward, 1936. *La Fin de la nuit*, Grasset, 1935; *The End of the Night*, see *Thérèse Desqueyroux*. *Genitrix*, Grasset, 1923; *Genitrix* (in *The Family: The Kiss to the Leper and Genitrix*) (Lewis Galantière), Covici-Friede, 1930; also *A Kiss for the Leper and Genitrix* (Gerard Hopkins), London: Eyre & Spottiswoode, 1950. *Le Jeune Homme*, Hachette, 1926. *Le Mal*, Grasset, 1924; *The Enemy* (in *The Weakling* and *The Enemy*) (Gerard Hopkins), Pellegrini & Cudahy, 1952. *Le Noeud de Vipères*, Grasset, 1932; *Vipers' Tangle* (Warre B. Wells), London: Gollancz, 1933; *The Knot of Vipers* (Gerard Hopkins), London: Eyre & Spottiswoode, 1952. *La Pharisienne*, Grasset, 1941; *A Woman of the Pharisees* (Gerard Hopkins), Holt, 1946; London: Eyre & Spottiswoode, 1946. *Le Sagouin*, Plon, 1951; *The Little Misery* (Gerard Hopkins), London: Eyre & Spottiswoode, 1952; also *The Weakling* in *The Weakling* and *The Enemy*. *Thérèse Desqueyroux*, Grasset, 1922; *Thérèse, A Portrait in Four Parts* (Gerard Hopkins) includes: *Thérèse Desqueyroux*, *Thérèse and the Doctor*, *Thérèse at the Hotel*, *The End of the Night*, Holt, 1947.

MAUROIS, André. *Bernard Quesnay*, Gallimard, 1926; *Bernard Quesnay* (Brian W. Downs), Appleton, 1927; London: Jonathan Cape, 1927. *Le Cercle de famille*, Grasset, 1932; *The Family Circle* (Hamish Miles), Appleton, 1932. *Climats*, Grasset, 1928; *Atmosphere of Love* (Joseph Collins), Appleton, 1929. *L'Instinct du bonheur*, Grasset, 1934. *Les Silences du Colonel Bramble*, Grasset, 1918; *The Silence of Colonel Bramble* (Thurfrida Wake), Appleton, 1920; London: John Lane, 1920.

MERLE, Robert. *Weekend à Zuydcote*, Gallimard, 1949; *Weekend at Dunkirk* (K. Rebillon-Lambley), Knopf, 1950; as *Week-end at Zuydcoote*, London: J. Lehmann, 1950.

MOINOT, Pierre. *La Chasse royale*, Gallimard, 1954.

MOLAINE, Pierre. *Les Orgues de l'enfer*, Corrêa, 1950; *Strange Laughter* (Eithne Wilkins), Roy, 1953; London: A. Redman, 1953.

MONTHERLANT, Henry de. *Les Bestiaires*, Grasset, 1926. *Les Célibataires*, Grasset, 1934; *Perish in Their Pride* (Thomas McGreery), Knopf, 1936; as *Lament for the Death of an Upper Class*, London: J. Miles, 1935. *L'Histoire d'amour de la rose de sable*, Plon, 1954. *Les Jeunes Filles*, Grasset, 1936–9: (1) *Les Jeunes Filles*, 1936, (2) *Pitié pour les femmes*, 1936, (3) *Le Démon du bien*, 1937, (4) *Les Lépreuses*, 1939; *Pity for Women* contains 1, *Young Girls* (Thomas McGreevy) and 2, *Pity for Women* (John Rodker), Knopf, 1938; *Costals and the Hippogriff* contains 3, *The Demon of Good*, and 4, *The Lepers* (John Rodker), Knopf, 1940; Parts 3 and 4 as *The Lepers*, London: Routledge, 1940. *Le Songe*, Grasset, 1922.

MORAND, Paul. *Bouddha vivant*, Gallimard, 1927; *The Living Buddha* (Madeleine Boyd), Holt, 1928. *Fermé la nuit*, Gallimard, 1922; *Closed All Night* (G.P.C., C.B.P., and H.M.), T. Seltzer, 1925. *Ouvert la nuit*, Gallimard, 1923; *Open All Night* (H.B.V.), T. Seltzer, 1923.

NELS, Jacques. *Poussière de temps*, Bateau ivre, 1946; *A Man of Means* (Elaine Halperin), Chicago: Ziff-Davis, 1948.

NIMIER, Roger, *Le Hussard bleu*, Gallimard, 1950; *The Blue Hussar*

(Jacques LeClerq), Messner, 1953; *The Blue Hussar* (John Russell and Anthony Rhodes), London: McGibbon & Kee, 1953.

PERRET, Jacques. *Le Carporal épinglé*, Gallimard, 1951. *Le Vent dans les voiles*, Gallimard, 1948; *The Wind in the Sails* (F. G. Renier and Anne Cliff), London: Hart-Davis, 1954.

PERRY, Jacques. *L'Amour de rien*, Julliard, 1952. *Monsieur d'Ustelles*, Julliard, 1954. *Le Mouton noir*, Julliard, 1953.

PEYREFITTE, Roger. *Les Ambassades*, Flammarion, 1951; *Diplomatic Diversions* (James FitzMaurice), London: Thames & Hudson, 1953. *Les Amitiés particulières*, Vigneau, 1945; *Special Friendships* (Felix Giovanelli), Vanguard, 1950. *La Fin des ambassades*, Flammarion, 1953.

PROUST, Marcel. *Jean Santeuil*, 3 vols., Gallimard, 1952. *Pastiches et Mélanges*, Gallimard, 1919. *Les Plaisirs et les jours*, C. Lévy, 1896; *Pleasures and Regrets* (Louise Varèse), Crown, 1948. *A la Recherche du temps perdu*, 16 vols., Gallimard, 1913–27, (1) *Du Côté de chez Swann*, Grasset (subsequently Gallimard), 1913; *Swann's Way* (C. K. Scott-Moncrieff), London: Chatto & Windus, 1922; Holt, 1922; The Modern Library, 1928. (2) *A l'Ombre des jeunes filles en fleur*, Gallimard, 1918; *Within a Budding Grove* (C. K. Scott-Moncrieff), London: Chatto & Windus, 1924; Seltzer, 1924; The Modern Library, 1930. (3) *Le Côté de Guermantes*, Gallimard, 1921; *The Guermantes Way* (C. K. Scott-Moncrieff), London: Chatto & Windus, 1925; Seltzer, 1925; The Modern Library, 1933. (4) *Le Côté de Guermantes, II; Sodome et Gomorrhe*, Gallimard, 1922; *Cities of the Plain* (C. K. Scott-Moncrieff), Boni, 1927 (subsequently Knopf); The Modern Library, 1938. (5) *La Prisonnière*, Gallimard, 1923; *The Captive* (C. K. Scott-Moncrieff), Boni, 1929 (subsequently Knopf); The Modern Library, 1934. (6) *Albertine disparue*, Gallimard, 1925; *The Sweet Cheat Gone* (C. K. Scott-Moncrieff), Boni, 1930 (subsequently Knopf); The Modern Library, 1934. (7) *Le Temps retrouvé*, Gallimard, 1927; *Time Regained* (Stephen Hudson), London: Chatto & Windus, 1931; *The Past Recaptured* (Frederick A. Blossom), Boni, 1932; The Modern Library, 1951; *Remembrance of Things Past* (C. K. Scott-Moncrieff), Random House, 1934, 2 vols. (Vol. I: Parts 1–3; Vol. II: Parts 4–7).

QUEFFELEC, Henri. *Un Recteur de l'Isle de Sein*, Stock, 1945; *Island Priest* (James Whitall), Dutton, 1952; *God Needs Men* is the film derived from this work.

RADIGUET, Raymond. *Le Bal du Comte d'Orgel*, Grasset, 1924; *The Count's Ball* (Malcolm Cowley), Norton, 1929; *Count d'Orgel Opens the Ball* (Violet Schiff), London: Harvill Press, 1952; as *Count d'Orgel*, Grove Press, 1953. *Le Diable au corps*, Grasset, 1923; *The Devil in the Flesh* (Kay Boyle), H. Smith, 1932; New American Library, 1949.

RAMUZ, Charles-Ferdinand. *La Beauté sur la terre*, Genève: Mermod, 1927; Grasset, 1928; *Beauty on Earth*, London & New York: G. P. Putnam, 1929. *Derborence*, Grasset, 1936; *When the Mountain Fell* (Sarah Fisher), Pantheon, 1947. *La Grande Peur dans la montagne*, Grasset, 1926. *Présence de la mort*, Lausanne: Mermod, 1922; *The Triumph of Death* (Allan Ross Macdougall), Pantheon, 1946; London: Routledge, 1946. *Le Règne de l'esprit malin*, Lausanne: Editions des cahiers vaudois (s.d.); Geneva: Georg, 1917; *The Reign of the Evil One* (James Whitall), Harcourt, Brace, 1922.

ROBLÈS, Emmanuel. *Cela s'appelle l'aurore*, Seuil, 1953; *Dawn on Our Darkness* (Thérèse Pol), Messner, 1954.

ROMAINS, Jules. *Les Copains*, Figuière, 1913; *The Boys in the Back Room* (Jacques LeClerq), McBride, 1937. *Les Hommes de bonne volonté*, 27 vol., Flammarion, 1932–52 (Warre B. Wells, vol. I–III, Gerard Hopkins, vol. IV–XIV), Knopf, 1933–46. I. *Men of Good Will* contains (1) *The Sixth of October* (*Le 6 octobre*), (2) *Quinette's Crime* (*Le Crime de Quinette*), II. *Passion's Pilgrims* contains (3) *Childhood's Loves* (*Les Amours enfantines*), (4) *Eros in Paris* (*Eros de Paris*), III. *The Proud and the Meek* contains (5) *The Proud* (*Les Superbs*), (6) *The Meek* (*Les Humbles*), IV. *The World from Below* contains (7) *The Lonely* (*Recherche d'une église*), (8) *Provincial Interlude* (*Province*), V. *The Earth Trembles* contains (9) *Floor Warning* (*Montée des périls*), (10) *The Powers That Be* (*Les Pouvoirs*), VI. *The Depths and the Heights* contains (11) *To the Gutter* (*Recours à l'abîme*), (12) *To the Stars* (*Les Créatures*), VII. *Death of a World* contains (13) *Mission to Rome* (*Mission à Rome*), (14) *The Black Flag* (*Le Drapeau noir*), VIII. *Verdun* contains (15) *The Prelude* (*Prélude à Verdun*), (16) *The Battle* (*Verdun*), IX. *Aftermath* contains (17) *Vorge against Quinette* (*Vorge contre Quinette*), (18) *The Sweets of Life* (*La Douceur de la vie*), X. *The New Day* contains (19) *Promise of Dawn* (*Cette Grande Lueur à l'est*), (20) *The World Is Your Adventure* (*Le Monde est ton aventure*), XI. *Work and Play* contains (21) *Mountain Days* (*Journée dans la Montagne*), (22) *Work and Play* (*Les Travaux et les joies*), XII. *The Wind Is Rising* contains (23) *The Gathering of the Gangs* (*Naissance de la bande*), (24) *Offered in Evidence* (*Comparutions*), XIII. *Escape in Passion* contains (25) *The Magic Carpet* (*Le Tapis magique*), (26) *Françoise* (*Françoise*), XIV. *The Seventh of October* (*Le 7 octobre*).

Mort de Quelqu'un, Gallimard, 1911; *The Death of a Nobody* (Desmond MacCarthy and Sidney Waterlow), London: Latimer, 1914; Huebsch, 1914; Knopf, 1944. *Psyché*, Gallimard, 1922–9; (1) *Lucienne*, Gallimard, 1922; *Lucienne* (Waldo Frank), Boni & Liveright, 1925, (2) *Le Dieu des corps*, Gallimard, 1925; *The Body's Rapture* (John Rodker), Liveright, 1937; Pocket Books, 1953, (3) *Quand le navire*, Gallimard, 1929.

ROSSI, Jean-Baptiste. *Les Mal-Partis*, Laffont, 1950; *Awakening* (Prudence Griffin), Harper, 1952; Signet Books, 1954; as *The False Start*, London: Secker & Warburg, 1952.

ROY, Jules. *Le Navigateur*, Gallimard, 1954.

SACHS, Maurice. *Le Sabbat*, Corrêa, 1946; *Day of Wrath* (Robin King), London: Arthur Baker, 1953.

SAINT-EXUPÉRY, Antoine de. *Citadelle*, Gallimard, 1948; *The Wisdom of the Sands* (Stuart Gilbert), Harcourt, Brace, 1950. *Courrier-Sud*, Gallimard, 1929; *Southern Mail* (Stuart Gilbert), H. Smith & R. Haas, 1933. *Le Petit Prince*, Gallimard, 1945; Reynal & Hitchcock, 1943; *The Little Prince* (Katherine Woods), Reynal & Hitchcock, 1943. *Pilote de guerre*, Maison française, 1942; Gallimard, 1942; *Flight to Arras* (Lewis Galantière), Reynal & Hitchcock, 1942. *Terre des hommes*, Gallimard, 1939; *Wind, Sand and Stars* (Lewis Galantière), Reynal & Hitchcock, 1939. *Vol de nuit*, Gallimard, 1931; *Night Flight* (Stuart Gilbert), New York and London: The Century Co., 1932; also in *Airman's Odyssey* (contains *Wind, Sand and Stars, Night Flight, Flight to Arras*), Reynal & Hitchcock, 1943.

SARTRE, Jean-Paul. *Les Chemins de la liberté*, 3 vols., Gallimard, 1945–9: *L'Age de raison*, Gallimard, 1945; *The Age of Reason* (Eric Sutton), Knopf, 1947; London: Hamilton, 1947, (2) *Le Sursis*, Gallimard, 1945; *The Reprieve* (Eric Sutton), Knopf, 1947; London: Hamilton, 1947, (3) *La Mort dans l'âme*, Gallimard, 1949; *Iron in the Soul* (Gerard Hopkins), London: Hamilton, 1950; as

Troubled Sleep, Knopf, 1951. *L'Etre et le néant,* Gallimard, 1943; only two long essays extracted from this book have been translated and published as *Existential Psychoanalysis* (Hazel Barnes), Philosophical Library, 1953. *Le Mur,* Gallimard, 1939; *Intimacy and Other Stories* (Lloyd Alexander), New Directions, 1948. *La Nausée,* Gallimard, 1938; *Nausea* (Lloyd Alexander), New Directions, 1949; *The Diary of Antoine Roquentin* (Lloyd Alexander), London: J. Lehmann, 1949. 'Qu'est-ce que la littérature?' in *Situations ii,* Gallimard, 1948; *What Is Literature?* (Bernard Frechtman), Philosophical Library, 1949; London: Methuen, 1950. *Réflexions sur la question juive,* Morihien, 1946; 'Portrait of the Antisemite' (Mary Geggenheim), *The Partisan Review,* 1946; *Anti-Semite and Jew* (George J. Becker), Schocken Books, 1948; *Portrait of the Anti-Semite* (Erik de Mauny), London: Secker & Warburg, 1948.

TOURVILLE, Anne de. *Jabadao,* Stock, 1952; *Jabadao* (Mervyn Savill), London: Britannicus Liber, 1952; *Wedding Dance* (Mervyn Savill), Farrar, Straus & Young, 1953.

TRIOLET, Elsa. *Le Premier Accroc coûte deux cents francs,* Egloff, 1945; also Denoël, *A Fine of Two Hundred Francs* (n.t.), Reynal & Hitchcock, 1947 (includes also *The Lovers of Avignon, The Private Life of Alexis Slavsky, Notebooks Buried under a Peach Tree*).

TROYAT, Henri. *L'Araigne,* Plon, 1938. *Faux Jour,* Plon, 1935. *Grandeur nature,* Plon, 1936; *One Minus Two* (James Whitall), Washburn, 1938. *Judith Madrier,* Plon, 1940; *Judith Madrier* (James Whitall), Washburn, 1941. *La Neige en deuil,* Flammarion, 1952; *The Mountain* (Constantine Fitz Gibbon), Simon & Schuster, 1953. *Tant que la terre durera,* 3 vols., Table ronde, 1947–50: (1) *Tant que la terre durera,* 1947; *My Father's House* (David Hapgood), Duell, Sloan & Pearce, 1951, (2) *Le Sac et la cendre,* 1948, (3) *Etrangers sur la terre,* 1950.

VERCORS (Jean Bruller). *Les Armes de la nuit,* Editions de minuit, 1946. *Les Animaux dénaturés,* Albin Michel, 1952; *You Shall Know Them* (Rita Barisse), Boston: Little, Brown & Co., 1953. *L'Imprimerie de Verdun,* La Bibliothèque française, 1947; *The Verdun Press,* see *Le Silence de la mer.* *La Marche à l'étoile,* Editions de minuit, Cahiers du Silence, 1943; also French Pantheon Books, vol. 8, 1946. *Le Silence de la mer,* London & Paris: Editions de Minuit, Cahiers du Silence, 1943; *The Silence of the Sea* (Cyril Connolly), Macmillan, 1944. *Three Short Novels* (includes: *Guiding Star* (*La Marche à l'étoile*) (Eric Sutton), *Night and Fog* (*La Nuit et le brouillard*) (Haakon M. Chevalier), *The Verdun Press* (*L'Imprimerie de Verdun*) (Haakon M. Chevalier), Boston: Little, Brown & Co., 1947.

VILMORIN, Louise de. *Julietta,* Gallimard, 1951; *Julietta* (Alison Brothers), Messner, 1952. *Madame de,* Gallimard, 1951; *Madame de* (Duff Cooper), Messner, 1954. *Le Retour d'Erica,* Gallimard, 1948; *Erica's Return* (Sarah Fisher Scott), Random House, 1948. *Les Belles Amours,* Gallimard, 1954.

YOURCENAR, Marguerite. *Mémoires d'Hadrien,* Plon, 1951; *Hadrian's Memoirs* (Grace Frick), Farrar, Straus & Young, 1954.

ZERAFFA, Michel. *Le Temps des rencontres,* Albin-Michel, 1948; *The Living and the Lost* (J. M. Cohen), London: The Bodley Head, 1952; Roy, 1953.

BIBLIOGRAPHY *of Essential General Works on the Novel*

ALBÉRÈS, R. M., *Portrait de notre héros: Essai sur le roman actuel*, Le Portulan, Paris, 1945.
——, *La Révolte des écrivains d'aujourd'hui*, Corrêa, Paris, 1949.
ALDINGTON, Richard, 'Knowledge and the Novelist,' *The Times Literary Supplement*, July 2, 1938.
ALDRIDGE, John W., *After the Lost Generation*, McGraw-Hill Book Company, New York, 1951.
AMES, Van Meter, *Aesthetics of the Novel*, University of Chicago Press, Chicago, 1928.
——, 'Enjoying the Novel,' in *The Enjoyment of the Arts*, Max Schoen, ed., The Philosophical Library, New York, 1944.
ARLAND, Marcel, 'Sur le roman.' *Nouvelle Revue Française*, No. 305, February 1939, pp. 332-7.
AUERBACH, Erich, *Mimesis: Dargestellte Wirklichkeit in der abendländischen Literatur*, Francke, Bern, 1946.
BARTHES, Roland, *Le Degré zéro de l'écriture*. Editions du Seuil, Paris, 1953. (Chapter on *L'écriture du roman*.)
BEACH, Joseph Warren, *The Twentieth Century Novel: Studies in Technique*, Appleton-Century-Crofts, New York, 1932.
BENTLEY, Phyllis, 'The Armistice Period in British Fiction,' *The New York Times Book Review*, August 31, 1941.
BLANCHOT, Maurice, *Faux-Pas*, Gallimard, Paris, 1943. (Contains eighteen brief chapters on novelists.)
——, *La Part du feu*, Gallimard, Paris, 1949. (Essays on Kafka, Malraux, and Sartre.)
BONNET, Henri, *Roman et poésie*, Nizet, Paris, 1951.
BOWEN, Elizabeth, *English Novelists*, Collins, London, 1942.
BOYLESVE, René, *Opinions sur le roman*, Plon, Paris, 1929.
BROOKS, Cleanth, and WARREN, Robert Penn, *Understanding Fiction*, Appleton-Century-Crofts, New York, 1943.
BURGUM, Edwin Berry, *The Novel and the World's Dilemma*, Oxford University Press, New York, 1947. (Contains chapters on Proust and Malraux, as well as on Kafka, Mann, Joyce, and others.)
CAILLOIS, Roger, *Puissances du roman*, Sagittaire, Marseille, 1943.

347

CAMUS, Albert, 'L'intelligence et l'échafaud,' in *Problèmes du Roman*, Jean Prévost, ed., Confluences, Lyon et Paris, 1943, pp. 218–23.

CANBY, Henry S., 'A Certain Condescension toward Fiction,' in *Definitions*, Harcourt, Brace and Company, New York, 1922.

CATHER, Willa, 'The Novel *démeublé*,' in *Not under Forty*, Alfred A. Knopf, New York, 1936.

CHARBONNEAU, Robert, *Connaissance du Personnage*, L'Arbre, Montreal, 1944.

CHAUVEAU, Paul, 'A propos du roman,' *Les Nouvelles Littéraires*, April 14, 1928.

CHEVALLEY, Abel, *Le Roman anglais de notre temps*, The Clarendon Press, Oxford, 1921.

COMFORT, Alexander, *The Novel and Our Time*, Phoenix House, London, 1948.

CONRAD, Joseph, *A Personal Record*, Harper and Brothers, New York, 1912.

———, *Prefaces to His Works*, J. M. Dent & Sons, London, 1937. (With an introductory essay by Edward Garnett.)

CORMEAU, Nelly, *Physiologie du roman*, La Renaissance du Livre, Brussels, 1947.

DAICHES, David, *The Novel and the Modern World*, University of Chicago Press, Chicago, 1939.

———, 'Problems for Modern Novelists,' *Accent*, spring 1943, pp. 144–51.

DANIEL-ROPS, 'Les Problèmes actuels du roman français,' *Bibliothèque Universelle et Revue de Genève*, August 1928, pp. 932–45.

DATALLER, Roger, *The Plain Man and the Novel*, Nelson, London, 1940.

DAVIS, Robert Gorham, 'Fiction as Thinking,' *Epoch*, I, 3, spring 1948, pp. 87–96.

DE VOTO, Bernard, *The World of Fiction*, Houghton Mifflin Company, Boston, 1950.

DUHAMEL, Georges, *Essai sur le roman*. Marcelle Lesage, Paris, 1925.

———, *Remarques sur les mémoires imaginaires*, Mercure de France, Paris, 1934.

EDGAR, Pelham, *The Art of the Novel from 1700 to the Present Time*, The Macmillan Company, New York, 1933.

FERNANDEZ, Ramon, *Messages*, Gallimard, Paris, 1926.

———, 'Poétique du roman,' *Nouvelle Revue Française*, April 1929, pp. 544–50.

FERRERO, Guglielmo and Leo, 'Remarques sur le roman,' *Les Nouvelles Littéraires*, March 23, 1929.

FOLLETT, Wilson, *The Modern Novel: A Study of the Purpose and the Meaning of Fiction*, Alfred A. Knopf, New York, 1918.

FORD, Ford Madox, *The English Novel*, Constable, London, 1930.

FORSTER, E. M., *Aspects of the Novel*, Harcourt, Brace and Company, New York, 1927.

FRANK, Waldo, 'The Novel as Poem,' *The New Republic*, August 20, 1945.

FRIERSON, William C., *The English Novel in Transition, 1885–1940*, University of Oklahoma Press, Norman, Oklahoma, 1942.

FROHOCK, Wilbur M., *The Novel of Violence in America*, Southern Methodist Press, Dallas, Texas, 1950.

GADENNE, Paul, 'Efficacité du roman,' in *Problèmes du Roman*, Jean Prévost, ed., Confluences, Lyon and Paris, 1943, pp. 248–57.

GALSWORTHY, John, *Castles in Spain and Other Scripts*, Heinemann, London, 1927.

——, *The Creation of Character in Fiction*, The Romanes Lecture, Clarendon Press, Oxford, 1931.

GEROULD, Gordon Hall, *How to Read Fiction*, Princeton University Press, Princeton, New Jersey, 1937.

GIDE, André, *Interviews imaginaires*, Pantheon Books, New York, 1943. (Interviews VIII–IX touch upon problems of the novel. The American translation was published in 1944 by Alfred A. Knopf.)

GLASGOW, Ellen, *A Certain Measure*, Harcourt Brace & Co., New York, 1943.

GMELIN, Hermann, *Der Französische Zyklenroman der Gegenwart*, Quelle und Meyer, Heidelberg, 1950.

HACKETT, Francis, 'The Novel and Human Personality,' *The New York Times Book Review*, August 15, 1948.

HAEDENS, Kleber, *Paradoxe sur le Roman*, Sagittaire, Marseille, 1941.

HAMILTON, Clayton, *Materials and Methods of Fiction*, The Chautauqua Press, Chautauqua, New York, 1911.

HENDERSON, Philip, *The Novel Today: Studies in Contemporary Attitudes*, John Lane, London, 1936.

HOFFMANN, Frederick J., *Freudianism and the Literary Mind*, Louisiana University Press, Baton Rouge, Louisiana, 1945.

HYTIER, Jean, *Les Arts de littérature*, Charlot, Alger, 1945. (Contains five very suggestive chapters on the art of fiction.)

JALOUX, Edmond, *Au Pays du roman*, Corrêa, Paris, 1931.

——, 'Préface à un roman mythique,' *Le Temps*, April 15, 1938.

——, 'Roman français et roman étranger,' *Le Temps*, March 1, 1939.

JONES, Howard Mumford, 'Fiction and the Art of Fiction,' *The New York Times Book Review*, July 26, 1946.

KRUTCH, Joseph Wood, *Five Masters: A Study in the Mutations of the Novel*, Jonathan Cape, London, 1930.

LALOU, René, *Le Roman français depuis 1900*, Presses Universitaires, Collection Que sais-je, Paris, 1943.

LAWRENCE, D. H., 'The Novel,' in his *Reflections on the Death of a Porcupine*, Martin Secker, London, 1934.

——, 'Surgery for the Novel, or a Bomb,' 'Morality and the Novel,' 'Why the Novel Matters,' in *Phoenix: The Posthumous Papers of D.H.L.*, Heinemann, London, 1936, pp. 517–20, 522–32, 533–8.

LEAVIS, D. Q., *Fiction and the Reading Public*, Chatto and Windus, London, 1932.

LEAVIS, F. R., *The Great Tradition*, Chatto and Windus, London, 1949.

LESORT, Paul A., 'Notes sur le roman,' *La Nef*, V, 40, March 1948, pp. 7–18.

LIDDELL, Robert, *A Treatise on the Novel*, Jonathan Cape, London, 1947.

LUBBOCK, Percy, *The Craft of Fiction*, Jonathan Cape, London, 1929; Charles Scribner's Sons, New York, 1929.

MAGNY, Claude-Edmonde, *L'Age du roman américain*, Editions du Seuil, Paris, 1948.

——, *Histoire du roman français depuis 1918*, I, Editions du Seuil, Paris, 1950.

MARTIN-CHAUFFIER, Louis, 'Proust and the double "I," ' *The Partisan Review*, XVI, 10, October 1949, pp. 1,011–26. (Published in *Problèmes du Roman*, Jean Prévost, ed., Confluences, Lyon and Paris, 1943.)

MASSIS, Henri, *Réflexions sur l'art du roman*, Plon, Paris, 1927.

MAURIAC, François, See Bibliographical Note to Chapter VI.

MAUROIS, André, *Le Roman et le romancier*, Société des Conférences, Monaco, 1929.

MERLEAU-PONTY, Maurice, 'Le Roman et la métaphysique,' in *Sens et nonsens*, Nagel, Paris, 1948.

MICHA, René, 'La Marquise sortit à cinq heures,' *Cahiers du Sud*, No. 299, 1950, pp. 120–32.

MILLE, Pierre, *Le Roman français*, Firmin-Didot, Paris, 1930.

MOELLER, Charles, *Littérature du XXe Siècle et Christianisme*, Casterman, Paris et Tournai, 1953, Vol. 1.

MONROE, Elizabeth, *The Novel and Society: A Critical Study of the Modern Novel*, University of North Carolina Press, Chapel Hill, North Carolina, 1941.

MONTESINOS, José F., 'Imperfect Myths: Being an Observation on Detective Stories by a Continental Reader,' *Chimera*, V, 4, summer 1947, pp. 2–11.

MORGAN, Charles, 'L'Avenir du roman,' *La Nouvelle Relève*, IV, 5, November 1945, pp. 367–83.

MOTTRAM, R. H., and BERESFORD, J. D., 'Tradition in the Novel,' 'Experiment in the Novel,' *Tradition and Experiment*, Oxford University Press, London, 1929.

MOUNIN, Georges, 'Mythologies de l'adolescence dans le roman contemporain,' in *Problèmes du Roman*, Jean Prévost, ed., Confluences, Lyon and Paris, 1943, pp. 36–52.

MUIR, Edwin, *The Structure of the Novel*, Harcourt, Brace and Company, New York, 1929.

MULLER, Herbert J., *Modern Fiction: A Study of Values*. Funk and Wagnalls Company, New York, 1937.

MURRY, John Middleton, 'The Breakup of the Novel,' in his *Discoveries*, Collins, London, 1924.

THE NOVEL of To-morrow and the Scope of Fiction, by twelve American novelists, Bobbs-Merrill Company, Indianapolis, 1922.

THE NOVELIST AS THINKER, B. Rajan, ed., Dennis Dobson, London, 1947.

O'BRIEN, Justin, *The Novel of Adolescence in France*, Columbia University Press, New York, 1937.

ONIMUS, Jean, 'l'Expression du temps dans le roman contemporain,' *Revue de Littérature Comparée*, XXVIII, 3, July–Sept. 1954, 299–317.

ORTEGA Y GASSET, José, *The Dehumanization of Art and Notes on the Novel*, Princeton University Press, Princeton, New Jersey, 1948.

OVERTON, Grant, *The Philosophy of Fiction*, Appleton-Century-Crofts, New York, 1928.

PAUL, David, 'Time and the Novelist,' *Partisan Review*, XXI, 6, Nov.–Dec. 1954, 636–49.

PEÑA, Carlos Hector de la, *La Novela moderna: Su Sentido y su Mensaje*, Editorial Jus, Mexico, 1944.

PENTON, Brian, 'Note on Form in the Novel,' in *Scrutinies*, Edgell Rickword, ed., Wishart, London, 1931, II, 235–61.

PEYRADE, Jean, *Recherche de la joie à travers le roman français contemporain*, Spes, Paris, 1946. (Mostly on Catholic novelists by a Catholic.)

PEYRE, Henri, 'Le Roman français,' in *Esquisse de la France*, Parizeau, Montreal, 1946, pp. 243–78.

PICON, Gaëtan, 'Définition du roman,' *La Gazette des lettres*, August 9, 1947.

——, 'D'une Philosophie du roman,' *Fontaine*, No. 57, December 1946–January 1947, pp. 795–802.

POUILLON, Jean, *Temps et roman*, Gallimard, Paris, 1946.

POULET, Georges, *La Distance intérieure*, Plon, Paris, 1952.

——, *Etudes sur le temps humain*, Plon, Paris, 1950.

PRÉVOST, Jean, 'Le Métier de romancier,' *La Revue des Vivants*, February 1935, pp. 248–50.

——, Several articles in *Problèmes du roman*, Jean Prévost, ed., Confluences, Lyon and Paris, 1943.

PRITCHETT, Victor J., *The Living Novel*, Chatto and Windus, London, 1946.

RAMBAUD, Henri, 'Sur le Génie du roman,' in *Problèmes du roman*, Jean Prévost, ed., Confluences, Lyon and Paris, 1943, pp. 233–47.

RANSOM, John Crowe, 'The Understanding of Fiction,' *The Kenyon Review*, XII, 2, spring 1950, pp. 189–218.

RIVIÈRE, Jacques, 'De Dostoevski et de l'insondable,' 'Marcel Proust et la tradition classique,' 'Le Roman d'aventures,' articles collected in *Nouvelles Etudes*, Gallimard, Paris, 1947.

SARTRE, Jean-Paul, Preface to *Portrait d'un inconnu* by Nathalie Sarraute, Marin, Paris, 1948, pp. 7–16. (On the negative novels that Sartre defines as anti-novels.)

SELDES, Gilbert, 'Form and the Novel,' *The Bookman*, October 1929, pp. 128–31.

STANSBURY, Milton H., *French Novelists of Today*, University of Pennsylvania Press, Philadelphia, 1935.

SWINNERTON, Frank, 'Variations on Form in the Novel,' in *Essays and Studies by the English Association*, The Clarendon Press, Oxford, XXIII, 1938, pp. 79–92.

THIBAUDET, Albert, *Réflexions sur le roman*, Gallimard, Paris, 1938. (Much of the author's earlier volume, *Le Liseur de romans*, Crès, Paris, 1925, is reprinted here.)

UNDSET, Sigrid, 'Some Notes on Undercurrents of American Literature,' *The New York Times Book Review*, March 21, 1943.

VALÉRY, Paul, 'L'Art de Charles Morgan,' *Carrefours*, July 27, 1945.

———, 'Hommage' (to Marcel Proust) in *Variété* I, Gallimard, Paris, 1924, pp. 149–59.

———, Letter on the novel in *Problèmes du roman*, Jean Prévost, ed., Confluences, Lyon and Paris, 1943, pp. 193–4.

WALPOLE, Hugh, and others, *Tendencies of the Modern Novel*, Allen and Unwin, London, 1934. (Contains a sketchy chapter, by Hamish Miles, on French fiction.)

WHARTON, Edith, *The Writing of Fiction*, Charles Scribner's Sons, New York, 1925.

WHAT'S NOVEL IN THE NOVEL, Yale French Studies, No. 8, 1951. (Articles by thirteen authors.)

WOOLF, Virginia, *Mr. Bennett and Mrs. Brown*, Hogarth Press, London, 1928.

———, 'The Russian Point of View,' 'Modern Fiction,' 'How It Strikes a Contemporary' in *The Common Reader*, First Series, Harcourt Brace, New York, 1929.

———, 'Phases of Fiction,' *The Bookman*, New York, April, May, and June 1929, pp. 123–32, 269–79, 404–12. (See Solomon Fishman, 'Virginia Woolf and the Novel,' *The Sewanee Review*, XLI, summer 1943, pp. 321–40.)

Index of PROPER NAMES